Albert Gore, Sr.

POLITICS AND CULTURE IN MODERN AMERICA

Series Editors: Margot Canaday, Glenda Gilmore,
Michael Kazin, Stephen Pitti, and Thomas J. Sugrue

Volumes in the series narrate and analyze political and social change
in the broadest dimensions from 1865 to the present, including
ideas about the ways people have sought and wielded power in
the public sphere and the language and institutions of politics at
all levels—local, national, and transnational. The series is motivated
by a desire to reverse the fragmentation of modern U.S. history and
to encourage synthetic perspectives on social movements and the
state, on gender, race, and labor, and on intellectual history and
popular culture.

Albert Gore, Sr.

A POLITICAL LIFE

Anthony J. Badger

PENN

UNIVERSITY OF PENNSYLVANIA PRESS

PHILADELPHIA

Publication of this volume was aided
by a grant from the Albert Gore Research Center.

Published by
University of Pennsylvania Press
Philadelphia, Pennsylvania 19104-4112
www.upenn.edu/pennpress

Printed in the United States of America
on acid-free paper

10 9 8 7 6 5 4 3 2 1

Library of Congress Cataloging-in-Publication Data
Names: Badger, Anthony J., author.
    Title: Albert Gore, Sr. : a political life / Anthony J. Badger.
    Other titles: Politics and culture in modern America.
    Description: 1st edition. | Philadelphia : University of
Pennsylvania Press, [2019] | Series: Politics and culture in modern
America | Includes bibliographical references and index.
    Identifiers: LCCN 2018022859 | ISBN 978-0-8122-5072-5
(hardcover)
    Subjects: LCSH: Gore, Albert, 1907-1998. | United
States. Congress. Senate—Biography. | Legislators—
United States—Biography. | Southern States—Politics
and government—1865-1950. | Southern States—Politics
and government—1951- | United States—Politics and
government—1933-1945. | United States—Politics and
government—1945-1989.
    Classification: LCC E748.G689 B33 2019 | DDC 328.73092 [B]—
dc23
    LC record available at https://lccn.loc.gov/2018022859

CONTENTS

Illustrations follow page 172

Albert Gore, Sr.

Introduction

A WARM SUMMER'S EVENING on the lawn of Ted Kennedy's house in McLean, Virginia, in early August 1970: The guests were a microcosm of the national Democratic Party's liberal wing. Clark Clifford and Averell Harriman from the foreign policy establishment attended. Officials from the Machinists, the Auto Workers, the Electrical Workers, and the Teamsters represented labor. The chairman of the Senate Foreign Relations Committee, J. William Fulbright, joined Majority Leader Mike Mansfield and other senators. They were there to raise money for Albert Gore's reelection campaign. Senator Daniel Inouye from Hawaii explained that Gore was the only senator to receive such a reception because "this election is of historical importance." Inouye added, "We are responding to the President [Nixon]. We are picking up his gauntlet." Ted Kennedy praised Gore's courage for casting votes in the Senate that were unpopular in Tennessee, adding, "His constituency is all of this great nation." The guests also presented Gore with a memento—a tree stump. He climbed up and gave a characteristically powerful stump speech.[1]

The funds raised in McLean that evening went to hire Charles Guggenheim, the Kennedys' favorite filmmaker, to produce six television advertisements for Gore's campaign against his Republican opponent, William Brock. Guggenheim's cinema vérité technique produced beautifully crafted ads stressing that Gore represented the values of his home, Smith County, in the hill country of Tennessee. The adverts captured Gore playing checkers with an elderly voter, talking to his uniformed son, Al, about the values of patriotism, and riding on a white horse in the Tennessee countryside.[2]

Expensive TV ads were a far cry from Albert Gore's first race for Congress in 1938. Then the state commissioner of labor, and former county superintendent of schools for Smith County, he had been the youngest of six candidates in the Democratic primary for Tennessee's Fourth Congressional District. The six were vying for the seat made vacant by the incumbent's decision to run for the governorship. Gore needed name recognition to compete with his better-known and older opponents. So he would liven up his stump speech by playing his fiddle, accompanied by musician friends who traveled round the large Fourth District with him. Gore's fiddle-playing at the six or seven campaign stops he made each day distinguished him from the other candidates when there were, in practice, few significant policy issues to separate them.

The fiddle remained useful. While he was a congressman, Gore's weekly radio show, broadcast every Sunday morning, was legendary in middle Tennessee. If a guest did not turn up or Gore was short of material, he would sometimes take up the fiddle again. But Gore was also alert to the possibilities of another medium. In 1951 Gore played on television in Nashville on Amateur Hour. "My eyes have been opened about television," he reported. "People whom I had never seen before would call me by name, mentioning having seen the television program. It is the coming of the future." He would use television in his 1952 campaign to unseat veteran senator Kenneth McKellar. Gore rarely had the funds for expensive TV advertisements in his subsequent campaigns, but he always had a sharp eye for the possibility of free coverage on local TV news programs. In 1969 and 1970, as he prepared to defend his Senate seat for the third time, he organized his week so that he would be in Nashville on Friday afternoons to catch the newscasts that night; in Knoxville and Chattanooga on Saturdays to catch the newscasts that day there; and in Memphis on Sundays to achieve the same effect.[3]

But it was more than changes in modern campaigning techniques that characterized Gore's political career. The young politician went to Congress when the four pillars of conservative control of the South identified by political scientist V. O. Key, Jr., were very much in place—the one-party system, African American disfranchisement, segregation, and malapportionment of state legislatures. Remove these, Key argued, and the forces of liberalism would be immeasurably strengthened.[4]

During Gore's thirty-two years in Washington, these pillars were comprehensively dismantled. African Americans were already voting in significant numbers by the 1950s. Even before the 1965 Voting Rights Act, those voters were providing the margin of victory for Democratic candidates in Tennessee The physical edifice of segregation crumbled under the combined weight of a civil rights movement, often led by Nashville students, and the federal government, through the Civil Rights Act of 1964. Rural overrepresentation in state legislatures was eliminated by the 1962 U.S. Supreme Court in light of the *Baker v. Carr* case, which originated in Tennessee. By the late 1960s Tennessee had the most competitive two-party system in the South. And yet Gore was defeated by a conservative Republican congressman in 1970.[5]

This biography seeks to explain the underlying rhythms of Gore's political career. That career is emblematic of several important themes in postwar U.S. politics and society. First and foremost it was the product of a modernizing South. Gore exemplified the "new generation of Southerners" that Franklin Roosevelt believed would take over from the conservatives in the economically changing South. Like other young Southerners, especially after World War II, Gore believed that the federal government was the solution and not the problem. New Deal-style measures could transform the position of the South as the nation's number one problem. Social welfare measures, union organization, and farm programs could raise the purchasing power of ordinary Southerners and tackle the region's problem of chronic underconsumption. Above all investment in the region's infrastructure could modernize the South and produce a mechanized, diversified agriculture and a consumer-oriented, high-wage industry. The federal government could sponsor water-resource development, provide cheap electrical power, and make cheap credit available to a region that had previously been starved of investment. Indeed, the Tennessee Valley Authority provided the model of how the region could be transformed, and Albert Gore was a quintessential "TVA liberal," as Alabama Senator John Sparkman described like-minded politicians. Gore was a passionate defender of the TVA, an enthusiastic advocate of nuclear power, and the legislative driving force behind the Interstate Highway Act of 1956. The consequences in the modern South are there for all to see.[6]

This "new generation of Southerners" hoped economic modernization would bring gradual racial change and Gore was the prototypical Southern white racial moderate. White racial moderates who were praised for their courage in the 1950s, particularly by white Northern liberals, have not always received good press since. Critics have described them as "closet moderates" who "surrendered to the mob before it even gathered." Through the prism of the dramatic change of the 1960s, their courage appears less evident than their fatalism and caution.[7]

Gore in the 1950s was committed to gradualism, but he was more courageous than many Southern moderates. As reporter David Halberstam observed in 1958, Gore "probably comes as close as anyone in Washington to fitting the description of the much discussed highly sought and rarely found Southern moderate." There were few African Americans in Smith County, where Gore grew up and started his political career. Service in Washington exposed him to national liberal pressures on civil rights, but there was no evidence that he would actively hasten the demise of segregation. Above all else he advocated compliance with the law of the land. Therefore in 1956 he refused to sign the Southern Manifesto, that blast of defiance against the Supreme Court. He was a long-standing opponent of the poll tax and a supporter of the right to vote for all Americans, so he voted for the 1957 Civil Rights Act. Given the segregationist nature of his opponents, he received the support of the steadily increasing African American electorate. But like other moderate politicians of his generation, he campaigned for the African American vote at a distance, dealing with African American leaders through intermediaries. Thus Gore was not exposed personally and directly to the urgency of African Americans in the way that he experienced the passions of his white supporters.[8]

Before 1960 civil rights for Gore was largely an issue that arose from white resistance to judicially mandated federal intervention. Gore was operating in a world where whites essentially were dictating the timetable of racial change. It is a truism that there was a "long civil rights movement." But the nature of that civil rights movement changed in 1960. Now, immediate racial change would be coerced from a reluctant white South by a pincer movement of direct action from below by African Americans and intervention from outside the South by the federal courts and the federal government. Gore had to adjust to this new dynamic. His lack of personal exposure to African American impatience partly explains why he voted against the Civil Rights Act of 1964. But the Voting Rights Act the following year was a different matter: White violence at Selma and the egregious denial of the vote to African Americans in the Deep South was indefensible. Similarly Gore had little truck with the realtors' opposition to open housing in 1968. By the time of Nixon's nomination of two Southerners, Clement Haynsworth and Harrold Carswell, to the Supreme Court in 1969 and 1970, Gore's sensitivity to the demands of the increasing number of African American voters was acute.

Gore's story enables us to examine the role of race in the creation of the modern Republican Party in the South. For some historians, race is at the heart of the realignment of white voters behind the Republican Party—a realignment Gore experienced firsthand in his narrow election victory in 1964 and in his defeat in 1970. A Southern strategy aimed at winning over white Democrats and supporters of George Wallace was at the heart of Republican appeals under both Barry Goldwater and Richard Nixon, even if the language was now racially coded rather than racially explicit. For some political scientists, social class is the key to explaining Republican success. According to this line of thinking, the move of Southern whites to the Republican Party was led by upper-income voters. Only later did white, working-class Democrats also switch their allegiance. Economic issues, not race, were at stake. Historians of the suburban South similarly suggest that the shift of white voters to the GOP resulted not from simple white backlash but from a sense of middle-class entitlement that was national, not merely Southern, in scope. Voters in residentially segregated suburbs that had been made possible by federal subsidies for housing and transport developed a middle-class sense of entitlement as taxpayers that was threatened by African American activism and liberal social and economic policies in the 1960s.[9]

Gore was certainly alarmed by the strength of Goldwater support in 1963 and 1964, particularly in the black belt of western Tennessee. In 1970 he tried to emphasize bread-and-butter economic issues to win over Wallace supporters. His supporters were convinced that race played a major role in his defeat in 1970. But the Republican Party we see develop in Tennessee during Gore's political career is also the result of young businessmen returning from military service or coming from outside the state. Their resentment of the corruption of an entrenched local oligarchy in a one-party system led them to political activism on behalf of the GOP.

Religion is another aspect of Gore's career that bears on the debate over race and class in Southern politics. Gore came from a generation of Southern politicians who had witnessed at firsthand the power of religious fundamentalism in Tennessee in the 1920s and the damage done by anti-Catholicism in the 1928 campaign against Democratic presidential candidate Al Smith. These politicians were part of a "religious truce" that shaped American politics from 1932 to the 1970s. Gore was a Southern Baptist who believed strongly in the separation of church and state. But like many of his contemporaries, he was uneasy with public religiosity and he rarely went to church in Washington. Nor did he attend the Senate prayer breakfasts hosted by Senator John Stennis. In 1964 Gore's Republican opponent, Dan Kuykendall, called for the restoration of America under God. That restoration, he argued, was needed because of the 1963 Supreme Court decisions against state-sponsored school prayer. In 1970 the issue came right to the forefront of William Brock's successful efforts to defeat Gore. This defeat, and that of Gore's close friend Ralph Yarborough earlier that summer in Texas, were the first times that school prayer became a major campaign issue in the South.[10]

⌐

WHEN ONE LOOKS back over Gore's remarkably productive political career, the importance of his generational cohort becomes clear. When Gore arrived in the Senate in 1953, he was a member of one of the most important freshman classes in the institution's history. In addition to Gore, it included John F. Kennedy, Stuart Symington, Mike Mansfield, and Henry Jackson. Kennedy would become president and Mansfield Senate majority leader, while Gore, Symington, and Jackson would make serious bids for the Democratic Party's nomination for the presidency or vice presidency. Historians have highlighted even more the memorable liberal classes of 1958 and 1962. Looking back from the gridlocked, partisan, and polarized Senate of today, observers have celebrated "the Last Great Senate" when bipartisan leadership ruled. Senators from the 1970s like Dale Bumpers and John Culver similarly remember a very different Senate from that of today. It was a Senate not obsessed with fundraising and reelection. It was a Senate that attempted to make laws, and to do so you needed to work across the aisles. Nowadays, Washington veterans lament, senators all too often simply find a polarizing hot-button symbolic issue—an issue on which quite possibly the legislature cannot act in any case—and force opponents to take a stand on the "wrong side." Then they can nail their opponents with negative TV advertisements. In that earlier era, Gore was part of the Last Great Senate.[11]

The Senate that Gore joined in 1953 did not necessarily have the same reputation it would a decade later. The alliance of conservative Southern Democrats and Republicans that had been so powerful since 1938 was blamed for the "deadlock of democracy": the failure to address the unfinished business of the New Deal or the cause of civil rights. When Mary McGrory, legendary Washington correspondent, started to cover Congress in the 1950s, the institution was far more florid than it is today. As her biographer wrote, "Congressmen slurped down bourbon, conducted tawdry affairs, and exchanged cash for votes with startling brazenness." By contrast, *New York Times* correspondent William S. White celebrated "the Club that is the U.S. Senate." The "Senate types" who ran the Senate in what White called "the Inner Club" did their work in places more remote than the committee rooms. They eschewed publicity. They valued colleagues who were workhorses not show horses. They operated under certain self-imposed limitations on demagoguery. They disliked senators who took themselves too seriously, and they disliked hypocrisy. They had an overriding sense of national responsibility. Under their leadership, particularly that of the Southern committee chairs, the Senate of the United States was "elevated to its highest plateau of power in history." This Senate, according to White, was "a forum largely of big men." By the 1980s, when White looked back, the Senate had become "a forum of little men."[12]

Gore was not a member of the Senate's inner club. As White described him, "he was a very unsouthern kind of fellow. He really wasn't liked in the southern caucus." Members of the inner club despised Gore's fellow Tennessee senator, Estes Kefauver. When Kefauver ran for the presidency in 1952, Senator Tom Connally of Texas observed that the womanizing Kefauver was "out running for president with his cock in one hand and the Bible in the other." The Senate insiders had little time for Kefauver's headline-grabbing investigations and his exploitation of television. They detected a combination of hypocrisy and naked ambition that they scorned. Gore was not treated with the same disdain. They recognized that he was ambitious but also serious-minded and hard-working. He was not engaged in self-publicizing crusades at the expense of his colleagues. But there was what they saw as a certain self-righteousness and a tendency toward pomposity and self-importance. As Russell Baker observed in 1960, he "stands a bit too solidly on principle to win any popularity contests," and he had a "talent for picking colorless or profitless causes." Gore was not a clubbable man, and his "abstinence from tobacco, spirits and blue language is a subject of comment." A hell-raising stump speaker, Gore in his formal Senate speeches at that time ran to a "Ciceronian solemnity."[13]

Above all Gore marched to his own drumbeat. Hubert Humphrey advised Sargent Shriver and Bill Moyers in 1961 on how to handle members of the Senate Foreign Relations Committee when they were seeking support for the Peace Corps. When he came to Gore, he said, "Albert's a very fine senator, very distinguished, hard-working. But Albert's a loner; Albert's a maverick." He would need "a little loving." Peace Corps officials had to go and see him, pay close attention to what he said, thank him for his advice, make certain that Gore knew he was not being taken for granted. Humphrey concluded, "Albert's very independent and this is what we'll have to do to make sure of his vote." Later Senate secretary Francis Valeo was less flattering. Gore, Valeo said, "was a very egotistical man. He really loved the sound of his own voice, which he used beautifully, I must say. I don't think he really needed any support, or wanted any support in anything he did. He just felt that he was on top of just about anything he picked up." Valeo acknowledged his intellectual competence and conceded he was always very pleasant but, along with Wayne

Morse of Oregon, they "were not club-men in the Senate sense. They were part of it, but not part of it." Valeo ended with the note: "One can almost say they were looking at the presidency." To members of "the inner club," loyalty to the Senate as an institution came above presidential ambitions. Gore, especially in the 1950s, could not escape the suspicion that he had these higher goals.[14]

Gore's status as an outsider was confirmed by the sort of friends and allies he made in the Senate, none of whom were in "the inner club": Mike Monroney from Oklahoma, Paul Douglas from Illinois, Ralph Yarborough from Texas, Herbert Lehman from New York, and Clinton Anderson from New Mexico. These were all independent-minded individuals; they were all more liberal than members of the club; and they had often had careers outside the Senate which were at least as important as their days in the Senate: Clinton Anderson, whose memoirs were actually called *Outsider in the Senate*, had been Truman's secretary of agriculture. Herbert Lehman had been governor of New York and director-general of the United Nations Relief and Rehabilitation Administration. Independent-mindedness was not a recipe for success, however, in the Senate of the 1950s. Gore and the people he associated with were not necessarily cavalier mavericks, but they would not conform at all costs.[15]

If Gore was not an insider, he nevertheless shared in what observers described as the obligation to make the Senate work. He was a fierce partisan but would work across the aisles not only with east Tennessee Republican congressmen but also with conservative national Republicans like Honest John Williams of Delaware. And he had important legislative achievements to his name with regard to Medicare, finance, nuclear disarmament, and, above all, the Interstate Highway Act of 1956. The Senate changed in his time there. The cohort of senators elected in 1958 began to assert themselves; the veteran Southerners began to lose influence. Mike Mansfield ran the Senate in a much more inclusive way than LBJ, and LBJ as president broke the legislative gridlock that had stymied reform. The changes paved the way for the Last Great Senate, and Gore flourished in the more permissive environment.

⤻

GORE'S RELATIONSHIP WITH Johnson shaped almost his entire Senate career. It was a story of a great personal rivalry and illuminates as much about the president as it does the senator from Tennessee. Lyndon Johnson and Albert Gore were elected to the House of Representatives within a year of each other. They came from similar backgrounds in the poor rural South, worked their way through minor colleges, and then taught school. They were both internationalists and passionate supporters of what the New Deal could do for the South. Both were Southern racial moderates. Gore gloried in Johnson's election to the Senate in 1948. When Gore followed LBJ to the Senate four years later, Johnson gave him favorable committee assignments and lined up votes for him to get his bills on highways and atomic energy passed. Johnson threw Texas's support behind Gore's vice-presidential candidacy in 1956. Gore was a strong supporter of Great Society legislation. They stayed at each other's houses; their wives were friendly with each other; they shared a passion for cattle. Yet they hated each other. Both thought they might be the first Southern president in modern times. Gore believed Johnson was cruel and entirely too indebted to conservative financial interests, while Johnson and his staff could not abide what they saw as Gore's self-righteousness.[16]

What sealed the hostility between LBJ and Gore was Vietnam, the defining issue in Gore's later career. Gore was a committed internationalist and supporter of the Cold War. He advocated ending the Korean War by the use of nuclear weapons to create a dehumanized atomic belt across the Korean peninsula. Though not innocent about Soviet intentions, he developed an expertise on nuclear disarmament, and his approach underlay the eventual efforts to secure the 1963 test-ban treaty. He was always anxious to improve relations with the Soviet Union, and he recognized the futility of a conflict with Red China. America's involvement in Vietnam he regarded as "one of the most tragic mistakes in American history." He never forgave himself for voting for the Gulf of Tonkin resolution. His skepticism about Vietnam dated back to a visit to Vietnam in 1959 to investigate corruption in the aid program. He understood the unpopularity of successive regimes in Saigon, doubted that the Americans could win militarily while burdened with Saigon as an "albatross," and worried about the impact on Soviet–U.S. relations and the possibility of a direct confrontation with China. He told Kennedy he should withdraw from Vietnam and early advocated a negotiated settlement in Vietnam. He was one of the members of the Senate Foreign Relations Committee whom Chairman Fulbright could trust. Gore's forensic and contemptuous dissection of administration spokesmen in the committee's hearings confirmed all of LBJ's hostility toward him. Vietnam was also the most difficult issue for Gore to face at home in the "Volunteer State." Tennessee was a microcosm of the South. A large majority of white Southerners supported the war. Most disapproved of a limited war and favored a campaign for all-out victory. The region suffered greater casualties than any other. Fulbright and Gore were the only Southern senators to oppose the war from 1965 onward. Despite the political dangers, Gore never doubted that he was right to oppose the war.[17]

↜

TENNESSEE HAS A rich history of leaders in the Senate, effective lawmakers, and national office-holders in Washington: Cordell Hull, Howard Baker, Jim Sasser, Al Gore, Bill Frist, and Lamar Alexander. In April 2015 a correspondent for the *Economist* detailed the rather surprising role of Senator Bob Corker on the Senate Foreign Relations Committee in providing a nonpartisan, dispassionate analysis of the Iran nuclear deal. Corker explained the pros and cons of the deal to what would normally be a skeptical audience of Rotarians in Chattanooga. When the journalist expressed surprise, "several Rotarians independently volunteered that Tennessee has a history of sending 'pragmatic' statesmen to the Senate."[18]

This biography attempts to explore the successes and failures of a Tennessee politician who was in the national eye for more than thirty years and whose son would become vice president of the United States. For all the paradoxical support for political dynasties in the most democratic society in the world, Albert Gore remains the only modern Southern senator whose son has achieved high national office. I hope to draw out the political courage, the serious-minded intent, the concern for policy, the commitment to both the environment and economic growth, and the restless entrepreneurialism that father and son shared. This biography focuses on the public life of a politician. It does not intend to provide a day-by-day account of Albert Gore's life. I have written elsewhere of the limitations of biography in explaining major social and political changes like the New Deal, but I hope in this biography of Albert Gore not only to reveal the successes and struggles of this most significant figure in regional and national politics but also to explain the dramatic changes that created the modern South.[19]

CHAPTER 1

From Possum Hollow to Capitol Hill

IN THE YEARS BETWEEN 1944 and 1952, Americans elected a remarkable generation of talented political leaders to the United States Senate. They included three future presidents, three vice presidents, several presidential candidates, and a host of contenders for their party's nomination for the presidency. Many of them had been born of modest means in small rural communities in the 1890s and the first fifteen years of the twentieth century. Lyndon Johnson, Clinton Anderson, Estes Kefauver, William Fulbright, Mike Mansfield, John Stennis, Mike Monroney, Hubert Humphrey, and Richard Nixon were born into what was still a "horse and buggy" age. Rail and the steamboat were then the main means of long-distance travel. The only governments that mattered were those at county and state levels. The United States had never intervened militarily overseas outside the Caribbean and the Philippines. Once in the Senate these men would develop atomic energy programs, build interstate highways, regulate commercial aviation, send men into space, see the United States station its armed forces across the globe, and confront the Soviet Union both head-on in Europe and, by proxy, in Korea and Vietnam. Albert Gore was one of these men.[1]

⤸

GORE WAS BORN in the Upper Cumberland hills in Granville, Jackson County, Tennessee, on 26 December 1907. When he was five, the family moved down from the hills to Possum Hollow, a small rural community in Smith County about fifteen miles from the county seat, Carthage. His father, Allen Gore, like most other hill country farmers, owned his farm, and the Gores were largely self-sufficient. Their own chickens, hogs, and cows gave them their own eggs, milk, pork, and beef. The pork could be cured and kept;

beef could not. So local farmers formed a cooperative beef club and slaughtered one cow a month. Gore and his elder brother, Reginald, hunted and would sometimes add squirrel, rabbit, groundhog, and white-crest chicken hawk to the diet. Gore's mother, Margie, canned "everything." She made kraut and pickles and mixed the ashes from the wood stove with water to produce soap. Any extra eggs, milk, and butter could be sold to help pay off the mortgage or barter for commodities like salt and pepper. Throughout the South the butter and egg trade was vital to farm women. Although they managed most of the subsistence activities of the farm, they were producing not just for home use but also to barter with peddlers at the back door or at the local store. As elsewhere in the Upper Cumberland, it was Gore's mother who was the family member who provided the link with a market and cash economy. Lumber was another possible source of cash. Gore's father rode logs down the river to sell in Carthage, and the river was the only means of traveling any distance. When the railroad finally came to Smith County, livestock and poultry could be transported farther to market. Cars did not come to the Upper Cumberland until the 1920s: As late as 1926 there were only four stretches of paved highway in the area. Graveled roads rapidly disappeared into dirt tracks. While Gore was growing up, counties like Smith would not use contractors to repair roads—rather they relied on local residents to do the job. This "public work" was another link of farmers to a cash market.[2]

Life was hard, and Gore recalled that "there was but one way to go from Possum Hollow—that was up and out! . . . You couldn't get out except by going up, and once you got out, you were still pretty far down the pole." But the Gores were not dirt poor. Allen Gore had savings of $8,000 invested in local banks on the eve of the Depression.[3]

Life for young Albert revolved around school, the church, and the outdoors. The school was a typical one-room school just like the one in which Gore would later teach in Overton County. Although he progressed to high school in Gordonsville, he was to discover that his education in Possum Hollow had not prepared him for college. The teachers were ill-trained, appointed not even by the county but by directors of local school districts. Few teachers had had even four years of high school. They received little on-the-job training and taught a curriculum that was set by the local school directors under very loose state guidelines, offering little more than instruction in reading and writing. The school year was short, designed not to interrupt work on the farms. Until 1913 education was not compulsory in Tennessee. Most students in Upper Cumberland did not attend school past the fourth grade. Even after 1913 few went beyond the eighth grade. When Gore went to Gordonsville High, he was one of only sixty-four high school students in the entire Upper Cumberland to do so.[4]

Gore never lost his love of hunting and fishing or working on the farm. At the age of eighty-three, he could still be found fixing poles that had been blown down on the farm on a Saturday afternoon. Almost all his early social life centered around the church and Sunday school. The local minister was a significant figure in the local intelligentsia. Few men could afford the cost of training to be a doctor and a lawyer, but training to be a minister was more feasible. Unlike the ill-trained local teachers, the preachers lived and worked in the community all year round. But while the church had more influence than school, family trumped both. Gore believed that the "most profound influence on me and on my life and on my outlook on moral and social values" was the almost puritanical "mores and moral codes that are traditional with the fundamentalist religion of this area and Scotch-Irish independence." The moral code, which he learned from his parents, left a greater mark on Gore than the directly spiritual effect of religion. His father, Allen, was a life-long Baptist church-goer, both evangelical and stern. Albert was a disciplinarian, but he wore his spirituality much more lightly. Organized religion would never play a major part in his personal or political life once he left Possum Hollow.[5]

ↄ

THE YOUNG GORE was ambitious. He wanted to get out of Possum Hollow, and he wanted to become a lawyer. Importantly he was also open to new ideas. Sociologists would discover, perhaps unsurprisingly, that the people who stayed behind in the Upper Cumberland were the ones most committed to traditional values. They crafted communities with a very flat social hierarchy: "Getting ahead" individually was not a prominent value of the villages in the hills. Gore was the only boy of his generation in his community to go to college. In 1924 the representative from Smith County in the state legislature voted against appropriations for the University of Tennessee on the grounds that nobody in his community went to university. Law school was out of reach financially for Gore, but training to be a teacher and a career in teaching might in time enable him to put aside the money to pay for his legal education. He briefly worked tables at the University of Tennessee at Knoxville, but he could ill afford the fees of the leading state college. Instead in 1925 he went back to Middle Tennessee State Teachers College (MTSC) at Murfreesboro.[6]

Middle Tennessee had been established in 1911 as one of the three two-year "normal" schools in the state provided for by the General Education Bill of 1909. Progressive reformers in Tennessee wanted to compensate for the lack of high school graduates who could teach in the state's elementary schools. The normal schools were designed to provide a speedy high school education for future teachers. The Murfreesboro school was the one chosen for the Middle Division of Tennessee, but its funding was bitterly resisted by those who saw it as taking money away from existing high schools. Successful lobbying, notably by the school's first president, saved that funding and extended its remit. The college that Gore entered in 1925 had therefore just become a four-year, degree-awarding teachers' training college.[7]

Like Lyndon Johnson, who was attending San Marcos Teachers' College in Texas at the same time, Gore could not afford to enroll for four uninterrupted years at college. Instead, he studied at Murfreesboro for one or two quarters, and then went back home to raise a tobacco crop, work the farm, teach school, or do odd jobs, including one fruitless summer working in Detroit, until he had enough money to return to school.[8]

Gore was not conventionally academically gifted. Failing his first English class, he was taken in hand by an instructor who told him that, despite his omnivorous reading, he had been inadequately taught in rudimentary English grammar. Gore was a keen student and, in later life, "became a stickler for correct punctuation, sentence structure, and paragraphing." According to his transcripts at MTSC, his grades were largely Cs and Ds. In forty-eight courses in Murfreesboro, he obtained only two As—in 100-level courses in European history and geography. He majored in history and English, in which he claimed to have had inspirational teachers. But he regarded all his specifically education-related courses as a "virtual waste of time." Indeed he almost failed his practical teaching course. His contemporaries remembered him as a keen, even flamboyant, actor and as a man already with an eye on a political career. Pressed to go out on Saturday night, he would frequently stay in his room, writing postcards to people back in Smith County. He explained to roommate Rollie Holden that these letters were to and from students he had taught at grammar school. He was going to run for county superintendent of schools: "I expect all of those kids to get their mothers and fathers to vote for me."[9]

Gore developed friendships at the college that would still be providing him with support in his final campaign in 1970. But he was always conscious that his education had been unsophisticated. His peers in Tennessee politics—Estes Kefauver, Frank Clement, Gordon Browning, and Prentice Cooper—were graduates of the more prestigious University of Tennessee, Vanderbilt University, the Cumberland School of Law, and the Yale and Harvard law schools. However gifted a stump orator Gore would become, his written and spoken style occasionally had the stilted quality, studded with long words, of the autodidact. He confessed to an interviewer much later that he shared her difficulty in spelling a particular word. She thought this was a charming anecdote that would humanize the rather stiff Gore. He was adamant that she should not use it in her article.[10]

Gore finally graduated in 1931. He had already had experience teaching in one-room schools deep in the Cumberland hills. His uncle, Charlie Gore, who lived in Livingston, arranged for him to teach at Highland, in Overton County, known as "Booze" because it was a center for the production of moonshine liquor. His uncle drove him to the foot of the mountain, and the eighteen-year-old Gore walked the five miles to Booze. He boarded with another Gore, who may have been a distant cousin, who rode a mule every day to work in the coal mine five miles away on the other side of the mountain. Gore saw the impact of abject poverty. Overton County ranked near the bottom of the state in per capita income. Timber clearance in the early twentieth century, coal strip-mining, and overgrazing had denuded its soil. Only once in the four months he was there did the family have meat on the table, except on those occasions when Albert brought in the results of his hunting. Gore later recalled a most beautiful teenager who came to school when he started teaching there. He saw her again in a crowd ten years later when he was on the campaign trail. Still only in her twenties, she looked an old woman. Later, he taught two fall semesters at Little Creek in his home county. After graduation Gore taught at Pleasant Shade, a few miles outside Carthage, and he then ran for county superintendent of education. Narrowly defeated that year, he found himself without a teaching job. Nevertheless he invested in a small farm outside Carthage and received $89 for his tobacco crop. He added to his income by selling furniture as a traveling salesman for $12.50 a week. However, when the newly elected county superintendent died of cancer the following year, Gore was appointed to the position by the county court. At the age of twenty-five, he was in charge of Smith County schools, with an office in Carthage. No one who knew Gore could doubt his ambition and his determination. At various times he had led a hand-to-mouth existence. His solution to his difficulties was always hard work.[11]

↜

CARTHAGE WAS, like most county seats in the South, a hotbed of Democratic Party politics as factions struggled for local patronage. Former governor Benton McMillin lived there. It was also the home of Cordell Hull, who
had served as congressman for the Fourth District for twenty-two years before being elected to the Senate in 1931. In the House of Representatives, Hull
was the sponsor of the bills that established the federal income tax. His first
speech in Congress had been in favor of free trade: Lowering tariffs became
a crusade for him. Hull had been chair of the Democratic National Committee when Franklin D. Roosevelt began reaching out to party leaders across
the country in an effort establish more of a national profile for himself after
he was paralyzed by polio in 1921. Like other Southern and Western leaders,
Hull shared FDR's view that the party needed to move in a progressive direction. One of the earliest backers of Roosevelt's presidential bid, Hull would
be rewarded with the post of secretary of state, and he would go on to be the
longest-serving secretary of state in American history. He received the Nobel
Peace Prize in 1945 for his contribution to the formation of the United Nations.[12]

Gore's father greatly admired Hull. As a younger man Allen Gore had
ridden rafts of logs down the Cumberland River from Carthage to Nashville
with Hull, returning upriver by steamboat. Albert Gore as a young teacher
used to drive over to Carthage at the end of the workday in Pleasant Shade
and watch and listen as Hull talked to the men playing checkers in the courthouse square. That memory lasted with Gore. In 1970 Gore's campaign ads
filmed by Charles Guggenheim featured Gore playing checkers and talking
about Medicare on that same courthouse square.[13]

When political scientist V. O. Key, Jr.'s assistant Alexander Heard un-
dertook fieldwork in Tennessee in 1947 for Key's monumental survey of
Southern politics, Carthage and Smith County were singled out as examples
of bitter factional local politics that involved both corruption and electoral
skullduggery. Veteran Tennessee journalist Larry Daughtrey would describe
the Tennessee state legislature as "a rollicking rural fiefdom" controlled by
leaders like I. D. Beasley, of Carthage, who had been first elected to the state
House of Representatives in 1923. Like other rural leaders, Beasley ran his
fiefdom into the 1960s. When Heard visited Carthage in 1947, he described
the courthouse as "a run down affair in the worst rural tradition." He met a
local lawyer, a member of the state Democratic executive committee, whose
office had a "shabbiness . . . that was characteristic of the public institutions

of the county." The lawyer admitted to Heard that Smith was one of the counties where money was used to buy votes. Earlier in the twentieth century, it had been even more blatant. On election day in Defeated Creek, men would come out of the hills and go down to the polling place. In the morning they would sell their votes for one dollar each. Later in the day the price would go down to fifty cents, and about the time the polls would close, the price would probably go down to twenty-five cents. They would go home and not vote at all if they were not paid enough. The lawyer explained to Heard that Circuit Judge Clint Beasley, I. D. Beasley's brother, was the most powerful man in the county, with a group of followers who constituted an "informal alliance of ins." Periodically people would change sides for no apparent reason.[14]

Heard interviewed Clint Beasley, who had been appointed a county judge in 1930. They talked about the New Deal and about anti-communism. "Every nuance of speech," reported Heard, "and every piece of office equipment and every client in the reception room and every prop of local scenery outside contributed to my belief that Judge Beasley would hold the conventional small town southern politician's view towards these things." But instead Heard found a Roosevelt Democrat and a staunch defender of Henry Wallace. Heard was further shocked when Beasley continued that, whatever the prejudices he had grown up with, "I have persuaded myself we were all wet about that proposition, we were dead wrong. . . . That there is no question about it that we were wrong in the Civil War." These were heretical words for a Democratic politician in the 1940s. Judge Beasley was effectively chief executive of Smith County. He chaired the county court, which set the county tax rate and appropriated county funds. It was Clint Beasley who appointed Gore as school superintendent, and it was Beasley, more than any other single person, who was Albert Gore's political mentor.[15]

⤳

AS COUNTY SUPERINTENDENT Albert Gore was clearly a coming man in local politics. Progressive reformers in Tennessee had long seen schools as the entry point to improve the life of rural communities: School was a bridge to the rural home, the linchpin of an improved country life. But in the Upper Cumberland, local resistance to taxation and spending hampered reform initiatives. Under the 1925 Education Act, in Tennessee there were now incentives for counties like Smith to levy taxes that would give them access to equalization funds from the state. Funds were available first from the state, and then from the federal government in the New Deal to build new schools.

When roads were built, children could travel for the first time to larger, consolidated schools. District school boards might still appoint teachers, but the county superintendent had the opportunity to provide training for these teachers in annual normal schools or institutes. Gore was fully engaged with this modernizing agenda. In 1998 C. L. Powell could still remember inspirational visits by the county superintendent to his school. Powell lived in Difficult, a small community with a grade school. It was only fifteen miles from Carthage, but Powell had never been to Carthage. Regular visits from Gore, who talked to pupils like Powell as if they were adults, left a lasting impression. For all his engagement with the local schools, Gore did not lose sight of his desire to get a law degree. Although he dabbled in trading livestock and land, and grew tobacco, Gore could not afford to enroll at a university law school. Instead he studied part time for three years at the Nashville School of Law, a night school at the YMCA.[16]

Three times a week for three years, Albert drove the fifty-two miles from Carthage for classes that took place between seven and ten p.m. It was his habit to have coffee in the Andrew Jackson Hotel at end of the class to keep himself awake on the return journey. One of the waitresses at the hotel was Pauline Annette LaFon, who was living in the YMCA and waiting tables to pay her way through Vanderbilt Law School. Pauline LaFon was born in Palmersville, Weakley County, in northwest Tennessee, close to the Kentucky border. She had walked to school with the mother of future Tennessee governor Ned McWherter. She grew up in a poor family, the third of six children, whose mother had been swindled out of the family property by distant relatives. Her father's country store at Cold Corner went bust in the Great Depression. Her elder sister had gone blind at the age of thirteen. Her younger brother, Whit, became a circuit court judge in Jackson. Pauline was ambitious and determined not to be held back by conventional restrictions on opportunities for women. As she recalled, "It never occurred to me that I couldn't go to college. I just knew it was up to me to find a way." She borrowed a hundred dollars from the Jackson Rotary Club to attend Union College, a small Christian college in Jackson, where she enrolled in the fall of 1931. She waited tables at Miss Snipes' Restaurant in downtown Jackson to help pay her way. She insisted on bringing her sister, Thelma, with her to Union. She took notes and read lessons for both of them. Pauline, her brother Whit recalled, "had a burning desire to better herself." She was briefly and unsatisfactorily married, and then, not content with the limited offerings at Union, she determined to go to Vanderbilt Law School in the state capital. At the Andrew Jackson Hotel, she was attracted to the handsome and politically ambitious county school super-intendent who came in for his late-night coffee, and she and Albert studied together for the state bar exam. Eventually, in 1936, Pauline was rewarded by becoming only the tenth woman to graduate from Vanderbilt Law School. There were no barriers that she did not believe could be climbed—and she climbed most of them.[17]

Pauline may have graduated well from the law school, but there were no openings for her in Nashville law firms. Indeed half the graduating class failed to get jobs at all. The law school dean, however, recommended her to a Vanderbilt graduate who had a practice in Texarkana, just across the west Tennessee border in Arkansas. Pauline's time in Texarkana was not a happy one. Texarkana may have been too much like Palmersville and Jackson, from which she had worked so hard to escape. In addition, she told journalist Pamela Hess in 1993, she had been sexually harassed by the partner, Bert Larey. She told the dean who had recommended her simply that Larey was impossible to work with. In 1993 she said Larey's behavior had been worse than that of either Supreme Court Justice Clarence Thomas or Senator Robert Packwood, whose records of unwanted sexual advances to subordinates were in the headlines in the early 1990s. After seven months she had paid off her loans and could return to Tennessee to marry Albert, who had regularly driven over to Texarkana to see her. They were married in a quiet ceremony over the Kentucky border in 1937.[18]

Pauline may not have carved out the pioneering role in the law that she had envisaged. But she did carve out a major political role for herself. Like her good friend Martha Ragland, she combined a formal domestic role with a clearly visible political role. Al Gore recalled, she "was my father's closest adviser." She spoke on Albert's behalf and joined him on the campaign trail, and they made policy and strategy decisions jointly. Pauline Gore was a natural politician. Gregarious and sociable where her husband could be aloof, she possessed a politician's memory for names that neither Gore, nor indeed his folksy contemporary Estes Kefauver, had. Albert Gore acknowledged that she compensated for his political weaknesses: "Her political judgment is excellent. She could sense trouble many times more quickly than I. And, as adroitly, she remembers people, names, faces, personalities excellently, better than I. Her personality was always warmer than mine. Though I was sometimes described as magisterial, she was never so described."[19]

Fiercely independent, loyal, competitive, and intellectually sharp, she was part of a formidable political partnership. Pauline told her daughter-in-law Tipper that her "tough-minded approach to politics had got Albert further than he could have got on his rich oratory and high principles alone." In 1988 she noted that her son, Al, was by nature "more of a pragmatist than his father. As am I. I tried to persuade Albert not to butt at a stone wall just for the sheer joy of butting. If there's no chance of victory, there's no sense in bloodying yourself." As a friend of Nancy, her daughter, observed, "If it had been left up to him, Albert would lose touch with reality. To me he was head in the clouds. Smart but not much horse sense." Nancy spoke to the fact that her mother compensated for Albert Gore's lack of a common touch. "He just doesn't know how to gossip, how to make small talk. He doesn't like to pull off his shoes, drink beer, and shoot the bull. Mother will talk 45 minutes to a person and Daddy will talk 10." One Gore staffer spoke for many when he said Pauline "was the most politically astute member of the Gore family, more so than her husband." She was, Hodding Carter III recalled, an "exceptional woman" who, while unfailingly polite, was forthright in her opinions at a time when Southern women were generally expected to be reticent.[20]

Brought up in the Stone-Campbell Church of Christ, she would attend the Methodist church in Carthage while her husband attended First Baptist. She also brought an understanding of, and contacts with, western Tennessee politics through her brother Whit. Whit LaFon had followed Pauline to Vanderbilt, but after war service in the air force and law school studies, he returned to Jackson to practice law. In 1987 Governor Ned McWherter, the son of one of Pauline's school companions, appointed him as a circuit judge. For years Whit would be associated with the dominant Murray political organization in Madison County.[21]

⇿

GORE HAD BEEN involved in the newly formed state Young Democrats and had made speeches in support of Franklin Roosevelt in 1932, but his first real exposure to statewide politics came in 1934. Tennessee congressman Gordon Browning invited him that year to run his statewide campaign for the U.S. Senate against the incumbent, Nathan Bachman, who had been appointed to replace Cordell Hull when Hull became secretary of state.

Tennessee was a Southern state whose politics displayed many of the features of the typical state politics of the white supremacist South: black disfranchisement, a restricted white electorate, and one-party Democratic control of state government. What made Tennessee different in the South was, on the one hand, the size of the Republican Party based in its mountain redoubt of eastern Tennessee and, on the other, the city machine politics of Memphis in the west under its boss, Edward H. Crump. The mountain Republicans of eastern Tennessee had owned few slaves and had been opposed to secession. Many had either supported the Union or engaged in guerilla warfare during the Civil War. They had remained Republican throughout Reconstruction and Redemption. They profited by federal patronage during the years when the Republicans were the national majority party and usually sent two congressmen to Washington. In 1920 they carried the state for Harding, just as they would for Hoover in 1928, and they elected a Republican governor in 1920.[22]

Boss Crump ran one of the few authentic city machines in the South. A successful insurance broker who had moved to Memphis from Mississippi in 1893, Crump was elected mayor during the Progressive Era as a businessman anxious to produce cheaper, efficient government for the city's business community. He promised a city-owned electric light plant, regulation of the rates charged by streetcars, phone companies, and taxicabs, and, after the flood of 1912, proper flood control for Memphis. While he worked for strict law enforcement and the elimination of graft, he shocked some reformers by his refusal to enforce prohibition, and he was ousted from office in 1915 because of it. Crump never entirely lost his power base in the city, however, and by 1920 he had regained firm control of Memphis's politics and retained that power until 1948. Behind the scenes in Memphis and the state, he dictated the choice of both the mayor and, with rare exceptions, the governor. His power rested on control of the electoral machinery, selective granting of city contracts, and the provision of services for low-income constituents.[23]

Included among those constituents were African Americans who voted in Memphis, in stark contrast to the surrounding black-belt counties of western Tennessee, which ruthlessly disfranchised black tenants and sharecroppers. Crump's defense of black voting had nothing to do with racial liberalism, though he retained a self-image of benign paternalism. Crump encouraged African Americans to vote because they supported his candidates. He subcontracted control of the African American community to loyal African American leaders who faithfully delivered the entire black vote to Crump's slate of candidates. The reward for African Americans was some provision of local government services that were absent from many Southern towns, and a tolerance of African American social activity, including the music and speakeasies on Beale Street. Crump fought the Klan and censored anti-black and anti-Semitic films and literature.[24]

Nevertheless Crump was a staunch segregationist. If an African American leader chose to attempt to be more independent, he or she soon learned how traditional Crump was. Successful Republican insurance man Robert R. Church was forced out of town. Earlier, the anti-lynching crusader Ida Wells-Barnett had to flee Memphis. Thus Crump maintained a gentlemanly image, but his control of machine politics always rested on a measure of intimidation, although that would become blatant only when Congress of Industrial Organizations (CIO) unions came to Memphis in the late 1930s.[25]

The poll tax not only prevented African Americans from voting in most parts of the state but also suppressed lower-income white voting. A statewide electorate of 450,000 was no more than 40 percent of the voting-age population. Of those voters Republicans contributed 100,000. Crump, who paid the poll tax for his black voters in Memphis, controlled 50,000 Shelby County votes. In a primary battle of perhaps 300,000 votes, any successful Democratic candidate running for state office had to seek out Crump's support. Crump did not usually hand-pick candidates at the state level; rather he chose who to endorse among candidates who came forward, and that endorsement usually guaranteed victory.[26]

But Crump's influence in the state was much greater than the bloc of votes he controlled in Memphis. While the state legislature was in session, Crump maintained a permanent presence in Nashville to make sure that Shelby County's interests were protected. In addition to controlling western Tennessee Democrats, Crump also worked with the eastern Tennessee Republicans. While Republicans were permanently out of power in the state, their best chance of getting local state patronage and contracts lay in working in alliance with Crump.[27]

Crump's other source of power lay in Washington. The state's senior U.S. senator, Kenneth McKellar, had been in the Senate since 1917. Before that he had been the congressman from Memphis from 1911. Powerful positions on both the post office and appropriations committees of the Senate ensured that jobs and appropriations flowed to Tennessee, particularly in the 1930s. McKellar was an old Wilsonian, but preeminently a patronage politician. There were few people in Tennessee who did not have a family member who owed their job to McKellar. McKellar had a genuinely statewide organization of his own, partially independent of Crump's. Crump and McKellar were allies, even though they fell out periodically. Both saw the potential of the New Deal for jobs and projects. Indeed Crump served in Congress from 1931 to 1935 as a loyal FDR supporter.[28]

As Gordon Browning's state campaign manager in 1934, Gore was exposed to Crump's power. Browning was a lawyer and World War I veteran from Huntington, Carroll County, in the western Tennessee uplands. He served in Congress from 1922 to 1934, when he decided to run for the Senate. Like other Tennessee congressmen, he was a late convert to George Norris's fight for the public development of the Muscle Shoals dam in the Tennessee Valley to provide cheap electricity. Even when FDR firmly backed Norris in 1933, Browning still favored leasing the dams to private enterprise. He was no great fan of FDR, whom he regarded as "two-faced." He cast himself as a defender of World War I veterans and voted against the Economy Act in 1933 because it would "slaughter" disabled benefits. Roosevelt's attempts to get him to give in were unsuccessful. Though denounced by many state newspapers, Browning seemed able to get enough support from veterans to consider opposing incumbent senator Nathan Bachman in 1934.[29]

His decision to appoint the twenty-seven-year-old Albert Gore as his state campaign manager was in part testimony to Gore's prominence among young Democrats. In addition Gore could help Browning in the middle section of the state. The sitting senator, Bachman, came from Chattanooga, in east Tennessee. Since McKellar, like Browning, came from the west, Browning had to fight the tradition that both senators should not come from the same section of the state. But Gore's selection more substantially reflected the fact that no single important political figure in the state would commit to Browning. The congressman was up against an incumbent candidate who was backed by Senator McKellar, Governor Hill McAlister, and Boss Crump. Browning had no alternative than to turn to a political neophyte like Gore to run his campaign.[30]

His work for Browning's campaign took Gore all over the state. Even so Browning was comfortably defeated by 166,293 votes (57.85 percent) to 121,169 (42.15 percent). Gore could see the impact of Crump's power in Memphis. Browning received only 5,444 votes in Shelby County. By contrast, Bachman's vote in Shelby alone was greater than his entire statewide margin of victory.[31]

By 1936, when Browning ran for governor, he no longer needed Gore as campaign manager. Browning ran pledging to reorganize state finances and to refinance the growing state debt. He was able to turn for help to the man who had masterminded Governor Austin Peay's successful state campaigns in the 1920s. In addition, he acquired Boss Crump as an ally. Crump had fallen out with Governor McAlister when McAlister tried to introduce a sales tax. Crump had also fallen out, temporarily, with McKellar. As a result,

Crump, who had had an amicable working relationship with Browning when they were in Congress together, endorsed Browning. He approved of his opposition to a sales tax. Crump's endorsement did not in itself elect Browning: Crump endorsed him because he thought Browning was going to win. But Crump's backing did guarantee victory. Shelby County, which had rejected Browning in 1934, now delivered 59,874 votes to Browning in 1936. His opponent, handpicked by McKellar, got only three votes in McKellar's home precinct in Memphis.[32]

If Browning did not need Gore in the 1936 election, he did not forget him when he entered the state house. He appointed Gore as state labor commissioner. Gore's main task was to bring Tennessee into the unemployment compensation program of the new national Social Security scheme. Under the New Deal's Social Security Act, unemployment compensation was to be funded by a payroll tax, but 90 percent of that tax would be offset in any state that adopted a satisfactory unemployment insurance scheme. In addition, although Tennessee did not have a state minimum-wage law, Gore would have to implement the national 1938 Fair Labor Standards Act, which he supported, but which most Southern manufacturers opposed. As labor commissioner he was also responsible for mine inspection. As a member of Browning's administration, Gore had a ringside seat as Crump and Browning fell out over patronage and, with McKellar's active encouragement, over the Tennessee Valley Authority (TVA). Browning would therefore be humiliatingly defeated in his reelection bid in 1938, this time getting only 9,815 votes from Shelby County voters in Crump's fiefdom.[33]

⤺

BY 1938 GORE'S political future was uncertain. He knew that Browning was likely to be defeated and that his own position as state labor commissioner would almost certainly come to an end. Suddenly the four-term congressman from the Fourth District, J. Ridley Mitchell, announced that he would not stand for reelection; the conservative representative from Cookeville announced he was going to run for the U.S. Senate. Although Gore's daughter was only one month old, Gore took the plunge and joined five older men in attempting to capture the nomination to succeed Mitchell as congressman for the Fourth District.[34]

In seeking to represent Tennessee's Fourth District on the national political stage, all the candidates had to confront the fact that the New Deal had dramatically changed not only the national political landscape but also the physical landscape of the constituency. For the first time, the federal government under the New Deal had become a reality in the experience of ordinary Tennesseans. The federal government told farmers what they could and could not plant, told manufacturers what they could and could not pay their workers, and guaranteed workers the right to unionize. The New Deal paid people on relief and gave them jobs, provided every worker social insurance against unemployment and old age, and left its physical mark in its public works and work-relief projects on all but two of Tennessee's counties. Above all the Tennessee Valley Authority built dams to provide flood control and cheap electricity for the state's municipalities and farmers. Its headquarters were located in Norris, a new town built in Anderson County, eastern Tennessee. Little wonder liberal Chattanooga newspaper publisher George Fort Milton, Jr., proclaimed in 1939 that the state and the South as a whole had "undergone more fundamental change than has any other region of the country."[35]

As late as September 1930, Tennesseans had prided themselves on having avoided the worst of the Depression, but in November of that year, the Bank of Tennessee failed. The bank was part of the empire of Rogers Caldwell, whose investment house had dramatically expanded in the 1920s. Caldwell marketed bonds for Southern municipalities which then deposited funds in the Bank of Tennessee, which then could fund further expansion of Caldwell and Co. The firm benefitted from, and helped finance, Colonel Luke Lea's political and publishing empire in Tennessee as publisher of the *Tennessean* in Nashville, the *Memphis Commercial Appeal*, and the *Knoxville Journal*. Financial irregularities and the unauthorized funding of Rogers Caldwell's lavish lifestyle were exposed in November 1930, and the bank went into receivership. As a result banks in seven Southern states failed. Thanks to the political influence of Colonel Lea, the state of Tennessee had five million dollars on deposit in the Bank of Tennessee. The state lost that money when the bank collapsed. At the same time, the effects of the Depression eroded the state's tax revenues. The state thus was hard-pressed to pay off the debts it had incurred when, like other Southern states, it had invested heavily in roads and schools in the 1920s. After 1930 Tennessee was in no position to continue spending or to cope with the urgent relief demands of the swelling numbers of the unemployed and needy.[36]

First under Hoover, and subsequently under Roosevelt, the federal government came in and paid for what the state could no longer provide. Under Hoover funds from the Reconstruction Finance Corporation aided some 50,000 families in Tennessee. Under the New Deal, the Emergency Relief Administration, the Civil Works Administration (CWA), and lastly the Works Progress Administration (WPA) helped jobless Tennesseans. Between 1933 and 1935, 118,000 families—an estimated 526,000 people—received direct assistance or jobs from the CWA and Emergency Relief Administration. The Civilian Conservation Corps employed 46,000 young men over a five-year period.[37]

The help offered to individuals and families through the recovery and relief programs of the New Deal solidified the loyalty of the majority of Tennesseans to Roosevelt. The almost unanimous support for New Deal legislation from the Tennessee congressional delegation testified to the demands of their constituents that they back the president. Despite business opposition to the labor and minimum-wage legislation, the Tennessee senators voted for both the Wagner Act of 1935 and the Fair Labor Standards Act of 1938. But nowhere was there greater unanimity than in their support for the Tennessee Valley Authority in its battles to distribute cheap power to the state's cities and farmers. Even so the full impact of the TVA was not felt until the later 1930s and 1940s. The private power companies tied up the TVA in the courts over the right of the authority not merely to produce but to distribute electrical power. Not until 1939 was the constitutional threat to the TVA lifted.[38]

But if the full impact of the TVA was delayed, the impact on the infrastructure of the state of the relief program and the projects of the WPA and the Public Works Administration was immediate, and still shapes the physical landscape of the state today. At its height two-thirds of New Deal spending in the state of Tennessee was on infrastructure projects; the relief program rescued both the state's highway program and its education system. In 1931 the cash-strapped state almost had to eliminate its highway department, and it laid off four thousand workers. The state and local school boards could not afford to build new schools and had to lay off teachers. Student enrollments fell away. By contrast the New Deal poured money into schools and roads. Under the New Deal 47 percent of federal spending in the state between 1935 and 1938 ($37 million) was on highways, roads, and streets in towns and cities. The CWA and the WPA worked on seventeen airport projects and built five new major airports. According to Carroll Van West, the New Deal launched the largest program of school building in the state's history. The WPA built new schools and renovated others. The National Youth Administration (NYA) not only enabled students to stay in school and college but also provided the labor for many of these construction projects.[39]

The Fourth District provided ample testimony to this dramatic transformation. In Smith County, in his role as school superintendent, Gore had successfully secured funds for the WPA to level the high school playing field. By 1940 the WPA had built a new high school. Above all Carthage had the new, 605-foot-long Cordell Hull Bridge across the Cumberland River. It also had a modern sewer system. At Gore's old college, MTSC, falling enrollments halted any new construction in the 1930s, but into the breech stepped the WPA, which worked on the football stadium, and the NYA supported landscaping projects and the construction of a new industrial arts building. Murfreesboro now had a large Veterans Administration hospital, a new school gymnasium, and a new Boy and Girl Scout lodge, and the county had a new African American school in Almaville to replace the old one-room school. Dirt-poor Overton County, where Gore first taught, now had two new schools on Highway 52, a renovated courthouse, a new state park, and a new post office in Livingston. In Woodbury, county seat of Cannon County, the New Deal provided the town's first concrete sidewalks, a new school, and a new waterworks and sewage system.[40]

ᔕ

HOW DID ALBERT GORE respond to the New Deal?

As with most rural Americans, Gore had not experienced pre-1929 prosperity, but the Depression had a devastating impact on his father, Allen. His hard-earned money had been deposited in a number of banks so that if one failed, the deposits in the others would be secure. After all, small, rural, undercapitalized banks had collapsed through even the supposedly prosperous 1920s. It was certainly wise to be cautious. But during the Depression all the banks in which Gore's father had left his money failed. These failures forever fueled Albert Gore's traditional distrust of financial institutions. Thomas Jefferson, Andrew Jackson, and the populists were Gore's political heroes. What they had in common was the defense of credit-starved farmers and small businessmen against large financial institutions. Given his family's admiration for Cordell Hull, who had led the drive for progressive taxation and financial regulation under Woodrow Wilson, it was not surprising that Gore spoke enthusiastically in support of Franklin D. Roosevelt in the 1932 presidential campaign. Fellow Carthage resident and former governor Benton McMillin headed up FDR's campaign in Tennessee. But, Gore's was not a personal loyalty or appreciation of Roosevelt. As he recalled, Roosevelt was the antidote to Hoover, and that was enough for Gore.[41]

Gore was an enthusiastic supporter of the early New Deal measures, but work relief and its political uses gave him pause. He retained a rural hostility to relief dependency: He had seen how New Deal patronage, linked to the relief programs, could be used when the McKellar–Crump alliance in 1934 pulled the patronage strings against Gordon Browning. The political manipulation of the WPA after 1935 further confirmed this hostility. How local New Deal patronage operated was brought home even more closely in 1937, when Gore was implementing the Social Security Act's provision for unemployment compensation. Senator McKellar secured the appointment of his unsuccessful candidate for governor, Burgin E. Dossett, to head the Social Security office in Nashville.[42]

But national politics was not an issue in the 1938 Fourth Congressional District primary. Gore was running in a one-party system in which the only election was the primary. All the candidates were pro-Roosevelt. It was a classic Southern congressional election for an open seat. A plethora of candidates ran, with no party organization to back them and with no clear ideological issues to divide them. It was not politics in which national issues resonated; it was local and highly personal. Political allegiances were based on personal ties and alliances with small-town, county-seat elites.

The problem for any candidate was to establish a distinctive identity with the voters. Gore's five opponents were a district judge, two district attorneys general, a former state senator and prominent lawyer, and a current member of the state legislature. They all had local reputations and name recognition. To carve out an identity, a successful candidate would have to mount a vigorous personal campaign in all the district's eighteen counties. Gore also had to fight what he perceived to be the opposition of the "federal crowd"—local federal appointees, particularly in the work-relief program. Armed with a campaign war chest of $10,000, Gore campaigned across the district, speaking every day at crossroads communities and at night in rural schools and all the county seats. He was a good stump speaker, with a natural gift for rural storytelling coupled with an ability to relate his standard speech to the local community concerns of local individuals. Nevertheless, to cover the whole district required a punishing schedule. He was immensely helped by the fact that Pauline was with him on the trail, despite the fact that their new baby, Nancy, was only one month old. As his son, Al Gore, described it, "In that first campaign, my mother would talk with any voter she could find, and speak at any club meeting that would have her." Pauline walked the dirt roads of the district, and on rainy days, she'd pull off her shoes and wade through the mud to reach people's homes. Between them, Albert and Pauline covered the district. Ivy Agee, a former classmate of Albert Gore's at Gordonsville High School, recalled him visiting up to five small towns a day—towns that might be several miles apart. The district covered 7,467 square miles; even in the 1930s it was the largest district in the state and one of the largest east of the Mississippi. It was a formidable task for Gore to make himself known across the whole of the district.[43]

Gore recognized that, to attract crowds, to pack the rural schools, and to get two thousand at the meetings in the county seats, he needed more than his speaking ability—the ability to speak "loudly and forcefully," as one listener recalled. He needed to provide some sort of entertainment. So he paid a group of youngsters to play guitar and banjo and sing at meetings, and Albert would join them on the fiddle. He played an acceptable fiddle, having learned how at hoedowns in Possum Hollow. Larry Richards, whose father was superintendent of schools in Woodbury, in Cannon County, remembered that Gore would "go around to all the little country stores and whatever and get out his fiddle and play it." When Gore went to Woodbury, word would get out through the county newspaper, and, Richards recalled, "He would stand on the courthouse steps and make a speech and there would be several hundred people would gather round the courthouse yard and hear him." In pre-television days, many people who lived out of town did not even have access to a radio because they did not have electricity. Gore's "little road show" was "a source of entertainment" that would bring out the people of Woodbury. When he spoke in county towns on Saturdays, his crowds ranged from two thousand to four thousand attendees. In one week he made thirty-four speeches to an estimated twenty thousand listeners.[44]

Gore acknowledged the role of the fiddle in getting the crowds out. But he also believed these meetings gave the electorate the chance to weigh up the candidates. "It was necessary to impress the voters that the candidate had the capacity to get worked up on an issue and give a good accounting of himself in debate." It was, Gore summed up, "a personality contest." The precise nature of issues themselves did not matter: "So far as my position on issues contrasting with other candidates, I don't think it played any part at all." Indeed, the ten-point program he laid out when he announced his candidacy was blandly in favor of everything: farm and conservation programs, good roads, bank deposit insurance, and social insurance. He wanted an "Adequate National Defense," but "America should not become involved in foreign wars or entanglements." He pledged support of Roosevelt's policies but reserved the right at all times to make his independent judgment. Like almost all Southern politicians, he deplored freight-rate discrimination against the South. He campaigned less on FDR's coattails and more on Cordell Hull's. He shamelessly invoked the secretary of state: "Having sat at the feet of Judge Hull during many summer evenings and having had him bless me with a discussion of the ideals of his Congressional life and his tariff and trade ambitions for the United States. . . . I frankly say that he is my ideal in public life. To be of meager assistance to him would be a happy privilege. I pledge to you now that when elected to Congress I will seek the advice and guidance of Judge Hull."[45]

The most distinctive issue Gore campaigned on was not the New Deal but immigration. Gore attacked aliens as, "the seven to nine million foreigners in the United States . . . being supported by the American taxpayer." They were not schooled in democracy, rather they "are possessed of various concepts of government to which they attempt to convert America." They had taken jobs that should have gone to American citizens: "We already have too much unemployment—too many traitors to Americanism." In reports of his first campaign speech, reporters identified immigration as his strongest point. In his early days in Congress, he would go on to praise the "splendid work" of the Dies Committee, lament the fact that American taxpayers supported "thousands of foreigners on the WPA rolls," and ask why should "alien enemies, dope peddlers, prostitutes, criminals etc. be turned free to further promote debauchery and subversiveness." He was echoing his political mentor Gordon Browning, who took a strong anti-immigrant stance. As Browning said, "I've always been opposed to immigration for we have a virile and strong people and they'll stay strong by not being mixed with any other race."[46]

Harry McPherson recalled that Gore never lost that concern about immigration and racial purity. In the 1950s, when McPherson was controlling the Senate calendar for Majority Leader Lyndon Johnson, senators asked to be alerted about particular specialist bills that might otherwise slip through unnoticed. Gore wanted to be told about any bill that came out of the Immigration Committee which waived the requirement that mentally deficient immigrants not be admitted to the United States. One of Gore's office staff explained to McPherson, "In the Tennessee Hills there was . . . incest [that] would produce mentally deficient children, and he [Gore] didn't want there to be more mentally deficient children allowed into the United States who would then produce mentally deficient children."[47]

Gore's campaign climaxed with a rally in his hometown, Carthage. An estimated 7,500 people packed into the town on a Saturday, a bonanza for local merchants who took advertising space in a full-page ad in the *Car-*

thage Courier, which announced the sequence of events to celebrate the final "homecoming" speech of their local boy. Twelve or fifteen hundred automobiles parked on the streets of Carthage. The crowds could shop, listen to Gore, and also listen to the Carthage Modern Woodmen Brass Band and Rambling Cowboys.[48]

Gore won only just over a third of the votes in the district, but he had a comfortable majority. His vigorous campaigning all over the district, the majorities he piled up among his home-turf Smith County voters, and his pull in his old college town of Murfreesboro in Rutherford County saw him safely home. The margin of victory over his nearest rival was large enough to discourage any significant challengers for his seat for the next fourteen years.[49]

～

IN JANUARY 1939, at the age of thirty-one, Albert Gore set off for Washington, D.C., with his wife and baby daughter. It was a grueling journey: a two-day trip on two-lane roads through the mountains of Tennessee and Virginia. As the Gores attempted to break the journey on the first night in eastern Tennessee, they could not find a motel that would let their African American nanny stay with them. They had to detour to a cousin's house in the mountains to find somewhere to stay. Subsequently they came to an agreement with a motel that would allow them to stay with the nanny, provided they arrived after dark and left before other guests got up in the morning. Seventeen years later Gore would be responsible for the Interstate Highway Act, which in time would transform the drive into a fifteen-hour stretch along four-lane roads. But it would take a quarter of a century to open up public accommodations across the South to African Americans.[50]

CHAPTER 2

A Washington Education

IN 1936 PRESIDENT ROOSEVELT explained to the leader of the Socialist Party, Norman Thomas, that he could not achieve what Thomas wanted for Southern sharecroppers because he was hamstrung by the power of Southern conservatives in Congress. But he counseled Thomas to be patient because "there was a new generation of Southerners" on the horizon. By 1945 Gore had emerged as part of that new generation of Southern New Dealers.[1]

But when Gore arrived in Washington in January 1939, he was not a committed New Dealer. He had, in his own words, a provincial attitude toward both the New Deal and the world. He had a hill country faith in self-sufficiency and individualism that made him fearful of dependency on government handouts. He disliked machine politics and the manipulation of WPA patronage. He was suspicious of immigrants and the cities into which they were flooding. He knew little about foreign policy. In his first term in Congress, he behaved, predictably, like a young rural congressman whose enthusiasm for the New Deal was restrained. Wilbur Mills, the future titan of the House Ways and Means Committee who was elected at the same time, remembered Gore as a conservative at the time.[2]

But like many young Southerners who went to Washington in the 1930s, Gore soon became convinced of what the federal government and New Deal liberalism could do to help the South. Congressional leaders and the White House courted him as an up-and-coming lawmaker. Inspired by Roosevelt and his personal hero, Cordell Hull, Gore became a staunch supporter of an interventionist, internationalist foreign policy during both World War II and the Cold War. That made him no different from most Southern congressmen. But the realities of wartime mobilization also convinced him of the importance of government economic regulation, and the TVA convinced him of the possibilities of infrastructure investment in the South. He soon learned that the problems of the nation were not the same as the problems of the hill country.

&

WHEN GORE ARRIVED in Washington, he arranged to see Secretary of State Cordell Hull. Gore usually called him "Judge Hull" because Hull had served as a state circuit court judge early in his career. Hull remembered Gore's father from Smith County. He advised the new congressman to spend as much time as possible on the floor of the House so that he could watch, listen, and learn the parliamentary rules. Following the judge's advice, Gore soon would make himself useful to the House leadership, particularly Majority Leader Sam Rayburn.[3]

But initially Gore made a name for himself in the House as an independent, conservative voice. He had joined a Tennessee congressional delegation whose members, like most Southern Democrats, had been enthusiastic supporters of the New Deal. They had overwhelmingly backed the emergency measures of the New Deal, which provided desperately needed relief to their hard-pressed constituents, particularly farmers. After 1936, as the worst of the Depression eased, some Southern congressman saw less need to support the administration's reform program. The nonemergency New Deal to them seemed to benefit the urban North, not the rural South. The 1937–38 recession damaged the recovery credentials of the administration, and congressional leaders worried about the extension of presidential and executive power envisaged in Supreme Court reform, executive reorganization, and FDR's attempted purge of conservative congressmen in the 1938 midterm primaries.

Gore arrived in Washington, therefore, just as a potentially obstructive conservative bipartisan coalition of Southern Democrats and Republicans, strengthened by Republican gains in 1938, began to flex its political muscle. No measure aroused the suspicion of Southerners concerned about the Northern, urban thrust of the New Deal more than public housing. An $800-million appropriation for the United States Housing Authority (USHA), which enabled slum clearance and the construction of low-cost housing, was part of Roosevelt's spending program in the summer of 1939 that provoked opposition from the conservative coalition. Albert Gore first made his mark in Congress as a vocal and effective opponent of this quintessentially liberal New Deal measure.[4]

Gore had been appointed to the House Banking and Currency Committee. At hearings on the housing bill, USHA administrator Nathan Straus had angered Gore by his perfunctory and patronizing answers. Gore retaliated by going against his committee chair and testifying before the Rules Committee, already a road block for New Deal legislation, against allowing the housing bill on to the floor. Urban congressmen made it clear to Southern representatives that there would be no action on a cotton barter bill unless the housing bill was allowed onto the floor. But when the bill got to the floor, Gore put what the *Tennessean* described as a "tuneful stiletto" into the legislation. The fact that Nashville was in line to get a $9 million grant for badly needed slum clearance and housing construction did not deter Gore. He denounced the cost of the bill, the cost of individual USHA projects, and the burden of debt placed on the occupants. The bill, he said, "promotes and perpetuates tenancy." The USHA, he charged, "is guilty of disseminating the most reprehensible, deceptive and misleading information." He slammed a book down on the well table so hard that it bounced into the lap of a Missouri congressman. This passionate denunciation of a New Deal spending program brought Gore an ovation for a full minute—rare for anybody in their first term—and he was mobbed by Republicans, who swarmed across the aisle to congratulate him. His flamboyant speech, laced with scorn, "stopped the show," according to the *New York Times*. The paper's Washington correspondent, the legendary Arthur Krock, singled out Gore shortly after the first session as one of the small number of freshman representatives who had won a "single-handed victory" over the administration. Republican minority leader Joseph Martin of Massachusetts stood aside to allow Gore to "deliver the coup de grace" in his maiden speech on the floor of the House.[5]

The *Washington Post* heralded the role of three "seldom heard of Congressmen"—Gore, Mike Monroney, and Wilbur Mills—in the bill's defeat. All three were freshmen. Monroney and Gore would be steadfast friends and allies—first in the House, then in the Senate—for the next thirty years. As Jack Robinson Sr. recalled, if you wanted to know where Gore was likely to stand on an issue, the easiest way was to see where Monroney stood. A few years older than Gore, Monroney had been a reporter in Oklahoma City before entering the family furniture business. He moved from the presidency of the Oklahoma City Rotary Club to Congress in the 1938 elections. Gore and Monroney would work closely together on price controls and congressional reform. While Gore worked on atomic energy and roads, Monroney, who had interviewed Charles Lindbergh after his flight to Paris in 1927, worked on aviation and masterminded the creation of the Federal Aviation Agency. Gore described Monroney to Bernard Baruch as his "inseparable friend."[6]

Gore further demonstrated his hostility to the Northern cities through his support for the House Un-American Activities Committee and by his opposition to any moves to relax immigration controls to allow in those who had served in the allied armies in World War I. Back in Murfreesboro he would celebrate Tennessee's Anglo-Saxon stock, ninety-nine and a half percent native-born, which he believed would "offset the unfortunate infiltration of inferior foreign blood in other regions." Gore had grown up in a homogeneous culture. There were few sources of "sophisticated cosmopolitanism" in the South, and Gore and other Southern congressmen reflected that provincialism.[7]

≈

GORE WAS UNEASY, however, in his role as a hero of the anti–New Deal coalition. The administration moved to bring him into the New Deal fold. The first step was to invite Gore to lead off the on the second day of the debate over revision of the Neutrality Acts in November 1939.

In Tennessee, foreign policy had featured scarcely at all in Gore's career. In Washington, Gore found himself in a maelstrom of controversy about preparedness and America's appropriate stance in the event of a European conflict. At first Gore simply used his weekly newsletters to explain to constituents the opposing viewpoints on foreign policy issues. In the summer of 1939, he told them that it was "reassuring to find that the members of the House and Senate are unanimous in their efforts to keep American at peace." He made the standard argument in defense of the arms embargo in June 1939 that "if England can't count on our help, and if Hitler can't count on our isolation, there won't be any war." What was important was that "as long as the desperado dictator nations threaten the peace of the world, America should prepare adequately to defend itself and to let the world know that she is invincible."[8]

Roosevelt, by contrast, believed that the Neutrality Acts designed to prevent America from being sucked into a European conflict were actually encouraging Hitler. An arms embargo that prevented the United States from supplying arms to any combatant would in effect benefit a strong aggressor like Hitler, who had built up his armed forces, but harm nations like Britain. In the summer of 1939, Roosevelt and Hull tried to revise the Neutrality Acts to allow arms to be sent to a belligerent provided they were paid for and transported in the belligerents' ships. Given the British navy's power, this was a move that would potentially benefit the British. Gore and other Southerners backed FDR and Hull, but Congress as a whole still preferred to stay on the sidelines as tension mounted in Europe.[9]

Once Hitler invaded Poland in September 1939, and Britain went to war against Germany, Roosevelt was determined to aid the British without risking going to war himself. He called Congress into special session to repeal the arms embargo and enact a "cash and carry" provision so the United States could shore up British defenses.

Southern congressmen were almost unanimously internationalist in these years. They revered Woodrow Wilson. They did not readily forgive Henry Cabot Lodge and the irreconcilables who had kept the United States out of the League of Nations. They supported FDR's moves to join the World Court. They were pro-British both for reasons of ethnic sentiment and economic self-interest. Representing a rural region dependent on exports, they favored free trade and supported Cordell Hull's drive for reciprocal trade agreements. Whatever their views on the domestic New Deal, they were keen to support the British in any European conflict. Indeed, some of Roosevelt's most unyielding conservative critics were the keenest to get into a "shooting war" on behalf of the British. They were, as Gore described them, in a state of "ready belligerency." Historian Arthur Schlesinger, Jr. remembered that the debate over possible American intervention in World War II provoked "the most savage political debate in my lifetime," but in Tennessee and the South that debate simply did not take place. Support in the region for the Allies crossed political and ideological divides.[10]

Majority Leader Sam Rayburn and the Southern chairmen took the lead in the legislative efforts to change the Neutrality Acts. Polls showed that more than three-quarters of Southerners favored revision of the acts. It was no surprise that they and the White House turned to a freshman with a reputation for independence and proven rhetorical ability to open the debate on November 2. They also knew that Gore was a self-confessed admirer of Secretary of State Hull and that he could protect himself against any local isolationists in Tennessee by wrapping himself in Hull's mantle. Any resentment Gore might have felt against the administration over the housing bill was offset by his own pro-British views, his loyalty to Hull, and his desire to ingratiate himself with both the House and executive leadership. Gore repelled personal attacks on Hull in the debate and argued that repeal of the arms embargo would deter aggressors. But he also said that it would stimulate the United States' own preparedness program and buy that program time. "By supplying belligerents with arms and implements of war," he argued, "the United States will be able to gear its own industrial plant to production schedule in the event we should be called upon to defend ourselves from aggression."[11]

From this point on Gore was a staunch supporter of Roosevelt's policy of providing as much assistance as possible to the British without going to war. Although he was Cordell Hull's point man at the 1940 Chicago convention, Gore was a supporter of the unprecedented third term for the president. When Roosevelt swapped supposedly obsolete destroyers for British bases in the Western Hemisphere after the fall of France in 1940, Gore hailed the "daring and courageous far-sighted move" that "forged a chain of Atlantic defenses which this country badly needed." If people queried FDR's constitutional right to hand over the destroyers, Gore noted that similar criticisms had been made of Jefferson's Louisiana Purchase and Theodore Roosevelt's acquisition of the Panama Canal. Gore was an outspoken supporter of conscription. It would be a "reckless act" not to be prepared to defend the United States. Conversely, "If we are prepared to defend this nation and its hemispheric outposts, we likely will not be attacked." Only two Southern Democrats in Congress voted against the Conscription Act; only six against its extension in 1941.[12]

When it became clear after Roosevelt's reelection that the British could no longer pay for the arms they needed from the Americans, Gore emerged as a congressional leader in the early 1941 fight for lend-lease. He rejoiced that fellow Tennessean Wirt Courtney put isolationist poster boy Charles Lindbergh on "a hotter spot" than any other member of the House Foreign Affairs Committee. Then, throughout 1941, Gore strongly supported the moves by the administration to protect supplies to Britain by extending the area of the North Atlantic where the U.S. Navy could convoy and protect British merchantmen. He backed the arming of U.S. merchantmen. Some thought the administration was intent on provoking an attack from German submarines to justify American entry into the war. Gore was untroubled by such fears. He was increasingly convinced that the successful defense of Britain was vital to U.S. self-interest. The British navy was the guarantor of the "safety belt" of the Atlantic and Pacific for the United States. Control of the seas was critical for the future of American trade and its supply of raw materials. If that defense could be secured only by American entry into the war, Gore accepted that necessity. He dismissed isolationist arguments: "The day when we can wait until we see the whites of our enemy's eyes is gone. Tomorrow's Bunker Hill or King Mountain may be thousands of miles away." Hitler, he said, had been the enemy of the United States "since long ago." Most Southerners shared Gore's views. By September 1941, 88 percent of Southerners believed it was more important to defeat Germany than to avoid war. Gore also praised the firmness of the administration's stance against Japan in the Far East. He viewed a possible war with Japan with equanimity. His casual racism about the Japanese was vivid. As he told his Tennessee radio audience, "If those scrubby, malignant Japs think they are going to scare the American people they have another thought coming which will open their eyes wider than their usual oriental slant."[13]

For Gore the declaration of war in December 1941 following the Japanese attack at Pearl Harbor confirmed the futility of isolationist policies. He believed the seeds of the war lay in the U.S. decision to walk away from its responsibilities in 1920. He therefore emerged as an early supporter of the creation of a postwar organization to maintain security, in which the United States must play a leading role. Such an organization must be able to keep the peace by force. He dismissed fears of the "bugaboo" of a super state. Although he disclaimed any intention of advocating a specific form of international organization, he strongly supported a joint resolution sponsored by Joseph Ball of Minnesota and William Fulbright of Arkansas. In 1943 he was invited to go on a ten-day trip with Ball to California, Washington, Oregon, Nevada, and Colorado, under the auspices of the Carnegie Endowment for International Peace. The purpose of campaigning in some isolationist strongholds was to begin a campaign for U.S. leadership in ensuring peace after the war. The issue was clear-cut, according to Gore: "Foreign affairs are no longer foreign affairs. They have come home to this nation; they have cost too many lives in too many homes. Out of this cauldron of suffering and sacrifice, America must mold an inflexible resolution that never again shall war come about for lack of American leadership, cooperation, and courage." Gore was an attractive proposition for this assignment, according to the press, because it could be assumed that he represented the views of Secretary of State Cordell Hull. Southerners as a whole supported the formation of the United Nations. During World War II the South was the region most committed to intervention and to a postwar international organization. For many it was a matter of partisan loyalty and an appreciation of the importance of defense spending in rebalancing the Southern economy. Support in the region for a more nationalist and unilateralist foreign policy might come to the fore after the war. But for Gore, like Hull, support for an internationalist foreign policy had become an article of faith that would shape his entire foreign-policy outlook.[14]

⤳

FOREIGN POLICY MADE Gore an administration supporter, but so too did exposure to FDR's personal charm. Gore's leadership in the housing fight brought an invitation to the White House. Like many newcomers to Washington, Gore went to the White House to make a case to the president but ended up charmed and mesmerized. On 3 May 1940, the president invited Gore and Mike Monroney to meet with him in an effort by the White House to head off the congressmen's continued obstruction of housing legislation. Gore brought a new briefcase for the meeting and loaded it with data to support his case. But as Gore vividly recalled, "Every time I would reach for that briefcase, Roosevelt would either tell a new story or he'd bring up another issue, other than the one I'd been invited to talk about! We never did get around to it. He really mesmerized me. I felt so jubilant as a young congressman that I thought that I had arrived, and he was regaling me with humor." But Roosevelt also talked to him about a guaranteed annual income and full employment, concepts that Gore had never heard discussed before. What they did not discuss was the housing bill. When an aide came in to end the meeting, Gore was walking on air—and reached the front door of the White House before realizing that he had left his briefcase behind.[15]

That fall party leaders used Gore to campaign for the ticket outside Tennessee. Scott Lucas of Illinois arranged for Gore to spend a week campaigning in the Midwest in 1940. Four years later he would spend another five days on the stump in the Midwest, including a speech in Missouri where he served as a last-minute replacement, something a grateful vice-presidential candidate, Harry S. Truman, never forgot.[16]

The administration would also turn to Gore to defend the president and his family. In 1942 Congressman William Pheiffer (R-NY) complained that the armed forces showed favoritism in awarding commissions to the sons of prominent leaders and singled out President Roosevelt's son Navy Lt. Franklin D. Roosevelt Jr. as a prime example. Gore sprang to FDR's defense. In 1943, when Rep. William P. Lambertson (R-Kansas) alleged that FDR ordered two of his sons (James and Franklin Jr.) withdrawn from active service (in Guadalcanal and North Africa, respectively), Majority Leader John McCormack arranged for Gore to respond. Gore contended that Lambertson was "stabbing at the heart of unity. I must brand his insinuations the nastiest, below-the-belt disservice yet uttered in this house. He says he is on the spot. I say he is on the altar of shame before the country and the Congress." He detailed the exemplary service records of Roosevelt's four sons, documenting the bravery of the three who were serving overseas. He cited eyewitness testimony to the front-line service of James Roosevelt. Gore's combativeness was recognized when, after Republican gains in the midterm elections of 1942, Sam Rayburn put him on a rapid-response team of young Democratic representatives tasked with reacting instantly to the charges of the newly confident Republicans in the House.[17]

↩

FIGHTING A WORLD WAR, as Americans had discovered in 1917–18, was immensely expensive and produced massive inflationary pressures. In the summer of 1941, as industrial production cranked up both to supply the Allies and to rebuild the U.S. military, the administration and Congress began to develop plans to control inflation. On the whole the United States relied on voluntarism wherever possible in fighting World War II at home. Nevertheless the administration augmented voluntarism with wage and price controls, and the Roosevelt government consistently tried to fund the war through progressive taxation and the sale of war bonds to restrain inflation. Gore established a national reputation as an advocate of comprehensive wage and price controls and compulsory savings. It was a simple matter for him: "I could not see how we could successfully have price controls without wage controls. Plummeted into a world war, I felt it absolutely necessary that there be some rigid controls and regulations on our economy. Or else we would have rampant inflation, perhaps economic disaster. And I thought it was necessary to have overall control." Other moderate congressman from the South—Wilbur Mills, Mike Monroney, and Georgia's Paul Brown—shared Gore's insistence that any price controls be complemented by wage controls. The GOP also supported wage controls because they wished to curb labor. The administration was more concerned about prices, whereas congressmen with rural interests were concerned with protecting producers and farm income. Leon Henderson, of the Office of Price Administration (OPA), wanted to protect workers in their role as consumers.[18]

When price control first became an issue, Gore admitted a lack of expertise, but he immediately immersed himself in the subject, taking home stacks of books from the Congressional library. His conclusion, as he testified before the Banking and Currency Committee in October 1941, was that the piecemeal or selective price controls advocated by the administration "[leave] the general price level free to skyrocket. Nowhere is a halt called to the rise of general prices." He predicted that it would be "utterly futile" to control the general price level by selecting a few prices to which to apply ceilings. "It would be like trying to prevent the general growth of a forest by chopping down a few of the big trees," he argued. "The more big trees you cut down, the faster the others grow towards the sky." That, for Gore, was the lesson of World War I. Gore proposed that, in addition to wages, prices and rents had to be controlled. Unlike many of his rural colleagues, he also argued that farm prices should be limited to the prices they fetched in the week ending October 12 (unless they were below parity). Many of his colleagues instead wanted a guarantee of farm prices above parity.[19]

Gore's views might not have attracted any public attention if it had not been for the testimony of Bernard Baruch, the legendary financier and mobilization czar during World War I. Baruch felt that he had been sidelined during the New Deal. Deprived of direct power, he maintained influence by funding the careers of prominent Democrats like James F. Byrnes. In the defense buildup and mobilization for war in 1941–42, Baruch expected to be called back to the colors to utilize the enormous expertise and prestige he had acquired as chair of the War Industries Board in 1917 and 1918. His advocacy for comprehensive price and wage controls at the same time as Gore in 1941 was his first attempt to wield decisive influence. The efforts of Gore and Baruch were unsuccessful. Gore's bill for comprehensive controls including wages was defeated in the House by a vote of 218 to 63.[20]

Baruch never "forgot the Gore amendment and the support you and Monroney gave me in WWII on price controls. If only we had put them into effect. What a different world we would now be living in." Baruch believed that the delays in introducing controls which even then were manifestly inadequate "affected manpower and production enormously. It has cost thousands of lives because it has slowed up production and the whole industrial and financial mobilization." Gore and his associates, Baruch believed, had fought a "brave fight." Baruch and Gore would work together again when the need to control inflation became a major issue in 1946 and again during the Korean War. Baruch deplored the "scuttle and run" on controls after the 1946 elections. Baruch kept a benign eye on the young Gore's career. He prided himself on spotting "coming" politicians and would take satisfaction in the success of a number of them in the 1952 Senate elections. There was no evidence that Gore was especially favored and no evidence that Baruch financially underwrote his career. But he consistently gave Gore advice on both his business career and politics. For his part Gore always admired successful businessmen. He flattered Baruch, and he kept him up-to-date with his plans and the current political situation in D.C. When Baruch visited Washington, Gore arranged sympathetic audiences of like-minded young Southern congressmen to hear the older man's views and to make him feel appreciated.[21]

Gore's unsuccessful fight for more comprehensive price controls also put him in touch with young New Dealers at the Office of Price Administration, including John Kenneth Galbraith. It took Pearl Harbor to persuade Congress to implement a price control act. But it became clear in 1942 that piecemeal controls were failing, and the views of OPA administrator Leon Henderson and the president began to dovetail with Gore's. The *Saturday Evening Post* paid for Gore to go to Canada to study the Canadian overall price-control plan. He returned to introduce a price-control bill that would have frozen wages and restricted agricultural price increases by placing the floor under farm prices at parity rather than 110 percent of parity (110 percent of heaven, as one critic noted). Gore's prescience in 1941 was now acknowledged even by Republicans. As Representative Carl Hinshaw (R-CA) commented: "It is quite evident that if we had adopted the Gore bill a year ago we would not be in this mess today." Gore never succeeded in lowering the floor on farm prices, but the administration moved ever closer to his stance on wage controls. Like his mentor Sam Rayburn, Gore could be exasperated by the president's combination of indifference and bluster. FDR tended to leave congressional leaders to deliver satisfactory legislation without clarifying what the administration expected, but then he denounced them and threatened vetoes when Congress failed to deliver a satisfactory bill. At one point Gore was driven to explode, "I just don't trust him [FDR]. He had a chance to get wage controls in the first bill. . . . The farm bloc would not have been able to write in these parity formulae if it had not become evident that the administration intended to do nothing about advancing wages." Gore, like Baruch, remained adamant that, if his proposals had been accepted, "price increases which added billions to the cost of the war would have been avoided."[22]

The other, related central question was how to raise the huge sums of money needed to finance the war. Gore consistently backed Roosevelt's calls for progressive wartime taxation, but he also believed in compulsory savings. Again he put the issue simply: "Dependence upon voluntary savings is as archaic and inadequate for 'total war' as reliance on voluntary enlistment into the armed forces." In parallel to his 1942 price-control bill, he introduced legislation that would withhold some income from all wage-earners subject to Social Security that could be redeemed in war stamps and bonds. The proposal linked up with FDR's desire for a ceiling on higher incomes: Employees would be compelled to purchase war bonds at progressively higher rates that ensured that no one could take home more than $25,000 per year. The administration preferred to see how voluntary bond sales progressed before pushing for compulsory savings, but both Henderson and Secretary of the Treasury Henry Morgenthau acknowledged that they might have to move toward compulsion. In the end the administration financed a much larger proportion of the costs of war through taxation than had the Wilson administration during World War I, and, despite the repeated criticism of price and wage controls, and the difficulties of implementation, the administration mounted a relatively effective drive against inflation.[23]

The anti-inflation drive certainly gave Gore a national platform. He appeared on several radio forums to discuss inflation, wrote an article for the *Washington Daily News*, and spoke to regional meetings of bankers in Minnesota and New York. But the links he made to young liberals in Washington were greater and longer-lasting. He established friendships with both John Kenneth Galbraith and Chester Bowles, Leon Henderson's successor at OPA. Over the years Galbraith and Gore would find common cause in opposition to the tight money policies of the Treasury and the Federal Reserve. Gore, Bowles, and Galbraith also would be allies in their early skepticism of, and ultimate opposition to, the Vietnam War.

⤶

IF PREPARING FOR and fighting a war convinced Gore of the need for the government to exercise blanket economic controls, the war also convinced Gore of the importance of federal investment in Tennessee's infrastructure and the potential for the federal government to transform a poor, backward region.

The Tennessee Valley Authority had had a major impact on Tennessee in the 1930s, and all the state's politicians were united in its defense. The authority represented a unique Depression-era opportunity for jobs and patronage, and in Memphis Boss Crump was able to fulfill his career-long goal of establishing a municipally owned power company through the distribution of TVA power. But the lure of cheap electricity, especially for farmers, was put on hold for many until the late 1930s, in part because of ferocious differences among the three-man TVA board. Chairman Arthur E. Morgan had a holistic vision of planned development that focused on sustainable growth of local communities engaged in subsistence agriculture and part-time craft industries. His academic expertise was in flood-control engineering. He was happy for the TVA to generate electricity as a byproduct of flood control, but he was content to sell that power to private power companies for them to distribute over their own transmission lines. Harcourt A. Morgan, former president of the University of Tennessee, had a growth-oriented philosophy that saw the TVA as a tool for modernized agriculture and industrial development. David Lilienthal, former foe of private utilities in Wisconsin, wanted to build dams, generate large amounts of cheap electrical power, and distribute it over TVA-owned transmission lines to local rural electrification cooperatives and municipal power companies. The bitter dispute took place while the TVA was hamstrung by legal actions by the utility companies, which challenged the constitutionality of the TVA's generating and distributing its own electricity. When the courts upheld the TVA in 1938 and FDR dismissed Arthur E. Morgan, the way was clear for Harcourt Morgan and Lilienthal to set about fulfilling their ambitions of building hydroelectric dams, and of producing enough power to electrify the farms and attract major industry to the region. Industrial giants like Alcoa relocated to the valley, and the TVA produced enough power to make possible the development of an atomic bomb for the Manhattan Project in Oak Ridge, a new, secret community, in Anderson and Roane counties.[24]

David Lilienthal, who became chair of the TVA in 1941, later recalled, "Back in about 1940 or '41 I drove young Albert Gore to the site on the French Broad [River] where, after a violent battle with McKellar, Douglas Dam was rising. He walked out on a hillside overlooking the magnificent confusion of a big dam at that stage and what he said was: 'What we are seeing is not just a dam: it may be more important still; the end of a political regime.'" The TVA provided Gore and fellow congressman Estes Kefauver a model for the economic transformation of Tennessee. They welcomed the cheap power for the farmers and looked forward to the industry that would come with available electricity and ample, controlled water. Tennessee governor Gordon Browning recalled that Harcourt Morgan persuaded him that the TVA's distribution of power would bring industry to every county in the state. Browning acknowledged that "it turned out like he said."[25]

But the model in Tennessee was more than that to a new generation of Southern politicians. Like Gore and Kefauver, these New Dealers believed that the TVA was a model for what the federal government might do for the South, the poorest region in the country, as a whole. They became, in north Alabama John Sparkman's words, "TVA liberals." Just as the federal government had rejuvenated a whole valley, so too could the federal government rejuvenate a whole region—federal assistance through flood control, cheap power, and water-resource development could be the engine of economic growth, modernizing agriculture and stimulating industry; aid to education could transform the schools; federal assistance could provide everything from hospital construction to rural telephones. The TVA was the exemplar of the New Deal policies that would liberate the South from the colonial domination of the Northeast.

Of course, all politicians in Tennessee were in favor of the TVA. Senator Kenneth McKellar claimed to have been the founder of the TVA and bitterly resented any claim that George Norris might have had anything to do with it. With some justification he could point to his role as chair of the Senate Appropriations Committee in securing TVA appropriations through the 1930s. The story circulated in Tennessee that FDR asked McKellar to hide a secret appropriation for the Manhattan Project in an appropriations bill. McKellar replied, "And just where in Tennessee, Mr. President, will the plant be located?" The manufacturing plant for the atomic program was located at Oak Ridge, in eastern Tennessee. Not only would it have access to TVA power, but it was far from the coast, and the high valley ridges made it easier to keep secret and afforded a measure of containment in the event of explosions. Oak Ridge would employ as many as 120,000 workers at its peak and become the fifth-largest city in the state. But McKellar did not see the TVA as a model for federal intervention in the region's economy—he saw it as a piece of pork barrel and a source of jobs he wished to control. As Governor Browning described it, McKellar "wanted to make a patronage heap dump out of it [the TVA]." He wanted to "name everybody in that outfit."[26]

Relations between McKellar and the TVA were satisfactory until September 1941. Lilienthal was under pressure from the defense production agencies to increase dramatically the TVA production of electric power. Lilienthal believed the only way to do that was to construct the giant Douglas Dam in Sevier County. McKellar, who had been ill, preferred the construction of two smaller dams. He objected to the flooding of forty million acres of productive farmland that served the local canning industry. Lilienthal saw McKellar's stance as a blatant attempt to politicize decision-making in the TVA. McKellar viewed Lilienthal's determination to build the Douglas Dam as willful, discourteous, and ungrateful. Lilienthal won the battle, but only after Pearl Harbor allowed the TVA to argue that McKellar had "rolled a pork-barrel over every one of our boys in the armed services of our country." McKellar came to hate Lilienthal and aimed to maintain control of TVA appointments and the distribution of funds. McKellar sponsored a succession of bills that sought to require senatorial confirmation for most TVA appointments and the return of all TVA revenues to the Treasury so that Congress, in the form of McKellar, not the TVA in the form of Lilienthal, could determine how TVA money should be spent.[27]

Such was McKellar's power in the Senate—and the political debts he could cash in as chair of the Appropriations Committee,—that the Senate usually voted in favor of these amendments. The defense of the TVA therefore rested with Tennessee congressmen in the House. The younger Tennessee congressmen—Gore, Kefauver, Percy Priest from Nashville, and Ways and Means stalwart (and administration backer) Jere Cooper—firmly lined up with Lilienthal against the senior senator. They successfully fought to pre-serve the TVA's independence from outside political pressures. This support for a nonpolitical TVA, of course, was a useful shield against importunate job-hunters and, at the same time, ensured that the TVA community supported representatives like Gore. Gore made sure that he chaired the appropriations subcommittee that oversaw the TVA and would later in the Senate became a member of the Joint Committee on Atomic Energy, which monitored the development of nuclear energy. Although Oak Ridge was not in Albert's con-stituency, he worked with Republican congressmen—first John Jennings and then Howard H. Baker, Sr.—to look after the community. In turn Gore's office soon became the first port of call for Oak Ridgers seeking political help from their congressman. They believed they would gain more from a Democratic congressman in a neighboring district than from their local Republican con-gressman, given that the Democrats were in power nationally.[28]

The TVA issue was simple for Gore: "The people who depend upon TVA for electricity don't want it operated by political hacks of either the Democrat-ic or Republican parties." Under McKellar's proposals, "should congress try to operate a public-utility business, we would soon find ourselves knee-deep in highly technical details, guess estimates and unpredictable contingencies. If it should prove unworkable from the standpoint of congress it would be calami-tous to the region served by the TVA." For all the talk of the TVA as an ex-ercise in "grass-roots democracy," however, Erwin Hargrove has shown that this protective, nonpolitical ideology espoused by Gore and Kefauver served bureaucratic as much as democratic needs. "Lilienthal's strategy of a nonpo-litical protective stance had an anti-democratic edge to it that was not appar-ent at first." It made the TVA more progressive, but also less accountable to Congress. In the long run the TVA would become a self-perpetuating, giant, dam-building, power company that was insensitive both to local concerns and to national environmental concerns. But in the 1940s the issues seemed clear-cut. McKellar represented an older generation of patronage-oriented politicians; Gore and the other younger politicians represented a new, issue-oriented politics.[29]

Support of New Deal infrastructure politics turned Gore into a consistent supporter of a New Deal–style domestic policy that backed redistributive, social justice policies. He was part of what Ira Katznelson, Kim Geiger, and Daniel Kryder have described—especially in the House—as a "party-based liberal coalition of non-southern and southern Democrats on welfare state, fiscal and regulatory issues." Gore, like other Southern liberals, supported "much of the party's social democratic agenda with a level of enthusiasm appropriate to a poor region with a heritage of opposition to big business and a history of support for regulation and redistribution."[30]

But there were limits to Gore's New Deal liberalism. The social-democratic program supported by the Southern coalition did not extend to trades unions, and Gore was no exception. His rural suspicion of immigrants extended to a lack of sympathy for organized labor. From the early days of the preparedness program, when strikes disrupted the defense buildup, to the confrontations with John L. Lewis and striking coal miners, to the passage of the anti–union labor Smith–Connally War Labor Disputes Act, Gore denounced labor, both its leaders and its rank and file.

When Gore was promoting lend-lease, he clearly entertained the idea that strikes should be banned in navy work. Labor, he warned, would be making the "mistake of their lives if they try to get bigger than the government itself." Celebrating the passage of the Lend-Lease Act, he sounded like a classic Southern conservative, ridiculing Secretary of Labor "Madam Perkins" (Frances Perkins) for working to standardize ladies' hats but not to control strikes. He returned to the theme in May 1941: "Great Britain desperately needs ships and we urgently need ships and yet our workers are striking, striking, striking. What's wrong with us? Are we not a united people? Is our system decaying from within?" Just before Pearl Harbor Gore equated labor leaders with the Wall Street barons of 1929. He warned them that they would be regulated just as the mighty business leaders had been, because "the safety of all America is jeopardized by the abuses of the labor barons." In 1943 Gore denounced mineworkers leader John L. Lewis, whose striking coal miners were threatening to bring the economy to a halt. The bristle-browed Lewis, according to Gore, was a "mad egoist." Unions had been allowed to grow to such proportions that they now "threatened the sovereignty of the government itself." Gore believed that the Wagner Act had to be rebalanced to make labor leaders more responsible both to the public and to their own members. Just as the Wagner Act outlawed unfair employer anti-union practices, so too should the government should act to impose a similar code of fair practices on the trade unions. He believed that all strikes in war work should have been outlawed. He vociferously spoke in favor of the Smith–Connally Act, which allowed the federal government to seize and operate industries threatened by or under strikes that would interfere with war production. "We have permitted political organization," he warned, "under the name of organized labor, to grow to such proportions that they now threaten the sovereignty of the Government itself." He voted to override FDR's veto of Smith-Connally, and paved the way for his postwar support of the Taft-Hartley Act. Small wonder that, when the CIO rated Southern congressmen according to how they voted on ten issues, it found that Gore scored eight anti-labor votes to two pro-labor votes. In this regard he was less part of a national liberal coalition than part of the South that crucially restricted American policymaking to what Ira Katznelson describes as "the southern cage."[31]

When Gore first went to Washington, he spoke approvingly of Martin Dies, Jr. and the House Un-American Activities Committee, particularly when it was dealing with the supposed threat of subversive aliens. He possessed neither an absolutist commitment to civil liberties nor the cosmopolitan experience of his new congressional colleague, Estes Kefauver. But he soon realized that the committee's zeal for finding communists was a smokescreen for the chairman's anti-statism and opposition to the New Deal. Russia's entry into the war against Hitler did nothing to diminish Dies's passion. In October 1941 he sent Attorney General Francis Biddle a list of 1,212 communists or fellow travelers whom he asserted were working in the federal government. The indifferent response of the administration only exercised Dies further. After Republican successes in the 1942 midterm elections, he returned to the theme and publicly named thirty-nine government employees as affiliates of communist-front organizations. He proposed that, instead of waiting for the administration to act, Congress, through the Appropriations Committee, could deny funding for their salaries.[32]

The House leadership distrusted the demagogic Dies. Speaker Sam Rayburn despised his fellow Texan. Both the leadership and the White House saw the damage that Dies could do to the Democratic Party and the White House, especially since Republicans were only too keen to jump on the anti-communist bandwagon. Dies may have been something of a lone wolf—conducting hearings, for example, on his own—but the Democratic leadership realized that Dies had created a climate, with GOP support, where the congressional leadership was obliged to respond. Rayburn and Appropriations Committee Chair Clarence Cannon sought to contain the issue by establishing a subcommittee on subversive activities to be led by North Carolina congressman John H. Kerr, a stalwart defender of tobacco farmers and, like Gore, a friend of Cordell Hull. Kerr had been in the House for twenty years and had previously served as a state superior court judge. He was a run-of-the mill segregationist and anti-communist, but not a zealot. Kerr, leaders felt, could be relied on to avoid a witch hunt and conduct a sober investigation, while his conservative credentials might placate critics on the right. A careful investigation with reliable pro-administration stalwarts on the subcommittee might douse the flames that Dies had lit.[33]

Cannon and Kerr chose two Southern and Western moderates to serve on the subcommittee, Clinton B. Anderson from New Mexico and Albert Gore. It was the first time Gore and Anderson had worked together. They would both go to the Senate and later cooperate on farm policy, atomic energy, and health insurance. The subcommittee did act more responsibly than some investigatory committees. It established a definition of subversive activity. Witnesses were not browbeaten. Indeed, its measured pace drew Republican criticism. In its final report it recommended termination of the pay of only three of the thirty-nine officials Dies had targeted. But in important respects the committee was not so very different from HUAC or later McCarthy investigations. Its definition of subversion was sweeping: Past and present opinions and associations, rather than actions, were the legitimate subjects of investigation. The committee did not always avoid accusations of guilt by association and relied too readily on professional informers. Gore later recalled the causal way with which the FBI handled evidence and individual rights. The evidence against the three officials the subcommittee named did not appear significantly different from the evidence against the ones they cleared. It was too easy still to equate 1930s pro-labor and pro–New Deal radicalism with subversion. The *Tennessean* summed up its efforts as a "kangaroo court."[34]

When Arthur (Tex) Goldschmidt was summoned before the subcommittee, his boss at the Department of Interior, Abe Fortas, warned him that Albert Gore asked all witnesses if they believed in God, under the assumption that if they answered in the affirmative, they could not be a communist. Goldschmidt, a former New Deal relief administrator and a friend of LBJ's, thought it would be impossible, despite Fortas's entreaties, to answer that question in the way Gore wanted, given Goldschmidt's atheism. In the end Gore missed the hearing (Goldschmidt believed LBJ arranged this happenstance), and Goldschmidt found himself answering questions about his donations to the Washington Friends of Spanish Democracy in the 1930s. At first sight it was strange that Gore, a Baptist who believed in the separation of church and state, should question an official's religious beliefs. It appears to have been a tactical move by Gore to enable the accused to protect themselves and cut off further lines of inquiry.[35]

The Kerr Committee largely failed to fulfill the leadership's goals of neutering Dies and HUAC. The committee inflamed rather than calmed the passions Dies aroused and effectively legitimized the stance that liberal positions in the 1930s constituted prima facie evidence of subversive activity. For Gore his work for the committee highlighted the pragmatic limitations of his commitment to civil liberties. It was consistent with the later liberal position of Gore and likeminded liberals that, rather than an absolute commitment to First Amendment rights, they should try and defuse the anti-communist issue by establishing their own impeccable anti-communist credentials. Gore had voted against an earlier attempt to deprive William Pickens, an African American federal official, of his salary, and he professed to be opposed to "people being lampooned unjustly and unfairly." But he also had voted for the continuation of the Dies Committee. Later, unlike Kefauver, Gore would vote for the McCarran Internal Security Act and the Communist Control bill.[36]

FOR MANY POLITICIANS who came to national prominence after World War II, service in the military during the war was what defined their political careers. For young politicians in Congress during the war, the question of whether to serve in the armed forces was a difficult one. To vote for conscription but not to join one's peers in the military was a troubling political conundrum. Lyndon Johnson immediately enlisted, was commissioned, and had high-profile tours in the Far East, but he was rapidly summoned back to Congress—apparently to his relief. Roosevelt, anxious to avoid the hemorrhaging of young supporters out of Congress and into the military, banned congressmen from receiving commissions. But the option to enlist as privates was still open to young representatives like Albert Gore and Henry "Scoop" Jackson.[37]

When he voted for the draft in September 1940, Gore insisted on registering and waiving any exemption as a member of Congress. His attempts to get a commission and serve in the U.S. Office of Military Government were unsuccessful. In November 1943, when draft boards started drafting men who were fathers before Pearl Harbor, Gore prepared to be drafted. The ban on congressmen holding commissions did not apply to enlisted men. Pauline gave up her job with the Red Cross in Washington. On December 29 Gore reported for service at Fort Oglethorpe. But Roosevelt was worried that losing Gore and others would have a drastic impact on the Democrats' slender working majority in the House. As Gore recounted during his 1944 election campaign, FDR sent for him and personally asked him in January 1944 to remain in Congress: "You are needed here; you can best serve here." Gore argued that "the President is supreme commander of our armed forces as well as our leader on the home front. The way he put it up to me, there was no truly patriotic alternative but to serve where the highest authority said I was most needed and could best serve."[38]

To Gore's opponents back in the Fourth District, this arrangement smacked of politically inspired stage management, masked by Gore's self-righteous rhetoric. W. H. Turner, a World War I veteran from Gore's own county and former state utilities commissioner, challenged Gore in the 1944 primary—the only challenge Gore ever faced in his House career. Turner bluntly asserted that Gore should have served. Gore comfortably survived that challenge, but he remained anxious to see military service. In December 1944 he resigned his seat from the 78th Congress (knowing that he could serve in the 79th Congress) and was sent to Europe by FDR to report on issues of military governance for the future occupation. Bryce Harlow, then an aide to General George Marshall, listed Gore as one of a number of congressmen for whom he had to arrange brief military assignments that would spare them embarrassment when they were up for reelection. In Gore's case the chronology does not exactly fit, but the issue of his military service would again surface in his 1952 Senate campaign. In fact Gore was in Europe for three months. He came under fire crossing the Roer River with the invading force.[39]

Gore was struck by the utter devastation in Germany and the formidable obstacles to the country's postwar reconstruction. He foresaw that finding Germans who were not Nazis to take part in that reconstruction was going to be difficult. He understood the policy of nonfraternization of military personnel with local people, but he recognized that would soon be an impractical policy. He thought the repatriation of refugees would inevitably be slow. He believed the justice meted out by the military courts was rough but fair. He himself had prosecuted a German civilian for harboring a German soldier and a spy in civilian clothes behind U.S. lines. He emphasized to Congress the magnitude of the task of feeding the Germans. Every German civilian, male and female, regardless of previous occupation, should be forced into the fields. Those fields should be cleared of mines by Germans, not by American soldiers. There would have to be rigid and severe credit controls, but he was under no illusion that implementing these initiatives would be an easy task.

As for the longer-term challenge of reconstructing a democratic Germany, Gore was fearful of a strong, centralized country that would be the economic heart of Europe. To create a new Germany purged of the Nazi past would be an immense and long-term task, not one casually imposed overnight by the victors: "We will have to reach much deeper into the German social and political structure than the schools, and over more than one generation." To create a new German national conscience that would withstand "the inevitable backlash following our withdrawal from Germany, whether that be early or late" would require long-range social, economic, and political programs. The length of time necessary could not be estimated in years: "A flexible estimate in terms of generations would be a more fitting measure of time." The scale of the task of winning over hearts and minds, even after overwhelming military victory, made him skeptical of the claims, fifteen years later, of the success of the "pacification" programs in Vietnam.[40]

Gore took part in Veterans of Foreign Wars encampments after the war. He cultivated Jack Woodall, Congressman Tom Murray's secretary, who was state commander of the VFW in Tennessee, and he took a keen interest in VFW facilities. Woodall became a law partner of Gore's brother-in-law, Whit LaFon. But Gore's military service did not have the same defining influence on his political career as did the war experiences of other politicians who had fought their way through Europe or in the Far East. For example, his future Senate colleague Philip Hart was overseeing German governance at the same time as Gore. But Hart had been badly wounded in the D-Day landings and had insisted on rejoining his company at the same time Gore was in Germany. For John F. Kennedy, with whom Gore later formed a friendship, heroism in the Pacific was a prerequisite for a postwar political career. The war did not create a network of supporters that Gore could tap into after 1945 as it did for Southern politicians like Sid McMath in Arkansas or deLesseps Morrison in New Orleans.[41]

∽

IN DRAWING ATTENTION to Gore's primary election battle in 1944, the *New York Times* had praised Albert Gore's "outstanding record," his uncommon national vision, and his "astonishing courage" in the face of interest-group opposition. Jennings Perry, veteran opponent of the poll tax in Tennessee, told the *Times* readers that Gore, alongside Lyndon Johnson and Estes Kefauver, was a promising younger Southerner. This was not the national prominence that had come to Gore when he first arrived in Congress in 1939. Then he had made his mark as a highly vocal opponent of the federal housing program, an archetypal New Deal measure aimed at Democratic, Northern, urban, low-income voters. He was suspicious of the patronage excesses of the relief program of the New Deal. He had a provincial suspicion of immigrants and radical aliens. He remained hostile to organized labor throughout the war.[42]

Gore had been singled out and mentored by Sam Rayburn, John Mc-Cormack, and the House Democratic leadership. He had been courted by the White House. He was much in demand as a speaker by Democratic regulars across the nation. His dogged, if unsuccessful, battle to introduce comprehensive price and wage controls had led him to a friendship with Bernard Baruch on the one hand and young New Deal officials on the other. He had come to "admire extravagantly" Roosevelt and in retrospect acknowledged that "the way in which he succeeded in controlling inflation of wages, prices and interest rates was remarkable." As befitted the congressman from Cordell Hull's hometown, he had become a passionate advocate of American interventionism in the lead-up to the war, and of international cooperation and free trade in the postwar world. As America came to terms with its new superpower status in an atomic age and the South came to terms with the dramatic economic and demographic changes brought about by the war, Albert Gore in 1945 had every chance to play a significant role in mediating those changes.[43]

CHAPTER 3

"Think Some More and Vote for Gore"

GORE HAD GREAT RESPECT for Harry S. Truman. Though he was not in awe of the former senator from Missouri, as he had been of FDR, Gore admired Truman's courage and appreciated his work exposing corruption in military contracts during World War II. In turn Truman was grateful for the gestures and speeches Gore had made to help him in Missouri politics. Gore was less at ease with the cronyism and revelations of corruption in the Truman circle, and he saw Truman as too reliant on city bosses and machine politics. As he later recalled, he generally supported the Truman administration, but "I must say that some of the little irritants—his conduct, the cronyism of his administration, his excesses such as his language—these humiliated me to some extent."[1]

The Truman administration witnessed mounting tensions with the Soviet Union, the decision to contain communist expansion first in Europe and then in Korea, and the start of an atomic arms race. But the thrust of national politics very much represented continuity—New Deal internationalism abroad, the consolidation of the New Deal state at home. In the South, however, much spoke of change rather than continuity. John Egerton, the journalist-chronicler of the New South and the Americanization of Dixie, recalled: "One of the things I have come to see in retrospect is how favorable the conditions were in the four or five years after World War II. It appears to have been the last and best time—perhaps the only time—when the South might have moved boldly and decisively to heal itself voluntarily."[2]

The war had transformed Tennessee. The state ranked only twenty-seventh in the nation in war-supply contracts but thirteenth in publicly funded industrial and manufacturing facilities, sixteenth in private-sector and non-war-related federal agencies, and twenty-first in military facilities funded by public money. (Memphis ranked thirteenth among the nation's cities in these military facilities.) Thousands of Tennesseans, black and white, were on the move from the land to the cities, both inside and outside the state. Prospering farmers, urban consumers, and the new atomic-research facility at Oak Ridge generated a huge demand for power, which was met by new dams and steam-power plants built by the TVA. Abundant electrical power in turn attracted war-related giant industrial plants like Alcoa, which relocated to eastern Tennessee. Metropolitan elites in cities like Nashville began to see the public sector as something that could serve, rather than thwart, their needs. In Memphis the percentage of workers in industrial manufacturing tripled in the 1940s.[3]

Even conservative whites acknowledged that World War II had changed Tennessee. Clifford Davis, the congressman from Memphis, was, according to fellow congressman Percy Priest, a "servant of Mr. Crump." But in December 1948 Davis, wrote to fellow representative Thomas Jefferson Murray: "I think you and I must recognize that these students coming out of the colleges—many men who have returned from the war—have more flexible ideas about a lot of things than your generation and mine. I do not care enough about this office to go off in the deep end on a lot of this stuff, but I believe a change here and there may be helpful, and certainly will not destroy our ideals and respect for the fundamentals of government."[4]

Murray, by contrast, saw little need for change. He was an old-style, conservative, patronage- and courthouse-oriented politician who depended on the black belt counties of Fayette and Hayward, where the regime of terror prevented African Americans from voting until the 1960s. But he anticipated trouble. As he wrote to a constituent, he was "on the radical Communistic CIO PAC purge list," unfairly targeted by labor forces that advocated "race equality, repeal of our Jim Crow laws in the South, abolition of our segregation laws and a permanent FEPC," and were "making every effort to re-make the South and bring equality between the races."[5]

Would Gore take advantage of these liberal opportunities? How would he cope with the obstacles of race?

⤺

GORE WAS AN almost unquestioning supporter of the Cold War foreign policy of the Truman administration. In September 1946 he had some sympathy with Henry A. Wallace's foreign policy speech, at Madison Square Garden which called for greater understanding of Russia. Surely, said Gore,

Russia had reason to be suspicious of a centralized Germany. Russia had legitimate interests in Eastern Europe, just as the United States had in the Pacific Islands, which it was occupying. Though he supported the president when Wallace was dismissed, he heralded Wallace's "extraordinary courage" and noted that the principles of the New Deal farm policy which he instituted were still supported by millions who subsequently denounced him. But when Truman in 1947 called for economic and military aid to Greece and Turkey, Gore came to be a strong defender of the Truman Doctrine. The alternatives to containment, he said, were uninviting, but he believed the consequences of appeasement might bring about a repetition of Munich. "Unpleasant and undesirable though the course of action recommended by the President is, I believe it offers the course most likely to bring world peace." The United States, Gore told his constituents, "will oppose totalitarian aggression under whatever name and by whatever means it seeks to subjugate and oppress." He worried over the isolationist forces that opposed aid to Britain. If Britain were to collapse, America might lose access to the enormous markets of the British Empire. Britain and other European countries needed credits to restore their buying power, but they also needed to be able to sell their goods in America, which made extension of reciprocal trade agreements imperative. Whatever doubts he may have later entertained about United States overreach, he took pains in 1947 to point out—and praise—the global nature of the commitment to containment, not merely aid to Greece and Turkey.[6]

It was logical therefore that Gore, like all the Tennessee congressmen, fully and enthusiastically endorsed the Marshall Plan designed to promote European recovery.

He feared that, unless the Marshall Plan were endorsed by Congress and the American people, the chance to spread U.S. democracy into Europe and the Balkans would be lost. "The might of America has placed tremendous responsibilities upon us," he asserted. "If we reject the opportunity for world leadership as the spearhead of world democracy and freedom, another system is not only ready but anxious to take over." For Gore there was no intelligent alternative "but to do what we can to preserve what is left of the free world." If America did not act, not merely would it have no friends left but, equally important, it would have no customers. Once again America needed to demonstrate resolve and avoid the mistakes of the 1930s. He was an enthusiastic supporter of the creation of NATO in 1949.[7]

Gore was a staunch supporter of the expansion of American air power to counter the Soviet Union. He was a leader in the fight in 1948 to secure full funding for the 70-group air force proposed by Secretary of the Air Force Stuart Symington. In language reflecting that of George Kennan in his "Long Telegram" and his "X" article in *Foreign Affairs*, Gore noted similarities between the Soviet "program" and "the historic expansionist policy of Russia under the Czars," although he described the Soviet Union as "more powerful than ever before, better organized and, therefore, more menacing." He asserted that "only the United States has the power and influence to give effective world leadership against the onrushing scourge of despotic communism." He argued that "unless we have the power and force to back our words with actions there is no way either to convince Russia to the contrary or apparently to even command her respect for our position." The Soviets must "know that America is convinced that world peace is not secure anywhere unless it is."[8]

Not surprisingly, Gore supported the globalization of containment when the United States secured United Nations authorization to drive back the North Korean invasion of South Korea in 1950. But within a year he despaired of the stalemate that developed once the North Koreans had been driven back, and Douglas MacArthur's attempt to invade the North had been halted.

Gore was certain that it was impossible to win a war of attrition against the Chinese. This conviction led him to support Truman when he dismissed MacArthur as U.S. commander in Korea. He was deluged with criticism of the president. Constituents saw no reason to support a limited war and called for a policy of total victory in Korea. In the region as a whole, 69 percent of white Southerners, compared to 55 percent of Northerners, backed MacArthur. Only 17 percent of white Southerners endorsed Truman's position. In Gore's district MacArthur's popularity was also sustained by the fact that his wife came from Murfreesboro. Gore had met MacArthur on a tour of the Far East theater in June 1945. Gore, however, like Estes Kefauver, supported the president. As he told Truman, he believed many situations could have been handled differently, but "once the supremacy of civil government was challenged by a military commander, particularly in a manner calculated to intensify the danger of World War III, there must be but one choice under our constitution. The military must be subordinate to civil government authority."[9]

But Gore made one concession to his critics. While he recognized that Truman was adamant in his faith in Secretary of State Dean Acheson, Gore believed Acheson was dispensable. The replacement of Acheson was a staple demand for many of his conservative, anti-communist constituents. Gore did not believe that there could be "unity in foreign policy" if Acheson remained in office. He needed to be replaced by a "less controversial figure whose appointment can contribute to the unity and solidarity of the country."[10]

Gore despaired of American victory in Korea. As he felt later about the Vietnam War, he believed a South Asian country had become a "meat grinder of American manhood." No matter how bravely Americans fought and how many casualties they inflicted on the enemy, the communists had the capacity "to continue this meat grinder operation indefinitely." Gore's solution drew on his experiences taking part in the subcommittee hearings on the Atomic Energy Commission of the Appropriations Committee. He proposed to "dehumanize a belt across the Korean peninsula by surface radiological contamination." According to Gore's plan, the belt would be regularly recontaminated until a peace agreement had been reached. In the meantime atomic weapons should be ready to be used to fight off a submarine attack on America's naval forces or an attempted invasion of Japan. He believed the use of atomic weapons in such cases would be morally justifiable. The atomic death belt in Korea would do little more than maintain the existing stalemate, but that was preferable to maintaining that stalemate with existing methods, which could be "tremendously costly" to American lives. Gore's proposal reflected an early enthusiasm for atomic energy both for military and peaceful purposes. He chaired the appropriations subcommittee that oversaw TVA and Atomic Energy Commission appropriations. In October 1951 he was lyrical about the "spectacular and magnificent" nuclear test he witnessed in Nevada which had left him speechless. The flash of the explosion outshone the morning sun and left a "white hot multi-colored afterglow." He viewed the use of tactical nuclear weapons with equanimity. He was convinced that "we can now use the atomic bomb in a tactical way against enemy troops in the field . . . without serious risk to our own troops." He envisaged the development of small and large bombs that could be used as "artillery shells, guided missiles, torpedoes, rockets, and bombs for ground supporting aircraft." Only later, after the development of the hydrogen bomb, would Gore come to appreciate the dangers of nuclear fallout, put his faith in eliminating testing in the atmosphere, and concentrate on the peaceful development of atomic energy.[11]

～

IN DOMESTIC POLICY Gore was a staunch defender of the Fair Deal. Truman continued New Deal policies in terms of economic growth and social justice. Key elements of Truman's policies appealed to the "new generation of Southerners": support for public power and water-resource development by the Department of the Interior, headed by former TVA power engineer Julius Krug; price support for farmers, as driven forward by Clinton Anderson and Charles Brannan; extensions of minimum wage and Social Security benefits; and proposals to extend the New Deal through federal aid to education and a national health insurance plan. Gore was part of a bloc of young liberal Southern congressmen, many of whom he introduced to Bernard Baruch in 1946. Gore could turn to men elected in the late thirties and forties in the House: his Tennessee colleagues Percy Priest and Estes Kefauver; John Sparkman, Carl Elliott, Robert Jones, and Albert Rains in Alabama; Frank Smith in Mississippi; Henderson Lanham in Georgia; William Fulbright, James Trimble, and Brooks Hays in Arkansas; and Lyndon Johnson in Texas. Sparkman, Johnson, Fulbright, and Kefauver preceded Gore in making the move from the House to the Senate.[12]

Gore developed close ties with the national Democratic leadership in the House. In early 1946 Gore became the head of an unofficial "ready debaters' committee" of fifteen young representatives dedicated to asserting Democratic positions—administration policies—and countering Republican "propaganda" in the coming elections. Committee members believed that the Democrats responded too passively to Republican attacks. The new group was intended not only to reply quickly to Republican criticism in Washington but also to give speeches around the country to assist Democratic candidates in tough elections and maintain the Democratic majority in the House. Gore gave a speech in Akron, Ohio, on behalf of Congressman Walter Huber, who had narrowly won the last election (and would be reelected for his second term in 1946). The group also compiled materials to be used in speeches or otherwise inserted into the *Congressional Record* and then mailed to voters. The group coordinated its work with the Democratic National Committee and the congressional campaign committee. Party leaders wanted the young congressmen to establish close ties with congressional and administration leaders as well. Sam Rayburn rewarded Gore with a greatly improved office located near the House leadership. Some older Southern Democrats were less impressed. One dismissed Gore's "committee," which he claimed did not represent the Democratic Party in the House. It was, he said, "made up mostly of left-wingers and the so-called liberals of the party."[13]

Gore came into his own as an attack dog when Republicans took control of Congress after the 1946 elections. Gore was among six young House Democrat "watchmen" tasked by party leaders with challenging Republicans in congressional debates. Gore was described as "one of the house's ablest spur-of-the-moment speakers." The other five were all freshmen: John Bell Williams (Mississippi), Carl Albert (Oklahoma), John Carroll (Colorado), George Smathers (Florida), and John Blatnik (Minnesota). Assistant leader John McCormack of Massachusetts described their task: "The purpose of these watchmen will be to spotlight mistakes of the opposition." Gore took the lead in blasting irresponsible Republican tax cuts, which departed from the "democratic principle" of ability to pay and had returned to the taxation philosophy "of the Middle Ages." He stated that one Republican tax proposal came "right out of the Andrew Mellon primer of special privileges. It was the economic theory that worked so well that it brought on the panic of 1929 and the utter defeat of the Republican Party in 1930 and 1932."[14]

Egged on by Sam Rayburn, Gore also used his position on the Appropriations Committee relentlessly to expose what he considered the "phony nature" of Republican claims to having saved billions of dollars in government spending. After a national radio broadcast by Gore laid bare those claims, Rep. Clare Hoffman (Michigan) labeled him "General Gore" of the "Rayburn-McCormack Goon-Squad."[15]

Gore took care of matters nearer to home. He continued to lead the fight to defend the TVA against both Republican attempts to eviscerate the agency and Senator McKellar's efforts to control appointments and return TVA revenues to the Treasury. Here Gore was helped by his membership on a new, but small, subcommittee of Appropriations that was set up under the Government Corporation Control Act of 1945. The subcommittee was to supervise government corporations and independent executive agencies, including the TVA. Gore was able to work across the aisle on this committee, on issues as diverse as those involving the Inland Waterways Corporation and the Farm Credit Administration, both when the Democrats controlled the group under George Mahon of Texas and when the Republicans ran it under Ben Jensen of Iowa. He used the subcommittee to work out a compromise to protect the TVA from demands that it repay money to the government more quickly and at unfavorable interest rates; to secure permission for the authority to build a phosphate fertilizer plant in Mobile, Alabama; to build the two dams on the Watauga and Holston rivers (the subjects of his quarrel with McKellar); and to build a new steam plant in Johnsonville to supply badly needed power for western Tennessee once the existing hydroelectric plants in eastern Tennessee reached full capacity.[16]

The battle with McKellar continued unabated. Gore protested that McKellar wanted to make the TVA a "political football." He used his influence with the rest of the Tennessee delegation in the House to defeat any Senate attempt to return TVA revenues to the Treasury. When McKellar attempted to block the Senate Public Works Committee's nomination of Gordon Clapp as David Lilienthal's successor, Gore testified in favor of Clapp alongside Percy Priest and Estes Kefauver and enlisted the support of Lister Hill and John Sparkman of Alabama, as well as the American Farm Bureau Federation. McKellar's prime target was his old enemy Lilienthal, who had been nominated as chair of the Atomic Energy Commission. Failing in that battle, McKellar next targeted Clapp, who had risen from a minor clerk's job at the TVA to become first director of personnel then general manager of the authority. McKellar used the confirmation hearings to try and leverage the changes in TVA policy and practice that he wanted. When McKellar alleged that Clapp had harbored communists at the TVA, Gore cited Tennessee Republican congressman John Jennings's defense of a former TVA employee alleged to have had communist leanings. Jennings had angrily stated: "I do not know whether Buck Borah was a Communist, but he was killed in defense of his country and it looks to me like his blood should wash away whatever taint may be on his record." Clapp was nominated.[17]

Once the Democrats regained control of Congress after the 1948 elections, Gore became an enthusiastic advocate of Truman's efforts to complete the unfinished work of the New Deal in housing, education, and health care. With the exception of the 1949 Housing Act, which benefited Southern as well as Northern cities and therefore won the support of Southern senators, this support was largely unavailing in the face of the sustained power of the conservative coalition of Southern Democrats and Republicans, particularly in the Senate.

Gore had some legislative success in agriculture, but he lined up with Truman's opponents to achieve it. Gore did not favor the plan under which Truman's secretary of agriculture, Charles Brannan, attempted to marry the demands of the Democrats' diverse constituencies of farmers and urban consumers "to cement the tentative alliance of farmers and laborers that had elected Truman in 1948." Brannan argued for the end of price supports and the implementation of a cheap food policy. He believed that domestic demand for farm products would increase and that transfer payments to farmers would compensate for any loss of farm income, particularly payments to small farmers. The transfer or production payments would also help farmers to shift from commodities for which there was usually a surplus—for example, wheat and cotton—to livestock, for which there was rapidly increasing urban demand. It was the last serious effort to rationalize American agricultural policies until the 1990s.[18]

Brannan and his advisers thought his proposals "a reasonable program for changing what had been an embarrassment . . . to everybody. It [the price support system] had just grown like Topsy and it was just all out of whack, and somebody had to do it, sometime." But the opposition to the Brannan plan was ferocious. The Farm Bureau, academic economists, and Republicans assailed the plan. The Farm Bureau always maintained the fiction that all farmers wanted was a fair price, not a government subsidy. Republicans and economists balked at what they thought the Brannan Plan would cost. The Farm Bureau and Republicans raised the specter of government regimentation. In the South, where the Farm Bureau was strong, large, established cotton producers objected to the plan's alleged bias in favor of small producers. Many Southern congressmen were also suspicious of any farm plan that had the support of organized labor. Gore responded with gusto to these pressures by introducing a bill that would keep the guaranteed price level support at 90 percent of parity for the basic storable commodities. Despite the efforts of the House Democratic leadership and Midwestern and Northern Democrats, Gore's bill passed 239 to 170, with 60 percent of the Southern Democrats supporting the legislation.[19]

In the Senate the key figure for farm legislation was Clinton P. Anderson from New Mexico, Gore's old colleague from the House Appropriations Committee. Anderson had served as Truman's secretary of agriculture but then returned to New Mexico to run for the Senate in 1948. A small-town boy and successful businessmen, he was independently wealthy, which Gore always respected. Anderson's relationship with his successor, Brannan, turned sour when Anderson went on the Senate Agriculture committee. He proved more adept than Brannan when it came to legislative management and farm politics. Anderson set his sights on achieving a more flexible system of price supports, but in the end he had to concede the continuation of the rigid 90 percent price supports. An initial one-vote victory for Anderson turned around when Gore went to the Senate chamber. He warned Kentucky senator Garrett L. Withers that the House would vote to eliminate 90 percent supports for tobacco if the Senate failed to keep the 90 percent support level on the other basic commodities. Withers persuaded Vice President Alben Barkley, also from Kentucky, to cast the decisive vote in favor of rigid 90 percent price supports. In the final analysis, the Anderson–Gore Farm Act of 1949 did little to make price supports more flexible. It updated the base periods for calculating the level of support but left the fundamentals of New Deal farm policy outlined in the Farm Act of 1938 largely untouched. Republican gains in the 1950 midterm elections and the Korean War sounded the death knell for any effort to revive the Brannan plan. Gore was unapologetic in his defense of what many liberals would describe as agrarian fundamentalism. He believed suspicion of the price-support programs stemmed from consumer prejudice and misinformation. The high cost of food was the result not of a "politics of scarcity" but of increasing distribution costs. The Brannan plan, he told the North Carolina Farm Bureau in a thinly veiled anticommunist smear, was the program of Henry Wallace and the 1948 Progressive Party. Gore wanted no part of such a program. All the farmer wanted to do was "to stand on our own feet, think our own thoughts, speak our own words, be independent, proud, and the masters of our own fate." He told voters in 1952: "Farmers were in no mood to depend upon whims of Congress to feed them and their families with a subsidy." He took credit for his bill as "the basic Farm Law of the land."[20]

Gore also departed from the national liberal perspective on the labor question, an issue on which he had already made his dissent known. After the end of the war, labor attempted to make up for the wage gains it believed it had foresworn during the war. At the same time employers tried to recapture the shop-floor managerial prerogatives they believed they had surrendered in the war years. The result was a great national strike wave in 1946.

In Tennessee organized labor saw new opportunities both in World War II and in Operation Dixie which it launched to organize the South in 1946. As the CIO's Paul Christopher said, even anti-union bastion Nashville was "exceptionally ripe for organizing." There were also left-led interracial unions in the state which flourished in Memphis and in the phosphate mines of Maury County. Boss Crump had tolerated the more conservative AFL unions in Memphis, but he had no intention of allowing "CIO nigger unions in Memphis." Before the war whites at the Firestone plant voted overwhelmingly for the AFL union; blacks, who constituted about a third of the workforce, voted equally solidly for the CIO. During the war, however, the labor shortage, federal protection, and the need for federal defense money all served to restrain Boss Crump and his police force. White workers in the new manufacturing plants saw the real gains unions—even biracial ones—could achieve. Communist leadership in United Cannery, Agricultural, Packing, and Allied Workers of America (UCAPAWA) and the International Woodworkers Union instilled great loyalty in its African American members that enabled the unions to organize the traditional cotton-compressing, cotton-seed-oil and woodworking plants where black workers were in the majority. In the long run CIO regional organizers' caution in Operation Dixie, and the anticommunism of both Crump and liberal CIO leaders, all militated against unions' success.[21]

Gore joined most Tennessee politicians in opposing militant labor. Miners' leader John Lewis remained his bête noire. Gore supported Truman's emergency strike bill in 1946. He rejoiced when the Supreme Court upheld Lewis's conviction for contempt of court in 1947. He told listeners a year later that the American people would be "pleased to see this home-grown dictator hauled into the court of law and justice." In 1947, alongside every Tennessee congressmen except Kefauver, Gore voted for the Case Bill, which aimed to prevent strikes by making unions liable to injunctions, outlawing violent picketing and organized boycotts, and allowing civil suits against employers or workers who violated contracts. The Case Bill was the forerunner of the Taft–Hartley Act, which, following the lead of the wartime Smith–Connally Act, redressed the balance of the Wagner Act of 1935. Whereas the Wagner Act outlawed a raft of unfair employer anti-union practices, Taft–Hartley proscribed a series of unfair union practices. Gore voted for Taft–Hartley along with the other Tennessee congressmen, excluding Estes Kefauver and east Tennessee Republican Dayton Phillips. Gore then voted to override Truman's veto. Labor in Tennessee would strongly support Kefauver when he ran for the Senate in 1948. By contrast, there was still considerable distance between labor and Gore four years later when he challenged McKellar.[22]

The other major domestic issue on which Gore parted company from his party was civil rights. Truman made civil rights for African Americans a major plank of national liberalism in a way Roosevelt had largely managed to avoid, despite African American voters' shift to the Democrats in Northern cities. Truman attempted to make the wartime Fair Employment Practice Committee permanent. In response to postwar violence against African Americans in the South, including returning GIs, he set up a Commission on Civil Rights. He endorsed its findings, "To Secure These Rights," in the expectation that Southern Democrats would not bolt the party and that African American voters in the North would retain their Democratic allegiance. His caution when Southerners protested was undermined by liberals at the Democratic national convention in 1948 who voted for a strong civil rights plank. Delegates from the Deep South states who walked out went on to support Dixiecrat candidate Strom Thurmond in the general election.[23]

African Americans in Tennessee were not passive observers of these developments in the 1940s. They were part of what historians now call the "long civil rights movement." They registered to vote, joined the NAACP, supported litigation to challenge segregation, returned from service overseas to assert their rights, and joined industrial unions. NAACP membership surged in cities like Nashville, where wartime overcrowding and the presence of servicemen of both races on nearby military bases inflamed racial tensions and sparked police brutality. In Tennessee in 1947 national NAACP official Gloster Current noted that the destruction of "corrupt political machinery" rather than the right to vote was the issue confronting liberal groups. He observed that "Negroes in this state represented a considerable voting force," having voted in the Republican primary in this state since the Reconstruction period, and "with the exception of two counties directly above the Alabama border, they voted in the Democratic primary as well." The exceptions to Current's generally positive assessment were Fayette and Haywood counties. As activist lawyer Z. Alexander Looby noted, "In Haywood County, however, where Negroes comprise a majority of the population, the aggregate situation there amounts to not letting Negroes vote. Within the recent past two Negroes had been killed and nothing at all had been done about it," even though the NAACP gave local officials the names of those responsible.[24]

Black political mobilization became more independent during the war years. In Nashville, the City-County Democratic League had been founded in 1938 under the control of William B. "The Pie" Hardiman. Hardiman, who was given a nonexistent job as deputy coroner at city hall, simply delivered the black vote to whomever he decided to back. Looby complained bitterly about self-defeating factionalism in the black community. Joe Hatcher, the political correspondent of the *Tennessean*, said that African American leader Grant "is the smartest politician in Nashville. He regularly sold out to both sides for money. He promises 2000 negro votes. The negro vote splits up anyway—only a couple of times has it gone heavily one-sided—and therefore both sides get their 2000 votes. Mr. Grant keeps all of the money." But to dilute the black vote in Nashville, the city redrew the districts in 1949 to create two small, black-majority wards. In 1951 Looby and another black lawyer, Robert E. Lillard, were elected to the city council. Looby would serve on the city council as a Republican until his death in 1971.[25]

Blacks in Memphis had always voted thanks to Boss Crump. In return Crump made city jobs available, offered a degree of police protection, and extended city services to the black community. Crump intimidated and controlled black voters as his black henchmen brought up poll tax receipts and used tax assessors and city inspectors to drive any independent businessmen out of the city. The black banker Robert Church, who controlled federal patronage in Memphis when Republicans were in power, was instrumental to Crump's operation until 1933. Once FDR came to power, Crump abandoned and bankrupted Church. But in 1948 African American insurance executive Joseph E. Walker threw in his lot with the white elite reformers in Memphis who were backing Estes Kefauver in his race for the Senate. Although a majority of blacks in Memphis may still have voted for Crump's candidate, three black-majority precincts, in a display of unprecedented independence, voted for Kefauver.[26]

Independent political activity was also matched by black middle-class leaders' rejection of the deference and paternalism of the old interracial movement, a paternalism that assumed that African Americans were content with segregation and gradualism. Leaders like Fisk sociologist Charles S. Johnson for the first time publicly discussed the contradictions of democracy and segregation. Johnson reported "a great deal of objective evidence that his [Negro's] attitude is increasingly becoming one of protest. . . . We have, then in the South, on the one hand, a situation in which the great majority of southern Negroes are becoming increasingly dissatisfied with the present pattern of race relations and want a change." Johnson launched an annual Race Relations Institute at Fisk, which operated on an integrated basis. When conservative whites protested, the trustees responded by making Johnson the president of the university.[27]

The attitudes of African American leaders might have been changing but, as Johnson had noted, these changes reflected grassroots changes. None was more important than African Americans' service in the armed forces, and nowhere was this clearer than during the Columbia, Tennessee, race riot of 1946. World War II gave returning black veterans a sense of esteem and comradeship, as well as new skills and access to arms. The original incident in Columbia involved an attack on a black navy veteran whose mother was being cheated by a white repair store. When a lynching threatened, a corps of armed black veterans deterred a white mob from entering the black section of town. The highway patrol wrecked the black business district in a dawn raid, and the overwhelming number of arrests were of black veterans. Remarkably, Looby, Maurice Weaver, and Thurgood Marshall, attorneys for the NAACP, secured acquittals on first-degree murder charges for twenty-three of the twenty-five defendants; the majority of the acquitted were veterans.

In the spring U.S. senator Kenneth McKellar told Crump that "a late report says that negroes are going to try to enter the Democratic primary in Maury County. You know that is where they had trouble not long ago. I have heard no such intention on their part in any other county." Henry Harlan, a member of the African American community in Columbia, told black journalist Carl Rowan that the lessons of armed self-defense in the town were clear: "No, there will be no more trouble. That's the one thing I learned from 1946. They know now that Negroes have guts. They were the first Columbia Negroes ever to stand up like men. Blood was shed, but it paid off. . . . Times have changed. A Colored man used to not have the chance of a sheep-killing dog. But 1946 changed that."[28]

But the limitations of this black activism were just as noticeable as its strengths. The wartime boom in members and activity for the NAACP did not last. When the organization created a state conference of branches in 1947, nobody in the national office or locally knew what happened to the state president, a minister from Chattanooga. (He had left to take up a new pastorate in Philadelphia.) Two years later the state president reported that "our local membership campaign has hit the rocks." By August 1950 the state organization had lost two-thirds of its membership. The state president noted that the flagship branch in Memphis was struggling and that funds were parlous. The two-dollar membership was too great a burden, he argued. In May 1951 Ruby Hurley, regional secretary of the NAACP, reported gloomily on her visit to Tennessee. At Fisk University she was certain that the NAACP "runs a very poor second to fraternities and sororities. I found a complete lack of knowledge of both Negro history and NAACP history among both the campus and city youth." By that summer statewide membership of the NAACP languished at 4,770, a far cry from its 1946 peak of almost 19,000.[29]

It was the litigative strategy masterminded by Thurgood Marshall and implemented by Looby that yielded effective results. The threat of an NAACP lawsuit increased Chattanooga teachers' salaries in 1941. Looby secured the equalization of Nashville teachers' salaries in 1942. In 1951 the University of Tennessee at Knoxville admitted three black students to graduate school rather than allow the NAACP case to go to the Supreme Court. In 1950 Looby and Williams filed suit on behalf of Anderson County African Americans who were bussed eighteen miles to Knoxville rather than to the local Clinton High School.[30]

Political action should also have been effective. Tennessee had the highest percentage of voting-age African Americans registered in the South.

Tennessee's African Americans participated in what can be called the first postwar system of biracial politics in the South, where a small but slowly increasing black electorate used its political leverage to help elect moderate white politicians and to extract concessions from them that would soften the edges of segregation and provide public services and spending for blacks. In Nashville African Americans supported challenges to the old city machine (as they eventually did in Memphis). In return they secured the black-majority districts that elected Looby and Robert Lillard to the state legislature, increased spending for the state-funded, historically black Tennessee State University, eliminated the worst black slums, increased hiring of blacks by the city government, secured desegregation of the city buses, and even won the city's support for Looby's challenges to segregation at the Nashville airport and municipal golf courses.[31]

It is tempting to celebrate the history of African American activism during and after World War II as a forerunner to, and an integral part of, the direct-action phase of the civil rights movement. But to acknowledge assertive individuals is not the same as identifying a continuous thread of protest that culminated in the modern civil rights movement. After the war the radical left-led unions were defeated. Armed self-defense gave violent whites pause but did little to enhance African American power. Litigation and political participation before the landmark *Brown* decision of 1954 had won some limited concessions on the margins of segregation but little more.

It was a measure of the relative lack of local success for African Americans in Tennessee that Albert Gore could largely ignore this history of the "long civil rights movement." There were few African Americans back home in Smith County, or indeed in the Fourth District overall. Murfreesboro, where Gore had gone to college and which was brought into his district before he went to the Senate, had only thirteen NAACP branch members in 1947, and then none in 1948 and 1949. But the hill country did give Gore a distrust of conservative elites and, by implication, their racial excesses. Gore also had a national and international perspective that made him uneasy with the white supremacy certitudes of Southern conservatives. In Washington his wife, Pauline, who worked for the Red Cross in Washington during the war, found the customs of white supremacy to be strictly enforced in the nation's capital. Stepping out from the office to the street, she outraged the wife of another Tennessee congressman by addressing an African American woman with the prefix "Mrs."[32]

These perspectives helped Gore support the right to vote for African

Americans. In 1942 he joined Percy Priest and Estes Kefauver in voting to abolish the poll tax. But the vote on the poll tax in 1942 had as much to do with a fight for political democracy for white Tennesseans as it did with black rights. The drive against the poll tax in Tennessee was a drive against Crump, dictatorship, and corruption rather than a drive for black rights. Similarly Gore's support for the federal provision of the soldier's vote, rather than the eventual Rankin Bill, which retained state control, had more to do with his fear of bosses in Tennessee and their restraint of white voters than with a desire to protect African American voting.[33]

Gore saw no need to alarm his low-income white supporters by talking about racial change. Gore, like most Southern white moderates, genuinely believed that the economic progress he was so earnestly fighting for would gradually eliminate the evils of racism. He had no strong personal feeling for the evils and humiliation of segregation. Nor did he have the brutal experience of fighting overseas, which had given some of his white contemporaries a conviction that a new racial order was needed.[34]

Gore's speeches in Congress, the press coverage devoted to him, and his weekly radio broadcasts scarcely mentioned the race issue. Occasionally, he had to refer to it. On the Appropriations Committee he consistently opposed riders to appropriations bills that sought to deny federal funds to segregated institutions. When Truman proposed civil rights measures in 1948, however, Gore refused to sign the resolution of the Southern caucus for a "fight to the finish" against President Truman and his civil rights program, on the grounds that it constituted a "threat of bolting" from the Democratic party.[35]

Gore seemed to feel that that he had done enough to improve race relations. After all he had opposed the poll tax and he could claim antilynching legislation had been rendered obsolete in the modern South, but he could not avoid the proposal for a Fair Employment Practice Committee, a lightning rod for conservative opposition to FDR and Truman. Gore publicly opposed the FEPC in 1949 with considerable rhetorical vigor. His explanation for his opposition on the radio distilled the essence of white Southern racial moderation—the commitment to gradualism, the faith in economic progress, and the hostility to change imposed from outside.

> There is no denying that serious discriminations are practiced
> against some of our racial minority groups. Nor are these
> discriminations confined to the South. Of course, very very
> rapid strides in the direction of understanding, tolerance, and

Christian brotherhood have been made in recent years and are in
rapid progress now. This move will continue unless interrupted
by some similar attempt to force the issue too rapidly. It is my
opinion that all of us as individual citizens, that we as a community
and as a Nation must examine our own hearts and as a result of
this introspection approach this problem, truly one of the most
troublesome of our day, with compassion, understanding, and
tolerance. This method of education and social consciousness
would have been largely ignored by the FEPC proposal that was
brought before the Congress. It would have substituted instead the
force of law.

The FEPC proposal, concluded Gore, was a "naked and ugly" "despotic
infringement upon the liberty of the whole people."[36]

Gore's attempt to finesse the race issue largely dictated silence. While
Gore later acknowledged that he was "no shining knight" on civil rights, his
constituents would have been justifiably surprised to learn of his other claim
that he had been "upfront" on the race issue during this period. Like other
Southern moderates, Gore resented any effort by the Truman administration
or Northern liberals that forced him to be explicit on the race issue. As he
complained to Bernard Baruch, the FEPC and other such demagogic proposals had made the South a whipping post. He deplored the efforts of the
"recent leadership, Truman et al," which had "oriented [the party] to the Har-
lems and Hamtramyks."[37]

All the upheaval regarding race during the war years—African American
activism in Tennessee in the 1940s, the white backlash to it, and flashpoints of
tension like the Williams lynching and the Columbia riot—therefore seems
to have had no impact on Gore. He seems to have had no personal contact
with African American leaders. Because the race issue did not yet drive a
wedge between his low-income black and white supporters, Gore could focus
on economic issues and avoid discussing race.

෴

AT HOME DRAMATIC political change came in 1948. The Crump forces'
hold over Tennessee was memorably loosened when the kingmaker's candidates for governor and senator were defeated by his former protégé, Gordon
Browning, and by the Sixth District congressman Estes Kefauver, respectively. According to George Barrett, Crump had no doubt about who was

responsible for his defeat: "You know, the niggers and labor had a heyday." New forces were thus emerging in Tennessee politics—a small but increasing black electorate, returning veterans, and women. Kefauver marshalled these forces in 1948.[38]

No group was more vocal about the deficiencies of the old ways in Tennessee than returning white servicemen. They mounted GI revolts to overturn the local power structures. They were not always successful—the GI Joe ticket in Nashville lost in 1946. Their role in the 1948 victories of Browning, a former military governor in Germany, and Kefauver, a new breed of liberal, was obvious.[39]

Gore was talked of as a possible anti-Crump candidate in 1948. He was, in many ways, the most prominent Tennessee congressman, and he had established a national reputation. He appealed to the same reforming supporters that Kefauver and Gore's old mentor, Gordon Browning attracted, with the exception of organized labor. But in 1948 Gore had just seen the long-awaited birth of a son, Albert Jr., and he told Baruch that he was anxious to put his family finances on a firmer footing. He had just started a feed mill in Smith County with Grady Nixon. Still, Gore was ambitious, and Kefauver's victory showed the possibilities for young reformers. But could Gore defeat the veteran McKellar in 1952?[40]

Albert Gore had established an enviable record in the House. His role on the Appropriations Committee enabled him to protect the interests of the TVA and Tennessee farmers. He was favored by the Democratic House leadership of Sam Rayburn and John McCormack. He had good relations with the White House and was much in demand as a speaker for Democratic candidates across the nation.

One very clear career path was to build on this enviable position of strength on the Appropriations Committee and simply to accumulate more and more power in the House. That was the path Gore's neighboring congressman, Joe Evins, took. Evins had come back from the war and was elected to Congress in 1946 as part of a GI revolt in his Fifth District. In Rutherford County, John Bragg recalled: "When the war was over, the next election we had a very strong VFW and American Legion. And in every office there was a veteran running and just cleaned out the courthouse. There wasn't a civilian left. It was all soldiers running the county."

Evins decided that climbing the seniority ladder in the House, and the influence over patronage and pork-barrel projects that it brought, was the way to power. At election time he would simply go back to his district, go to a county, and announce he was going to speak at the courthouse square. He would then reach into his pocket, pull out a list of projects and appropriations he had secured for the county, and read it out. He would finally thank the audience for its attention and leave. As a former attorney for the Federal Trade Commission, his chairmanship of the House Small Business Committee enabled him to guide his district's businessmen through the regulatory thicket in Washington and help direct procurement contracts their way. His seniority and the give-and-take of pork-barrel politics ensured that everything from dams to model-cities projects came to his district. He kept getting elected year after year, with merely token opposition, and only gave up his seat in 1976, when he tired of driving back and forth to Washington, since he would not fly.[41]

That career path was not an appealing one to the ambitious Albert Gore. Like Lyndon B. Johnson in Texas in 1948, Gore did not relish the prospect of years of patiently building up seniority in a congressional committee. Relying for years to come on Appropriations chair Clarence Cannon, with whom he had an uneasy relationship, was an unappetizing prospect for Gore. His wider policy interests for his state and region and his fascination with foreign policy would remain stunted if he stayed in the House. After ten years in the House, he recalled, you had to decide to go up, or get out. The Senate was the natural stepping stone, as it had been for his Tennessee colleague, Estes Kefauver, in 1948, and his close friend from Oklahoma, Mike Monroney, in 1950. If he needed any further persuading, Tennessee was to lose one of its congressional seats in 1952, and Joe Evins would be competing with Gore for the Fourth District nomination.[42]

The prospects for a Southern New Dealer like Gore were greatly enhanced by the dramatic political changes in Tennessee after the war: The war and TVA inspired economic development, the migration from the land, the demands of urban leaders for change, the increased breathing space for both organized labor and African Americans.

Boss Crump in Memphis was troubled by the impact of these changes. He had remained loyal to Roosevelt, even though he, like many conservative Southerners, detested Eleanor Roosevelt, "who the people hate." FDR, he noted sympathetically in the summer of 1944, "sounded tired, but why shouldn't he be? A man who had more to contend with than any five men in the world—world war, national politics, and the big-monied interests at his throat." But what worried Crump was that "the negro proposition is becoming tremendous." Truman exacerbated the problem. Crump saw in the president's civil rights proposals a "Civil Rights Commission with police powers everywhere. They will have charge of Memphis and Shelby County and other towns and counties in the state—all southern states." Truman was selling the South down the river.[43]

There was increasingly a disconnect between Crump's view of himself as a benign force for good and his critics' perspective. Crump's old close associates had been blunt in their advice to the boss. Increasingly after 1940 they were succeeded by acolytes who fawned and told Crump what he wanted to hear. In 1947 Shelby District Attorney Will Gerber told New York columnist Walter Winchell that, thanks to Mr. Crump's beneficence, Memphis operated its own light, gas, and water facilities. It boasted a magnificent park system, fine colleges and schools, and was the "Hospital Center of the South." It had the lowest fire insurance rates of any city in America and was known as a noiseless city "where the sound of the automobile horn is almost extinct."[44]

Crump was puzzled that not everybody could see that Memphis was a great city with a great future. He would not tolerate any graft in the city administration and therefore could not see how anybody could equate him with corrupt city bosses in the North, like Ed Flynn of Brooklyn, whose appointment by FDR as ambassador to Australia was bitterly opposed by Crump. There could be only one explanation—the activities of a lying press. Crump told Edward J. Meeman of the *Memphis Press-Scimitar*: "Your nature is so steeped in suspicion, disappointment, vanity, hate, envy and lust for power, you are a deadly enemy to fair play, charity and truth." Crump accused Meeman: "You loathe me. You would resort to anything that might injure this town if you thought you could in the slightest way hurt me. You are a murderer at heart even though your hands may not have moved to kill."[45]

But however sensitive Crump was to criticism, in the end he regarded Meeman as ineffective. His real venom was reserved for the *Nashville Tennessean*, with whom, as he saw it, he had vied for control of the state since the days when it was owned by Colonel Luke Lea. Now the paper was controlled by Silliman Evans from Texas, who had been bankrolled by Jesse Jones and the Reconstruction Finance Corporation, and who, much to Crump's disgust, enjoyed the good favors of the New Deal and the national Democratic Party. Evans was a "white livered coward." The proprietor, his editor, Jennings Perry, and his political correspondent, Joe Hatcher, were publicly denounced by Crump as "three slimy, mangy, bubonic, rats."[46]

What Crump could not see was that his methods sat uneasily during an American war against fascism. The London *Economist* reported that Memphis lived under "a totalitarian government." Crump was "less the traditional American political boss, more the modern dictator." Agnes Meyer, wife of the owner of the *Washington Post*, called Crump "Hitler." *Time* noted that thirty-seven years of benign but iron despotism had "given Memphis citizens almost everything but the right to vote for a candidate of their own choosing." Crump's election workers smashed newsmen's cameras on election day and imprisoned reporters. CIO organizers were beaten up. Assertive African American businessmen were driven out of town.[47]

And so it was that in 1948 Crump's power was shaken to its foundations. His former protégé from the 1930s—but then bitter rival—Gordon Browning, returned from service as a military governor in Germany and ran for governor of Tennessee. "I made," Browning recalled, "three hundred speeches over an hour long in that campaign and most of them were directed at Crump." In the Senate race Crump disowned the incumbent, Tom Stewart, whom he regarded as a lazy officeholder and a poor campaigner. He endorsed a challenger, Judge John Mitchell of Cookeville, whom he scarcely knew. Crump thought Mitchell would be a strong candidate because of his military record—he was a veteran of both wars—but he turned out to be an uninspired candidate. Stewart and Mitchell were both upset by the man who marshalled the new forces in Tennessee politics—returning veterans, the small but increasing black electorate, women, and organized labor—Estes Kefauver, the Chattanooga congressman. The homespun but Ivy League–educated Kefauver had countered his lack of a political organization or significant financial backing or name recognition by crossing the state back and forth, shaking hands with everybody he could. He capitalized on the GI revolts, like the one that took over Rutherford County and sent Joe Evins to Washington. Veterans who had organized to overturn local power structures now voted to overturn the state's power structure. Kefauver was the first statewide candidate to appoint a female state campaign manager with special responsibility for female voters, Martha Ragland, and female campaign managers in each county. Organized labor backed him because of his votes against Taft–Hartley, although his campaign manager, Charlie Neese, made sure that checks from labor were cashed outside the state.[48]

Above all, Kefauver cracked open Memphis. The wartime contradictions of fighting dictatorship overseas and living under Boss Crump's rule at home were stark for white elite reformers. International concerns troubled *Memphis Press-Scimitar* editor Edward Meeman, aristocratic lawyers like Lucius Burch, and businessman Edmund Orgill. They favored a federal "Atlantic

Union," a form of integration of the democracies of the North Atlantic. Such a union might have halted Hitler but would now be necessary to halt Stalin. They were acutely conscious that they lived in a "totalitarian democracy" in Memphis. When Estes Kefauver indicated his willingness to support the Atlantic Union, these Memphis businessmen were willing to forgive him his vote against Taft-Hartley. Kefauver also picked up labor votes in Memphis, and Crump's "drum-tight control of the Negro vote" finally ended as a result of police brutality and the reluctance of Crump's mayor to appoint black police officers. White middle-class reformers, labor, and African Americans delivered Kefauver enough votes in Shelby County to win statewide. Crump himself blamed "the heavy CIO vote" in Shelby. He heard the CIO "went all over the state strong, with a lot of money."[49]

﹏

WOULD ALBERT GORE be able to take advantage of these new forces in Tennessee politics? He was, in many ways, the most prominent Tennessee congressman, and he had established a national reputation. Reformers like newspaper editor Meeman in Memphis and fellow liberal congressmen like J. Percy Priest in Nashville favored him as the up-and-coming man in state politics. Estes Kefauver and Gore talked to each other about one of them running for the Senate in 1948. Kefauver announced his candidacy in November 1947 without consulting Gore, but Gore claimed to be neither surprised nor disappointed.[50]

In that 1948 campaign Albert put his energies, instead, into campaigning for Gordon Browning for governor. Gore had been his campaign manager and a member of his cabinet in the 1930s, and he admired Browning as a reformer and an administrator. Gore claimed he made more speeches in the campaign than anybody other than Browning and Kefauver—more than forty speeches in the final three weeks. He opposed the Crump machine by name because he had been targeted himself by Crump's lieutenant, Will Gerber. Gore did not have to back Kefauver publicly—he was a friend of one of Kefauver's opponents, Judge Mitchell—but he knew that the Browning and Kefauver campaigns were closely linked.[51]

From 1950 it was clear that Gore was seriously contemplating a bid for the Senate. He accepted invitations to speak all across the state, and he helped candidates for reelection, particularly Democrats in eastern Tennessee. At the start he may have taken at face value Senator McKellar's 1946 pronouncement that he would not run again in 1952. But the senator put the record straight in the summer of 1951, when he announced that he would offer himself for reelection.[52]

McKellar would be eighty-three in 1952; he was not in good health, and he was rarely back in the state. But Gore could be under no illusion about the scale of the task. McKellar was, he knew, "deeply entrenched" in Tennessee. His seniority and chairmanship of the Senate Appropriations Committee, his ability to bring federal money to the state, and his ruthless pursuit of patronage made him a formidable foe. In 1946 McKellar had been reelected without even making a campaign speech. As the hostile David Lilienthal observed, there was "hardly a person in the state for whom the old boy [McKellar] hasn't done a personal favor." Whereas in 1948 the Crump forces had been divided, in 1952 they would be united behind the incumbent. No wonder a Washington columnist thought that Gore would be "tilting against one of the most redoubtable windmills on the national political skyline."[53]

How could Gore attack McKellar for his age and ill health without sounding deeply personal and indelicate? "It is," he told Bernard Baruch, "a very touchy and tricky matter to run against a man with a long, honorable record." Some of his campaign team thought that he should be direct—McKellar could "no longer cut the mustard." However Gore took the calculated, but apparently high-minded, position not to attack the incumbent personally. "Not one time did I call his name during the campaign or criticize on a single issue." After all, despite early tensions, Gore and McKellar in the late 1940s cooperated on many issues concerning the TVA and atomic energy, with McKellar sometimes rescuing appropriations in the Senate that Gore had been unsuccessful in securing in the House. Instead Gore professed to concentrate on policies and programs for the future, while acknowledging what McKellar had achieved in the past. He made it clear that he would not allude to the age or general decrepitude of his opponent "because I'd have to change my character to do such a thing. I've never done that in my campaign." Nevertheless, his tactics "indirectly [made] the point of his [McKellar's] advanced age without ever making specific mention of it."[54]

Kefauver's success in 1948 had shown that even such "deeply entrenched" forces could be undermined. Gore had significant resources of his own at his disposal. Frequent redistricting since 1938 meant that twenty-four of the ninety-five counties in the state had at some point been in his congressional district. His work on appropriations for the TVA and his efforts to develop Oak Ridge had benefitted the entire state, not just his district. Former Republican congressman Judge John Jennings, who had worked so closely with

Gore on Oak Ridge, reported in January 1951 that Gore was well ahead in his section of east Tennessee. Gore had maintained close ties with the Farm Bureau and sponsored major farm legislation. He tried never to miss a VFW or an American Legion encampment.[55]

Gore also knew the value of television and radio. His weekly radio broadcasts on WSM in Nashville had given him an audience far beyond the state capital or his own district. They were carried by ten stations in the state. Al Gore Jr. would recall that, when he made his own first race for Congress in 1976, people still remembered his father's weekly radio broadcasts. After the success of his appearance playing the fiddle on television in Nashville in 1951, Gore launched a weekly television show, which necessitated his flying back to Nashville each weekend. The Sunday before Christmas 1951, he brought his family on the show. The proud father reported that "Al stole the show." In the middle of a conversation among Nancy, Albert, and Pauline to which Al appeared oblivious, Al "dropped his crayons and climbed up in my lap in full view of the TV camera close-up, put his arms around my neck and in a clear voice said, 'Now Daddy, tell me what old Santa Claus said he's gonna bring me.'" It made Al, said Gore, "the talk of the town."[56]

He could also draw on the Kefauver organization that had been so successful in 1948. Whereas Crump and McKellar had particular local lieutenants or managers, Kefauver had set up committees in every county, and Gore followed suit. He talked a lot to Kefauver about the upcoming campaign, and he endorsed Kefauver when he made his dark-horse bid for the presidency in 1952, where he surprised everybody by winning the New Hampshire primary. Reform-minded women had been mobilized for Kefauver in 1948 by Martha Ragland. Gore appointed Ragland as one of his campaign managers in 1952. She was, remembered Jack Robinson Sr., one of the small number of people Gore turned to for political advice. His wife, Pauline, worked to target women voters and was an expert campaigner in her own right. Pauline took over campaigning from Albert for two weeks at the start of June 1952, when Gore had to be in Washington for the ARO/AEDC investigations.[57]

Gore could not rely on Governor Browning's supporters. Having campaigned so vigorously for his mentor in 1948, Gore had a marked falling-out with Browning. In retrospect, both Gore and Browning downplayed the split. Clearly Gore believed that Browning had thought of running for the Senate in 1952, and there was a competitive edge to their relations. Browning, in turn, remembered it this way: "Well, Albert and my friends got into a terrible row after I became governor. I couldn't stop them fussing at each other. I just decided I'd not put my hands on the Gore situation anymore, and I didn't. McKellar really got a lot of my friends in 1952. They got mad at Albert about something, two or three things maybe but I stayed out if it entirely and they just went ahead and voted the way they wanted to."[58]

In fact in 1951 Browning told Lucius Burch in Memphis that "when you talk of my obligations to Albert Gore you do not know all of our relationships from the beginning. My feeling is easy on the fact that I have done more for him than he has for me." As governor Browning had had to work with McKellar, particularly on the development of the wind tunnel and the major aircraft research facility at Tullahoma, and there was some talk of a federal judgeship for Browning. Gore believed that Browning, like other politicians in the state, thought that, if McKellar won, there would soon be a vacant Senate seat. An appointment by the governor would be a far easier and cheaper route to the Senate than running against a veteran incumbent. In any event, in the 1952 campaign Browning's aides desperately tried to keep out of the Senate race. One leading aide acknowledged that some Browning supporters would vote for Gore but predicted that the bulk of their supporters would vote for McKellar. The Browning and McKellar teams were closely linked in eastern Tennessee, and McKellar himself was convinced after the election that he owed half his votes to Browning's supporters.[59]

In running for reelection as governor, Browning found himself up against a young, reform-minded, stirring Methodist orator and war veteran, Frank Clement. Clement ran a reform campaign, latching on to financial scandals in the Browning administration and the governor's support for the sales tax. But crucially Clement also received the endorsement of Boss Crump. There was little affinity between the boss and Clement—but Crump listened to legionnaires in his inner circle who told him that Clement could beat his long-standing enemy Browning. For Browning and the *Tennessean*, Clement's alliance with Crump was the antithesis of reform. As in 1948 Browning campaigned as much against Crump as against his opponent, "the stooge candidate." The *Tennessean* was vituperative, and its political correspondent, Joe Hatcher, denounced Clement every day for his corrupt links with Memphis.[60]

In contrast to Browning, Gore did not go out of his way to attack Crump in his election. He stressed that, unlike his opponent, he had no political machine behind him, and he courted the Memphis newspaper editors Edward Meeman and Frank Ahlgren, other Memphis reformers, and African American voters. But he also tried to see Crump when he visited Memphis, thanked Crump effusively for some kind words the boss had offered about Gore over a TVA issue, and said nothing hostile about Crump when he campaigned in Memphis.[61]

Above all Gore followed in Kefauver's footsteps in taking his campaign to people all over the state to compensate for the lack of a party organization or substantial campaign funds. Getting out to the county crossroads, not merely the county seats, was the standard path for Southern candidates challenging incumbents or established organizations in a one-party system. It had been Kefauver's approach. It had been Lyndon Johnson's approach in his run against Coke Stevenson for the Senate in 1948 in Texas. It had been the approach of liberal Southern "good ole' boy" politicians like Big Jim Folsom in Alabama and Kerr Scott in North Carolina. Gore had, at most, $50,000 for his campaign. The McKellar forces were envisaging spending $167,000. Gore needed to take his case beyond county-seat elites and established powerbrokers to the people—and in the absence of major funding, the only way to do that was in person.[62]

Throughout 1950 and 1951 Gore accepted almost every invitation to speak in Tennessee and to help local candidates. He had no primary opposition in 1950 in his own district and only token opposition in the general election. He made more than two hundred speeches in the state that year. In October he spent a week campaigning for his Oak Ridge political ally, Frank Wilson, in his congressional race for the Second District. He rigged himself up with a sound truck and even turned down an invitation to the Tennessee–Alabama football game on the grounds that Saturday afternoon was a particularly good time to campaign in crowded county seats.[63]

In 1951 Gore's schedule reflected a constant diet of speaking to farm bureaus, Rotary, Kiwanis, and Lions Clubs, American Legion posts, Jaycees, and high school commencements, usually from Friday to Monday so that he could spend the week in Washington. He spoke at the state farm bureau and CIO conventions, the American Legion state convention, and the VFW encampment. By March he had already made thirty speeches in the state. In 1951 a typical weekend saw Gore speaking at the Rhea County Farm Bureau in Dayton on Friday evening, then returning to Washington for a newspaper editors' banquet on Saturday before flying back to Nashville for his Sunday TV program. The next day, Monday, 23 April, he was at the Lions Club at Halls; on Tuesday, 24 April, at the Rutherford, Dyer, and neighboring Lions Clubs; on Wednesday, 25 April, at another Lions Club in Covington; on Thursday, 26 April, at Hornbeak High School; on Friday, 27 April, at the Dixon County Teachers Association; and finally, on Saturday, 28 April, at the state convention of the Knights of Columbus in Chattanooga. In May he reported from Nashville that he had given three speeches in middle Tennessee the day before and was heading to west Tennessee the next day to speak there. He was optimistic: "Things continue to look very good to me." In July and August the pace quickened. Between 23 July and 23 August, he made nineteen speeches and flew back to Washington three times. On 15 August he left for two weeks to visit Europe and the Middle East with the Inter-Parliamentary Union. Gore lamented to his uncle, Charlie Gore, that the speaking and handshaking strategy was an expensive one. The once-a-week roundtrip from Washington cost about $100 out of his own pocket. He was "beginning to be mashed out pretty thin." The only way he could afford the plane fares was because of his business operation in Carthage.[64]

In a much-heralded move, on 2 February 1952, Gore formally announced his candidacy. In a series of firsts in Tennessee politics, he and Pauline boarded a plane in Washington, DC, which stopped at the Tri-Cities airport in upper eastern Tennessee, then Knoxville, and on to Nashville, and Memphis. Greeted by friends at each stop, he handed out copies of his announcement to local newspapermen. In Nashville his children joined the plane, and in Memphis, McKellar's hometown, he made his formal announcement. In Nashville and Memphis his announcement was made on television. He also made a short, fifty-second recording for each of the fifty-nine radio stations in the state which they could use along with the press release and the television announcement.[65]

Gore stressed his record, in particular his leadership in defending the TVA program and its funding in the House. He cited his role in the defeat of the Brannan farm plan and the passage of substitute price-support legislation, the Gore–Anderson Bill, and his battle to control inflation during World War II. He portrayed himself as beholden to no one: "I have no political machine supporting me. I am running on my own. The plan of my campaign will be simple—go to the people." He saw himself as a "middle of the road" candidate who would not please extremists on either the left or the right. He criticized the "unnecessary free-handed spending policies of the present administration." Gore said he viewed the mounting spending "with an active hostility." But perhaps what was most striking about his plans for the future was his ambition to make Tennessee "the atomic capital" of the nation. He had been chairing meetings of the Appropriations Independent Offices subcommittee on atomic energy. Gore held out the hope that the huge expansion of atomic power promised by Gordon Dean, the chair of the Atomic Energy Commission, would mean new nuclear facilities in Tennessee—which had TVA power, the "world's largest reservoir of atomic energy technicians and professionals at Oak Ridge," and a secure strategic location.[66]

To take his campaign to the people, Gore became a "Tuesday-to-Thursday" congressman. In Washington, however, he maintained his profile by defending the TVA plans to develop high dams and hydroelectric plants on the Cumberland River to meet the expected increase in demand for electricity. He also robustly defended the agency against charges that it had extravagantly mishandled its coal-purchasing contracts. He also maintained his watchdog role on federal spending by arguing that the deplorable backlog of cases in the federal district court in Nashville should *not* be met by creating a new, highly paid judgeship. Above all he sustained a prolonged investigation into the cost-plus contract for the operation of the Arnold Engineering Development Center at Tullahoma. It had been a great coup for Senator McKellar and Governor Browning when the Air Engineering Development Center (renamed in 1950 after the first general of the air force, Hap Arnold) was located in Tennessee. The first secretary of the air force, Stuart Symington, had identified the need for a center to study jet propulsion, supersonic aircraft, and ballistic missiles to maintain the air force's technological supremacy. The main part of the flight simulation facility was a gigantic wind tunnel. McKellar and Browning offered the air force the forty-thousand-acre Camp Forest, a World War II army base and POW camp—land, security, and abundant water and electrical power made it an attractive proposition. The operation of the center was contracted out to Arnold Research Organization. It was this contract that aroused Gore's suspicions. ARO had been established by a St. Louis civil-engineering company specifically to service the center. Its leaders had close contacts with the air force department under the Missourian Symington. Gore mounted something like a one-man crusade to expose "the fat contract on a silver platter" that had been handed to the St. Louis businessmen. The whole contract reeked of cost-plus profiteering and favoritism. It provided, he alleged, "a gravy train pipeline to the taxpayer's pockets." Investigating waste and corruption was a role Gore adopted with relish. He liked to portray himself as a lone operator, without any staff help (a fact he lamented earlier when examining costs of the Atomic Energy Commission), up against lobbyists working out of the Ritz-Carlton Hotel. Others were less impressed. Memphis businessman Lewis T. Berringer, a close friend of both McKellar and President Truman, recalled that Gore spoke many times when he should have been listening. He did concede that after Gore had fully investigated the operation of the wind tunnels, Gore later became a big supporter of the project.[67]

Away from Washington Gore appointed three young veterans—George Cloys (west Tennessee), Harry Phillips (middle), and Frank Wilson (east)— as well as Martha Ragland as his campaign managers. He went to Memphis to stress that he would be ringing doorbells and shaking hands there. Shelby County had too many votes to be left uncontested. Each weekend he came back and campaigned vigorously. During the Easter recess he mounted a cross-the-state meet-the-people drive. He started in Jackson on Thursday, 10 April, where he met his western campaign team. On Friday he campaigned in Fayette, Haywood, and Henderson counties. Saturday and Sunday he tackled Memphis. His Monday itinerary started in Covington at 8:30, then Henning (noon), Ripley (1:00), Gates (4:00), and Halls (4:30). He ended up spending the night in Union City. He then headed to Nashville and spent the last part of the week in eastern Tennessee. The following week he was back in the middle part of the state: Monday, Dickson, Waverly, and Humphries and William- son counties; Tuesday morning, Columbia and Maury county; Tuesday af- ternoon, Pulaski and Giles County; Tuesday night, Fayetteville and Lincoln County; Wednesday, Murfreesboro and Rutherford County, Woodbury and Cannon County, McMinnville and Warren county, Spencer and Van Buren county; Thursday, Sparta and Crossville. Finally, on Friday, he spoke at the high school commencement exercises at Pikeville.[68]

↬

HOW WOULD MCKELLAR respond to this highly visible, energetic chal- lenge, which highlighted the disparity between the challenger candidate's youth and vigor and the incumbent's age and frailty?

Crump was intensely loyal to Senator McKellar. In March 1945 he had re- sisted President Roosevelt's plea to deter McKellar from running again. Instead he worked flat out to secure McKellar's reelection in 1946. In 1952 McKellar ignored Crump's repeated warnings that he would face serious opposition. As late as January of that year, days before Gore announced, McKellar retained the hope that he might not be opposed.

Crump fully understood the basic problem McKellar faced. The senator had not been over the entire state for many years. "To the hundreds of new people in Tennessee, and very many young people grown to maturity in their native environment," Crump pointed out, McKellar was "just a distinguished name in the papers, and they are utterly ignorant of the personality that put him there." Crump worked with Herbert "Hub" S. Walters, an east Tennessee banker, former highway commissioner, and McKellar's devoted henchman, to take the steps necessary to counter that ignorance among new voters and to offset Gore's barnstorming campaign. Since the senator could not appear because of his Washington duties and declining health, Crump wanted three men appointed to cover each division of the state who would speak constantly, in every county, between March and the election. Every county had to be organized. There was no time to lose.[69]

Crump was always paranoid about the failure of candidates to put in enough work across the state. He resented what he saw as the assumption of some candidates that the boss would deliver enough votes in Shelby to carry them through to a statewide majority. But in this case Crump's pessimism was justified. At a meeting on 7 May, it was clear that only forty-five of the ninety-five counties had been organized. Walters despondently reported that east Tennessee was deluged with rumors of McKellar's ill health, and he seemed at a loss as to how to counter those allegations. Crump despaired of the lists of supporters he received from McKellar's office. They were out of date: Some people on the list had died. What Crump wanted was not people who had occasionally written to the senator but people who had a real debt to the McKellar, who could be leaned on to get supporters to the polls.[70]

Finally, Crump decided McKellar should withdraw. There had been repeated speculation in the *Tennessean* and in Drew Pearson's columns in April that McKellar was going to withdraw because of his health and that Seventh District congressman Pat Sutton would run in his place. Crump and McKellar had consistently refuted these suggestions, and McKellar invited journalists to his Washington, DC, apartment to show how vigorous he was. But Crump's survey of the campaign in early May convinced him that McKellar should stand down. He sent Walters to Washington. Walters and Lonnie Ormes, federal marshal for Middle Tennessee, saw McKellar and laid out a "doleful" story of newspaper opposition, the doubts about his age, the ugly things being said about him. However when McKellar asked them directly whether they wanted him to stand down, neither could say that to his face. They felt only Crump could do that. The next day Crump rang his old friend. In the painful conversation, it became clear that McKellar could not contemplate standing down. He called on their fifty years of friendship, defended his record of achievement for the state, pointed out that William Gladstone had been prime minister of the strongest nation in the world at the age of eighty, and claimed to be in better health than in a long time. Confronted by the pained accusation of betrayal, Crump had to accept McKellar's decision and, with a heavy heart, do the best he could for a campaign he was convinced was doomed.[71]

Crump despaired that McKellar would ever get started. But finally McKellar launched his campaign at Cookeville on 14 July, in Gore's home district. He downplayed his age and frailty. His fitness to do the job in Washington, he said, was indicated by the fact that he'd worked harder in the previous six months than at any time in his career. He spoke for fifty-five minutes, in the heat of the day, without notes. But this was not the start of a vigorous campaign by the senator. He had spent the day resting in his hotel in Nashville so he could give the Cookeville speech, and he skipped a scheduled meeting with the press immediately afterward. It was a killing time to campaign: Not only was June 1952 the hottest June on record in Nashville and middle Tennessee, it was also the hottest month ever to that date. The high temperatures reached 105.6 degrees Fahrenheit on 30 June, the twelfth straight day over 100 degrees. July brought no relief. McKellar gave only six further speeches in the campaign—and four of those were in Memphis and Shelby County. When the American Legion post at Donelson invited him to attend their open house, McKellar declined, even though he was staying in a hotel in Nashville. Gore accepted. McKellar rarely left his hotel rooms. Surrogates went around the state on his behalf. Plans to use a helicopter had to be abandoned because the only one available in the South was being used by Congressman Boyd Tackett in Arkansas. Veteran state lawmaker John Bragg recalled the McKellar campaign: "McKellar didn't come back but once. He came back up to Cookeville and that was all he did."[72]

Instead, McKellar stayed in his air-conditioned hotel rooms and consulted with friends, supporters, and campaign officials. Press accounts of these meetings served merely to emphasize that the senator was too feeble to campaign. To compensate, McKellar had surrogates go around the state not only making speeches on his behalf but also traveling in motorcades and stopping to shake hands with voters.[73]

The campaign themes were simple. McKellar's seniority and power enabled him to be of great service to Tennessee. He could obtain money for the TVA, public roads, and other public works. McKellar proposed a number of federally financed four-lane highways and condemned financial aid to foreign countries. Boss Crump compared McKellar to Winston Churchill, who had also been attacked because of his age. His organization paid for advertisements in the Memphis newspapers touting, "There Is No Substitute for Experience." McKellar's friends then attacked Gore for neglecting his House duties in pursuit of a Senate seat and for generally being ineffective in his fourteen years in the House. They claimed he had failed even to land a promised new post office for Carthage and had few or no laws to his show for his time in Congress. The Gore–Anderson farm bill, they claimed, had little to do with Gore. They tried to dent Gore's image as a friend of the TVA. McKellar alleged that the South Holston and Watauga dams were being built despite Gore's opposition, and that he, not Gore, had had to secure dams on the Cumberland River which ran through Gore's district. McKellar put that failure down to his opponent's "continuous absenteeism" from the House.[74]

The senator's friends also attacked Gore's war record. In June Ward Hudgins, music industry lawyer, criticized Gore's military record. According to Gore, McKellar wrote to a friend that he was sure he would never commend Gore's war record, "as he never got near a battlefield and certainly not until after the war." Veterans for McKellar published a paid advertisement as an open letter to Gore, signed by a number of veterans, which challenged Gore's account of his war service. Why had he not served from December 1943? They poured scorn on his ninety-five days of service "in some capacity as a writer on military matters." Why had he returned home when the war was not over either in Europe or the Pacific? Clearly, they said, his minimal service had been a political stunt designed to protect his political future. They accused him of "merely playing tag with your country's uniform for your own benefit and without any desire to serve your country." Gore was compelled to recount his story of being blocked by FDR from serving but then carrying out his mission for the War Department, traveling incognito on the front lines with the infantry, coming under enemy fire, and firing back. McKellar also charged that subsequently Gore had opposed increased combat pay for Korean War veterans. Since McKellar had never served in the military, it was not clear how much effect these charges had. As Gordon Browning recalled, McKellar was simply wrong on Gore's war record.[75]

It was a small step from impugning Gore's war record to attacking his stance on race. But it is a measure of Gore's success in defusing the racial issue that he did not have to spend much time defending himself on race. Only once, late in the campaign, did one of McKellar's surrogates raise the race question. Roane Waring, a Memphis attorney and longtime ally of Boss Crump and McKellar, went on television and alleged that a "pink tinged north group" which included "radical thinkers and Communist-minded individuals" had been raising money on Gore's behalf to defeat McKellar. Their aim, Waring asserted, was to "destroy the influence of the South." By the standards of the Red-baiting and race-baiting campaigns mounted against Claude Pepper and Frank Graham in 1950, this attack was fairly tame. Waring was attacking the National Committee for an Effective Congress, a liberal pressure group founded by Eleanor Roosevelt in 1948. Gore ignored the racial dimension and used his television address later that evening to distance himself from the National Committee. As soon as he learned about the activities of the committee, he said that had told the group to stop using his name and announced he would not accept any money from them. As Gore recalled, he focused on his liberal economic record to secure black support and "let the deceptive dogs of racism lie as best I could." Campaigning in western Tennessee, he alarmed some of his local allies by "shaking hands with the niggers" when he pressed the flesh enthusiastically at crossroads communities. Gore himself conceded that McKellar never once stooped to racism in the campaign, and to outside observers, Gore and McKellar were both "South-oriented" on the civil rights issues.[76]

Gore spent some time rebutting both McKellar's attacks and the defence of the senator's record. Before McKellar came back to the state, Gore had largely refrained from mentioning the senator by name. Now he repeatedly argued that seniority was not essential for influence in the Senate. Rather, junior senators had often been successful, and some senators, like Carter Glass, had clung on too long. His own experience in the House had trained him for the Senate. When McKellar's supporters plastered the state with slogans, "Thinking Feller? Vote for McKellar," Pauline Gore organized the reply, "Think some more and vote for Gore." Gore targeted McKellar for his crude patronage politics. As chair of the Senate Appropriations Committee, McKellar was "the chief architect of our mounting national debt." While Gore stressed his own support for the TVA through shepherding TVA appropriations through his House subcommittee, he blamed McKellar, without mentioning his name, for endangering the TVA's technocratic success. He attacked McKellar for seeking to make TVA appointments a matter of congressional patronage, for attempting to increase congressional control over TVA spending, and for attacking the TVA's directors.[77]

But in the main Gore hammered away at the theme that he, as part of a new generation of Southern politicians, would deliver Tennesseans a New Deal–style program for economic development: investment in the infrastructure—roads, public power, and atomic energy—and redistributive policies in favor of farmers and labor. He did not let up on his ferocious travel pace and kept furiously campaigning right to the end.

Gore not merely defeated McKellar, he overwhelmed him. Gore received almost 335,000 votes. He and the successful gubernatorial candidate, Frank Clement, were the first Tennessee candidates to amass more than 300,000 votes in a primary. McKellar carried only the eastern Republican congressional districts, Memphis, and Shelby County, but significantly, McKellar won Shelby by only 5,000 votes, whereas the Crump-backed Frank Clement won the county by more than 20,000 votes. For historian James B. Gardner, Gore's "careful avoidance of any derogatory comments about the Crump machine" had been rewarded by "the boss's unusual silence on Gore's candidacy." By contrast, Browning felt the full force of Crump's opposition in the governor's race.[78]

In fact the victories of both Gore and Clement highlighted the success of young, new candidates against older incumbents. They both brought new voters to the polls. It was the first election in which all Tennessee voters could take part without paying a poll tax. Gore reaped the reward for his punishing campaign schedule, traveling back and forth across the state. Farmers recognized his championing of price supports and rural electrification, middle-class reformers in Memphis welcomed his independence and integrity, and African Americans acknowledged his racial moderation. Matt Lynch, head of the Tennessee CIO, may not have quite forgiven Gore for his support of Taft–Hartley and his distance from trades unions. The Labor Non-Partisan League claimed that coalminers in Tennessee would support McKellar because of Gore's support for "vicious anti-union legislation." But Lynch relied on what George Barrett had done to educate Gore on labor, and there was no incentive to back anti-union McKellar. Women like Martha Ragland may have owed their first loyalty and real passion to Kefauver, but they had been recognized by Gore as well, and they responded positively to Pauline Gore. Above all, Tennesseans supported Gore's vision of the federal government as an engine of the state's economic growth. They were not about to renounce the legacy of the TVA. One of the first to congratulate Gore was David Lilienthal, McKellar's nemesis and head of the TVA and then the AEC. He hailed Gore as "new Twentieth Century Senator," in a telegram sent with "special feelings."[79]

Free from any serious threat to his senate seat from Republicans in the general election in Tennessee, Gore was able to campaign out of state in the autumn as the Democrats tried to stop the momentum for General Dwight

Eisenhower and the Republicans. His old friend Mike Monroney arranged for him to speak in Oklahoma, Rochester, New York, Pittsburgh, and Eunice, Louisiana. But Gore was still needed in Tennessee, where his efforts on behalf of the Stevenson–Sparkman ticket were unavailing: The state went for the Republicans in the presidential election, as it would again in 1956 and 1960.[80]

John Popham in the *New York Times* described Gore's victory as a "youth victory." Gore's defeat of the chair of the Senate Appropriations Committee, the decision of Tom Connally, chair of the Foreign Relations Committee, not to seek reelection, and the death of Brien McMahon, chair of the joint committee on atomic energy, guaranteed a "major upheaval" in the Senate, even if the Democrats did not retain control. As a young, new face in the Senate from the South, Gore also had reasons to be ambitious. A Washington columnist described him as a "Tennessee hills version of Tom Dewey without the moustache: smart as a whip, bright as a new silver dollar, with a gift for ardent oratory." "You might take him," the columnist continued, "for a successful young Baptist preacher who coaches freshwater college football on the side. He has a marked enthusiasm for down-to-earth things." Racially moderate, economically liberal Southerners like Gore were inevitably of interest to the national Democratic Party. Its leaders were anxious, on the one hand, not to damage their civil rights credentials with African Americans and, on the other, not to lose the South. In 1952 the party had turned to John Sparkman of Alabama as its vice presidential candidate. It was hoped that Sparkman, who described himself as a TVA liberal, would be acceptable to both wings of the Democratic Party. An Alabama politician would, however, inevitably face increasing pressure on the race issue. Racial moderates from Tennessee might be a more attractive proposition in the future.[81]

But Gore would not be the only new young face in the Senate. John F. Kennedy was elected from Massachusetts at the same time. Stuart Symington, who had been one of Gore's targets in the ARO investigation, was elected from Missouri. There were other senators who, though still young, would be senior to Gore and had already established their reputations—Lyndon Johnson, Hubert Humphrey, and Estes Kefauver elected in 1948, and Gore's friend Mike Monroney and George Smathers of Florida elected in 1950. Albert Gore as the new junior senator from Tennessee faced a real challenge if he was to carve out a distinctive and substantial role for himself in the U.S. Senate.

The Infrastructure Senator
from the Sunbelt

ON 9 JANUARY 1953, Albert Gore wrote to the newly elected minority leader and chair of the Democratic Steering Committee, Lyndon Johnson, confidently giving his choice of committee assignments. His preference was for Appropriations, then Agriculture, and, finally, Foreign Relations. His other request was that he not be assigned a committee chaired by Senator Joe McCarthy.[1]

Gore got none of those assignments. But this failure was not a sign of the uneasy relationship, even hatred, between Johnson and Gore that developed so forcefully over the years. Instead, as Gore recalled, "There was a very good equation between Senator Johnson and me at that time." Johnson as a new minority leader wanted to reward effective freshman senators and other hard-working young men. He had some leeway because nine standing committees had been increased in size by two members. He persuaded the Steering Committee that no senator could serve on more than one of the five more desirable committees until all other Democrats had had a first choice or favorable assignment. He was therefore able to put Mike Mansfield and Hubert Humphrey on Foreign Relations, Stuart Symington on Armed Services, John F. Kennedy, Price Daniel, and Russell Long on Finance, and George Smathers on Interstate and Foreign Commerce. Gore was given Public Works—an assignment that would lead to his most important legislative achievement. Johnson wanted the Democrats in the Senate to be a loyal but effective opposition. He and Sam Rayburn, minority leader in the House, wanted to show that their own party was not fatally divided between North and South. Instead, LBJ wanted to exploit the divisions in the Republican Party between the isolationists who had supported Ohio senator Robert Taft and the internationalists who had supported Eisenhower. Rayburn and Johnson knew that Eisenhower would have to rely on the Democrats to pass foreign policy legislation. What Johnson wanted his party colleagues in the Senate to provide was constructive, responsible opposition. Gore could contribute policy specifics to that process—and Johnson would always welcome that, no matter how exasperating he found Gore at other times.[2]

Gore was not one of the inner club of Johnson acolytes that assembled in his office every day to drink and plot. He was not really a core member of what William S. White celebrated as "the Citadel." But he was a member of the Senate club in a way that his fellow Tennessean, Kefauver, never was. And he had another bond with heavyweights in the Senate: cattle. Robert Kerr of Oklahoma, Wayne Morse of Oregon, Lyndon Johnson, and Albert Gore all owned herds of purebred cattle. This was a shared passion that cut across all ideological divisions. In Gore's case in particular, it made him an unlikely friend of the senior senator from Oklahoma, the richest man in the Senate, Robert Kerr. They would exchange sales catalogs, invite each other to their own sales, and sometimes tease each other and muse about cattle in almost rhapsodic terms on the Senate floor. Russell Long of Louisiana noted wistfully that he had got out of the cattle business because there were better ways to lose money. Gore was "the only person I know of who makes money in cattle. . . . People have to pay $1000 to have their cows make the acquaintance of one of his bulls." One of the reasons Gore made money was that he was in business with Armand Hammer, the billionaire who shared his passion for fine cattle. They went into a partnership by which Hammer sent some of his herd to Tennessee to feed and breed on Gore's farm at Carthage, particularly Hammer's prize bull, Prince Sunbeam 328. At the end of December 1957, Gore had to tell Hammer that "the 328 is dead." Gore reported that the bull broke down in his hind quarters and had to be killed. "Actually," he went on, "I had not been able to get usable semen from him for nearly a year. Despite some exceptions, he was a great bull and left his imprint on the breed." Hammer agreed he was a great bull and asked Gore to get his secretary to notify the *Angus Journal* to see if they would run an obituary for the 328. Cattle was the start of what in the end was a lucrative friendship for Gore.[3]

It was a perhaps an indicator of Gore's distance from the Senate's inner club that in 1954 he incurred the lasting hostility of J. Edgar Hoover and the FBI. Until 1954 Gore had been cultivated by the FBI, as many up-and-coming congressmen were. A local FBI agent in Tennessee assured associate director Clyde Tolson in 1947 that Gore was ambitious, but that though he was a "very good backer" of the New Deal, he was "by no means too liberal or a left-winger." The agent thought Gore seemed "very friendly to the bureau and could be depended upon to render assistance where necessary." Another special agent reported on Gore's praise of the FBI in a speech at the Memphis Exchange Club. But alarm bells rang in the bureau after a colloquy on the floor of the Senate between Gore and his friend Paul Douglas on 8 March 1954. Gore complained that the FBI was passing on derogatory information without evaluating it and without revealing the source of the information. He was clearly annoyed by a specific case involving a constituent, but he lamented generally that under the Federal Employee Loyalty Program "thousands of persons are being wrongfully accused and wrongfully convicted, without having the privilege of disproving their guilt, without having an opportunity to establish their innocence, without knowing who is accusing them or of what they are being accused."[4]

Cartha DeLoach, deputy associate director of the agency, was dispatched to see Gore and put him right. DeLoach primly reported that he courteously approached the senator but that Gore responded "without showing any decency or courtesy." He launched an attack on "a snooping police agency" that furnished "raw information on poor innocent people without first evaluating the information." He denounced "guilt by association" smears. Gore dismissed the claim that FBI files were inviolate and that the agency did not evaluate information. He had seen hundreds of files when he was on the Kerr Committee, and Hoover had had no qualms about evaluating information about Harry Dexter White for the benefit of the Jenner Committee—something that clearly upset Gore. DeLoach was outraged that Gore refused to listen to reason and also refused to apologize when he was corrected regarding the specific case he had referred to in Congress. DeLoach's righteous indignation was further reinforced by the fact that he discovered, as he left, that Bill Allen, Gore's administrative assistant, had been standing behind the door taking notes. The irony of an FBI agent complaining about being spied on seems to have escaped DeLoach's notice.[5]

The FBI's reaction was instantaneous. Gore's name was to be placed on the list "not to be approached at any time." Hoover concluded that Gore was now "openly hostile towards the FBI." Agents in Tennessee were told of Gore's "self-chosen hostility and uncooperative attitude" and told not make any contact with him without the specific approval of the bureau.[6]

A visit by Bill Allen to FBI headquarters was to no avail. There was amusement that he "was overly polite and courteous." His invitation to the

FBI officials to drop in to see him and Gore if they were in the vicinity cut no ice. The FBI did arrange for the young Al Gore and friends to tour the bureau, and the bureau mailed him two souvenir targets as mementos. Gore was occasionally reported to have said nice things about the FBI, but as late as 1967 he was said to have launched a tirade about the bureau and its failure to deal with the mafia. "It is apparent," the official continued, that "Gore harbors strong personal animosity towards the Bureau and is uninterested in facts." M. A. Jones, a special agent in Memphis, noted that he "is regarded by many in his own state as being stupid and completely no good." Any more "baseless accusations" by "this disreputable individual" needed to be forcefully refuted. DeLoach meanwhile lobbied hard to make sure that the proposal Gore supported for a congressional committee for oversight of the FBI was defeated.[7]

THE TVA WAS ALWAYS a priority issue for a Tennessee senator. But in the 1950s producing enough power to sustain economic growth at an unprecedented level and to meet ever-increasing consumer needs was also a national issue. Who was to provide that electricity was of particular importance to Southern and Western politicians who saw cheap power as the key for the "takeoff" of their regions into self-sustaining economic growth. In 1953, with Eisenhower in the White House, the issue took on a particular salience. When, in 1952, Eisenhower campaigned successfully in Tennessee, he had denounced as unfounded any notion that he would sell off the Tennessee Valley Authority to private enterprise. But Tennessee politicians had reason to be suspicious. Lyndon Johnson allegedly overheard the president saying, "We will sell the [expletive deleted] thing." Even Eisenhower supporters believed he would have liked to sell off the TVA if he could.

Gore and Kefauver feared that Eisenhower would appoint TVA board members who would be hostile to public power. They waged a constant battle during the 1950s to sustain sympathetic members of the board of directors of the TVA. The Tennessee senators shared the Lilienthal philosophy that the TVA should produce as much power as possible: Demand would always increase to meet supply. Private utilities, by contrast, saw no reason why they should be denied access to these consumers: They demanded protection from unfair competition from the government-subsidized TVA. This battle aroused the greatest interest in Tennessee and in the valley itself, although some Western senators committed to public power helped out lest unhelpful precedents were established that could be applied in the West. But the battle for public power would unexpectedly become a national issue. The attempt by the Atomic Energy Commission to provide private rather than public power for the city of Memphis started out as a policy debate but eventually raised questions of conflicts of interest, which went to the heart of the Eisenhower administration's relations with both big business and the TVA.

The demands of the nuclear facilities at Oak Ridge and the Atomic Energy Commission were insatiable and threatened to take up all the power the TVA could produce. In the first months of the Republican administration, the Tennessean congressional delegation was defeated over plans for the TVA to build a coal-fired steam plant near Fulton, Tennessee, the aim of which had been to produce enough electricity for Memphis, where TVA had the contract to supply power. The Eisenhower administration ordered the Atomic Energy Commission to reduce its demands on TVA power produced at Paducah, Kentucky, and instead buy private power. When private utilities balked at building a competing facility at Paducah, the AEC came to an ingenious agreement with Edgar Dixon of Mid-South Utilities and Eugene Yates of the Southern Generating Company. Dixon and Yates would form the Mississippi Valley Generating Company and supply Memphis, while the TVA would continue to supply the AEC plant at Paducah. The AEC was effectively substituting private for public power for Memphis.[8]

No one had bothered to consult Memphis—where politicians of all factions took pride in their own power plant and the supply of TVA electricity. In addition, in the summer of 1953, Adolphe H. Wenzel, a Boston securities man whose firm underwrote securities for private utilities, was secretly "loaned" to the Budget Bureau in Washington to produce a financial study of the TVA. He proposed to sell off the TVA's power system intact to a new private firm, although the TVA would retain its flood-control operations.[9]

The contract was written in December 1953 but not brought to public attention until Gore highlighted this threat to the TVA in a speech on the Senate floor in April 1954. The speech started out as a few extemporaneous comments, but, helped by sympathetic interventions by fellow Southern and Western defenders of public power, Gore held the floor for seven hours. He argued that the private utilities' proposal to supply the Paducah plant amounted to the thin edge of the wedge. "Dismemberment of the TVA service area is the goal." "Why," he asked, "should the United States government pay more for power for its own use than it costs the government to produce the power in its own plants?" Kefauver and Gore, backed by John Sparkman and Lister Hill from Alabama and John Sherman Cooper from Kentucky, doggedly kept the issue before the public. For all the technicalities of the issue, it was easy to cast it in terms of public versus private power; the people against the interests of high finance; the South and West against the financial might of the Northeast, which sought to handicap regional competition from the Sunbelt. At first it appeared to be largely a battle over policy between private and public power advocates. But thanks to the Joint Committee on Atomic Energy, the role of Adolphe Wenzel emerged. Wenzel's long-term plans for the selloff of the TVA were revealed. But then it became clear that he had been drafting a contract between the government and a private utility, Dixon–Yates, which his own firm was going to underwrite.[10]

Gore had just become a member of the Joint Committee on Atomic Energy. The only joint select committee that exercised both oversight and legislative functions, the JCAE had been established under the Atomic Energy Act of 1946. Johnson appointed Gore to the committee in 1953, despite Kefauver's own request to be appointed. There were plenty of good reasons to appoint Gore: He would be an active, hard-working watchdog; he agreed with the minority leader on the role of cheap power in stimulating regional economic growth; he was the Democrat most associated with the development of Oak Ridge; and, as chair of a subcommittee of the House Appropriations Committee, he had supervised appropriations for the AEC. But above all Johnson did not want to reward Estes Kefauver. Both the minority leader and Sam Rayburn distrusted the senior senator from Tennessee as a publicity-seeker who had also, through his televised hearings on crime, embarrassed Northern Democratic city machine politicians. Appointing Gore was a convenient way for LBJ to thwart Kefauver.

Gore joined fellow Democrats on the joint committee in investigating the Dixon–Yates contract with evangelical fervor. Gore insisted that the contract "is but the first step in a long-range program to destroy, at a profit to private power monopolies, the success of the Tennessee Valley [Authority]." Congressman Chet Holifield, who had served on the JCAE from the start, strongly objected to the AEC brokering a deal with a private utility company to supply electricity not to itself but to the TVA grid. He objected to the way the chairman of the AEC, Admiral Lewis Strauss, appeared to be overriding a majority of his commissioners. But the publicity did not stop Strauss from pushing ahead with the contract, and under the Atomic Energy Act of 1954, he had the power to do so. Strauss was unrepentant over his opposition to the TVA operation. Why should the Tennessee Valley get special privileges? He steadfastly maintained that the principle of private enterprise would serve both the valley and Memphis better. He was backed by the president. If Congress rejected Strauss's reasonable proposal, Eisenhower would veto any attempt to appropriate funds for the TVA to solve Memphis's power needs.[11]

The JCAE staff was able, however, to uncover the secret role of Adolphe Wenzel in the AEC's move to help the private utilities at the expense of public power in the TVA. The staff got access to the AEC's visitors' book and sifted through thirty thousand cards to show how often Wenzel was at the AEC, half the time signing himself as attached to the Budget Bureau, half the time attached to his firm, First Boston. As Senator Robert Kerr described it, "The story of Dixon–Yates is a sordid one. The First Boston Corporation, country's largest utility investment bankers, placed a man in the Bureau of the Budget for the purpose of advising the Director of the Budget of the Bureau how to get the government out of business (power business). While he was there, he supervised the writing of a contract which his bank was going to finance."[12]

Wenzel's role came to light in February 1955. Then Memphis voted to build its own municipal power plant, and the Tennessee legislature barred construction of the necessary power lines to enable the Dixon–Yates contract to proceed. The Senate voted to cancel the contract. As Bob Kerr asserted, "I am not in favor of giving any company or group of companies a monopoly which is protected by the government. To me, this is un-Americanism." Eisenhower might complain that "Wenzel's report . . . had no more to do with the contract than 'flying,'" but he was left with no alternative but to cancel the contract. Six years later the Supreme Court ruled that no termination costs were due Dixon–Yates because of Wenzel's undeclared conflict of interest. Gore and Kefauver's successful blocking of Dixon–Yates not merely protected the provision of TVA power to Tennessee. It was also an extremely effective way of preempting the Eisenhower administration's efforts to sell off the power operations of the entire TVA to private enterprise.[13]

THE TVA WAS NOT the only battleground between private and public development. The development of atomic energy put the public-power development advocates once more on a collision course with the Atomic Energy Commission. Gore enthusiastically promoted the peaceful development of nuclear energy. The first chair of the AEC had been Gore's TVA ally, David Lilienthal. Lilienthal's successor, Gordon Dean, married Gore's cousin Mary Benton Gore. But like other members of the JCAE, Gore was suspicious of the new chairman of the AEC, Admiral Strauss. Gore felt Strauss had an excessive faith in the ability of private utilities to make the investment necessary to develop nuclear power. Few commercial nuclear plants were on the drawing board let alone producing reliable power. Under the 1954 Atomic Energy Act, the AEC launched the Cooperative Power Demonstration Reactor Program. In the first stage four reactors were authorized near Chicago, Detroit, and in western Massachusetts and Nebraska. Private industry would build, own, and operate the reactors with some research and development assistance from the AEC.[14]

By the spring of 1956, no contracts had been signed. The previous July Gore had taken up a bill that was presented to New Mexico senator Clinton Anderson, a fellow civilian nuclear power enthusiast and the chair of the JCAE. Gore introduced the bill that authorized and directed the AEC to build six large-scale reactors. Gore was scathing about the failure of private industry under the parameters of the 1954 act:

> We were told that hundreds of millions of dollars were waiting
> to flow quickly into atomic-power reactors. We were told that
> if Congress would but tie the hands of government and take
> government out of the field of atomic power, private enterprise
> would move quickly and efficiently and certainly into the
> development of atomic power. Over the protests of several
> members of the Senate, that bill did pass. The government's
> hands were tied. A monopoly on the use of atomic power was
> given to private enterprise. We simply have not received the
> results that were granted. . . . Not one license has been granted,
> not one construction permit has been issued, and none is even in
> immediate prospect.

The price of the failure of this existing policy was high. Gore believed that both the Soviets and the British had overtaken the Americans in the peaceful development of nuclear power. The Soviet program dwarfed the U.S. effort: The Russians saw trade, prestige, and weapons advantages in pressing ahead. The loss of the race to the Russians would be "catastrophic," according to Gore, but he also pointed to the commercial consequences of losing to the British or the French. The first countries to develop reactors, he argued, would be the ones who would capture the first orders from foreign markets. The Americans would be stranded.[15]

Lyndon Johnson engineered a unanimous Democratic vote to ensure the passage of the Gore bill. Johnson was back on his ranch a few weeks later and unusually mellow. "The days are flowing peacefully and quietly down here in Texas. I get out in the morning to look at my cattle and my sheep and to see how my irrigation plans are coming along." He flattered Gore, saying that the Tennessee senator had been instrumental in the session's record of success: "I do not know that any single event gave me more pleasure than the day all 49 Democrats stood up on the Floor and voted for the Gore Reactor Bill. There we stood in all our strength and it was a pleasure to see that we showed it on your issue." From Oklahoma came Robert Kerr's imprimatur and praise for Gore's tenacity in the face of the AEC chair's regrettable and "outmoded views."[16]

In the House, Chet Holifield ran into opposition from the AEC, Eisenhower, private utilities, and congressmen from coal-mining and oil districts. Tom Pickett of the National Coal Association dismissed any need for new power. The Gore bill represented "partial abandonment of the free enterprise system and a long stride toward complete socialism." Any power produced would be high cost. It was yet another round in the argument between advocates of private and public power. A full-page ad in leading national daily papers costing $100,000 was sponsored by "America's Independent Electric Light and Power Companies." Titled "How America Will Keep Its Lead in Atomic-Electric Power," the ad claimed that fifty-five nuclear reactors were "completed as of 1956" and an additional thirty-five were "building or planned" in this country. "More than $300 million from individual investors is involved in the planning and construction of atomic-electric plants and related research." Clinton Anderson, Gore, and the JCAE were furious and labeled the ad wholly false. Gore and Anderson pointed out that only a single one of the atomic power undertakings with which private power had any connection had reached a stage nearing completion. Despite the efforts of the Senate sponsors, the bill was recommitted by the House.[17]

Gore did not lose his sense of urgency or abandon the issue. At the end of 1956, he made a five-week trip to the Far East that included a five-day stay in Japan. The Japanese AEC, he told Clinton Anderson, was about to contract with the British for a $75 million reactor like Calder Hall in England. The Japanese chairman had told Gore that they had visited Britain and the United States. The British reactor was up and running, whereas the Westinghouse reactor was theoretical and unproven. The Japanese told him that their "supply of conventional fuel is very short and therefore must be imported. Our demand for electricity is growing by leaps and bounds. We must have atomic power and soon." Gore saw the advantages the British would have—the nation that sold the first reactors would likely sell additional reactors, replacement parts, and reactor fuels. "The economies involved are important," he concluded. "The politics and prestige values are incalculable."[18]

The following year he went to Europe for three and a half weeks and studied atomic power in Great Britain, mainland Western Europe, and Russia. He wrote three articles for the *New York Herald Tribune* as a "serious indictment of the administration's shortsighted and atomic power program." He feared the cataclysmic effect on American security of permitting the country to slip behind in technology. Gore was cheered on from the sidelines by former president Harry Truman and former AEC chair David Lilienthal. Both wanted Gore to stress how the utilities had been subsidized by the taxpayer, protected from competition, yet still had failed to deliver the atomic reactors. By this time the JCAE had abandoned its efforts to pass Gore–Holifield. Instead, through Clarence Cannon, they used the appropriations power to deny the AEC operating expenses and instead approved appropriations only for specific projects, thus pushing the AEC down the road of research and development of large-scale reactors. Lewis Strauss remained convinced that there had been no need for the government to build civilian reactors. The Joint Committee, he argued, would never be satisfied. But in a few years "there were numerous civilian power reactors and reactor experiments in operation, under construction and planned." Gore, Anderson, and Holifield were unconvinced and retained their interest in civilian nuclear power for the rest of their careers in Washington.[19]

Gore had consistently been at odds with Lewis Strauss. Strauss had been a dissenting voice on the AEC under Lilienthal and Gordon Dean. But he was Eisenhower's special adviser on nuclear matters, and the president had appointed him to head the AEC. There, with Eisenhower's enthusiastic backing, he had relinquished civilian control of the nuclear stockpile to the military, and sought to involve private industry in nuclear development and prevent the AEC from becoming a "nuclear TVA." When Eisenhower appointed Strauss as secretary of commerce, Clinton Anderson and other Democrats sought to prevent his confirmation. But Gore retained a respect for Strauss as a dedicated public servant, broke ranks with his fellow Democrats, and voted to confirm him. Eisenhower was grateful. He could not, he wrote to

Gore, "fail to recognize the courage, wisdom, and spirit of fairness" that Gore displayed in that vote.[20]

~

FOR ALL OF GORE'S drive for the atomic reactor bill, what primarily occupied him in 1955 and 1956 was another infrastructure project: the launching of the national system of super highways, the interstates. For those two years, he recalled, "my principal interest in the Senate and in the country was holding hearings, visiting, making observations of the highway problems, and fighting the battle with the committee and later on the floor of the Senate and in conference."

The postwar roads crisis was obvious to everybody. After the war existing American roads, pounded by heavy military traffic during the war, were crumbling. At the same time automobile ownership increased two- to threefold. Car ownership, the GI Bill, and a federal mortgage policy that enabled people to think of buying a home and a garden plot made possible the flight to the suburbs. Those commuters gridlocked the roads into town. Everywhere the roads were clogged. The three-hour roundtrip that Albert had made three times a week from Carthage to Nashville in the 1930s to study law and to court Pauline seemed a far-off memory after 1945. Al Gore recalled as a child seeing "long, long, long lines of red tail lights stretching out of highway 70 at night and the equally long line of headlights coming in the opposite direction. And at that time, with simply one two-lane road representing the main east–west corridor for not only Tennessee but also the nation, Highway 70 North was the principal east–west route for the whole midsection of the country." American states and counties were building roads, but they simply did not build them fast enough to match America's capacity to manufacture and purchase cars.[21]

The federal government did play a financial role. As early as 1916 the Federal Aid Road Act provided for matching federal funds for highway construction and required states to have highway departments. The American Association of State Highway Officials (AASHO) became the most powerful road-building lobby in the country. At the state level the state highway commissions often became politically the most powerful agencies in state government, able to satisfy legislators' demands for roads in the communities and to award large contracts to construction companies. They jealously guarded the revenue which they derived from state gasoline taxes to prevent them from being diverted to nonroad spending. The 1916 act led to little road building, but the 1921 Federal Aid Highway Act committed the federal government to at least $75 million a year and required states to designate 7 percent of their roads as primary routes that linked to other states. The federal Bureau of Public Roads oversaw this expenditure and left decisions on routes to local states, but it engineered road construction to ever-increasingly stringent federal standards. In 1926 the bureau secured standardized road numbering and signs. The 1920s saw states like Tennessee embark on major road-building programs. The 1930s ushered in New Deal spending of more than $1.8 billion on road construction and repair. More than 225,000 miles of roads had been built with federal aid. In 1947 the South accounted for one-third of all federal funds allocated for road construction and maintenance.[22]

But the system had major deficiencies. Most roads were only two-lane. Businesses and residents demanded easy access to them. Multiple intersections, traffic lights, and railroad crossings interrupted any journey. The roads were designed to service local needs rather than to link major centers across the nation. Under the authorization of the 1944 Federal-Aid Highway Act, some sixty thousand miles were to be designated by the joint decisions of state highway officials as part of the interstate highway system, but this was merely a change of nomenclature for existing roads that had not been constructed with interstate travel in mind. Robert Moses had constructed parkways in New York state, however they were designed not for commercial traffic but rather to enable the car-owning middle class to get out to Moses's state parks. Some cities had constructed freeways to enable commuters to get to work more efficiently. The Pennsylvania turnpike, completed in 1940, had shown the potential for long-distance, limited-access, divided highways, but it was a toll road that was emulated only by New York, Maine, New Hampshire, and New Jersey.

Everyone agreed something had to be done. The construction and automobile industries, in conjunction with the state highway officials, were formidable lobbyists. But what exactly was to be done? There were powerful contradictory forces. Urban planners despaired of unclogging their cities while money was spent on rural roads. Governors of states like Arkansas and North Carolina, by contrast, called for farm-to-market roads to meet the long-standing demands of their farm supporters. After all, automobiles were advertised on billboards for their durability in withstanding the Arkansas mud test. State governors were jealous of the federal gasoline taxes; they felt that federal aid was too small and the demands of local, rather than interstate,

travel were too pressing. Truckers who would benefit most from improvements in long-distance travel were reluctant to pay higher taxes on diesel or
tires. The Bureau of Public Roads was unable to see beyond existing traffic
usage. Famously, the agency had once predicted that 715 cars a day would
use the Pennsylvania turnpike: In fact almost 10,000 cars did. The bureau was
unalterably opposed to toll roads. The 1954 Federal Highway Act authorized a
mere $175 million for interstate roads.[23]

One man had a vision of what was needed. In 1937 Franklin Roosevelt
called in Thomas Harris MacDonald, the legendary chief of the Bureau of Public Roads (BPR), and presented him with a map with six lines drawn on it—
three interstates north–south, three east–west. Roosevelt thought they could
be funded by taking land by eminent domain in sufficiently wide strips to sell
off. In 1941 he established the National Interregional Highway Committee.[24]

Road-building was a large part of New Deal public works spending. Historically in the United States, public works had three functions: to put people
to work during depression, to stabilize the economy by smoothing out the
economic cycle, and to invest in the nation's infrastructure. Road-building
was attractive to New Dealers because small projects could be initiated quickly in most of the counties of the United States, and they used local unskilled
labor. By the end of the New Deal, there were public-works projects in all
but three of the nation's 3,700 counties. That was the sort of distribution that
guaranteed widespread political support, and almost as a byproduct, the projects stimulated demand for steel and concrete. But more than any previous
administration program, the New Deal invested in infrastructure that would
sponsor economic development: military facilities, airports (five in Tennessee), and great hydroelectric and flood-control projects (notably the TVA).
Gore's constituents could be in no doubt as to the benefits of infrastructure
spending and the potential to expand it.[25]

Road-building took something of a backseat during the war, since there
were no new cars and tires were in short supply. Nevertheless the federal government worked to strengthen bridges, widen strategic roads, and serve the
populations of military bases. Federal Works Agency administrator Philip
Fleming recalled in 1948:

I do know from our war experience how vital our highway system
was to our existence then. Our highways really became part of our
production line. There were wings and fuselages and turrets and
engines moving over our highways to Kansas and Texas and being

assembled there in finished airplanes. There were mechanical parts moved up into New Hampshire, which became bombsights. So our highways really were part of our national effort. Without them I do not know where we would have been in our war effort.

He considered "the vital matter of highway construction" to be the greatest of all New Deal public-works contributions, since it linked all forms of government from federal to state to county. New Deal planners believed that a reserve of public-works projects, within which an interstate system would be a major item, was needed so that in a postwar recession the projects could be brought off the shelf to revive the economy.[26]

Grandiose New Deal road plans did not come to fruition immediately. MacDonald's BPR doubted in 1940 that the extra usage would justify the $6-billion cost of FDR's 29,000 miles. They even doubted that the $2.9-billion cost of 14,000 miles was justified. The BPR was skeptical about the value of spending on roads because officials thought there would never be enough cars to use the roads and low-income automobile owners could not afford tolls. The 1944 Federal-Aid Highway Act did little other than continue the same formulas and appropriations for highway spending. But New Deal infrastructure spending disproportionately benefited the South and the West. In 1947, for example, the South accounted for one-third of all funds allocated for road construction and maintenance in the nation.

President Eisenhower understood from a personal viewpoint the deficiencies of the current road systems and the potential for development which FDR had identified. In 1919, as a young officer Eisenhower had volunteered to join a motorized convoy that General John Pershing organized to travel from Washington, D.C., to San Francisco to test the suitability of the American road system to meet defense needs. The journey took fifty-six days. The convoy did well on "average to non-existent roads" to maintain a speed of five miles an hour over a day's driving.[27]

In 1945 Eisenhower sped through Germany and paid close attention to the autobahns—divided highways with limited access—in the debriefing reports he received. He believed the autobahn system enabled Germany to fight a two-front war. Eisenhower told a congressional delegation in 1955 that the efficiency of the autobahn system inspired him to create a similar network in the United States. "The old convoy," he recalled, "had started me thinking about good two-lane highways, but Germany had made me see the wisdom of broader ribbons across the land." By contrast, the head of the U.S. Bureau of

Public Roads, Thomas MacDonald, saw little justification for the autobahns. Having served six presidents, he was therefore retired at the start of the Republican administration in 1953.[28]

It was Eisenhower who broke the stalemate that seemed to paralyze road policy. Eisenhower was a fiscal conservative, committed to balanced budgets, concerned about inflation, hostile to the statism of the New Deal. But he understood the scale of the highway crisis. Freed from the concerns of the Korean War, he drafted a speech in July 1954 that electrified the nation's governors at their annual conference. Vice President Richard Nixon read the speech, in which Ike told the governors that the country needed to spend $50 billion over ten years. Eisenhower described the highways as "inadequate locally and obsolete as a national system." No wonder the governors were enthusiastic: The spending Eisenhower contemplated made the $175 million appropriated in 1954 seem paltry. The governors were sufficiently excited to give up their demands for the abolition of the federal gasoline tax. The president then established a commission to flesh out these ideas under General Lucius Clay, the logistical mastermind of the Berlin Airlift.[29]

Eisenhower argued that it would be impossible to evacuate citizens using existing roads in the event of a defense catastrophe "should an atomic war come." The first iteration of the House highway legislation in 1956 was called the "National System of Interstate and Defense Highways bill. But in reality defense did not play a major role in Eisenhower's thinking. What concerned him most was the threat to economic development that poor infrastructure posed. A massive road-building program would not cause inflation; not building a modern highway system would. "With our roads inadequate to handle an expanding industry, the results will be inflation and a disrupted economy," he told cabinet colleagues and Republican leaders. He told Congress that the costs of accidents totaled $4.3 billion a year. Increased business costs added up to $5 billion a year. Projected population, traffic, and business growth by 1965 meant that "existing traffic jams only faintly foreshadow those of ten years hence." In addition, though "we desperately need the roads," Eisenhower believed that the highway program was a good tool for the federal government to have "in its pocket" as insurance against a downturn.[30]

The commission General Clay assembled could be relied on to recognize the scale of the problem. The chairman of a car-parts manufacturer, a banker, and the corrupt president of the Teamsters Union joined the chairman of Bechtel, the giant construction company that had started on its international trajectory with contracts to build major New Deal public-works programs.

The commission calculated the system needed $101 billion in investment, 30 percent of which should be provided by the federal government. The cost of upgrading the 64,000 miles that would constitute the interstate system would be $27 billion. The federal government was designated to pay 90 percent of that cost.[31]

How would the United States fund that spending without unbalancing the budget? Eisenhower wanted toll roads to be built so that the system would pay for itself. But the commission, like the Bureau of Public Roads before it, believed that a toll system was impossible in many areas of the country where the interstate might be the only road. The commission's solution was to establish the Federal Highway Corporation, which would issue $25 billion in bonds. These would be financed over thirty years by existing federal gasoline and diesel taxes. The scheme would therefore not increase the national debt.[32]

The Clay Committee proposal was blown out of the water almost immediately. The veteran chair of the Senate Finance Committee, Harry F. Byrd, watched federal spending like a hawk. He had advocated "pay-as-you-go" funding of roads since he was governor of Virginia in the 1920s. He blasted the idea that the proposal did not increase the national debt. Byrd and the chair of the Senate Committee on Public Works, Dennis Chavez, complained that taxpayers would have to pay more than $11 billion in interest payments. Both the House and the Senate in 1955 rejected the Clay plan embodied in the administration's highway bill by margins of two to one.[33]

At this point Albert Gore, encouraged by Lyndon Johnson, seized his chance.

Now that the Democrats controlled Congress after the midterm elections, Johnson needed to be able to show that the Democrats could be a constructive governing body yet also hold the Republicans to account. He needed young articulate, aggressive, policy-oriented committee members to establish a Democratic record. A highway act that had a Democratic imprint fitted his needs perfectly. Gore, as chair of the roads subcommittee of the Committee on Public Works, could deliver that legislation. Johnson could ensure that Chavez, the chair of the committee, would support him. In turn Gore could rely on Johnson's mastery to guide any bill of his to the Senate floor and through to passage.[34]

Like Eisenhower, Gore had seen the benefits of the autobahns in Germany during the early months of 1945. Even before Eisenhower had submitted the Clay recommendations to Congress, Gore had announced hearings on his own highway bill. His bill provided for spending $10 billion on the interstate system of 68,400 miles through fiscal 1961 while continuing the usual federal aid for other roads. For the interstates the federal government would contribute 75 percent of the money. The attraction of Gore's bill was that it offered more money for rural communities and that it promised more spending on the interstates quickly. Governors, however, were leery of the 25 percent they would have to find to match federal funds. Governors from heavily populated Northeastern states worried about a spending allocation formula that took into account road mileage and land area as well as population. Contractors and Southern senators worried about the Davis–Bacon requirement that prevailing wages had to be paid. (This was a requirement for purely federal projects; traditionally it had not been applied to federal aid projects.) To meet these concerns Gore raised the federal contribution, satisfied the Northern governors on allocations, and conceded on the prevailing-wage provision. Lyndon Johnson was always uneasy with organized labor and listened to one of his most loyal financial backers, Herman Brown. LBJ personally engineered the elimination of the prevailing-wage provision on a voice vote rather than a roll call, which spared highway-bill supporters from risking the wrath of labor. But then Johnson moved to make sure that all Democrats supported the Gore bill when it came to the final vote. The only Democratic senator to defy Johnson and Gore was John Kennedy of Massachusetts.[35]

If the program was to be funded, the proposals for revenue-raising had to come from the House. There highway legislation was prepared by the chair of the House Public Works Committee, George H. Fallon, a Baltimore machine politician from Maryland. It was said that the initial "H" in Fallon's name stood for "highways." He produced his own bill with the help of Francis Turner, the future highway administrator and an adviser to the Clay Commission. The federal government could pay 90 percent of the interstate costs through FY 1968. The program would be funded by higher taxes on highway users: taxes on gas, diesel, tires, trucks, and buses would all increase. Fallon comfortably defeated the Republican bill based on the Clay report, but then saw his own bill defeated just as convincingly. Urban representatives did not see enough in it for them. The petroleum and tire industries and the truckers lobbied against the higher taxes they would have to pay if the bill passed.[36]

Eisenhower's attempt to devise an agreed expert solution to the roads crisis that would overcome special interests and congressional particularism had failed. He saw the Gore bill as a classic example of the faults of Congress and party politics. On the passage of the Gore bill in the Senate in 1955, Eisenhower wrote to a friend: "Being something of an impatient man, you can imagine the state of my blood pressure when I find measures, obviously designed for the welfare and advancement of the whole country, blocked by partisanship and selfish interests."[37]

The election year, however, concentrated minds in 1956. The roads crisis continued. Secretary of the Treasury George Humphrey accepted that there was no chance of persuading Congress to fund the program through bonds—and he himself had turned against that funding because of its projected effect on the deficit. Business leaders grew more alarmed at the delay. Highway-users began to have second thoughts about their opposition to user taxes. Urban congressmen were won over when the BPR designated the remaining miles in the interstate system. The BPR's "Yellow Book" sent to each congressman contained one hundred maps of urban areas showing just where the freeways might be in their cities. The funding dilemma was solved in the House Ways and Means Committee by New Orleans congressman Hale Boggs. He raised the federal gasoline tax from two cents to three cents a gallon and, on the suggestion of Secretary of the Treasury Humphrey, earmarked that revenue for the Highway Trust Fund. The Boggs funding bill was joined to the Fallon bill to provide for 65,000 miles of interstate at a cost of $24.8 billion, funded by the federal government for thirteen years on a 90 percent basis and allocated to states on a cost-of-completion basis. The Senate simply substituted the Gore bill for the Fallon bill, and labor managed to reinstitute the prevailing-wage provision. Gore boasted that he stood on his feet "from 10am until after midnight without any lunch or supper, and saw the bill through the Senate. Every amendment I accepted was added, and every amendment I rejected was voted down. We had a margin of 2 to 1 on the bill." LBJ avoided embarrassment by taking an earlier flight to the Mayo Clinic for a checkup and missing the prevailing-wage vote. At the conference there were compromises on the number of miles in the system (two thousand fewer than in the Gore bill) and on the allocation of funds. For the first three years, funds would be allocated on the Gore principle, which balanced population, land use, and mileage; thereafter it would be on the cost-of-completion principle. Gore and Fallon summed up their work as providing "the greatest construction program in the history of the world."[38]

Thirty years earlier the head of the Bureau of Public Roads had asserted, "There have been just three great programs of highway building within recorded history: that of the Roman Empire, beginning with Julius Caesar and extending to Constantine; that of France under the Emperor Napoleon; that of the U.S. during the last decade." Albert Gore and Fallon had just added a fourth. President Eisenhower, after his exasperation with what he considered petty politics, was pleased with the final result. He signed the bill without ceremony because he was in Walter Reed Hospital, but he sent Gore one of the pens he used to sign. Forty years later Bill Clinton retrieved that pen to sign the Telecommunications Act of 1996.[39]

Gore did not lose interest in highways with passage of the interstate act. When it looked as if tax receipts for the Highway Trust Fund would not be adequate to cover the expected costs on the interstates, he quickly moved to suspend the Byrd requirement for pay as you go and to fast-forward spending on both the interstates and other roads. Grudgingly the Eisenhower administration, concerned about recession, acquiesced in a compromise deal. Gore consistently aimed to ensure the administration honor its commitments about highway spending.[40]

The 1950s saw Albert Gore fight for atomic power, the Tennessee Valley Authority, and interstate highways. He believed federal investment in this infrastructure was the key to economic development in the South. This was the solution to what FDR had identified as the nation's number 1 economic problem: the poverty of the South. In time all three causes would arouse the ire of modern environmentalists. The rush to build roads saw the destruction of historic, especially black, neighborhoods, the casual relocation of poor people, and the precipitate decline of the central cities and of the business districts of small towns like Carthage. Critics lamented the end of Southern cultural distinctiveness as the region took on the homogenized appearance of the rest of the country: endless suburban development, shopping malls, and soulless and indistinguishable strips alongside highway interchanges.

But in 1956 it was striking that no one questioned the wisdom of highway construction. There were few visionary critics. Americans shared a common optimism about their country's unprecedented affluence and the ability of an interstate highway system to extend that affluence to all classes, to city and countryside, and to all regions.

Even with the wisdom of hindsight, it is difficult to say that Albert Gore was wrong as far as the South is concerned. A modernized highway system was a crucial ingredient in the creation of the Sunbelt. It made possible the shift of population, the relocation of industry, and the outside investment in the region. For the first time the South had a consumer purchasing power of its own that could serve a manufacturing base, house high-tech research parks, and buy the products of a diversified, rather than cotton-only, agriculture.

The South led the nation in securing federal funds for interstate construction and led the nation in devoting its state budgets to highway construction. In 1965 every Southern state but North Carolina exceeded the U.S. level of highway spending per thousand dollars of personal income. Indeed, Mississippi spent twice the national ratio.[41]

In 1992 Albert Gore, about to celebrate his eighty-fifth birthday, noted that Nashville was one of the few cities in the nation where three interstates intersect. In 2005 Al Gore illustrated the dramatic impact of those interstates. They had made Nashville the number-one city in the nation for attracting new industries and persuading others to relocate there—car manufacturers, high-tech computer companies. The interstates had made Nashville the center of gravity of a nation whose population was shifting to the Sunbelt. It is appropriate that, if the national interstate system is named after President Eisenhower, the sections of interstate in Tennessee close to the state lines are named after Albert Gore.[42]

↬

IN 1956 IT WAS SAID that "in America it is possible for any man to run for president. In Tennessee they all are." The previous March Wilma Dykeman wrote in *Harper's* that there was "too much talent in Tennessee." She identified the two senators, Kefauver and Gore, and the governor, Frank Clement, as all combining youth with "physical stamina, intellectual ability and moral courage; wives who combine brains with beauty; a generally high level of campaign techniques and public stewardship; and last—but perhaps most important—an ability to break all previous vote-getting records." In 1956, as if to confirm Dykeman's picture of an excess of nationally ambitious politicians in the same state, both senators and the governor had their eyes on national office. The senior senator, Estes Kefauver, in his second bid for the presidency, had won the New Hampshire Democratic primary unopposed and defeated Adlai Stevenson in Minnesota. He had enthusiastic volunteers in many delegations. But Stevenson defeated him in two tough primary fights for the delegate-rich states of Florida and California. Compared to Kefauver Stevenson had stronger support from state party organizations and greater financial resources. He was also prepared in the South to soft-pedal civil rights in a way that Kefauver could not afford to do and did not want to do. Kefauver recognized that he could not win the nomination, and he chose not to join New York governor Averell Harriman in a "stop Stevenson" movement. Kefauver's supporters believed that Stevenson owed him the vice-presidential nomination.[43]

The young governor, Frank Clement, had been lobbying hard to be chosen as the keynote speaker at the Democratic National Convention in Chicago. He made sense, his supporters believed, as a possible vice-presidential candidate. Clement was a reformer who, despite his youth, was renowned for his old-style oratory. Like William Jennings Bryan, he was open about his evangelical religious faith. A friend of Billy Graham, he spoke from time to time from pulpits across the state on Sundays. As an attractive, young, new face in Southern politics, he was the one Southern governor not compromised by campaigns designed to block the *Brown* school desegregation decision. He offered the hope that he could keep old-line Southerners in the Democratic fold: He was, after all, supported by the remnants of the Crump organization, not only in Memphis but also across the state. At the same time he was not fatally flawed on race in the eyes of Northern Democrats, unlike Deep South politicians, including previous vice-presidential nominee John Sparkman of Alabama, who could not escape the taint of Massive Resistance.[44]

Albert Gore, as the junior senator, had established a national reputation as a crusader for public power and as an effective legislator with passage of the Interstate Highway Act and the atomic reactor bill in the Senate. He made powerful presentations on atomic energy to the Democratic Platform Committee. Like Kefauver, he had refused to sign the Southern Manifesto and thus was not disqualified on civil rights grounds among national Democrats. Unlike Kefauver, he retained good working relations with Lyndon Johnson and with the Deep South politicians. One possible black mark against him among Northern Democrats was his vote for Taft–Hartley. Nevertheless, Harry Truman, still a force to be reckoned with in the Democratic Party, had been complimentary about him. Gore had every reason to believe he was also still well-regarded by Speaker Sam Rayburn. Indeed, in the fall of 1954, Rayburn double-barreled: "Clement is a bright boy. Gore is brilliant." Furthermore, whatever support Gore might lack in his own state delegation he could compensate for with support from Mike Monroney and Robert Kerr in Oklahoma. Leading Northern liberal Governor Abe Ribicoff drew Adlai Stevenson's attention to Gore's speech to the Connecticut Democratic Convention and recommended that he read it. Stevenson asked to meet Gore twice as he weighed vice-presidential options. The meetings appeared to go well, and the likely presidential nominee concluded the second meeting by telling Albert "it might be you." Since the vice-presidential nomination was traditionally in the hands of the party's nominee, there was little more that Gore could do about his own candidacy.[45]

Frank Clement opened the Chicago convention with a disastrous a key-note speech that went on far too long for impatient delegates on the convention floor. His preacher's style and arm-waving, so effective on the stump, looked provincial and unsophisticated to a television audience. There was now no chance that Clement would get the vice-presidential nod. But his forces still firmly controlled the Tennessee delegation.[46]

After he was nominated Stevenson threw the convention into chaos by announcing that he would leave the choice of running mate to the convention, a move that simply confirmed Sam Rayburn's worst fears about the candidate's indecision. It was a move that infuriated Kefauver's supporters, who saw it as a way for Stevenson to wriggle out of his obligations to the most powerful of his challengers. Six hours of frantic activity on the convention floor and in hotel rooms and bars followed. Kefauver—backed in particular by his enthusiastic followers in California—Hubert Humphrey, and Mayor Robert Wagner of New York emerged immediately as serious candidates. But another candidate emerged as a serious contender: a new face, but one that appealed to old-style Northern urban politicians—the handsome young Catholic war hero from Massachusetts, John Kennedy.[47]

As for Albert Gore, he was sitting and having a beer with reporter David Broder—who was covering his first convention for *Congressional Quarterly*—in the railroad lobby close to the International Amphitheater where the convention was being held. One of Gore's young staff ran up and announced that people wanted to put Gore's name in nomination. "And literally, in front of my eyes," Broder recalled, "this man who, you know, sort of straightened himself, threw his shoulders back and became, you know—you could just see it was all happening in his, in his mind. I saw a spark of the ambition that was there, you know, behind that, that relatively placid exterior in that moment." Gore's first move was to dash off to try and get hold of Lyndon Johnson and the Texas delegation. With their support, Gore could be a serious contender.[48]

In the hotel corridor near Johnson's headquarters, Gore ran into Johnson's assistants, Jim Rowe and George Reedy. They had been bemoaning the mess Stevenson's decision created for the party, and for Johnson, who had been placed in an awkward position. At first they didn't recognize Gore. "His eyes were glittering. He was mumbling out something that sounded like 'Where is Lyndon? Where is Lyndon? Where is Lyndon? Adlai's thrown this open, and I think I've got a chance for it if I can only get Texas. Where is Lyndon?'" Here was Albert Gore, a man they had both known well for almost twenty years, but his face was so distorted. Claimed Reedy: "I have never seen before or since such a complete, total example of a man so completely and absolutely wild with ambition, it had literally changed his features."[49]

To Rowe and Reedy, Gore's appearance was a godsend. They knew how unpopular Kefauver was in Texas. Here in Gore was a possible candidate who was conservative enough for Texas and the South but not a thorough-going racist, and he was a populist of a brand that was quite popular in Texas. "We greeted Albert Gore the way Custer would have greeted another regiment at the battle of the Little Big Horn," said Reedy. Johnson and Rayburn swung the Texas delegation behind Gore, and many of the same calculations put Oklahoma in the same camp. Gore told Kefauver that he could not put his Senate colleague's name in nomination under the circumstances. Once Frank Clement indicated that he would not run for vice president, his right-hand man on the Tennessee delegation, Buford Ellington, rushed to a caucus of Deep South states which decided to support Gore: Mississippi, Alabama, and South Carolina. Clara Shirpser, a Kefauver supporter from California, was seated behind Lyndon Johnson on the floor and found "senators, and governors, and congressmen, all asking him what he wanted them to do. They were running around that floor like messenger boys at his command." He was asking delegates what they wanted in terms of appointments and projects. "It's yours," Shirpser heard him say, "go back and tell them, 'not Kefauver,' that I'm going to back Gore from here on in. Gore is the candidate and he can stop Kefauver, and I'm for Gore. That's the message."[50]

On the first ballot Kefauver led with 483½ of the 686½ votes needed to win the nomination. Kennedy had 304 and Gore 178. Both Humphrey (134½) and Wagner (162½) effectively recognized their candidacies were finished. What would Gore do? His dilemma was that any success he might now have would be as a stop-Kefauver candidate, which would damage him with his base in Tennessee. The Tennessee delegation, despite the efforts of some Kefauver loyalists like the mayor of Knoxville, George Dempster, appeared determined to stick with Gore and not to transfer to Kefauver. They were committed to stick with Gore as long as he had a chance of winning. But it soon became clear that it was not Gore to whom the stop-Kefauver forces would go. Their votes started to go to Kennedy, beginning with Mississippi's twenty-two votes. Segregationist politicians in Mississippi would prefer a Catholic Northern liberal to the man they nicknamed "Cowfever," whom they regarded as a traitor to the region. (Kennedy had already won Georgia, Virginia, and Arkansas on the first ballot.) Gore turned to Lyndon Johnson to discover that Texas would be transferring its votes to Kennedy. Johnson had decided that only Kennedy could stop Kefauver, and he wanted to make sure that he and Texas got the credit for Kennedy's victory. It appeared that Kennedy already had 648 votes and was now leading Kefauver.[51]

The Kefauver forces both nationally and in the state could see victory slipping away. The Tennessee delegation seemed determined to stay with Gore unless Gore released their votes. Oklahoma remained hostile to a Catholic who voted against farm price supports and wanted Gore to hold firm. Eventually Martha Ragland made a personal plea on Kefauver's behalf to Gore, whose campaign she had helped manage in 1952. She was probably unsuccessful. J. Howard McGrath, Kefauver's floor manager, could not think what to do when Silliman Evans, Jr., publisher of the *Tennessean*, walked up. McGrath told him that the only way Kefauver could be saved was if Tennessee switched. Clara Shirpser pleaded with Evans to find Gore and threaten to withdraw his newspaper's support forever if Gore did not step aside. She ran alongside the publisher until the five-foot-tall Evans found the six-foot-tall Gore and raised his fist right under Gore's nose. He started swearing at Gore and then told him, "If you don't withdraw this minute, so help me God you'll never be reelected to anything—not as senator, not even as dog-catcher. You get up there and you withdraw." Certainly this was the version Drew Pearson believed—that Evans had warned Gore he could not be reelected in 1958 if Kefauver lost.[52]

These threats might have had little impact on Gore if he had not already received a signal from Lyndon Johnson that Texas would be transferring its votes to Kennedy. Gore stood up on the convention floor trying to get Sam Rayburn to recognize him. Rayburn first recognized Kentucky, which transferred its votes to Kennedy. The Kennedy forces and LBJ must have thought victory was in the bag. But Rayburn, who had no love for Kennedy, then recognized Gore, who announced his withdrawal and urged his supporters to vote for Kefauver. Starting with Tennessee and Oklahoma, followed by Missouri, states switched to Kefauver, and the senior senator from Tennessee won.[53]

Gore was not to know that this would be his last chance to win national office. He had received a great deal of national attention and won support from welcome sources (though not from Illinois, where he had hoped that Paul Douglas and Stevenson might have influenced the delegation to support him). The *Tennessean* and the Kefauver forces blamed Gore for allowing himself to be used by Governor Frank Clement and Lyndon Johnson in an unsavory stop-Kefauver maneuver backed by conservative Southerners. He was, they said, the "high school team trying to play in the big leagues." To Kefauver supporters Gore had only himself to blame for the fact that Kefauver had almost lost. They thought that, afterward, he was ashamed of what he had done. But that is to misunderstand the power relationships between Gore and Kefauver. Gore never felt he was in Kefauver's debt, that he was the junior partner who was indebted to the senior senator. Nevertheless Gore did admit that he had been carried away with the possibility of the nomination. He ruefully acknowledged that for six hours he had been in a "frenzy." But if Gore upset the Kefauver loyalists, who would come back to him in time, he upset even more the conservative delegates from Memphis. The representatives of the old Crump machine never forgave him for standing down, and in doing so paving the way for the victory of their hated enemy, Kefauver. Some of them would be involved in the effort to defeat Gore in 1958.[54]

The convention was also another stage in the problematic relationship between Gore and Lyndon Johnson. Johnson had never been interested in Gore's nomination of itself. He had been concerned to restore his own prestige, which had been threatened by his own half-baked effort to be nominated for the presidency. He made it clear he did not want the vice presidency. Where he hoped to get political credit was through being the key man to stop Kefauver. While Gore still had a chance, Johnson was for Gore. When Gore was no longer the candidate who could stop Kefauver, Johnson switched to Kennedy. But Gore, by standing down and switching Oklahoma and Tennessee votes to Kefauver, had prevented Johnson from even getting the satisfaction of backing the winner. The convention had been a disaster for Johnson from start to finish, and the vice-presidential debacle was another black mark against Gore's name in the majority leader's book.[55]

The Stevenson–Kefauver ticket was overwhelmed by Eisenhower and the Republicans in November 1956. Kefauver would gain more publicity subsequently with his Senate subcommittee investigating monopolies, attracting headlines for exposing corporations the way he had earlier exposed organized crime. The one person who did well coming out of Chicago was John Kennedy. His failure meant that he did not have to be associated with a losing ticket. His strong showing gave him links with Southern politicians and established his national, rather than state, reputation. It set him up perfectly for his 1960 bid for the presidency.[56]

One person who had observed closely the scramble for the vice presidency was JFK's brother Bobby, who ran John's vice-presidential bid and soon realized he was out of his depth. He learned that you do not win nominations on the Senate floor; you need an organization that had been working for years beforehand. He discovered that, while delegates liked John Kennedy as an up-and-coming man, they felt personally attached to Kefauver because of all the postcards and Christmas cards they had received from the Tennessee senator over the years. Bobby Kennedy learned that lesson for 1960. As David Halberstam noted, "Between 1956 and 1960 a lot of postcards were sent out by the Kennedys and a lot of homes visited." Gore did not learn the same lesson. Estes Kefauver was advised early in his career that "your votes and speeches may make you well-known and give you a reputation, but it's the way you handle the mail that determines your re-election." He invested in a staff that not only provided services for his constituents but also scoured the newspapers to find events or achievements for which they could send a congratulatory postcard from the senator. Gore maintained a small staff. Ted Brown recalls that once, in 1969, they tried the Kefauver tactic—but it was seen as too late and too transparent an exercise. Gore would never develop the sort of organization that Kefauver had worked so hard to cultivate.[57]

JOHNSON MAY HAVE used Gore cynically and, as it happened, unsuccessfully in Chicago, and there was little chance that Gore would join the Senate's inner club. But Johnson's strategy as majority leader of a loyal, constructive opposition needed the presence of men like Gore. Johnson needed to have real legislative achievements to avoid the criticism that he was prepared to compromise everything away to get some milquetoast law on the statute book. He was genuinely happy to be able to secure passage of Gore's atomic energy and highway bills in the Senate. Johnson also had to walk a tightrope between the Southern conservatives and the Northern liberals, whom he derided as bomb-throwers. The more that Johnson and Rayburn lined up in support of Eisenhower's foreign policy, the more liberals demanded an aggressively liberal opposition to Eisenhower's economic policy. Here Gore could play another pivotal role. Not only had he been part of the team Sam Rayburn had set up to harry and expose the majority GOP's economic pretensions in 1947–48, but public infrastructure investment advocated by Gore was a central part of Democratic criticism of the GOP's response to the Eisenhower recessions and the sluggish growth of the 1950s.

Gore was friendly with men like Herbert Lehman of New York and Paul Douglas of Illinois, who were both regularly humiliated by Johnson. Gore's positions on taxation and, in particular on high interest rates, were shared by the social-democratic wing of the national Democratic Party. He had been friendly with liberal economists like John Kenneth Galbraith since the battles over wartime price controls. Johnson was prepared to line up Gore on topics like these since they also appealed to Southern and Western suspicions of Eastern bankers. In the last week of the general election campaign of 1956, Johnson and Rayburn brought Gore over to speak in Texas in a final bid to keep Texas in the Democratic camp. Albert and Pauline stayed at the LBJ ranch. Gore sent a much-appreciated pig as a gift to the Johnsons.

But as Harry McPherson, LBJ's assistant, also recalled, "Gore had the damnedest ability to offend through a kind of righteous pomposity that would drive Johnson right up the wall and me too. I used to just despise it. He always looked like a Baptist bishop standing back there speaking of the outrageous thing that had just been perpetrated on the people by the Establishment." Johnson complained of Gore that the "little son of a bitch never had anything but political thoughts in his life."[58]

So at the same time as Johnson gave Gore his head on legislation and lined up the votes for success, he effectively neutered Gore in 1956 on two issues that got to the heart of money and politics: lobbying and election spending.

Oil and natural-gas producers, particularly in the South and West, wanted to deregulate the industry and remove the Federal Power Commission's authority to regulate prices. William Fulbright and his fellow Arkansas congressman Oren Harris introduced legislation to achieve this goal. Deregulation promised a bonanza for the producers but aroused the bitter opposition of liberal Democrats in the North representing the interests of consumers. A gigantic lobbying effort by the oil and gas forces, watched approvingly by Lyndon Johnson, went into action, aimed at buying off some Democratic opposition and securing pro-business Republican support. In a dramatic twist, however, Senator Francis Case of North Dakota announced that a Superior Oil lobbyist had left $2,500 at his campaign headquarters in Sioux Falls. Case said that he had been going to vote for the bill but now could not do so because of this bribery attempt.[59]

Gore was the ranking member of the three-man elections subcommittee of the Senate Rules Committee. Case's accusation was squarely within the subcommittee's jurisdiction. Subcommittee chair Thomas Hennings of Missouri, who would hand over control to Gore when he announced his own candidacy for reelection, joined Gore in announcing wide-ranging hearings on lobbying, and they summoned Case to testify. Johnson moved swiftly to block them. First, he and minority leader William F. Knowland secured unanimous consent for a special committee, chaired by the immensely respected Walter F. George of Georgia, to investigate the Case accusation. Then LBJ obtained the agreement of the special committee that Case would be instructed to testify before only them—and no other committee. Hennings and Gore let Johnson know that they intended to go ahead with the hearings. They left the meeting with LBJ to convene the subcommittee to hear Case's testimony only to find that Case turned up with a letter from Senator George forbidding him to testify. In vain, Hennings and Gore appealed to the full Rules Committee for support.[60]

Thwarted by Johnson in his attempt to investigate the Case bribery accusation, Gore, now chair of the elections subcommittee, promised a full-scale investigation of the issues involving campaign financing posed by the case, since lobbyists' "contributions are flagrant attempts to subvert the will of the people in smaller states. These funds are corrupting our electorate. It presents a real challenge to democracy. I intend to do everything I can to make the public aware of what is taking place." Gore received enthusiastic praise from national liberal journalists. The Alsop brothers called him "a born evangelist," given his commitment to opening the "'Pandora's Box' of the campaign contributions issue." James Reston of the *New York Times* described him as "one of the most respected, industrious and eloquent young men in the senate. . . . an outstanding critic of the present administration's tax policy, its power policy, and he is known to favor legislation which would place a strict limit on the amount of money that could be contributed by a donor in one state to a candidate in another." But such praise was to no avail in the eyes of Lyndon Johnson or the many senators who did not want too zealous an investigation of campaign contributions. Once again Gore was comprehensively outmaneuvered by Johnson, who was working in alliance with the Republican leadership. The Senate appointed a new committee to look into general lobbying activities. It was assumed at its first meeting that Gore would be chair, but Gore had to fume as Republican Styles Bridges, himself a recipient of oil-lobbyist money, made it clear that any chair would not have the usual power to hire staff and issue subpoenas. Gore left in impotent fury and leapt into a taxi before newsmen could catch up with him. Gore was forced to accept that the committee would have a limited mandate and that he would not be allowed to chair it. He had to acquiesce in the choice of John McClellan of Arkansas as chair. Lobbyists could relax. McClellan was Johnson's man. His law firm also represented Standard Oil, and Texas oilman H. L. Hunt had contributed to his 1954 reelection bid.[61]

Gore did not give up on his campaign-finance concerns. As chair of the elections subcommittee, Gore mounted a substantial investigation of general election campaign financing from 1 September through 30 November 1956. The investigation was based on voluminous statistical information captured on an IBM punch-card system, with data secured primarily from questionnaires to more than 700 political committees, 352 labor organizations, 4,000 radio and television stations, all the candidates for the U.S. Senate, and individuals who contributed more than $5,000. The committee's consultant and adviser was Alexander Heard of the University of North Carolina. (He later served as chancellor of Vanderbilt.) In 1952 Heard's "Money in Politics" project had attempted to track the contributions of large corporations, large oil companies, bankers, defense contractors, wealthy families, and labor. The investigations of Gore's committee in 1956 followed Heard's 1952 route closely, but his committee's resources and subpoena authority enabled it greatly to expand the quantity of information they could gather.[62]

The majority report submitted by Mike Mansfield and Gore amply documented that the laws on the statute book aimed at curbing election spending miserably failed to do so. It documented the sheer scale of campaign spending in 1956 as had never been done before. It painted a dramatic, if unsurprising, picture of corporations giving almost entirely to the Republicans and labor to the Democrats. (Carl Curtis of Nebraska, in his minority report, concentrated on the scale of labor donations, especially in the light of the "mammoth new union combine [the AFL-CIO].") It showed almost $10 million spent by both parties on radio and TV. Gore drew particular attention to the geographical concentration of large contributions. From contributions of $500 or more, the Republican Party received a larger sum from the state of Delaware, with a population of only 318,000, than the Democrats received from thirty states with a population of more than 54 million. The Republicans received more from Manhattan Island than the Democrats received from the entire United States and its possessions, Manhattan Island excluded. Gore and Mansfield thought the need for remedial legislation was "imperative and immediate." At the least they wanted limits on contributions and much tighter disclosure requirements.[63]

Gore and Mansfield may have been keen for reform, but public interest in the report was considerable as well. Unprecedentedly, the report sold out in the first couple of days after its publication. But when Gore tried to secure an extra printing, Lyndon Johnson and the new minority leader, Everett Dirksen, joined forces to make sure there was no reprint. As Gore told disappointed correspondents, "Since the report was not a public print, but a report of a Subcommittee to its full Committee, there was no authority for the Subcommittee to have additional printings." Johnson, Dirksen and most senators did not want more publicity for their sources of campaign finance, which helps explain why there was not meaningful campaign-finance reform until the 1970s. Neither party wanted further embarrassment for their major campaign contributors. Ironically, the one reform thrust in the 1950s was largely unintentional as far as Gore and Mansfield were concerned. Building on Carl Curtis's minority report, John McClellan's Special Committee to Investigate Political Activities, Lobbying, and Campaign Contributions focused on labor's political activities. Though no legislation resulted, McLellan's investigation of labor's political activity and its links to racketeering put unions on the defensive and also made them leery of campaign-finance reform in the future.[64]

⤷

ALBERT GORE'S INTERSTATE HIGHWAY ACT was one of two great federal government investments in the nation's infrastructure of the 1950s. The other, the National Defense Education Act, was sponsored by Senator Lister Hill of Alabama in 1958. These acts, which recognized glaring national deficiencies in transportation and education, both had Cold War justifications for the federal government's intervention. In the fall of 1957, the Soviets had launched a Sputnik satellite into space and created a panic in the United States that its Cold War rival was outstripping America in science and technology. The 1958 Education Act used this Cold War fear to commit the federal government to a program of massive assistance to education, funding fellowships for graduate study, foreign-language institutes, student loans, and assistance to elementary and secondary schools in need of scientific equipment.[65]

But it was also no coincidence that these two infrastructure initiatives were sponsored in the Senate by two Southern New Dealers. Hill, brother-in-law of Supreme Court justice Hugo Black, was elected to succeed Black in a special election in 1938, after a campaign in which Hill supported Roosevelt's minimum-wage legislation. He, like Gore, was a passionate advocate for a New Deal–style federal government to transform the South. For Hill everything from the region's lagging provision of rural telephones to the lack of hospital construction could be solved by federal intervention. Hill had succeeded in the 1940s in providing federal assistance for both telephones and hospitals, but he had been thwarted ever since his first term in the Senate in his effort to get federal aid for education. States-rights fears had always stymied his proposal. But in 1958 Hill was able to capitalize on Cold War fears and the administration's national-security concerns to secure this major commitment for educational assistance, which paved the way for LBJ's 1965 full-scale federal aid to education measure. Gore was a long-standing and enthusiastic supporter of Hill's efforts.[66]

But highways and education spending would also bring the economic growth that liberals like Gore and Hill believed would ultimately solve the region's racial problems. That faith in gradual racial change was genuine, but it was also prudential—it avoided the direct issue of segregation, which would otherwise likely drive a wedge between their low-income white and black supporters.

Racial backlash in the Deep South had already made such a balancing act difficult. The *Brown* school desegregation decision of 1954 and the Massive Resistance that it provoked made it even harder to sustain. Lister Hill had long decided that he could not afford to alienate his segregationist constituents and get reelected in Alabama. He deliberately gave up national party leadership positions that might embarrass him back home. He eschewed any hint of racial moderation in the years after 1954. He believed his continued formidable influence for liberal economic policies in Washington was more important for the South than allowing himself to be defeated by some right-wing racial zealot. Between 1954 and 1958 Albert Gore had to weigh the same political considerations. His calculations yielded a different result from that of Hill's balancing act—one that, as much as interstate highways or his later opposition to the Vietnam War, would define Gore's political identity.[67]

CHAPTER 5

The Triumph of a Racial Moderate

IT IS MARCH 1956 on the floor of the Senate. Strom Thurmond of South Carolina has in his hand a copy of the Southern Manifesto, the brainchild of Thurmond and Virginian Harry Byrd. Drafted by Richard Russell (Georgia), Sam Ervin (North Carolina), and John Stennis (Mississippi), the manifesto, even after it was modified by William Fulbright (Arkansas), Spessard Holland (Florida), and Price Daniel (Texas), remained a blast of defiance at the Supreme Court over the *Brown* school desegregation decision of 1954. Its signers promised to support resistance to the court by all lawful means. Despite the activities of the Citizens' Councils and the barrage of anti-desegregation measures passed by Southern state legislatures in the winter of 1956, the drafters were not trying to placate an outraged white citizenry. Rather they feared that too many Southerners were resigned to accept desegregation as inevitable. The first aim of the manifesto was to convince Southerners that the court could be defied. The second aim was to coerce wavering Southern senators, some of whom Richard Russell alleged actually favored the *Brown* decision, into the segregationist camp. The third aim was to convince the Supreme Court and the North, by this show of Southern unity, to delay enforcing the *Brown* decision.[1]

The speed with which liberal senators who were liberal on economic issues like John Sparkman and Lister Hill of Alabama rushed to sign the manifesto to establish their segregationist credentials suggests that the aim of coercing wavering Southern moderates would be successful. In their quest to display Southern unity, the drafters nevertheless did not ask Lyndon Johnson to sign. They did not wish to embarrass Johnson as majority leader. He was too useful to the South as majority leader to be compromised in the eyes of the wider party. Johnson, like Speaker Sam Rayburn, disliked measures like the manifesto, which to their minds gratuitously and unnecessarily highlighted the sectional divisions in the national Democratic Party. Johnson was not averse to receiving the plaudits of Northern liberals for refusing to sign something he was not even asked to sign. He also tried to dismiss the manifesto as a piece of domestic window-dressing designed to help the dean of the Southern senators, Georgia's Walter F. George, in his effort to defend his seat against the challenge of the young, militant segregationist Herman Talmadge.[2]

Nor had the manifesto organizers bothered to ask Estes Kefauver to sign. He was in the midst of battling for the 1956 presidential nomination in the Democratic primaries. As a Southerner chasing national office, he had little choice but to denounce the manifesto. He reiterated his 1954 stance that the *Brown* decision was the law of the land and had to be obeyed. He regarded as pure deceit "any attempt to lead the people into believing Congress could change the court's ruling." "People of goodwill" should be left to seek solutions at the local level. The federal government had an obligation to help much more vigorously to facilitate such solutions. He also saw the issue as one with an international dimension in the midst of the Cold War: "People all over the world with skin that is not white are restive."[3]

The organizers believed, by contrast, that they could put Albert Gore on the spot and force him to sign. Even Senator McKellar in 1952 had not accused Gore of being on the wrong side of the race issue. Wherever possible Gore had avoided the matter, which he regarded as a distraction from the real economic issues confronting black and white Tennesseans. Gore had been rather less emphatic than Kefauver in his endorsement of the *Brown* decision: It was the law of the land, but he stressed that the decision, fortunately, was not to be implemented immediately and that it had been taken out of the hands of Congress. He was at pains to point out to constituents that these views did not mean that he agreed with the *Brown* decision.[4]

Thurmond thus invited Gore to sign the manifesto on the floor of the Senate, waving the sheet with all the Southern signatures in front of him and jabbing him in the chest. After Gore replied, "Hell, no," he looked up to see that all the Southern pressmen, obviously primed in advance, were in the gallery. Gore had the distinction of being the only Southern senator to refuse to sign the manifesto when asked.[5]

Segregationist leaders in Tennessee were quick to denounce Gore and threaten political retribution in 1958. In Tennessee he soon heard from chapters of the Federation for Constitutional Government (the Tennessee version of the Citizens' Council), as his wife's old classmate Sims Crownover threatened that Gore faced "almost certain defeat in 1958." Crownover repeated a familiar theme: Voters expected Kefauver not to sign; but Gore was a different story. One correspondent claimed that Kefauver "has made it quite clear from the outset that he would sell the entire South to the NAACP in return for a few votes"; Crownover said that, by contrast, constituents felt Gore had "actually betrayed the South because people felt that you were on their side."[6]

Why did Gore refuse to sign? He expressed some surprise that constituents might have expected him to. He believed he had been "upfront" on the race issue, though constituents who had heard him denounce the Fair Employment Practices Committee and avoid giving a personal opinion on the *Brown* decision might have been forgiven for failing to recognize that. Gore regarded the manifesto as "the most spurious, inane, insulting document of a political nature claiming to be legally founded I had ever seen." It represented an act of secession. It was "utterly incomprehensible and unsupportable." Like Kefauver and Governor Clement, Gore of course had hopes of getting on the national Democratic ticket in 1956; signing the manifesto would have ruled that out.[7]

Although segregationist sentiment ran strong in the black belt counties of western Tennessee, the black belt was not the driving force that it was in Deep South states. The Federation for Constitutional Government was a pale reflection of militant Citizens' Councils elsewhere. Tennesseans had greeted the *Brown* decision with a measure of calm, perhaps, as Gore surmised, because they did not think anything was actually going to happen in the first two years after the decision. Governor Clement did not endorse anti-desegregation measures in the state legislature. Later the governor backed court-ordered desegregation in Nashville and Clinton so that African American children would not be barred from entering white schools, and he used the National Guard to protect the students against white mobs. A month after the manifesto was issued, Gore claimed that constituent mail on the subject had ceased. He had plenty of mail supporting his stand to counter the segregationist threats. Veteran congressman Percy Priest in Nashville had little difficulty defeating a challenger who had almost exclusively targeted Priest's failure to sign the manifesto. Two congressmen who did sign, Joe Evins and Ross Bass, both went out of their way to claim that the manifesto was meaningless.[8]

Gore never condemned Southern senators who made a different calculation than he had. Thirty years later he told a Birmingham newspaperman that Lister Hill and Congressman Carl Elliott in Alabama had no alternative but to sign, otherwise they would have been defeated by reactionary segregationists. He greatly admired William Fulbright and accepted his simple, unfussy political pragmatism. Fulbright's contention was that he could not afford to buck his constituents on the race issue; if he did, the Massive Resistance hero Orval Faubus would replace him in the Senate.[9]

It was true that the path of racial moderation was easier in Tennessee than in some Southern states: A greater percentage of voting-age blacks were registered to vote, organized labor was a force to be counted, the Tennessee Valley Authority had a liberalizing impact, and there were newspapers that supported compliance with the Supreme Court's ruling. John Kyle Day has even argued that Gore's decision not to sign was "the savvy political move in the Volunteer State." But in these respects Tennessee was not so very different from North Carolina and Arkansas. What distinguished Tennessee was that both senators and the governor chose to seek public support for compliance with the law of the land. As we have seen, all three had ambitions for national office and needed to appeal to Northern Democrats. Under such circumstances, when the three leading politicians ("you and coon-skin and pretty-boy," in the words of one of Gore's less friendly constituents), despite their rivalry, set the terms of the political debate in a particular way, racial moderation had a chance of success.[10]

∽

NOT ONLY DID the Tennessee senators refuse to sign the Southern Manifesto, but also, in the following year (1957), they both voted for the Civil Rights Act—the first civil rights act to pass Congress since 1875. They joined the two Texas senators, Lyndon Johnson and Ralph Yarborough, and Florida's George Smathers in breaking ranks with the Southern bloc.

By 1956 there was little to show for heightened African American aspirations, the success of the litigative civil rights strategy in the *Brown* decision, and a steady increase in African American urban voting in both Tennessee and the South. Some historians have argued that an "incipient amelioration of race relations" before 1954 was cut short by the *Brown* decision. But in most of the South, a backlash, often violent, against African American assertiveness predated the *Brown* decision. After *Brown* economic intimidation and outright violence had served both to deter African American voting and to frighten African American plaintiffs from pursuing school desegregation. The steady increase in black voting registration of the 1940s came to a juddering halt in the 1950s. State legislatures and local registrars raised the barricades against a further increase in the black electorate. The opposition of local school boards, the intimidation of black parents, and the caution of local federal district courts meant that only a tiny number of black children were going to attend previously white schools. In Tennessee the reign of terror in Fayette and Haywood counties in western Tennessee ensured that there was no African American voting in those black belt counties. In Nashville, where Z. Alexander Looby and Robert Lillard represented black-majority districts, there were more tangible benefits for black voting: increased spending on historically black Tennessee State University, elimination of the worst black slums, increased hiring of blacks by the city government, desegregation of the city buses, and even support by the city for Looby's challenges to segregation at the airport and the golf courses. But by 1958 only ten thousand of Nashville's seventy thousand African Americans were registered to vote. That lack of participation reflected a realistic assessment of what black political participation had brought. As one observer bitterly noted, "Talk about black voting will put a bunch of Negroes to sleep." Looby and Avon Williams had initiated school desegregation suits in Clinton and Nashville which would lead to token desegregation in 1956 and 1957, albeit in the face of mob violence and dynamiting of schools and synagogues. For most African Americans in Tennessee, the edifice of segregation and political exclusion was as firm in the years after the *Brown* decision as it had ever been.[11]

In Washington, Eisenhower was skeptical of the wisdom of the *Brown* decision and of the ability of law to change hearts and mind. But he was also mindful of the negative impact of America's racial excesses on the nation's international Cold War policies. His Justice Department, under Herbert Brownell and William Rogers, was institutionally committed to more interventionist policies. Republican senators, particularly liberal Northeasterners, traditionally supported civil rights and hoped to attract African American voters to the GOP. But they also saw civil rights legislation as a way of embarrassing the Democrats by exposing the sectional splits among them. They wanted to show that the liberal Northern Democrats were incapable of delivering on their civil rights promises because of their dependence on Southern segregationist Democrats. In 1956 therefore, the administration introduced a civil rights bill. In part it picked up on recommendations of Truman's Civil Rights Commission—the establishment of the Civil Rights Division in the Justice Department and the creation of the fact-finding U.S. Commission on Civil Rights. In part the bill addressed the two central issues of the segregationist backlash of the 1950s—school desegregation and voting rights. The burden of initiating local school-board compliance with the *Brown* decision lay with African American parents, who were vulnerable to economic reprisal and intimidation. They might be helped by the NAACP, but the NAACP was being harassed by Southern state legislatures and virtually put out of business in some states. Under the 1956 bill, the Justice Department could positively intervene and initiate school desegregation suits on its own initiative. Similarly, on voting rights the Justice Department would be empowered to file suit against local registrars who prevented African Americans from voting.[12]

These measures, particularly Title III on school desegregation, really threatened Massive Resistance and potentially would have a far more immediate impact on daily Southern life than the constitutional rhetoric of the Southern Manifesto. But in 1956 Lyndon Johnson was able to bury the bill in the Judiciary Committee. Democrats did not want their sectional splits advertised in a presidential election year. Possible national candidates from the South like Gore and Kefauver did not want to be put on the spot that summer. Possible national candidates from the North did not want to alienate Southern supporters. The civil rights bill aroused surprisingly little attention or alarm in the Tennessee press, partly because it was not introduced until mid-April 1956, with clearly no chance of passage in that congressional session. What aroused a good deal more interest in Tennessee was the issue of federal aid to education, something Gore had always supported. Like other supporters of federal aid, Gore was embarrassed by the Powell amendment, which passed the House in July 1956. African American New York congressman Adam Clayton Powell wanted to ensure that segregated schools did not receive federal aid. The amendment meant that there was no chance of enough Southern support to see federal aid to education get on the statute book.[13]

But 1957 was different. Until then Lyndon Johnson and Sam Rayburn wanted to avoid explosive sectional issues like civil rights, which exposed the regional fissures in the party. But in 1957 they knew that the Democrats had to pass national civil rights legislation to refute the charge that they were paralyzed by the Southern segregationists. In particular, if Lyndon Johnson hoped to be a credible presidential candidate in 1960, he had to show that he was a plausible national candidate, not the conservative pawn of the Southern bloc. If he could engineer passage of the first civil rights act since 1875, he would boost his national credentials enormously.[14]

The problem was that the bill as it stood was completely unacceptable to most Southerners. The *Nashville Banner* summed up segregationist opposition in Tennessee. From February 1957 to August 1957, the *Banner* hammered away at the theme that the bill was a "FORCE" bill designed to crush the South as it had been under Reconstruction. The pro-Eisenhower *Banner* avoided criticizing the president; instead it reserved its denunciation for the political-ly inspired machinations of Attorney General Brownell. Tensions over school desegregation increased in Tennessee. The General Assembly, responding to Frank Clement's leadership, passed five acts designed to maximize school segregation—laws on parental choice, pupil assignments, and provisions for transfer aimed at sustaining segregated schools while avoiding overtly racial classifications. In Massive Resistance states, these laws were merely the pre-lude to further laws that would close the schools if the courts ordered them to integrate. In Tennessee, however, Clement made it clear that he would not agree to closing schools the courts ordered to desegregate; nor would he end the state's compulsory attendance laws. Segregationists who were disap-pointed by the governor's moderation viewed the Eisenhower proposals as particularly dangerous.[15]

Johnson was convinced that the Eisenhower proposals would lead to a Southern filibuster that would prevent the passage of any legislation. Johnson knew that the Southern senators mobilized by Senator Richard Russell would not support any civil rights legislation. What Johnson had to engineer was a civil rights proposal moderate enough that he could persuade Southerners to oppose but not filibuster. He needed to be able to show the Southerners that if they filibustered on this occasion, angry Northerners would take steps to make votes for cloture (cutting off filibusters) easier in the future. The South-erners, LBJ would argue, needed to preserve the filibuster to deal with more threatening proposals in the years to come. At the same time, of course, John-son had to persuade Northern Democrats to accept compromise, and a more moderate civil rights bill than they wished for, to forestall a filibuster.[16]

Johnson was handed unexpected assistance by the president. Confront-ed by Senator Russell's denunciation of Title III, Eisenhower claimed at a press conference not to understand the full implications of parts of the bill. He effectively undercut his attorney general and, almost casually, sacrificed Title III and school desegregation. The bill now became essentially a voting-rights bill—much less threatening to the South. What continued to worry the Southern bloc was that voting registrars who were found in contempt of fed-eral injunctions would not have the benefit of a jury trial. Non-Southerners felt that a jury trial would emasculate the voting-rights provision—they did not believe that a white jury in the South would ever convict a registrar ac-cused of voting discrimination. Johnson's battle therefore was to get Northern liberals to accept a jury-trial amendment. He brilliantly orchestrated the historic hostility of organized labor to federal court injunctions, particularly the railroad brotherhoods and the United Mine Workers. He also lined up Southerners to support the construction of the Hell's Canyon dam on the border of Oregon, Washington, and Idaho. Thus Johnson had leverage over Western senators like Joseph O'Mahoney of Wyoming and freshman Frank Church of Idaho. To the chagrin of the unsuspecting Republicans, the jury-trial amendment passed.[17]

Gore and Kefauver were willing allies of the majority leader. Neither of them took part in the Southern strategy sessions that organized opposition to the bill, for which they were bitterly denounced by the *Nashville Banner*. Kefauver, with his excellent pro-labor record, was a key ally of O'Mahoney and Church in fashioning an acceptable jury-trial amendment. Gore told his constituents that he worked "to modify the bill into one the South could vote for." He claimed to be a leader in the Senate in the fight for five amendments that toned down the anti-South bill. He was able initially to attack the bill for its lack of a jury-trial provision in language that could resonate with segregationist constituents: "a vicious measure which smacks of coercion, totalitarianism, and the police state. . . . I will fight its enactment as strongly as I am capable of fighting for and for as long a time as may be necessary to prevent its passage." This overblown rhetoric was reminiscent of his denunciations of the FEPC. But with the jury trial on board, he was unapologetic in supporting a voting-rights bill, a stance consistent with his support for anti-poll tax legislation in 1942. As he said a year later on the stump, "I believe in the right to vote for every man—white or colored, rich or poor, Jew or Gentile—and I hope you do to."[18]

Segregationists in Tennessee despaired of Kefauver and Gore and their lack of militancy on the race issue. The *Banner* vowed never to forget that Tennessee's "two 'on again off again' Senators," Estes Kefauver and Albert Gore, ended up where they were expected to be—"on the side of the enemies of the South, namely the NAACP, the ADA, Herbert Brownell et al." Segregationist unease was sharpened after the passage of the 1957 bill. Despite the delaying tactics of the Nashville school board and the parental-choice legislation passed in early 1957, a resolute federal judge insisted on pressing ahead with grade-by-grade desegregation of Nashville's elementary schools. Unfazed by mob violence, the dynamiting of the newly opened Hattie Cotton school, boycotts, and the appearance in Nashville of segregationist firebrand John Kasper, the judge and the local police, backed by Governor Clement, kept the schools open. But events in Nashville were overshadowed by the crisis in Little Rock, where Governor Orval Faubus first used the National Guard to block nine African American students from entering Central High under court order and then allowed a mob to keep the students out. For segregationists in Tennessee, Faubus was a hero, a leader who had the nerve to do what their own governor, Frank Clement, had failed to do. They were incensed when Eisenhower, finally exasperated by the defiance of the federal courts and personally furious that Faubus had reneged on a commitment to uphold the law, sent in federal paratroopers to enforce the desegregation of Central High. The president's actions confirmed their conviction that the Civil Rights Act was a Force Act. The president was inflicting the evils of Reconstruction and trampling on state rights. Even moderate voices in the state who had condemned Faubus as a cheap demagogue were embarrassed and defensive over Eisenhower's actions.[19]

～

THE POLITICAL IMPACT of the Little Rock and Nashville crises could be seen in the bitter gubernatorial election of 1958. The example of Massive Resistance in other states had raised the political temperature dramatically in Tennessee for the defense of segregation. Two candidates, Buford Ellington and Andrew "Tip" Taylor, vied with each other over who had the most impeccable segregationist credentials. Taylor, a circuit-court judge from Jackson in Madison County, the urban center of the segregationist heartland of black belt West Tennessee, proclaimed that he was "unconditionally and irrevocably opposed to the integration of the white and Negro races in our public schools." He promised laws that would enable local school boards to close schools that had been ordered to desegregate by the courts. Ellington, Clement's original campaign manager and his commissioner of agriculture, drew on his Mississippi background to respond, "Yes, I'm a segregationist. I'm an old-fashioned segregationist, And I'm a states-righter." He promised to strengthen the laws to preserve segregation if necessary, and, finally, he had to match Taylor's promise to close the schools. He would not hesitate as governor to close a school to prevent violence or bloodshed.[20]

Two candidates did not engage in the segregationist bidding war. Clifford Allen, a perennial candidate backed by labor and African Americans, consistently maintained that local school boards had to obey the law and that it was pointless to pass state legislation to try and avoid that obligation. Allen would win just over 56,000 votes, but his time would come in the 1970s, when he was twice elected to Congress from Nashville. Edmund Orgill, successful businessman and reform mayor of Memphis, was a more compelling candidate than Allen. He pulled together historic anti-Crump forces and offered the classic racially moderate position: He would never advocate the integration of the public schools, but he would rely on the good faith of local school boards at the community level to handle their own school problems. He left unanswered the question of what he would do if those local school boards opted to defy the courts. Nevertheless, unlike Ellington and Taylor, he never advocated the closing of the public schools.[21]

The governor's race was intense and closely fought. Little more than 9,000 votes separated the three leading candidates. Ellington defeated Tip Taylor by 8,786 votes. But, however close Orgill had pushed the two avid segregationists, the fact remained that more than 410,000 Tennessee voters had supported candidates who were prepared to close the public schools rather than desegregate. Would Albert Gore, who had polled just over 300,000 votes in his 1952 campaign, be able to offset this formidable phalanx of segregationist votes when he ran for the Senate in 1958?

For a long time it looked as if Gore would not face serious opposition in 1958. The scale of his victory in 1952, his defense of the TVA and public power, his legislative achievements, and his national prominence all tended to discourage opponents. Frank Clement decided that Gore was too formidable an incumbent to challenge. But at the last minute, Prentice Cooper, a former governor, chose not to enter the packed governor's race field, but instead announced against Gore for the Senate. Cooper had been endorsed by Boss Crump when he challenged Gordon Browning for the governorship in 1938. He remained close to Crump throughout his three terms as governor. As a wartime governor he successfully led the fight for military and defense production facilities, but he also took advantage of the surge in state revenues during the war to achieve the largest debt reduction in the state's history. He increased funding for education by 66 percent, doubled old-age assistance, and provided free textbooks to children in the lower grades. He established a statewide tuberculosis hospital system and added lands to state parks and forests. He left office with a $10 million surplus in the state treasury. But he did not exude charm and goodwill. He turned down Roy Acuff's invitation to a 1943 gala celebrating the nationwide premier of the Grand Ole Opry. Cooper denounced Acuff and his "disgraceful" music for making Tennessee the "hillbilly capital of the United States." His son and future congressman, Jim

Cooper, remembered that he had a hot temper that scared his children. One legislator recalled that "Prentice is the only man who could commit assault and battery just by shaking hands."[22]

Cooper's reentry into state politics was primarily dictated by his desire to preserve segregated schools and his willingness to close schools rather than allow them to integrate; the governor's race was the logical battleground. When he spoke to the Rotary Club in Cleveland, Tennessee, on 22 April 1957, a supporter congratulated him on being the first candidate to take a stand on the issue. She was convinced that the candidate for governor who offered the strongest platform against integration would win. Like others who wrote to Cooper, she lambasted the NAACP and Governor Clement for his failure to furnish leadership to prevent integration. The voters, said another, want no more of Clement and Kefauver's brand of disloyalty. Only Cooper promised "to close schools in case of violent protest and resort to arms." After Clement had "aided in the rape of his own state and in returning Reconstruction terrors," the state, Cooper was assured, needed the healing efforts of his staunch conservatism. When railroad brotherhoods and a United Auto Workers local endorsed Cooper for governor in May, they did so because he was a "true-born Southerner," fair to both races, who would not "tolerate NAACP or order closed any school under attack by that organization or its agents." They were confident that he would not use troops against citizens in Tennessee to "aid outside interests seeking to destroy our Southern way of life."[23]

As late as the middle of May, Tennessee newspapers assumed that Cooper would run for governor and that Gore would have no opposition, but the pressure was mounting on Cooper to abandon the governor's race. In the battle for the segregationist vote, Cooper had to contend with the state government forces behind Ellington and the strength of Tip Taylor in the white supremacy heartlands of west Tennessee. The Clement–Ellington forces, with their links to the old Crump machine, were particularly keen to get Cooper to stand aside. Irrespective of racial issues, there were businessmen in the state who disliked Gore's stance in the Senate on national economic issues: public power and free trade in particular. Justin Potter, a Nashville industrialist, insurance executive, and former coal-mine operator, had long opposed Gore on atomic energy and the TVA. For Potter existing and future electricity needs could be met by the private sector. Roane Waring, former ally of Crump and McKellar, had raised both the race and the communist issue against Gore in the 1952 campaign. As a lawyer he had lobbied for the Dixon–Yates contract. Two textile manufacturers, A. G. Heinsohn of Knoxville and Pat French of Nashville, deplored Gore's refusal to countenance protectionist measures to safeguard textiles. Billboard interests in the state believed they had been let down by Gore's stand against advertising on the new interstate highways. It suited Gore to highlight wealthy business interests that opposed him, but there was also little doubt that these men helped persuade Cooper to run for the Senate seat and provided him with financial backing to run a well-oiled campaign. But the decisive forces came from the remnants of the old Crump machine and the supporters of Buford Ellington. The Citizens for Progress in Memphis, which was the successor organization to Crump's political empire, made it evident that they would endorse Cooper for the Senate race if he switched and cleared the way for the group to endorse Ellington for governor. In eastern Tennessee old supporters of McKellar also wanted to make a path for Ellington. They told Cooper that he had little chance in the crowded governor's race. Newsmen found many counties where there was little evidence of pro-Cooper activity. As the one unequivocal segregationist candidate against a racially moderate Senator Gore, Cooper could see much greater prospects of success in the Senate race than in the governor's race.[24]

Cooper therefore announced his candidacy for the U.S. Senate. He declared that he was targeting Gore on two issues: Gore's support of a "one-world, global giveaway program" of foreign aid and reciprocal trade agreements and his failure to defend segregation. A veteran observer of Tennessee politics, Joe Hatcher, had once been dismissive of the then-bachelor Cooper as rather effete and aloof, but now had to acknowledge what one journalist described as "one of the most intensive statewide campaigns in Tennessee history." "In less than two weeks of active campaigning," Hatcher observed, "Cooper has become a potent threat to unseat one of the three stars in the state's political firmament." Cooper might appear to lack the common touch, but he used different dictions to talk to urban and rural audiences. He may have once denounced the country-music industry, but now he promised to defend it vigorously and campaigned with Buddy Rose and His Country Tune Twisters or the Clinch Mountain Boys. The bachelor governor and ambassador was now married, with three children. His wife and children, including four-year-old future congressman, James, would appear at rallies with Cooper and take their turns at the microphones. Riding an air-conditioned bus, "the 62 year old former governor pursued his campaign at a pace that would have collapsed many a younger man" as he crossed the state back and forth. He also plastered the state's highways with 450 billboards and hit the airwaves. An envious Gore supporter complained that Cooper was spending $10,000 a day on radio and television. "If you listen to any radio or tv station as long as 30 minutes you will hear a flash for Cooper. There is no use switching stations," he concluded. A skeptical journalist would sometimes note the lack of audience response or the small crowds he attracted. Afterward Cooper was described as "aloof and uneasy in political crowds," but there was no doubt that he mounted a traditional Southern good-ole'-boy primary campaign with surprising vigor.[25]

The Eisenhower administration in the summer of 1958 was seeking an extension of the president's authority to negotiate reciprocal trade agreements to keep tariff barriers low between other countries and the United States. Gore was an enthusiastic supporter of the reciprocal trade program, which had been the brainchild of Cordell Hull. By contrast Cooper excoriated this program and foreign aid in general as a do-gooder's charter that wasted money, created unemployment in the United States, and failed to win Cold War allies abroad. This "global, one-world, give-away program" was responsible for throwing 70,000 men out of work in Tennessee, including 3,000 Alcoa employees in Maryville, 1,500 pottery workers in Erwin, hundreds of men in the zinc mines and textile mills of eastern Tennessee. To Cooper it was "neither reciprocal nor trade" but had "cut the throat of the American market and picked the pocket of American taxpayers." He asked his audiences if they could imagine a more futile waste of foreign aid than sending "millions of aspirin tablets to countries where they don't know anything about aspirin, electric microscopes where they have no need for them and water systems to small villages when many American small towns are without them."[26]

Traditionally, Southerners were internationalist and supported low tariffs because they depended on export markets for their cotton and tobacco. Cooper was appealing to the protectionist sentiments of Southern industries, particularly the extractive industries. But his isolationist or, more accurately, unilateralist line also appealed to a developing conservative suspicion of overseas nations and a straightforward anti-communism that went with segregationist fears of the corrupting, socialist, and possibly communist influence of other countries. Cooper's stand was one that would have been appreciated by such notorious opponents of foreign aid as Otto Passman and James Eastland, whose commitment to Massive Resistance was almost equaled by their sneering dismissal of American economic diplomacy. For Cooper it represented sound Americanism, but he also accused Gore of being soft on defense. In a speech in Clinton, Cooper warned his audience that Oak Ridge was a prime target for Russian bombs. He urged shoring up national defenses and ridiculed Senator Gore's "spaceship dreams that would squander billions." This strategy was part of a general attack on Gore's absenteeism (Cooper claimed he had missed 85 roll-call votes), his sixteen visits to Europe, and his nepotism (Gore family members were on the federal payroll, and Nancy Gore worked as a guide at the World Fair in Brussels that summer)—all of which, according to Cooper, made Gore the ideal senator for Russian leader Nikita Khrushchev.[27]

But it was not Cooper's trade policies that made him so passionate on the stump or stirred his listeners or attracted national attention. What gave Cooper's campaign its distinctive thrust was his full-scale defense of segregation and his denunciation of Gore for turning his back on the South. When Cooper formally opened his campaign on the steps of the Rutherford County courthouse in Murfreesboro, he blamed Gore for failing to sign the Southern Manifesto and for voting with the NAACP and the pink-tinged Americans for Democratic Action. By contrast Cooper pledged "to preserve the Southern way of life." After hearing this opening address, one observer said the speech sounded a good deal like a call on Southerners to open fire again on Fort Sumter. A journalist for the *Memphis Commercial Appeal* put it starkly, "For those who put segregation above all else, Mr. Cooper is just the man they've been seeking. Among his supporters are some of Tennessee's foremost champions of states' rights and race separation."[28]

At every campaign stop Cooper waved a copy of the manifesto. He promised that his first official act would be to sign it. By the end of July his copy of the manifesto was much-used and dog-eared. He condemned Gore for failing to sign it. He claimed that Gore's personal ambition and his desire to be on the national ticket in 1956 had led him to turn his back on Tennessee and follow instead the dictates of Northern radicals and zealots. The manifesto showed, according to Cooper, that the South did not need to be defeatist over school segregation. The first legislative act he would introduce in Congress, he promised, would be to restore the "separate but equal" doctrine that held before the *Brown* decision. He claimed to be a friend of "the colored," but he proclaimed his unalterable opposition to the forced mixing of children in schools. Grade-by-grade desegregation, as in Nashville, was no alternative. "Don't tell me that if the little ones are mixed, the big ones won't be mixed too," he shouted. He warned of the dangers of intermarriage. By contrast, he alleged, his opponent "has backed the NAACP policy designed to desegregate the South and mix the races in the schools." The manifesto was a "noble document." Gore's failure to sign was "the greatest betrayal of the South since the Civil War."[29]

According to Cooper, Gore "might as well have been a senator from Massachusetts or New Hampshire as far as helping preserve the Southern way of life." In Gore's "effort to curry favor with Northern radicals in pursuit of personal ambition for national office," not only had he failed to sign the manifesto, but he and Kefauver were working to weaken the power to filibuster, and had refused to support bills designed to restrict the right of the Supreme Court to nullify state laws. Finally, Gore had voted to confirm Gordon Tiffany, the new executive director of the Civil Rights Commission, established under the 1957 Civil Rights Act. The New Hampshire Republican lawyer, according to Cooper, had been "appointed to put the screws on the South." He was the "chief enforcer of the bill designed to punish the South and whip it into line in an effort to force race mixing in the schools." If the Tennessee people had not woken up to Gore's failings, it was because half the state's largest newspapers were owned by Northern radicals. Gore was endorsed, Cooper charged, by all four of the big daily Tennessee newspapers owned by Northern interests.[30]

For all the high-flown constitutional rhetoric Cooper employed, the appeal at the campaign stops was unequivocal, racist, and raw. A sound truck blaring out "Dixie" would precede Cooper into town. Don Oberdorfer, a young journalist sent by the *Charlotte Observer* to cover this campaign, explained what happened next. The Princeton-educated Oberdorfer had traveled on Cooper's air-conditioned campaign bus and was warmly received by the Ivy League–educated former governor. Cooper liked to come to the back of the bus, sit down, and eloquently recount for the young reporter his progressive ideals for good government, business development, and quality education. Then, Oberdorfer recalled, the bus would stop in an old courthouse square in western Tennessee. The sophisticated candidate got out of the bus. "He'd go into the center of Court House Square where there was a crowd, not a big crowd. And his line was 'I'm Prentice Cooper, and I'm gonna keep the niggers out of the schools!'" In a relatively understated description, fellow journalist David Halberstam wrote of Cooper's "earthy discussion of the race problem."[31]

National observers were in no doubt about the issues at stake. *Newsweek* said that segregation was the biggest single issue in the primary. *Time* labeled

Cooper "a white supremacist." Cooper himself took great encouragement from Orval Faubus's overwhelming reelection victory in neighboring Arkansas. The triumph of the poster boy of Massive Resistance, who had faced down the tyranny of the naked bayonet, gave segregationists in Tennessee great hope, and Cooper immediately fired off a telegram of congratulations. On a more mundane level on election day, Memphis policemen handed out to white voters copies of the black newspaper the *Tri-State Defender*, which had endorsed Gore, just to underline the danger to segregation that the apostate senator posed. An alarmed staffer at the Democratic National Committee warned former senator Herbert Lehman that Cooper was "pulling out all the stops on the racist issue." Although Lehman usually avoided involvement in primary elections, he immediately responded from the Hotel St. Moritz in Paris with a campaign contribution of five hundred dollars channeled through Mike Monroney.[32]

⤺

IN THE FACE of this well-financed segregationist onslaught, Gore had to move quickly. Unlike Estes Kefauver, he did not have a grassroots organization sustained by meticulous attention to the minutiae of constituent needs and personal loyalty. He had done little in 1958 to compensate for that deficiency because he was not expecting any serious opposition. Many of the people who had worked for him in 1952 were already committed to candidates in the governor's race. Martha Ragland, his campaign manager in 1952, was the state campaign comanager for Edmund Orgill. Journalist Neil Cunningham concluded that the Kefauver organization had simply adopted Orgill as its candidate. "In almost every county, Orgill has picked up the Kefauver organization for his own." "Kefauver has supplied Orgill with a ready-made political machine in every county; he has raised money for him [in the North] and even donated his own campaign financier to the cause; he has exerted pressure in every form to gain him support. Whether Orgill knows it or not, he's a cog in a potent political machine." It was not clear that these workers would be available to Gore.[33]

As *New York Times* reporter Claude Sitton noted, Albert Gore was "caught without a campaign organization" and "had allowed his organization to disintegrate." Pauline Gore recalled, "We only had 60-odd days to set up an entire campaign throughout the entire state." Memphis journalist Morris Cunningham captured the shock Gore felt when he realized he would face serious opposition. It was like that of a man whose house had been struck by lightning. Shocked at first, he seemed to think it could not possibly be his house. Then he discovered a hole in the roof. "Now, amid the threat of even worse thunderstorms, he's rushing about trying to fix the roof—and also to strengthen the foundations."[34]

Gore and the family closed the apartment in Washington, DC, and moved back to Tennessee. He returned to the capital for crucial votes on the TVA, atomic energy, a farm bill, and reciprocal trade. When he remained in Washington, Pauline, as fiercely combative as Gore himself, delivered several speeches in his stead. Gore planned to do what he did best, just as in 1938 and 1952, to take his case to the courthouse squares and small towns across the state. As Gore told reporters "He'll speak wherever he can get a crowd. And if he can't get a crowd, he'll shake hands." But formal speeches were only part of the campaign: "Rather than striving to arrange rallies and speeches in the traditional way, he indicated he will put emphasis on handshaking, breakfasts, luncheons, dinners and coffees." Here Pauline was essential as well, attending innumerable coffee and Coke parties put together by local women.[35]

Gore knew how to reach Tennessee crowds. Claude Sitton watched him talk in Brownsville, Haywood County. Gore started with the "air of a country school teacher which he was before his entry into politics. But the address that followed bore the marks of an orator seasoned by years of debate on the floors of the House and Senate." When he and Cooper addressed a Knoxville Democratic party gathering, Gore completely upstaged the former governor. Gore followed Cooper, said one observer, "like Elvis Presley coming on after a zither solo." Rather than traveling in an air-conditioned bus or a helicopter, Gore came into town in "the cheapest standard GM car from last year." But like Cooper, Gore brought a band with him, at least in western Tennessee: Slim Rhodes and the Mountaineers playing standards like "Blue-Eyed Sally" and "Got a Lot of Living to Do."[36]

Gore's response to Cooper's attacks was the classic response of the Southern racial moderate. He focused on economic issues and the benefits he and the federal government had brought to Tennessee. Of the five central issues he announced for his campaign, only one—his support for the 1957 Civil Rights Act, which he always called the right-to-vote bill—dealt directly with race. The other issues were the world trade program, the nature of his opposition, the national viewpoint of a senator, and how his legislative achievements refuted any notion that he had turned his back on Tennessee.[37]

Gore tackled the trade issue head on. Tennessee relied on exports. If other countries could not afford to buy American goods, where would the cotton farmers' markets be? As he told a western Tennessee audience: "I drove through this morning and I looked at your cotton crop and it looks good: it looks to be one of the best crops you ever had. Well, what are you going to do with it? . . . I know what you did last year. You sold sixty per cent of it to foreign markets. If you want to stop that and quit those foreign markets, there's a man running for the U S Senate who'll accommodate you. But I'm flying back to Washington tonight to vote for the extension of the Cordell Hull program." He warned his listeners that the cotton mill and textile people would love to buy the cotton crop dirt cheap—but the cotton farmers could not live off that. It was 1932-era economics to believe that "in some way we can continue to export our products in large volume without buying anything." "Exports protect present jobs," he asserted. "Expand exports and you create more jobs, more profits and more money in the farmer's pocket and the worker's pocket."[38]

As he always did on foreign policy issues, Gore wrapped himself in the mantle of Cordell Hull, still a revered figure in the state. He loftily proclaimed that he never dreamt he would see a race to tear out the capstone of Cordell Hull's legacy. But the evocation of Hull and the threat to export markets were joined to an unabashed Cold War perspective. Khrushchev had challenged the United States to compete in the peaceful field of trade. In the face of the Soviet trade challenge, Gore warned, "should we lapse into a state of economic isolationism, we will surely be inviting defeat in the economic cold war." The opposition "would give the Soviets customers and markets [that] would shift the balance of power against us and give a victory to the Soviets in the cold war without firing a shot." This dire warning was emphasized by a letter in support of Gore that was sent to newspapers by William L. Clayton, one of the architects of the Marshall Plan and a wealthy cotton broker in Houston. Clayton wondered how anybody from an export-dependent state like Tennessee could possibly oppose reciprocal trade. The stakes were high. "We are living in a dangerous world. Russia is trying to isolate us. If she succeeds, we are, of course, lost." Gore extended this analysis to a general attack on isolationism at a time of Cold War dangers, which were highlighted by the Middle East crisis that summer. "If we withdrew into an isolationist shell," he told his television audience, "we would invite defeat in the cold war. Tennessee cannot be free if America goes down. Tennessee cannot prosper if the other 48 states are in a depression. If we withdraw from world leadership we leave Russia free in the contest, not for world leadership, but for world domination."[39]

Gore continued with high-minded lectures on the national rather than parochial responsibilities of a U.S. Senator. Without national influence in

Washington, he said, he would have been unable to deliver tangible benefits to the state. At a time when Memphis was within a fifteen-minute range of an intercontinental ballistic missile, he needed to be a U.S. senator as well as a senator from Tennessee. He cited the national rather than local reputations of men like Alben Barkley, George Norris, and Cordell Hull. Without that influence, how could he protect the TVA, develop atomic energy at Oak Ridge, or deliver more than $90 million of highways to the state? He enticed his listeners in west Tennessee with the prospect that soon it would be possible "for Jackson people to go to a clover leaf outside Jackson and drive to Memphis—or Los Angeles—without seeing a stop light." In Nashville he promised that superhighways would lead to the city from five directions. This practical appeal to the voters regarding what Gore had delivered was reflected in newspaper advertisements toward the end of the campaign in which the race issue never got a mention: "TVA never had a better friend; a farmer knows the problems of farmers; an active senator gets things done; there's no substitute for experience; Albert Gore: an outstanding record of achievement."[40]

The men behind Prentice Cooper were an inviting target for Gore. Gore distinguished between his opponent, "a nice well-meaning man," and his opposition—"a strange conglomeration of special interests who confuse their own interest with the public interest" and had been trying to find a candidate for a year or more.[41]

With data assembled from his investigation into campaign finances, Gore could draw attention to a five-thousand-dollar check that one of these backers, Justin Potter, had paid to the GOP in 1956. That Republican link encouraged him to turn his fire also on Meade Alcorn and Lee Potter from the Republican National Committee and Guy Smith from the *Knoxville Journal* for interfering in a Democratic primary. Potter in particular was a godsend to Gore because of his vociferous opposition to the TVA. In July 1956 Potter had placed a two-page ad in *Farm and Ranch* magazine: "Is TVA Creeping Socialism or Rampant Communism?" He had also placed an ad in the *Chicago Tribune* calling the TVA a "Communist rathole." Gore mercilessly played on these ads, as well as on Roane Waring's role as a lobbyist for Dixon–Yates, to burnish his own credentials as a defender of the TVA. It was easy for Gore to develop a narrative of the people's candidate against "a little group of rich extremists" who were trying to buy the election. Gore was carrying his campaign directly to the people, he said, "because it's the only thing I can do. My opposition is spending half a million dollars on television alone to try and

buy a seat in the United States Senate." "More money," he asserted, "is being spent in this election to defeat me than has ever been spent in any other
political campaign in Tennessee." "The campaign," he intoned, "was designed
to deceive, planned to prejudice, and to deliver one of the Tennessee seats in
the United States Senate to a small group of special interests and extremists."[42]

However much Gore wanted to concentrate on nonracial issues, he knew
he had to address the racial concerns of the voters. Gore's legislative assistant,
Bill Allen, had carefully laid out the strategy for countering Cooper on the
issue of the manifesto. First, "minimize your disagreement with the text as a
matter of personal opinion. Your decision was based on the propriety of issuance of such a document as an official action of a public official." Second,
point out that an inflammatory statement of defiance was not conducive to
law and order. Third, note that "issuance of the statement could make no contribution to the solution to the problem. It had no legal effect whatsoever. Yet
its issuance held out false hopes to some that this document would somehow
change the situation." Finally, Gore could point out that, far from causing the
North to back off from confrontation with the South, the manifesto in fact
stimulated Northerners to introduce "extreme" legislation.[43]

In the event Gore completely ignored the manifesto. Instead he defended his role in the passage of the 1957 Civil Rights Act. He returned to rural
west Tennessee four times for separate two- and three-day trips, speaking ten
times a day on most days. As Jack Robinson drove the senator and Mrs. Gore
around the black belt, Gore joked that "I feel like Daniel going into the lion's
den." Robinson recalled tense, hostile crowds, at least at the start. Gore in part
explained away his vote by saying that he had led the battle to defeat a tough
civil rights bill. He patiently ticked off six successful amendments sponsored
by the Southern bloc to weaken the bill that he had supported. He quoted
praise from the leader of the Southerners, Richard Russell, for his constructive role regarding these amendments. The final bill was a "fair and moderate
bill [that] would postpone the enactment of a much more severe bill later."
He boasted: "We won a victory for the South. The bill represented a defeat
for the extremists." But increasingly he moved from the prudential defense of
his position to an unapologetic defense of the right to vote. As time went on
in the western part of the state, the crowds responded enthusiastically. There
was loud applause in Cleveland when he unequivocally stated, "The right to
vote is the very hallmark of a free man and it should not be denied to any
qualified citizen, man or woman, rich or poor, Jew or gentile, black or white."

As the days wore on, his speeches got "hotter and hotter"; a blistering civil rights speech in Somerville, Fayette County, according to one of the journalists following him, "turned an unenthusiastic crowd into one that caught the fervor of his delivery."[44]

∽

GORE'S STRATEGY WORKED. Prentice Cooper had been confident of victory. On election night he got in his car to make the one-hour drive from his home in Shelbyville to Nashville to deliver his victory speech. The car did not have a radio, so Cooper arrived in Nashville unaware that he had lost. For all the predictions of a close race with the uncompromising segregationist, Gore overwhelmed Cooper by 375,439 to 253,191. Gore received 50,000 more votes than in 1952, when race had not figured in the election. He won seventy of the state's ninety-five counties. He won Memphis by 18,000 votes. Cooper could not even win his home county.[45]

Tributes to Gore's victory poured in from fellow senators round the country: Oregon senator Richard L. Neuberger (another supporter of the regulation of billboards), Democratic majority whip Mike Mansfield, Oklahoma friends Mike Monroney and Robert Kerr, and Republican senators Francis Case and Thomas Kuchel. In the aftermath of Orval Faubus's overwhelming victory in Arkansas, national observers heralded Gore's victory as a triumph for Southern racial moderation. Syndicated columnist William S. White had earlier identified the stakes at play in the Tennessee senate race: "The result will tell whether a moderately liberal and forward looking Southern political view can survive in the tragic backwash of the racial crisis in Little Rock and elsewhere." If that moderate political view could not survive in Tennessee, what hope would there be elsewhere in the South? When both Gore and his friend Ralph Yarborough of Texas defeated conservative segregationists, White celebrated. These were the men, along with Lyndon Johnson and Estes Kefauver, who showed that Southern extremism could be defeated. "Both men are, by Southern standards, dangerously liberal on the racial question. Both had been marked by the Southern Old Guard for liquidation. Both won without abandoning unpopular convictions—and with the overwhelming endorsement of their own people." Their victories showed that "moderate and responsible politicians can still live in the South, given half a chance."[46]

In August 1958 Gore was at the peak of his political power in Tennessee. He had fought off well-financed segregationist opposition by taking his case to the people. He was still a master of personal politics, stump speaking, and handshaking tours. In 1958 that brand of personal politics—taking your case to the county seats and the crossroads—could still offset the more expensive, slicker politics of television and radio. He might not have the sort of political organization that Estes Kefauver possessed, but he could appeal to Kefauver's supporters. He could appeal to both African Americans and organized labor, not least because of his opponent's conservatism. He might run a lean Washington office that did not specialize in constituency service, but his legislative achievements and national influence brought tangible benefits to Tennessee—highways, defense of the TVA, advocacy for atomic energy and Oak Ridge, and, at the more mundane level, a federal building for Memphis and the tantalizing possibility of a farm bill to help cotton and tobacco growers. From that position he could take an internationalist lead on foreign aid and reciprocal trade at a time when isolationist sentiment was rising in the South, and a racially moderate lead on civil rights when segregationist sentiment was being stirred up.

Gore displayed real courage facing down hostile audiences in western Tennessee in 1958 and defending his support of the right to vote. But his style of racial moderation would be difficult to sustain after 1958. In the 1958 election he could uphold the rule of law, he could say that he had not voted to force children into racially mixed schools, he could talk about local control of the schools. He did not have to confront what would happen when local control of the schools conflicted with the federal courts. In 1958 he could talk about economic issues rather than race—foreign trade and prosperity for cotton farmers, the Eisenhower administration and recession, infrastructure investment—because most white Tennesseans had neither seen any desegregation nor experienced assertive African Americans demanding racial change.

Gore and his white supporters lived in a world where whites still dictated the timetable of racial change. William S. White feared that Northern liberals would make the position of white Southern moderates untenable with demands for radical action. But it was not Northern liberals who would make Gore's life difficult. It was African Americans who would ensure after 1960 that whites could no longer dictate the timetable of racial change in the South. The post-1945 tactics of litigation and political participation had brought some modest gains for African Americans in Tennessee. Before *Brown* they had won some limited concessions on the margins of segregation but little more. After *Brown* a significant but slowly increasing black electorate used its political leverage to help elect moderate white politicians like Gore and to extract concessions from them that would soften the edges of segregation and provide public services and spending for blacks. Litigation produced school desegregation on white terms—that is, token compliance—which, as in other moderate parts of the South, proved to be the most effective way of sustaining the maximum degree of segregation for the longest time. It is not surprising that a younger generation of Tennessee African American students saw the limited utility of those tactics and turned instead to direct action in late 1959 and 1960. African American assertiveness and challenges to the whole edifice of segregation in the public sphere would produce an often violent Southern white backlash and require federal intervention. The racially moderate stance that Gore sold to the Tennessee electorate in 1958 would be much harder to sell in the 1960s.

CHAPTER 6

Gore's Liberal Hopes and the Kennedy Promise

ON THE SATURDAY following the 1960 Democratic National Convention, nationally syndicated journalist Bob Novak flew from Los Angeles to Nashville. He planned to cover Estes Kefauver's battle for reelection against the segregationist Tip Taylor. When he called Albert Gore to ask about that campaign, he was surprised that Gore insisted he join him for family supper at home in Carthage. Certainly Novak had not been close to Gore in the two years he had covered the Senate.

Novak was under the incorrect impression that Gore was not sympathetic to Kefauver and his chances of success. But in fact Gore was confident that Kefauver would win more easily than expected, even if he ran a poor campaign, as Gore thought likely. Gore, who had beaten another segregationist, Prentice Cooper, two years earlier, told Novak that the day of segregationists like Tip Taylor was over. As they talked, Pauline, Nancy, and the notably polite twelve-year-old Al joined them for a fried-chicken dinner. Gore and Novak drank Budweiser from the can, but Novak surmised that Gore was not much of a drinker, as two cans of beer seemed to have loosened his tongue. Gore thus was more candid with the journalist than he had ever been before or since in the capital.

As they discussed the presidential campaign, Gore suddenly blurted out, "Bob, you were at Los Angeles last week. Tell me. Why would the Democratic Party pick Jack Kennedy when they could have had me?" Novak could not imagine how to answer, but Pauline saved him by yelling, "Albert! Now, you stop that."[1]

Bob Novak may have been surprised at the depths of Gore's presidential ambitions and his degree of self-importance, and he clearly thought Gore's aspirations were presumptuous. But in 1960 Gore was at the peak of his national prestige. He was a leading Democrat spokesman on nuclear disarmament. He was the most tenacious critic of the Eisenhower administration's conservative economic policy, and a relentless advocate of expansionist fiscal and monetary policies to combat the recession and sluggish growth. Northern liberals admired him for his moderate views on civil rights, his clashes with conservative congressional Democratic Party leadership, his support for tax reform, and his hostility to the influence of big business over economic policy and elections. He knew all the principal contenders for the 1960 nomination and had jousted verbally with them on equal terms. He brought the leading Democratic contenders to Tennessee—Kennedy, Humphrey, and Johnson— and had seen their strengths and weaknesses at first hand. He was much in demand across the nation for speeches to the party faithful, so it was not entirely unreasonable that he should, as he wryly admitted later, have had at least "occasional dreams of the Presidency."[2]

Whatever Gore said to Bob Novak, he both admired and liked John F. Kennedy. He would be able to play little role in Kennedy's campaign for the Democratic nomination, however, because Governor Buford Ellington had tied up the Tennessee delegation, which was officially an uninstructed delegation but committed to LBJ all the same. Gore would, however, play a significant role in the general election campaign and was on close personal terms with Kennedy throughout his administration, and he celebrated its achievements, particularly in foreign policy. Yet on some of the major issues of the Kennedy administration, Gore was either uninvolved or unsuccessful in persuading the president to change policy. Gore was sidelined by Vice President Johnson in the development of the test-ban treaty. He was silent on Kennedy's 1963 civil rights proposals, and he failed to persuade Kennedy to withdraw from Vietnam or to abandon tax-cut proposals. By 1963 Kennedy was referring to Gore as a "son of a bitch" because of his opposition to the administration's flagship proposal for a tax cut, which Kennedy hoped would kickstart a flagging economy. Gore nevertheless hoped that Kennedy, once safely elected for a second term in 1964, would pursue "economic, social policies traditional with the Democratic Party."[3]

༄

AS GORE WAS starting his second term as a U.S. Senator in 1959, he had reestablished a "passingly pleasant personal equation" with Majority Leader Lyndon Johnson. Johnson had visited Tennessee in October 1958 to speak for the Democratic ticket, and he stayed with the Gores. The trip had gone well and helped cast aside any doubts about Buford Ellington's election as governor in the general election. In Washington Johnson gave Gore two plum committee assignments that he had long sought—the Foreign Relations Committee and the Finance Committee. Gore's assignment to the Foreign Relations Committee was in part due to his proven expertise and interest in international affairs but was also part of an elaborate maneuver by Johnson to get his friend William Fulbright to replace the veteran Theodore Francis Green as chair of the committee.[4]

It was more surprising that he had been assigned to the Senate Finance Committee, given that Gore was opposed to the depletion allowance on oil and gas that allowed producers to exempt 27.5 percent of their income for tax purposes. Johnson took the "right" stand in favor of the depletion allowance to be a sine qua non of membership on the Finance Committee. Gore believed that his seniority entitled him to a place on the Finance Committee, as did his friend Paul Douglas of Illinois, an even more outspoken opponent of the depletion allowance. Johnson was unmoved by Gore's requests for a long time, but in 1957 he put both Douglas and Gore on the Finance Committee under veteran Virginia senator Harry F. Byrd. Johnson doubtless took comfort in the fact that Gore and Douglas had only two votes in a committee dominated by Byrd, and two passionate advocates of oil interests, Russell Long of Louisiana and Robert Kerr of Oklahoma. Kerr would remain the most powerful figure on the committee until his death in 1963, after which Gore would have to confront the equally effective, albeit less intellectually overpowering, Russell Long.[5]

In 1959 LBJ also put the newly elected Minnesota senator Eugene McCarthy on the Finance Committee. McCarthy later recalled sitting at the back of the Finance Committee with Gore, watching the latest depredation of the tax system by Kerr and Long. But McCarthy's support for the liberal cause was not immediately apparent to Gore and Douglas. It was difficult to escape the conclusion that LBJ, determined to thwart William Proxmire of Wisconsin—who desperately wanted the committee assignment—offered the freshman McCarthy the plum post after telling him to "clear it" with committee chair Robert Kerr. Kerr would have insisted that McCarthy be "right" on the oil and gas depletion allowance. In the first vote on the allowance in 1959, McCarthy, to Gore and Douglas's surprise, supported the conservatives. McCarthy's calculation was simply a recognition of political reality—there was no chance of defeating Robert Kerr and Russell Long. Gore and Douglas, he felt, were tilting at windmills. It was an early example of McCarthy's casual unreliability that irritated other Senate liberals over the years.[6]

Johnson had also endorsed Gore's selection as a Senate delegate to the nuclear-disarmament talks in Geneva in the fall of 1958. Ever since 1954, when the United States had exploded its first hydrogen bomb in the Bikini atoll, the national and international debate over the control of nuclear weapons and weapons testing had intensified dramatically. Atomic bombs (fission) had essentially been local bombs; hydrogen bombs (fusion) were global in impact. They could wipe out whole cities at a time but, as Western Europeans were only too aware, an H-bomb attack on Russia could also lead to millions of deaths in Western Europe from the nuclear fallout if the wind carried in the wrong direction. The security implications for the United States were similarly profound. If the Soviets could develop a deliverable hydrogen bomb, and by the end of November 1955 it was clear they could, they could at one stroke compensate for their existing shortfall in atomic weapons. Unlike the existing heavy atom bombs, which had to be carried in bombers, H-bombs could be packed into a missile warhead. The development of intercontinental ballistic missiles could give the Russians a first-strike capability and, as Gore pointed out in the 1958 election, put the Russians within fifteen minutes of hitting Memphis.[7]

Although the Eisenhower administration relied on a doctrine of massive nuclear retaliation to deter the Russians, the president himself was profoundly discouraged by the prospect of nuclear conflict. The first task he gave his new chair of the Atomic Energy Commission (AEC), Lewis Strauss, was to find some way of disarming atomic weapons. Throughout his presidency Eisenhower was looking to restrict nuclear testing, knowing that, with offers of a test ban, the Soviets won a large propaganda advantage in an international community concerned with dangers of nuclear fallout, particularly in the nonaligned Third World. But he was more worried by the prospect of nuclear war than nuclear fallout, so he saw a ban on nuclear testing as simply one part of a comprehensive disarmament package that had proved impossible to secure ever since the first American proposals for international control of atomic weapons in 1946.[8]

Both the Atomic Energy Commission and the Pentagon resisted any idea of a nuclear test ban. Chairman Strauss and the Joint Chiefs of Staff simply did not believe the Soviets could ever be trusted. The military wanted tests to maintain their nuclear superiority over the Russians and to develop battlefield nuclear weapons. Scientists like Edward Teller, "father" of the H bomb, held out the hope that testing would lead to the development of a "clean" H bomb with greatly reduced fallout. Meanwhile, the AEC consistently downplayed the effect of increased radiation as a result of fallout.[9]

Even so Eisenhower remained deeply unhappy with nuclear testing, while at the same time, Secretary of State Dulles was increasingly alarmed by the propaganda victories won by the Soviets. Eisenhower decided to secure alternative sources of scientific advice. The administration started seriously to consider suspending tests as a prelude to negotiation with the Soviets. Democratic politicians like Adlai Stevenson and Hubert Humphrey also advocated the possibility of a unilateral test moratorium. By the spring of 1958, Eisenhower was ready to reverse the American policy that test-ban negotiations had to be linked to other disarmament goals. He proposed technical talks on inspection as a prelude to test-ban negotiations in Geneva. The Russians responded positively, and 31 October was set as the date for the test-ban moratorium. Both sides tested furiously before the deadline: 1958 saw the largest number of tests in any one year.[10]

Gore had been appointed as one of the two Senate delegates or advisers to the American delegation at the Geneva talks. He briefed himself with the help of Thomas Murray, former AEC commissioner. Murray, appointed as a Democrat, had long been at odds with Lewis Strauss and had been a lone voice on the AEC in advocating for the suspension of tests. He was not overly concerned about the dangers of fallout, but he wanted instead to concentrate on the dangers of tactical nuclear weapons and limited war. What Gore saw at Geneva soon convinced him that Murray was right.[11]

After ten days of watching the Russians at the bargaining table and meeting them socially, Gore was convinced that they were at Geneva primarily for an exercise in propaganda. He also recognized, as he said in a handwritten letter to Lyndon Johnson, that the American military and the AEC had "been dragged into this by the ear, kicking and squalling." Gore feared that "we are undertaking to negotiate the unattainable" because he saw no way of ensuring adequate detection of underground tests. Even if the Russians agreed to inspection, what chance was there that the Chinese would also agree? He had learned from the experts that small explosions under four to five kilotons were impossible to detect and could not be distinguished from earthquakes. He noted how primitive the proposed means of detection were. What equipment would a mobile team of inspectors use? "An oil rig was the answer I got." Gore believed that the Americans should abandon "an endless hassle over the unattainable." Instead they should seek the limited goal of "permanent stoppage of atmospheric testing." Such an agreement would not impair the American military advantage: The Americans could achieve their military goals through underground testing. Detection of atmospheric testing was feasible, and an agreement did not rely on Russian promises. It would eliminate the most hazardous aspect of testing, and subsequently sub-oceanic and outer-space testing as well as large underground explosions could be eradicated.[12]

Gore returned to Washington and presented his ideas to Eisenhower, who was sufficiently interested to ask him to submit a paper elaborating on his ideas. Gore said that an American unilateral ban on atmospheric testing would not compromise American security because the United States could continue underground testing; but the ban would deprive the Soviets of a major propaganda advantage. Eisenhower was sympathetic but saw the Gore position as a fallback option should the talks in Geneva fail. Eventually Eisenhower and John McCone, the successor to Lewis Strauss at the AEC, came around to the idea of an atmospheric test ban and a ban on underground tests above a certain size threshold. Eisenhower had high hopes that the Paris summit conference in 1960 would bring progress, but the shooting down of a U2 reconnaissance plane dashed those hopes. Gore, who had been critical of the lack of planning for the Paris conference, publicly supported Eisenhower's test-ban aspirations. He often criticized drift in U.S. policy in the final years of the Republican administration. Like other Democrats he deplored Eisenhower's emphasis on a balanced budget at the expense of national security. But Gore came to admire Eisenhower's skepticism about the advice he received from the military. Gore praised Eisenhower's refusal to intervene militarily in Indochina in 1954, his willingness to entertain a nuclear test ban, and his valedictory warning against a military-industrial complex.[13]

⤷

GORE'S ENGAGEMENT WITH the nuclear testing issue, part of his long-term interest in atomic energy, showed that he was a serious-minded senator primarily interested in policy, albeit from a partisan perspective. At times he may have been worthy and earnest, but he clearly valued, and was able to understand, the importance of evidence-based policy. He served as secretary of a Democratic party roundtable that met regularly in 1959 to listen to expert speakers like Dean Acheson and George Kennan on subjects of current interest. From forty to sixty senators regularly attended, but Gore could never persuade heavyweight establishment senators like Lyndon Johnson and Bob Kerr to attend. The area where Gore worked hardest was economic policy. Throughout the Eisenhower administration, he had attacked Republican economic policy. His arguments had most weight during the Eisenhower recessions of 1954 and 1958. He was particularly alert to any rise in unemployment in addition to what he considered to be unacceptably low growth rates. Gore blamed the fiscal policy of the administration for the economic downturns: the combination of the president's desire to control the deficit and the monetary policy and high interest rates favored by Treasury Secretary George Humphrey and the Federal Reserve Board. His standard lament was of the "continuing Republican pattern of favoring the big financial interests at the expense of the public." Instead of deficit reduction, the drive for a balanced budget, and a tight money policy, Gore championed an economic stimulus of government spending and low interest rates. He was in regular contact with Leon Keyserling, the former chair of Truman's Council of Economic Advisers, who consistently argued for an expansionist economic policy. Gore was already alert to the counter argument that a tax cut would stimulate the economy. He was adamant "that acceleration of public works projects which would create more jobs would be more effective for this purpose than would a tax reduction. I am sure you will understand that a reduction of income tax is of little help to one who has no job and, therefore, no tax liability." He kept a sharp eye out for any effort to cut government spending, particularly on highways, and criticized Treasury and Federal Housing Administration policy that kept mortgage rates high. His speeches struck Eisenhower's advisers as advocating "regimentation" of the economy, but the speeches, especially those advocating a reversal of the administration's tight money policy, delighted former President Truman.[14]

Gore's advocacy of compensatory government spending in these postwar years was typical of what has been described as "commercial Keynesianism": the use of government spending in the postwar boom to create full employment, without increasing statist intervention in the economy. What made Gore different and aligned him with labor and Northern liberals in this period was his passionate advocacy of tax reform. There was a socialdemocratic, redistributionist tinge to his economic ideas that were part of a persistent "social Keynesianism" that historians have increasingly identified in the 1950s Democratic Party in the North, in particular the labor movement and California. Gore believed that the Senate Finance Committee perpetuated tax favoritism with special exemptions and loopholes engineered for the benefit of oil and gas companies and insurance companies, among others. He had a wide-ranging reform "shopping list" to modify or eliminate deductions

for business expenses and special treatment for investment income from corporate stocks, foreign investments, and pension and stock-option payments.
Gore would rarely get the support of the Senate Finance Committee, but he
did have surprising success in securing Senate backing for amendments he
presented on the floor. On one occasion sheer dogged determination secured
the closing of a loophole for manufactured goods in the oil and gas depletion
allowance by a vote of 87 to 0 on the floor of the Senate when he and Paul
Douglas had been the only members of the Finance Committee to support it.
He also introduced his own Medicare bill in 1960. Douglas and Gore became
accustomed to their joint, lonely dissents on the Finance Committee. On one
occasion Senator Eugene McCarthy of Minnesota murmured to Republican
Carl Curtis, "Diogenes spent all his life looking for an honest man: Paul and
Albert found each other."[15]

A *Congressional Quarterly* analysis in February 1960 identified those
Southern senators who regularly voted with the conservative Southern
Democrat–Republican coalition and those who voted with the Democratic
majority. Gore and Kefauver joined the Alabama senators Hill and Sparkman, Ralph Yarborough of Texas, and Russell Long of Louisiana, whose oil
interests had not entirely offset his father's populist legacy, as the small group
of Southerners who voted more than 50 percent of the time with the more
liberal Democratic majority. Gore's increasing identification with Northern
liberals and his estrangement from the Southern Senate establishment was
exemplified by his challenge to Lyndon Johnson at the start of 1960 over the
status of the Democratic Senate Conference and the Democratic Policy Committee, both of which the majority leader had wielded into instruments of his
own control.[16]

Older liberals in the Senate had either been coopted by LBJ, like Hubert Humphrey, or routinely humiliated and marginalized, like Paul Douglas.
But the class of 1958 brought to Congress a group of Democrats who were
less amenable to the "Johnson treatment." They chafed at the failure of the
Democrats to pose a consistently clear-cut liberal challenge to the Republicans. They resented the power wielded by older Southern conservatives, and
they blamed Lyndon Johnson for putting his acknowledged parliamentary
mastery to such unadventurous ends. The Democratic Conference of Senators, which met only when Johnson decided to call it, and the Policy Committee of nine senators, effectively chosen by the majority leader, exemplified for
them the problems of the cozy control exercised by Johnson. Joseph Clark of
Pennsylvania, newly elected, cantankerous, and unafraid, used the meeting of

the conference at the start of the 1960 session to propose that it should meet once every two weeks at the request of fifteen senators. Clark had already consulted Hubert Humphrey, Paul Douglas, William Proxmire, and Patrick McNamara (Michigan). Responding to this "revolt of the liberals," Johnson professed his willingness to call the conference whenever any senator wanted one called. Gore supported the thrust of the liberal complaints when he said that the conference should be called not when an individual senator happened to want one but in order to "try and get an overall approach to legislation." "Some of us not in the inner circle," he continued, "feel left out." He responded angrily to Johnson's statement that the Policy Committee was the "arm of the leadership." They agreed to return to the matter at an extra meeting on January 12.[17]

Gore presented himself as someone attempting to reach a compromise between the liberals and the majority leader, but on the floor of the Senate on January 11, he threw off the peacemaker role. He excoriated the party leadership: "With one compromise after another we stand before the country as a blurred image." He would not "weasel time and again to the point where it appeared to the country that we stood for nothing except compromise." He justified speaking about these divisions publicly. "Here," he told George Smathers, "one can be heard. Behind the closed door one can be steamrollered." The next day Gore gave notice to Johnson that he would introduce a motion at the rescheduled meeting of the conference to make the Policy Committee larger, more representative, and elected directly by all the Democratic senators. It reflected his concern with "the procedure, or lack thereof, for determining Democratic legislative policy." He believed it went to the heart of "the efficacy of the two-party system." Gore may have portrayed himself a peacemaker, but Johnson and his allies immediately identified him as a liberal enemy. At the meeting veteran senators denied that the Policy Committee was ever intended to have the policy-formulation role. Only Mike Monroney, Joseph Clark, and John Carroll publicly supported Gore. Young, new senators like Ed Muskie spoke against his stance. The debate was studded with professions of loyalty to the majority leader. The Gore resolution was defeated overwhelmingly by 51 votes to 12. Another motion for the conference to elect the members of the conference committee was defeated 51 to 11.[18]

Apart from Ralph Yarborough, not a single Southerner backed Gore. His friend Mike Monroney backed him, as did his long-time maverick colleague Wayne Morse of Oregon. His other supporters were the core of Northern liberals—Joe Clark, Paul Douglas, Philip Hart, and Pat McNamara, Hubert

Humphrey and Gene McCarthy from Minnesota, John Carroll of Colorado, and William Proxmire of Wisconsin. The names of his allies seemed to confirm the accusations of his opponents in Tennessee that he had cast his lot with Northern radicals. Even his loyal supporters on the *Tennessean* openly pondered the wisdom and purpose of his "crusade." Johnson's loyal henchman in Tennessee, Governor Ellington, said that he warned Gore against challenging the majority leader. He was surprised that Gore led the fight but not surprised at the results. Ellington identified with the majority who opposed Gore: "I kinda liked the group Mr. Gore was NOT running with on this question." Given Gore's assault on "one man leadership" of the Senate, it is not surprising that newspapers everywhere personalized the fight between Gore and LBJ. In vain on *Face the Nation* the following Sunday, Gore described Johnson as "the ablest majority leader in my lifetime." The long-festering personal rivalry between Gore and Johnson had come out into the open. It would be difficult for Johnson to forgive and forget.[19]

A measure of Gore's standing among Northern Democrats was demonstrated by renewed speculation that he might be a vice-presidential candidate and by their repeated invitations for Gore to speak in the North. But his identification with Northern liberals did not necessarily extend to a common cause on civil rights. In 1960 African American students across the South took part in sit-ins designed to force storeowners to desegregate lunch counters and downtown stores. The student sit-ins were a dramatic ratcheting up of black protest in that they forced a response from white Southerners. Whites could ignore a boycott if they were prepared to put up with the economic consequences. They could not ignore a sit-in. The storeowner had to choose whether to serve the students and desegregate the store, have the protesters arrested, or close the store. In Nashville students led by John Lewis and Diane Nash organized wave after wave of disciplined protests. White thugs violently assaulted the peaceful protesters, who were then routinely arrested by the police. Increasingly whites were fearful of shopping in downtown stores. The house of black lawyer and city councilman Z. Alexander Looby was dynamited. After a remarkable silent march, the students confronted Mayor Ben West on the steps of city hall and wrung from him the concession that he, as an individual, thought it wrong to serve African Americans in one part of a store but deny them service at the lunch counters in another part of the store. As a result Nashville businessmen set about negotiating the desegregation of their stores.[20]

Albert Gore remained silent about the racial conflict that was convulsing his state. He did write to Looby to express his regrets about the bombing of his house, but otherwise he ignored the black student protests and left any response to city and state authorities. However, as in 1958, he supported civil rights legislation in 1960. As in 1958 he announced his willingness to support reasonable voting-rights legislation but promised to eliminate all "punitive, unwise, and unacceptable" provisions. As in 1958 Gore and Kefauver followed Lyndon Johnson's lead. Although the Tennessee senators joined sixty-nine others to vote the final bill through, they had voted with the Southern bloc to water down the bill before final passage, an effort that Senator Harry Byrd boasted produced a Southern victory.[21]

~

IN THE 1960 race for the Democratic presidential nomination, Gore clearly favored John F. Kennedy but could do little actively to promote his candidacy. The governor, Buford Ellington, controlled the Tennessee delegation. The state delegates were uninstructed, but it was clear that the delegation intended to support Ellington's friend Lyndon Johnson for the nomination. Although Gore would be a delegate to the national convention, he had few allies in the state party hierarchy. All he could do was to arrange for John Kennedy to speak in Tennessee. Pauline Gore flew down from Washington for the speech with Kennedy and his wife, Jackie, on their plane *Caroline*. Pauline was the only spouse of Tennessee representatives who was not a member of the Wives for Johnson organization.[22]

Gore had known Kennedy since the young Massachusetts representative was elected to Congress in 1946. But they did not sit on the same committees, and they had no reason to collaborate closely. Their friendship blossomed after Charles Bartlett, the young liberal Washington correspondent from the *Chattanooga Times*, invited Pauline and Albert to a dinner in 1951 to which he also invited his friend Jack Kennedy and a young lady, Jacqueline Bouvier, whom Bartlett thought Jack should get to know. The Gores, the future president, and the first lady were good, if not close, friends from then on. At the start of 1952, they and Kentuckian John Sherman Cooper were together the day Albert, JFK, and Cooper all announced their candidacies for the Senate. They were freshman senators together.[23]

Gore respected Kennedy's thoughtful views on foreign policy, especially after he joined Kennedy on the Foreign Relations Committee in 1959. But as a senator from Massachusetts, Kennedy viewed programs like the TVA as federal subsidies that took industry away from the Northeast. He also voted against Gore's interstate highway bill because he believed its formula for distributing federal funds discriminated against the densely populated urban centers. A certain coolness came into the friendship after Gore's intervention at the 1956 Chicago Democratic convention, which effectively deprived Kennedy of the vice-presidential nomination. Since that setback spared Kennedy the damage of being associated with an overwhelming national election defeat, that coolness did not last long. In 1960 Gore was bound by the unit rule under which the Tennessee delegation operated at the Los Angeles convention, but when Kennedy's vote tally secured him a majority, Gore grabbed the Tennessee banner to join in the pro-Kennedy floor demonstration. Ellington was furious at Johnson's defeat. He was heard to say on the convention floor, "We've just elected a Republican," and most of the delegation left the floor when Kennedy won. Just a handful of Tennesseans joined the exuberant Gore as he waved the state banner.[24]

In Tennessee, Kennedy looked to Kefauver and Gore to set up the campaign but had to work through Ellington and the state organization. Ellington installed his own man, Secretary of State Joe Carr, as the chair. Although the Tennessee senators were largely frozen out from the state campaign, Gore had some national involvement. After his nomination Kennedy asked Gore to head up an advisory committee to provide him with behind-the-scenes policy advice for his campaign speeches. At Gore's insistence Kennedy chose the members of the group: William Fulbright, Clark Clifford (a lawyer and veteran presidential adviser with close ties to both Harry Truman and LBJ), Congressmen Richard Bolling and Fred Dutton. To avoid publicity the group met (usually without Bolling) at Fulbright's house or Gore's apartment at the Fairfax. Gore was responsible for nuclear issues and the economy, Fulbright for foreign policy, and Clifford for defense. Kennedy and Gore had similar criticisms of the Republican administration, citing its passivity regarding the economy and its tolerance of disappointing rates of economic growth. On nuclear weapons Kennedy largely accepted Gore's suggestions that it was worth exploring a test-ban treaty before resuming testing. Gore condemned Nixon for his irresponsible claim, without any evidence, that the Soviets had already resumed testing.[25]

The group's foreign-policy advice is a powerful reminder of how the Democrats and an enthusiastic Kennedy pursued an aggressive Cold War strategy that was committed to global containment. Democrats like Gore chided the Republicans for their inflexible yet lethargic response to the Soviet threat. Their excessive reliance on massive retaliation at the expense of conventional weapons, they argued, left America incapable of responding to low-level insurgencies in the Third World. Their commitment to a balanced budget and their lack of energetic leadership had left U.S. defenses dangerously exposed, most notably by allowing a missile gap that left Americans lagging behind the Soviets. Gore prepared Kennedy's comprehensive rebuttal to Nixon's claims that the nation's global struggle against communism had been successful:

> Within the lifetime of Mr. Nixon Communism was confined to a rented room in Zurich, Switzerland. Today it dominates 40% of the world's people, one-third of its geography, and one-third of its industrial power.
>
> Eight years ago Communism was being contained in Eastern Europe and Southeast Asia. Today its influence has penetrated the Middle East, notably the UAR and Iraq, Laos and Cambodia in Asian, Guinea and Ghana in Africa and Latin America, particularly Cuba.[26]

The text of Kennedy's statements during the televised debates with Nixon show his willingness to amplify several ideas from Gore's advisory group. Gore also advised Kennedy on the specific mechanics of the debates—making sure that Kennedy had a large clock in front of him, used his full allotted time, spoke more slowly, and stared at Nixon to make him nervous. Above all, "Keep hammering away. Sooner or later Nixon will feel the pressure and begin to make mistakes."[27]

Gore was deeply disappointed that Kennedy did not carry Tennessee. Nixon won by more than seventy-five thousand votes, a 7 percent margin. In addition to the mounting Republican support at the presidential level support that had taken Tennessee into the GOP column in 1952 and 1956, anti-Catholicism was still a strong force in 1960. Pollster Louis Harris offered a grim assessment in September 1960. Voters were two to one for Kefauver in the Senate race but 55 percent to 45 percent opposed Kennedy for president. Forty-seven percent of voters said outright that they were disturbed by the prospect of a Catholic president. This represented the highest proportion of opposition anywhere in the country—ten points higher than the sentiment even in Texas. Nixon secured more than ninety thousand more votes than Eisenhower had done in 1956. Gore had never forgotten the virulence of the issue in the campaign against Al Smith in 1928. Protestant ministers in the state inveighed against the Kennedy candidacy. Gore's own mother initially did not see how she could vote for a Catholic in the White House. It took all of Gore's persuasive powers and family loyalty to persuade her to vote for the Democrat. When Joe Hatcher noted in the *Tennessean* that the state had committed the political sin of voting wrong in a national victory, Gore said that he believed the religious issue was the key to the Tennessee vote.[28]

Gore had high hopes for the new administration. He was not part of Kennedy's inner circle, but he had access to the president, who encouraged him to stay in touch. Kennedy was prepared to listen to Gore at length, even when he was unpersuaded of either the political or policy stance Gore was advocating. Gore had long one-on-one sessions with Kennedy over economic policy, attended private family dinners in the White House, and was encouraged by Kennedy, behind the scenes, to put forward policies the president himself could not afford to articulate. Gore appreciated the president's willingness to listen, his wit, and his candor. He was a fierce defender of the president. But he was fated to be disappointed by many of Kennedy's actions. Gore was convinced that Kennedy was constrained by conservative advisers and the narrowness of his 1960 electoral victory. He retained the conviction that, reelected safely in 1964, his friend would be free to pursue liberal policies more to Gore's liking in the second term.[29]

⤺

THERE WAS SOME talk that Gore would be appointed secretary of the treasury. John Kenneth Galbraith certainly favored the choice of a liberal like Paul Douglas or Gore. The prospect of Gore's appointment alarmed the publisher of the *Washington Post*, Phil Graham. But there was never any real chance that Gore would be chosen. However conventional Kennedy might be, the business community suspected that he and the intellectuals close to him, like Galbraith and Arthur Schlesinger, were dangerously radical and antibusiness. Richard Neustadt, the political scientist who advised Kennedy on the presidential transition, stressed the importance of a treasury secretary who would reassure the markets. Neustadt believed Douglas Dillon, a moderate Republican and Wall Street investment broker, would reassure the financial community.[30]

Gore was appalled at what a Dillon appointment might mean for Kennedy's economic policy. Instead of the economic stimulus that Gore believed necessary, and which Kennedy had argued for during the campaign, Dillon's approach represented a policy of fiscal retrenchment and tight money: cuts in government spending and high interest rates. Gore laid out his arguments in a letter to Kennedy on 22 November and was summoned to the president-elect's Georgetown house for a two-hour one-on-one discussion. Gore argued that the government needed revenue to meet the country's infrastructure and social needs. The Federal Reserve needed to be reined in. It should operate the mechanics of the banking system, not formulate national economic policy. Monetary policy should be coordinated with fiscal, economic, debt-management, foreign and related policies. Dillon, he believed, was the wrong man to do that: "He was right out of Wall Street then." He was, Gore later conceded, an able, honorable gentleman, personally likable. But "his views on monetary policy, tax policy, are on all fours with the views of Andrew Mellon, Secretary of the Treasury, under Herbert Hoover."[31]

If monetary policy was not available as an economic stimulus, then that left fiscal policy. Gore advocated government spending to prime the pump. He believed that would provide a greater stimulus than a tax cut, which "primed the wrong pumps." He strongly advocated for tax reform to close revenue loopholes and end tax policies that favored the rich. He doubted Dillon could deliver tax reform. Kennedy responded that Congress was opposed to pump-priming and that Stuart Surrey, the new assistant secretary of the treasury, would deliver that tax reform. But Gore believed that the policies Kennedy felt constrained to advocate would inhibit an adequate policy for full employment, economic growth, and investment in education. Over the next three years, these arguments would be repeated. At times Kennedy's and Gore's priorities in economic policy coalesced, but on the major questions of spending, tax reform, and tax cuts, they did not. After the assassination Dillon lamented the fact that Gore had opposed him from the start and had not let up. He told John Seigenthaler that he admired Gore as a fine senator and did not understand his hostility. Seigenthaler explained to him that Gore was "a protégé of Cordell Hull and that in the part of the country that he came from, there was no such thing as a Republican in whom you could place absolute trust."[32]

In 1961 Gore fought a fairly lonely campaign against both Dillon and tax policy that favored big business. He denounced the Treasury decision to raise the ceiling on the interest rate for government bonds: He doubted the executive had the authority to do so. He had previously opposed such a move in the Eisenhower administration. Higher rates would trickle down to penalize small businesses and homeowners. He also campaigned against the stock-option schemes that companies like IBM operated for its senior executives.

They were paid bonuses in stock options. If the share price rose, they had the option to buy at the original, lower price. They were not taxed on the profit they made. Similarly, he campaigned against a bill providing special tax relief for DuPont shareholders for the income they received when the company was forced to divest shares in General Motors after a court order mandated divestiture. As so often, Gore saw himself in the role of David fighting Goliath: "I am really attacking the giant of giants. They have succeeded in misleading the vast majority of our people who are cognizant of the issues and most of the U.S. Congress about the contents and purposes of the bill."[33]

In August 1961 Gore aroused the further ire of the business community when he announced in the Senate that he saw no reason why the steel industry should raise its prices if the United Steel Workers negotiated a wage increase. The steel industry already colluded to set its prices; there was no economic case for passing on increased costs to the consumers. That fall and winter the Kennedy administration worked hard to persuade the steelworkers to moderate their wage demands in order to reduce inflationary pressures. On 10 April 1962 Gore had a message to phone the White House. Kennedy was incandescent that Roger Blough of US Steel had phoned to inform him that, notwithstanding the trade union restraint, the steel companies were going to increase their prices. Kennedy wanted Gore to stir up opposition to the steel companies in the Senate.[34]

Gore called staff in to work through the night drafting ten or twelve short speeches that could be delivered the next day on the Senate floor. At a congressional reception he lined up the senators who would speak. On 11 April some thirty senators condemned the steel companies. Five days later Gore introduced bills that would broaden powers under the Sherman Antitrust Act to punish collusive price-fixing; establish a national consumers' advisory board as a fact-finding body to examine price increases; and amend the Taft–Hartley Act to allow the president to mandate an eighty-day cooling-off period for price increases on basic commodities. The combined weight of presidential and congressional opposition forced the steel companies to back down.[35]

But Gore and the administration were not always singing from the same song sheet on monopolistic practices. Gore's Tennessee colleague Estes Kefauver chaired the Senate Commerce Committee's subcommittee on antitrust and monopoly; its well-publicized hearings were a vehicle for fierce denunciations of business practices in industry after industry. In 1962 Gore and Kefauver reacted angrily to a proposal by Senator Robert Kerr that the new satellite-communications industry—made possible by developments in space technology—should basically be in private hands. In neither the Commerce Committee nor the Foreign Relations Committee could the Tennessee senators derail a compromise proposal for a private-public partnership in the new Communications Satellite Corporation, COMSAT. Joined by Russell Long and Ernest Gruening, they took their case to the floor of the Senate in a liberal filibuster, charging that the complex regulatory procedure laid down in the bill would simply benefit AT&T and the other communications giants. It was a measure of Gore and Kefauver's outsider status that the Senate leadership and the administration were able to secure what the leadership signally had failed to do on the issue of civil rights: the first successful cloture vote to cut off debate in decades.[36]

Kennedy and Gore were nevertheless on the same wavelength on tax reform in 1962, but the legislative results were disappointing. Kennedy was worried about the deficit in the balance of payments. He was concerned about the export of jobs and capital, which he saw as linked to the tax breaks Americans received abroad such as the preferential treatment of income earned abroad and the existence of tax havens. Paul Douglas of Illinois and Gore worked closely together on the Finance Committee to eliminate tax loopholes and make the tax system fairer. Douglas recalled that Gore was an "ideal colleague." But they were usually defeated in the Finance Committee by 11 votes to 5, and then again on the floor of the Senate. Douglas, in particular, sought to collect taxes on the interest of stocks and bonds by withholding the taxes at their source. As Gore explained, "Individuals are still failing to report about $3 billion of dividend income and about $19 billion of interest income annually." It was not fair to withhold taxes from the salary of a workingman but not individuals receiving unearned income from dividends and interest. Douglas estimated that a billion dollars of additional tax revenue could be raised by taxing interest at the source.[37]

Instead the administration acquiesced in a requirement that financial institutions name individuals receiving such income to the IRS—a measure that raised only $250 million. Gore concentrated on overseas loopholes: He tried to tax the income of foreign subsidiaries of U.S. corporations and that of U.S. citizens living abroad. He lamented his failure to get a sufficiently stringent bill from the Finance Committee: "The only effective bill, in my view, is one which would subject United States taxpayers to taxation annually on the income and profits which they earn abroad through any type of activity or business organization. Such a rule is necessary in the interest of tax equity, maintaining the strength of our domestic economy, and assisting in the reduction of the current deficit in the balance of payments." At home he sought to eliminate expense-account abuses, and he wanted to tax pension lump sums, which he saw as a form of deferred compensation and therefore a way of avoiding income tax. Congress opted for an exemption of $30,000; Gore wanted to lower that to $6,000. In a foretaste of alliances to come, Douglas and Gore joined with conservative Harry Byrd of Virginia in unsuccessfully opposing an investment tax credit for business, which Byrd thought irresponsible at a time of budget deficits. Gore viewed the tax credit as "basically unsound" and an "unnecessary giveaway." Senator John Williams, a Republican from Delaware committed to transparent tax and spending regimes, was supported by Gore and Douglas when he tried, but failed, to reduce gas and oil depletion allowances. Overall Gore was disappointed by the results of tax reform in 1962. He felt that "the Kennedy Administration had not pushed for adoption of its own tax recommendations as strenuously as I did."[38]

Gore believed the Kennedy administration had been too cautious on tax reform, but soon the issue of how best to secure economic growth put the president and Gore on a collision course. Kennedy was acutely aware that recessions and sluggish growth had cost the Eisenhower administration and the Republicans dearly in the midterms of 1954 and 1958, and in the 1960 presidential election. During the 1960 campaign Kennedy had promised to get the country's economy moving again. The slow pace of economic recovery disturbed him during the first two years of his administration. He knew he needed "boom times" in 1964 to secure reelection. Kennedy's Council of Economic Advisers under Walter Heller advocated a substantial tax cut to stimulate the economy despite the budget deficit. They argued that the current tax regime exercised a "fiscal drag" on the economy, which greatly lessened the stimulating "multiplier" effect of government spending. What was new about this argument was that tax cuts historically followed budget surpluses. The aim was to balance the budget to pave the way for tax reductions. Here the administration was arguing that it should cut taxes despite the budget deficit. If the tax cut worked, it would secure economic growth, which would raise, not reduce, the total tax revenues.

Kennedy's ideas for a tax cut aroused opposition from two very different sources. Wilbur Mills, powerful chairman of the House Ways and Means Committee, was reluctant to give up revenue when the budget was unbalanced. Businessmen, so used to advocating for cuts to government spending to balance the budget, reflexively agreed. From the left, Gore's old ally in the price control battles of World War II, John Kenneth Galbraith, advised the president against a tax cut. What was needed, Galbraith argued, was tax reform. Tax cuts benefited those who needed it the least and were less likely to spend and increase consumer demand.

Gore instinctively agreed with Galbraith and argued strongly against a tax cut. Kennedy wanted to bring his friend around (and also, characteristically, wanted to hear counter-arguments). At Eleanor Roosevelt's funeral at Hyde Park, New York, on 10 November 1962, Kennedy stopped to talk at length to Gore, oblivious to the number of people anxious to talk to the president. When Gore joined other senators on the plane to return to Washington, an army jeep crossed the airfield; a messenger emerged and requested—to the derision of Gore's colleagues—that he join the president on Air Force One. On the flight back to Washington, the two debated the pros and cons.[39]

Kennedy told Gore that he had to have economic prosperity by 1964. Gore's advice was simple—spend. Kennedy, he said, should forget about a tax cut. Kennedy argued that Congress would not tolerate "pump-priming" spending. Gore retorted that a tax cut would unleash economic forces that would make it impossible to have a proper spending program again. Once taxes were cut Congress would never vote to reintroduce them. Proper tax reform, he predicted, would be impossible with a tax cut. He followed up, laying out his arguments in a letter to Kennedy on 15 November. A tax cut would set off a "howling campaign for reductions in expenditure." It would put the Kennedy administration "in an economic straitjacket," adversely affect foreign aid, and, most important, preclude any stimulus through public works. Those with large incomes would increase their take-home pay by between 50 and 200 percent. By contrast, lower-income earners would see an increase of at most 3 to 5 percent. He pleaded that the tax cut "simply cannot be justified—socially, economically, or politically. And I hold these sentiments passionately! This is something no Republican administration has dared do; it is something you must not do."[40]

Kennedy was unmoved. In his State of the Union address in 1963, he announced that the United States had an "obsolete tax system [which] exerts too heavy a drag on private purchasing power, profits, and employment." He proposed cutting individual income tax by $11 billion by reducing rates from the 20 to 91 percent range to that of 14 to 65 percent. In reducing the tax on corporations by $2.5 billion, Kennedy would reduce the corporate tax rate from 52 to 47 percent.[41]

Gore remained unconvinced. In light of the federal budget deficit, it made no sense to him to reduce government revenue. He continued to believe that spending would produce a greater stimulus than a tax cut: "a dollar of Federal spending generates more economic activity than does a dollar of tax cuts." When quizzed by White House assistant Arthur M. Schlesinger, Jr. about his opposition to the tax cut, Gore said he was an "old New Dealer—an old Populist who believed there were social imperatives that needed to be met which only government can provide."[42]

Gore acknowledged to Schlesinger that not many in the Senate shared his view. But he pointed out that he drew the greatest applause in Tennessee when he opposed the tax cut. As he admitted, the people who applauded him opposed the tax cut for reasons different from Gore's: They wanted to cut government spending. That was the national problem for Kennedy; he had to win over not the Gores of the world but businessmen.

It was not surprising that the tax bill was tied up for the best part of nine months in the House Ways and Means Committee chaired by Wilbur Mills. When it was finally prised out of the House, the Senate Finance Committee was in no mood to speed it on its way. For the conservatives Chairman Harry Byrd much preferred cutting federal spending. Liberals like Gore and Douglas rued the absence of any tax reform. Douglas approved the tax cut but told Treasury Secretary Dillon, "If this bill gets any worse, it is going to be very difficult for some of us to vote for it. It is going to be very difficult for some of us to vote for it as it is." Gore had no intention of rubber-stamping the House bill. Since the House bill did not close the loopholes Gore and Douglas had long identified and had tried to eradicate in 1962, the bill would increase the deficit. He was determined to continue to oppose it.[43]

Gore made it clear that he would continue to oppose the whole bill by "whatever means I can use." It might not be profitable to oppose a tax cut in an election year, but according to Gore the bill was "so unsound, so unprecedented and, I think, dangerous" that he had no alternative. The bill was "so horribly contrary to the public interest." He conceded to congressman Joe Evins that it was difficult to vote at odds with the entire Tennessee delegation, but "overall I consider it the most important single bill that I have dealt with since I have been in Congress and by all odds the worst."[44]

Gore joined the conservatives on the Finance Committee to insist on extensive hearings. He put down detailed amendments to try and resurrect the reforms that had failed in 1962. He sharply questioned Douglas Dillon about the bill. He did not let up. Kennedy was exasperated that his old friend was so obstructive. The president repeatedly called Gore a "son of a bitch" at a meeting with his advisers Dillon and Under Secretary of the Treasury Henry

Fowler on 30 September. "What did Albert Gore think he is up to?" was a question White House officials pondered. Kennedy noted, "If we get a good recession next summer, it's not going to do him [Gore] much good is it?" For his part Gore was incensed when a Democratic National Committee staffer tried to pressure Gore by planting and stories in the local Tennessee press to embarrass the senator, declaring, "Now is the time for Construction not obstruction." Gore was bitter that the administration had gone after him when it made no effort to coerce Robert Kerr or George Smathers for failing to toe the line. Mike Manatos, White House assistant for Senate Liaison, concluded: "We have softened Gore up. [But] we have a long way to go."[45]

ᔕ

ON THE EVE of Kennedy's assassination, the future of his tax cut was uncertain. Gore had contributed in no small measure to the stalemate in Congress over the president's proposals. The other great policy stalemate was over the president's civil rights proposals. Here Gore was not a major obstacle. He kept his head down, but, as with the tax cut and Vietnam, he was not giving any assistance to his friend in the White House on civil rights.

John Kennedy entered office determined to avoid sending troops into the South and to refrain from introducing coercive civil rights legislation. He was conscious of the blocking power of Southern segregationists in Congress and did not want to harm the prospects of economic and social legislation, such as an increase in the minimum wage, which would benefit African Americans as well as other low-income Americans. He put his faith instead in bolder executive actions (notably in the Justice Department headed by his brother) and in moderate Southern community leaders who he believed could be actively encouraged to lead their communities into accepting racial change.

But direct action by African Americans and an intransigent Southern white response severely limited Kennedy's policy options and forced him to do the two things he did not want to do: Send troops into the South and introduce meaningful civil rights legislation. The mobs at the University of Mississippi in the fall of 1962 forced him to send in federal troops to rescue the U.S. marshals and secure the court-ordered admission of James Meredith to Ole Miss. The police dogs and fire hoses that greeted children and civil rights protesters at Birmingham in May 1963 made him look for ways to avoid a summer of Birminghams and get black protesters off the streets and into the courts. The federal government successfully faced down Governor George Wallace of Alabama and secured the admission of two African Americans to the University of Alabama at Tuscaloosa. Kennedy took the opportunity to go on national television and call for civil rights legislation that would end segregation in public accommodations, allow the attorney general to initiate school desegregation lawsuits, and eliminate discrimination in employment.[46]

Like other Southern moderates Gore was ill equipped to cope with a new order in which African Americans dictated the timetable of racial change. He was shielded from the increasing impatience of blacks in Tennessee because he rarely dealt directly and personally with African American leaders, particularly the new generation of young leaders. He was largely silent on the challenges posed by the Freedom Rides, the Albany Movement, and Birmingham. These confrontations had to be dealt with by governors in other states and by the executive branch in Washington. Gore was comfortable with the very cautious approach of the Kennedy administration on civil rights legislation.

When Kennedy felt obliged to call for strong civil rights legislation, Gore was careful and noncommittal. He acknowledged the rights of all citizens to equal justice and treatment under the law. He conceded that more needed to be done, even if more progress had been made in Tennessee than elsewhere, thanks to local community leadership that operated with minimal discord and disturbance. He also agreed that the federal government properly had a role in ending discrimination. But he reserved the right to scrutinize carefully the far-reaching scope of Kennedy's proposals. What he explicitly hoped for was a repeat of 1957 and 1960: the sort of face-saving compromises and clarifications that would water down a civil rights bill and enable him to support it. But, he told his constituents, he was unable to forecast whether this would be the case.[47]

Gore had reason to be cautious. Overwhelmingly his correspondence ran against the civil rights bill. African Americans, his constituents argued, were blackmailing the federal government through violent protests organized by professional agitators and communists that bordered on anarchism. In particular constituents pinpointed the threat to the free-enterprise system through the public accommodations and employment provisions that would tell businessmen who they could and could not serve. As in 1957 segregationists complained that Gore and Kefauver were not joining the Southern bloc in devising strategies to defeat the bill.[48]

There is some evidence that the Kennedy administration was prepared to water down its proposals, particularly on employment, in order to break the deadlock in November 1963 over the civil rights proposals. It is possible that Gore might have been able to support the bill. But even before Kennedy's death, John Seigenthaler believed that Gore was suffering from "Goldwater fever," a fear that the resurgent right in Tennessee would produce a white backlash that a candidate like Goldwater could exploit to win the state. When Lyndon Johnson became president, the national political imperatives and LBJ's personal inclination, just as segregationists like James Eastland feared, made him unwilling to compromise on civil rights in any way that might let Gore off the hook. Finally, Gore was shocked and saddened by the sudden death, on 10 August 1963, of his fellow Tennessee senator, Estes Kefauver. Kefauver suffered a heart attack that proved fatal on the Senate floor as he and Gore were trying to amend a NASA authorization bill. They wanted to require that the private, profit-making communications satellite corporation (COMSAT) reimburse NASA for the cost of research and development from which COMSAT had benefitted. While Gore and Kefauver were not close personal friends, they had been long-time liberal political allies in Tennessee. They each offered the other a measure of political protection, especially on civil rights. Kefauver was replaced in the Senate by Herbert S. Walters, former ally and confidant of Senator McKellar and Boss Crump. Gore thereafter would be a more isolated liberal figure in Tennessee.[49]

GORE SAW TWO of the defining crises of the Kennedy presidency in close-up: the Bay of Pigs debacle in 1961 and the Cuban Missile Crisis in 1962. Gore was Kennedy's first appointment the day after the collapse of the Bay of Pigs invasion. Kennedy, Gore recalled, was very agitated: His tie was askew, his hair disheveled, and he talked too fast. The president excoriated the chairman of the Joint Chiefs of Staff, General Lyman Lemnitzer. Kennedy had refused to authorize the air support the general demanded to rescue the mission, air support the general had previously promised would not be necessary. When word filtered out to Gore that Lemnitzer had been forced to acknowledge his mistake in a closed session of the Foreign Relations Committee, Gore called for his resignation. Unable to cite that testimony or his White House conversation, Gore had to stand alone and accept the criticism laid at him in the press for undermining the military while Kennedy publicly proclaimed his trust in the chairman.[50]

The lessons Kennedy learned about uncritically accepting the advice of the military in part shaped his handling of the Cuban Missile Crisis eighteen months later. Gore represented the president's more calibrated approach to this later crisis in the United Nations, where Gore was the one of two senators appointed to the U.S. delegation in 1962–63. Overall Gore admired Kennedy's handling of foreign policy. He approved of the combination of Cold War determination on the one hand and flexibility on the other in seeking areas of accommodation with the Soviets. He supported a foreign-aid policy that focused on economic rather than military aid, and did not demonize neutral and third-world countries for their failure unquestioningly to espouse routine anticommunist policies.[51]

Gore succeeded Kennedy as chair of the Senate Foreign Relations Subcommittee on Africa. For the first and perhaps only time, Africa loomed large on an American government's agenda. Nowhere was the rising tide of nationalism more evident than in Africa, where some of the most brutal European colonial regimes had operated. Africa was the acid test of Kennedy's desire to refashion a new foreign policy that pursued the Cold War in a more sophisticated way. Resolution and military strength would contain the Soviet Union in Europe and maintain a status quo. Where the Cold War was more likely to be won and lost was in the third world. Kennedy argued that, to win the hearts and minds of newly independent countries, it was essential not to confuse nationalism and communism. The United States needed to acknowledge the right of newly independent nations to be nonaligned. Economic assistance was not to be dependent on countries' willingness to toe the line in the super-power conflict.

Africa had been an issue in the 1960 campaign. Once in office Kennedy appointed a committed liberal, G. Mennen Williams, as assistant secretary of state for African affairs and sought to make Africa a desirable posting for ambitious foreign service officers. Kennedy and Williams decisively tilted U.S. policy away from its Eurocentric concerns by resolutely opposing European colonialism, particularly Portugal's rule of its African colonies. Increased aid to Africa with no Cold War strings attached would be supported by the new Peace Corps, which sought volunteers to serve in Africa in particular. Both Kennedy and Williams went out of their way to establish personal relations with the African heads of state. Gore supported this strategy, which was based on acceptance of African neutrality, the promise of invigorated aid, and an end to deference to the old colonial powers.[52]

In 1961 liberal Senators Philip Hart and Maurine Neuberger accompanied Gore on a thirty-day visit to fifteen countries. The two most important stops were in Leopoldville, Congo, and Accra, Ghana. In the chaos of post-independence Congo, the Americans were troubled by the secession of mineral-rich Katanga, a secession supported by the Belgians and by a powerful lobby in the United States which particularly appealed to Southern segrega-tionists. But the United States also had to cope with a power vacuum left by the murder of President Patrice Lumumba, who the Americans feared had tilted his country increasingly toward Moscow. The Kennedy administration supported the UN invasion of Katanga: Whereas Kennedy had expressed lit-tle enthusiasm for the initial UN military action, he now recognized the need to support the UN and the central Congo government after the death of Sec-retary-General Dag Hammarskjöld. (Hammarskjöld had been killed when his plane was shot down—probably by Katanga mercenaries—while on his way to negotiate a ceasefire between the UN and the Katanga military.) The U.S. hoped to counter Lumumba's legacy as a Cold War martyr and to curb the power of his follower, Vice President Antoine Gizenga. The administra-tion instead backed Cyrille Adoula as president—a labor leader who aimed both to unite Congo and to contain the Lumumbist vice president.

When Gore and his colleagues reached Leopoldville, they were briefed by Ambassador Edmund Gullion, one of the most accomplished of the new breed of foreign service officers in Africa, and also by someone Gore knew well from Tennessee, young David Halberstam. Halberstam had been a reporter for the *Tennessean* in Nashville but, like many of his colleagues, had moved to the *New York Times*, where he was assigned to the Republic of Congo. The visiting senators were the first American politicians to meet Adoula, and they came away "deeply impressed." They viewed him as even more skilled than Tangan-yika's Julius Nyerere or Kenya's Jomo Kenyatta. The delegation's support for a united Congo and for the UN action in Katanga "genuinely heartened" both Adoula and the UN, according to Ambassador Gullion. It offset the impact of the pro-secessionist speeches of Senator Thomas Dodd of Connecticut, who had acted as a mouthpiece for the pro-Katanga lobby.[53]

In Accra Gore was less impressed by Ghana's Kwame Nkrumah. Gore believed that Nkrumah was a repressive ruler who strongly leaned toward the Soviet Union and China. Despite this negative assessment in Ghana, the del-egation overall had a positive view of both their trip and the administration's enlightened foreign policy, which they believed was winning the battle against communism. The senators noted two caveats: They warned against awarding aid to countries that did not respect basic human rights, and while they un-derstood that new nations wanted to avoid the Cold War, they believed these nations needed to be more than principled bystanders. The denial of human rights in East Germany ought to resonate with the African nations as much as the denial of rights in Algeria and Angola. The delegation strongly supported the Peace Corps against the criticisms of former president Eisenhower, who saw it as an unpopular juvenile experiment. To the contrary, Gore asserted, African countries wanted more Peace Corps volunteers. Indeed, it was better to send Peace Corps teachers to Africa, the senators argued, than to bring African students to the United States.[54]

The one area where Gore was unsympathetic to the reorientation of Africa policy was in Ghana. Should the United States continue with the Volta Dam hydroelectric policy? Gore doubted the wisdom of underwriting the increasingly dictatorial Nkrumah regime. He believed the erratic leader was lurching to the left. Many of Kennedy's advisers shared his concerns, but Kennedy was persuaded by more conservative African leaders and the British, who believed that refusal to fund the project would effectively drive Nkrumah into the arms of the Soviets.[55]

~

ON ANOTHER MAJOR foreign policy issue—the nuclear test-ban treaty—Gore's influence on administration policy was weak owing to his long-running feud with LBJ. The 1963 test-ban treaty Kennedy successfully concluded with the Soviet Union banned tests in the atmosphere, underwater, and in space. Such a partial treaty, which avoided the difficult issue of inspection of underground tests, was the culmination of the ideas put forward by Gore after his experiences in Geneva in 1958. Yet from 1961 onward Vice President Johnson had effectively sidelined Gore from influencing administration policy on nuclear tests. If Johnson had been disposed to forget Gore's challenge at the Democratic Senate conference in 1960, he had no intention of forgetting Gore's attack on the vice president-elect at the Democratic conference on 4 January 1961.

In December 1960 Senate liberals reportedly had been mapping their way to gain greater influence in the new administration with a new majority leader, the studious and consensus-building Mike Mansfield. Paul Douglas and Joseph Clark consulted with William Proxmire, Wayne Morse, and Gore. They sought increased representation on the steering and policy committees, especially for the Northern and Western wings of the party.[56]

If they thought they had rid themselves of the hated control of Lyndon Johnson, they were in for a rude awakening when the new Democratic conference met on 4 January 1961. The new majority leader Mansfield proposed that the new vice president LBJ chair future Democratic conferences. He argued that he was following the precedent established when Alben Barkley became vice president under Harry Truman. Barkley, like LBJ, had previously been minority and majority leader of the Democrats in the Senate. Gore was furious. It was a bad precedent, and the new majority leader should not be permitted to give up his powers. It violated the principle of separation of powers. "We might as well ask Jack [President-elect Kennedy] to come back and take his turn at presiding," said Gore afterward. What was different in 1961 was not merely that Gore was supported by liberals like Joseph Clark but that protests also came from senior senators like Clinton Anderson and Dennis Chavez and from Southerners like Spessard Holland. There was no doubt, however, that it was Gore who attracted the most publicity and who was angriest. Flushed, he spoke with the unguarded, pent-up passion of someone who assumed Lyndon Johnson would never again be in a position of power over his future. If Kennedy served two terms, Johnson would no longer be a force to be reckoned with in the Senate by 1968. A compromise was grudgingly passed at the conference whereby the vice president could be invited to attend all conference and caucus meetings and could be invited to preside. Embarrassed by the evident hostility, a furious Johnson did not take advantage of this compromise offer. The next day Gore was defeated on his proposal to a have the conference nominate members of the policy and steering committees. Kennedy telephoned Gore the day after the conference to say that he had done the right thing, but Johnson's revenge would be swift.[57]

When Kennedy convened a lunch meeting at the White House in March to discuss nuclear-testing policy, Gore was present to discuss whether the United States needed to resume testing, as Eisenhower had urged, whether the Soviets were cheating, and how many inspections should or could be agreed to with the Soviets. Gore agreed with Clinton Anderson about the need to be realistic regarding what the Soviets might agree to. Gore was in Geneva at the start of April for an Interparliamentary Union meeting and sat in on the disarmament talks. But on 5 May David Halberstam revealed in the *New York Times* that LBJ had stripped Gore of his appointment as Senate adviser to the U.S. delegation to Geneva. It was one of Johnson's more petty moves, removing one of the Senate's leading authorities on nuclear testing. It was also rare for a vice president to remove a senator who had been appointed in the previous Senate, but Mike Mansfield noted that Johnson, as presiding officer, had the authority to do so. In addition, it was difficult to argue that LBJ's nominee, Hubert Humphrey, chair of the disarmament subcommittee of the Foreign Relations Committee, was an inappropriate choice.

In vain Adrian Fisher, who became deputy director of the U.S. Arms Control and Disarmament Agency in 1961 and would be taking a major role in the test-ban treaty negotiations, tried to persuade Johnson to keep Gore. Fisher was born in Memphis; he had served as a law clerk to Justice Brandeis and as general counsel to the Atomic Energy Commission in 1948–49, where he got to know fellow Tennessean Gore when the congressman oversaw the AEC for the House Appropriations Committee. Fisher served as legal adviser to Secretary of State Dean Acheson. He admired both Johnson and Gore. But he recognized that, from LBJ's point of view, Gore was a difficult man to control; as soon as he raised the matter with Johnson, he realized it was a hopeless cause. Gore was at the White House again when Kennedy convened a meeting on 31 August 1961 to discuss the Russian resumption of nuclear testing. There, Gore reiterated his hard-nosed view of the Soviets: He believed their goal was world intimidation, and that they wanted to break the world's—and particularly Western Europe's—will to resist them. But he also retained his realistic view. He favored delaying announcement of the resumption of American tests and saw no need for alarm, since the United States had a superior stockpile of weapons. From then on Gore had little to do with U.S. policy-making on nuclear weapons during the Kennedy years.[58]

⌐

GORE HAD HAD little direct influence on the negotiations that led up to the test-ban treaty, but he was convinced that Kennedy was moving in the right direction. On Vietnam, Gore was convinced that the president was moving in the wrong direction. But he had equally little influence there.

Kennedy had inherited a worsening situation in Vietnam. The Americans had essentially taken over responsibility for supporting the South Vietnam regime after the Geneva conference, which had ended French involvement in Indochina. The Eisenhower administration had supported an independent South Vietnam, rather than have elections in the North and South, which they feared would hand over all of Vietnam to North Vietnam. The nationalist Ngo Dinh Diem regime in the south represented a Catholic elite and found itself increasingly facing a rural insurgency. The regime was covertly assisted by the United States. In neighboring Laos, where there was similar communist insurgency, one of Kennedy's first decisions was to not support Laos militarily but to start negotiations for a neutralized Laos. Kennedy's advisers were convinced that they could not afford a similar settlement in South Vietnam. Insurgency, which they interpreted as aggression from the communist north rather than as a domestic civil war, had to be resisted. Kennedy refused demands to send troops in to shore up the south, but he did send advisers—more than 15,000 by the time he died—who could assist the south. Kennedy believed that economic and technical assistance and special forces could together defeat a war of national liberation or a rural insurgency.

Gore was skeptical from the start. In 1954, as the French faced defeat, Gore had his staff provide background material on Indochina. Their findings led him and three other senators to meet with Lyndon Johnson and advise against U.S. military intervention at a time when the French were desperately seeking American air strikes to lift the siege of Dien Bien Phu. The four senators waited in the Democratic cloakroom as Johnson and congressional leaders were summoned to meet Secretary of State John Foster Dulles and the Joint Chiefs. When Johnson returned, as Gore recalled, he "gave us in the Johnson-manner, a vivid muscular and athletic recounting of the meeting. . . . He outlined his opposition and told us that he pounded the President's desk in the Oval Office to emphasize his opposition." The lack of congressional support doomed the proposal for air strikes. Most of Gore's constituents in Tennessee who wrote to him also opposed American intervention. Gore agreed that "it would be as disaster of great magnitude if we were to become directly involved in the fighting in the Indo-China area." But he did hope the Geneva conference would find some solution to the problem that "would not impose communist slavery upon the millions of people in Southeast Asia."[59]

Gore's skepticism about American policy in Vietnam was compounded by a visit he and Senator Gale McGee of Wyoming made to the country in December 1959. This was part of a two-month trip on behalf of the Senate Foreign Relations Committee, focused on examining allegations of corruption in the foreign-aid program. They visited the Middle East and India to examine the refugee problems and aid programs. But Gore had also planned a personal investigation of the administration of the aid program in Vietnam.[60]

In the years since 1954, the United States had essentially taken over from the French the role of sustaining an anticommunist South Vietnam. U.S. government officials strongly supported Ngo Dinh Diem as the ideal embodiment of an anti-communist leader. He had impeccable nationalist credentials, was a devout Catholic, and was apparently committed to reform, working with American advisers from Michigan State University led by Wesley Fishel to modernize Vietnam's economy and governance. In the United States he had been lionized by Catholic politicians like John Kennedy and Mike Mansfield, both when he was in exile and when he returned as president of South Vietnam. In 1957 Mansfield described Diem as "a man of the people; a man whom the Vietnamese admire and trust; and a man in whom the United States has unbounded confidence and great faith." Although Mansfield had to focus on domestic politics as Senate Democratic whip after 1958, he saw himself as the Senate's expert on South Vietnam and guardian of Diem's interests. The views of Mansfield, a former professor of Far Eastern history, carried great weight with the Foreign Relations Committee, and with the Eisenhower and Kennedy administrations.[61]

Gore had no such personal background in Vietnam, and Mansfield was worried that a clumsy intervention into the affairs of the Vietnamese by visiting senators would arouse "proper and indignant criticism." Mansfield was anxious that the senators should understand they were simply investigating American administration of the aid program. When Fulbright, as chair of the Foreign Relations Committee, authorized funding for the visit, he made clear the protocols that Mansfield had laid down: All statements by the visitors should make clear that they were investigating only administration of American programs, not the internal affairs of Vietnam; official inquiries should be only to American citizens; informal contacts with Vietnamese should be made with discretion; and meetings with Vietnamese officials should be guided by the embassy and arranged by embassy staff.[62]

But Gore and McGee arrived at a crucial time in the evolution of the relationship between the Diem regime and the American government. They arrived at the beginning of the Year of the Rat, the cumulative effect of which, according to Ronald Bruce Frankum, Jr., would become clear only with Diem's assassination in 1963. There was a fundamental disagreement within the U.S. team in Vietnam. Ambassador Elbridge Durbrow despaired of the increasingly authoritarian and corrupt Diem regime. A reign of terror had blighted land reform in the countryside. Dissent in Saigon had been snuffed out. He regarded the "miracle" that Diem had achieved—which had been celebrated in the United States—as a mirage. But the head of the Military Assistance Advisory Group, Samuel Williams, had close personal ties with Diem. He saw him as the only Vietnamese leader capable of delivering the modernization that he and the experts from Michigan State were trying to implement. There was little love lost between Williams and Durbrow. Williams regarded the ambassador as "better suited to be a senior salesman in a good ladies shoe store than to be representing the U.S. in an Asian country."[63]

Gore and McGee spent five days in Vietnam. They met Diem, the secretary of state, and the leader and president of the National Assembly. They apparently praised their work. But Gore criticized Diem in a media briefing afterward. Gore found some "basic faults and irregularities," especially in the way the South Vietnamese spent matching funds that had not been audited

FIGURE 1. Inspired by a traveling fiddler, Albert Gore pestered his parents to buy him a fiddle. In his first campaign for Congress in 1938 friends persuaded him to interrupt his speeches and play. His playing helped draw crowds and gave him recognition in a multicandidate field.
Courtesy Albert Gore Research Center.

FIGURE 2. Pauline LaFon was one of the earliest female graduates from Vanderbilt University. Albert Gore fell in love with her when she was working as a waitress in the Nashville YMCA and he was studying law at night school. They married in 1937. Perhaps the most natural politician in the Gore family, Pauline was Gore's closest political adviser for the rest of his life.
Courtesy Albert Gore Research Center.

FIGURE 3. Albert Gore made his
first impact in Washington with a
passionate conservative denunciation of the administration's
Housing Bill in 1939.
Courtesy Albert Gore Research Center.

FIGURE 4. Mike Monroney of Oklahoma, Wilbur Mills of Arkansas,
and Albert Gore were elected in 1938 to the House of Representatives. Monroney would become Gore's closest political friend in
Washington and would go to the Senate in 1950. Mills stayed in the
House and became the dominant congressman on all tax matters as
chair of the Ways and Means Committee. Gore as a member of the
Senate Finance Committee usually had a much more liberal position
on tax matters. *Courtesy Albert Gore Research Center.*

FIGURE 5. For all his suspicions of big business and corporate leaders, Albert Gore admired some businessmen like Bernard Baruch and Armand Hammer. Baruch and Gore shared a common belief in a more comprehensive and coercive price control wartime legislation than the Roosevelt administration proposed. Baruch and Gore flattered each other and maintained close contact throughout the 1940s and early 1950s. *Courtesy Albert Gore Research Center.*

FIGURE 6. Albert Gore on a tractor with wife, Pauline, and children, Nancy and Al. He never lost his pleasure in working on his farm in Carthage. *Courtesy Albert Gore Research Center.*

FIGURE 7. In 1970 Gore still campaigned in the traditional way, above "on the stump" at a rally in Memphis in his primary campaign against Hudley Crockett. In the general election he would supplement his old-style campaigning with expensively filmed television ads. *Courtesy Albert Gore Research Center.*

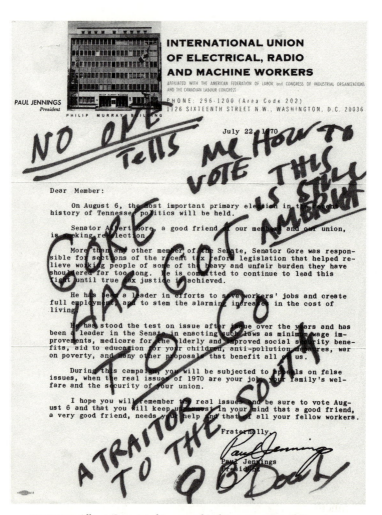

FIGURE 8. Albert Gore tried to appeal to lower-income white voters in 1970 by stressing economic issues. The anger of this white union member shows how difficult it was to overcome their hostility.

Source: "Jennings to Albert Gore 1970." Politics– General–1970 (Folder 1 of 3), Box C43 (6 of 6), Gore Senate Papers.

for four years. He cited "unauthorized use of deep freezers, improper use of automobiles and lack of follow through on the end use of commodities." He had been particularly concerned with the unauthorized purchase of freezers for the chief of the aid mission. As he departed Vietnam, however, he said, "The most encouraging thing we found was the military potential of the army and the effective leadership of the Vietnamese people by President Ngo Dinh Diem."[64]

McGee returned from Vietnam enthusing about "one of the most hopeful, exciting areas around the globe. . . one of the most imaginative and exciting land development programs anywhere in the world. Vietnam should be used as a showcase for what Americans could achieve in an undeveloped state." Gore did not share McGee's enthusiasm for the resettlement programs. During their visit the senators had been taken to see the strategic hamlets that had been established by clearing jungle in the highlands. Vietnamese inhabitants from the coast and Saigon were resettled there. Gore doubted that they wanted to be there. He noted that the bamboo fences round the villages could not prevent tigers leaping over them let alone armed Vietcong. Driving through the area, Gore and McGee were expected to be impressed with the sight of forty to fifty peasants clearing weeds. Looking out of the back window, Gore saw the peasants throw down their hoes in disgust as soon as they passed through. He found the aid policies extravagant "and, at least questionable, if not entirely mistaken." McGee was invited to join the National Committee of the Friends of Vietnam; Gore was not. Diem's Washington champion, Mike Mansfield, told Under Secretary of State Douglas Dillon that "he regretted the public findings by a certain Senator who was in Vietnam for only two days and whose findings did not accord with those of the sub-committee staff." Mansfield's views echoed those of his chief of staff, Francis Valeo, who did not greatly admire Gore. Valeo thought Gore "had his own way of getting interested for a brief period of time, and posing and displaying great erudition in regard to a problem, and then kind of dropping it and leaving it." It was difficult to justify this criticism as far as Gore and Vietnam were concerned. Gore was quicker to depart from the Cold War orthodoxy on Vietnam than the more expert Mansfield, and no one could deny Gore's tenacity on the Vietnam issue, at considerable political cost, from 1959 to 1970.[65]

If Gore had been polite about President Diem when in Vietnam, he told the *Washington Post* in January 1960 that he believed him to be a leader "whose authoritarian policies seem to be growing instead of diminishing." He had been particularly concerned with the denial of National Assembly seats to two leading Saigon intellectuals who opposed the Diem regime. Gore started to question U.S. policy in executive sessions of the Foreign Relations

Committee during the Kennedy administration. He later recalled that briefings from CIA director Richard Helms conflicted with official U.S. policy. When the Pentagon Papers were later published, Gore found little that he did not already know. Gore's skepticism was fueled by the views of people he trusted. Chester Bowles and J. K. Galbraith, old allies from price-control battles, both warned, from their vantage point as ambassadors to India, that military success in Vietnam was unlikely, and that nationalist sentiment should not be confused with communism. Albert and Pauline kept a keen eye on the young reporter David Halberstam, whom they had known since his time on the *Tennessean* in the 1950s. They took great pride in his achievements when he went to the *New York Times*. When Halberstam was sent by the *Times* from the Congo to South Vietnam, he wrote increasingly skeptical reports about the progress of the American effort. Gore, unlike Kennedy and Secretary of Defense Robert McNamara, was inclined to accept Halberstam's viewpoint. Halberstam's attempts to expose the reality behind the local officials' claims about the success of the resettlement programs resonated with Gore. Pauline Gore thought Halberstam had done a "terrific reporting job" and had played a great part in bolstering Buddhist morale in 1963.[66]

When the Diem regime became even more corrupt and unpopular in the summer of 1963, and its religious persecution became more intense, Gore made an appointment to see Kennedy. He tried to persuade the president, who was already deeply pessimistic given the difficulty of persuading Diem to reform, that in the light of the religious persecution it was a good time for the United States to withdraw. Gore's was not the only voice of concern that Kennedy heard in August and September 1963. Mike Mansfield had visited Vietnam at Kennedy's request in November 1962. He was rethinking his earlier high opinion of Ngo Dinh Diem. He now found him older, out of touch, and faltering, while his brother, Ngo Dinh Nhu, exercised more and more power without any popular mandate. On the ground in Vietnam, Mansfield met Halberstam and other members of the press corps and was impressed by their honesty. He, like the Gores, came to trust their reports. In August the majority leader repeated his gloomy assessment and recommended to the president at least a symbolic reduction in the number of military advisers. On the floor of the Senate in September, South Dakota senator George McGovern, Kennedy's former director of Food for Peace, gave what his biographer described as the earliest trenchant commentary by a senator on the U.S. entanglement in Southeast Asia. Vietnam, said McGovern, gave "clear demonstrations of the limitations of military power." Supporting a tyrannical government there, he proclaimed, was "a policy of moral debacle and political defeat."[67]

Unlike McGovern, Gore did not go public with his criticism of the Kennedy policy. He continued to express his strong opposition in executive sessions of the Foreign Relations Committee. At an 8 October 1963 meeting with Secretary McNamara, Fred Dutton reported that Gore, together with Wayne Morse, Frank Carlson, and Frank Church, all pressed the secretary on whether the Diem government could be effective, given the "repressions and political difficulties that had been encountered." They were sharply critical of the notion that the United States was winning the war. Gore kept pressing McNamara on whether Vietnam was a political or a military problem. If it was a political problem, as Gore clearly believed, then why, he asked, were officials in Defense rather than State reexamining U.S. policy?[68]

Kennedy listened to Mansfield and Gore and clearly had some sympathy with their concerns. Their advice was one of the factors prompting Kennedy and McNamara to announce the withdrawal of a thousand military advisers. Gore would see a basic inconsistency between that announcement and McNamara's subsequent call for increased military pressure in March 1964. But if Kennedy was sympathetic to the voices of dissent, he was also burdened by the persistence of the communist regime in Cuba and the example of the "loss" of China under Truman. No Democratic president could afford to lose Vietnam, he believed. In November 1963 Kennedy took the advice of his military advisers and his ambassador in Saigon and authorized a coup against Diem. The United States then found itself the prisoner of the successive military regimes that were neither popular nor effective. As each failed the pressure to shore up the next increased. Gore was disappointed, but he still trusted the president and would not publicly disavow Kennedy's policy.[69]

Gore would always believe that, even though Kennedy rejected the advice of the dissenters in 1963, the president, had he lived, would have sought to negotiate an exit from Vietnam in his second term. Gore, like other Kennedy admirers, thought that the president who had freed himself of one set of Cold War certainties to negotiate a test-ban treaty would have been buoyed by a reelection in 1964 to free himself of another set of Cold War certainties in Vietnam.

⤷

THE KENNEDY YEARS were some of the happiest the Gores spent in Washington. Gore and the Kennedy administration were largely on the same wavelength. Gore had ratings from the liberal pressure group the Americans for Democratic Action (ADA) that were virtually unheard of for a Southern Democrat during those years. Gore was not a Kennedy insider, and the president did not have to pay him the deference and constant attention that he might have had to pay powerful committee chairmen. But Gore was a respected national figure in his own right; the president often used him as a sounding board to test his own ideas, and in some cases as a mouthpiece who could trail possible administration policies. Pauline and Albert Gore were not prominent members of the Washington social scene or of the Camelot cohort. Pauline would not have been averse to a more active social life, but the senator was more staid. They were welcome at the White House for private dinner parties with the Kennedys. They were comfortably ensconced on the eighth floor of the Fairfax Hotel, owned by Albert's cousin Grady Gore. The hotel then was more a boarding house than the fashionable hotel that became the Ritz-Carlton. The apartment was by no means grandiose, although Pauline was always on the lookout for antiques to furnish it. She had excellent taste and a sharp eye for a bargain: As one friend noted, she filled the apartment and her house in Carthage with "gorgeous stuff on a budget." She could always rely on some expert upholsterers and repairers in Carthage who could refresh the furniture she bought. Grady Gore's children, Jimmy and Louise, opened a restaurant, the Jockey Club, on the ground floor of the Fairfax; it quickly became fashionable and attracted members of the administration as well as celebrity associates of the Kennedys like Peter Lawford and the Rat Pack.[70]

Pauline and Albert's son, Al, aged thirteen at the start of the Kennedy presidency, went to the prestigious private school St. Alban's and flourished in its disciplined atmosphere. He treasured the proximity to famous politicians and the highly informed discussions of hot-button current issues that he heard around the kitchen table. But the person who really came into her own during this time was his older sister, Nancy. In 1955 Nancy had gone to Vanderbilt, where she cut a spectacular figure on the Nashville campus. Only a quarter of the students at Vanderbilt were women. They were housed in old homes close to the campus and chaperoned by house mothers. Roommate Mary, the future wife of U.S. senator Jim Sasser, remembered how different Nancy was. Most of the students, like Mary, were middle-class, parochial, educated at public schools in the South. The extent of their travel might have been a family car trip to the West. Nancy was a senator's daughter, educated at the highly academic, private Holton Arms in Washington, DC. Cosmopolitan, well-traveled, and sophisticated, she seemed to know so much. She might not have appeared to study hard, but she read voraciously. While other students went home in the summer, Nancy worked on her father's reelection campaign in 1958 and then embarked on a European trip organized around her government job at the world's fair in Brussels. On campus she never flaunted her status as a senator's daughter and was known as a generous, sociable free spirit.[71]

Beautiful, high-spirited, and never short of male admirers, Nancy could drink and smoke with the hardest-drinking male students or with the remarkable young journalists who worked for the *Tennessean*. She was part of a circle that included David Halberstam and his roommate, Fred Graham. She was "spontaneous, unpredictable, irreverent," recalled Fred's brother, future historian Otis Graham, who dated her for one particularly intense summer. Always in motion, she had many irons in the fire, he remembered wistfully. The Graham boys and the young journalists adored her and recognized her powerful and innate political skills. Like her mother, she was a natural politician. As one observer noted, she knew what needed to be done and how to do it, but also the limits of what could be done. It was no surprise that she served as her father's campaign manager in 1964 and 1970. She was not afraid to take on male politicians, and she was fiercely protective of her father. John Seigenthaler remembered being chewed out by Nancy for the *Tennessean*'s criticism of Albert's vote against the 1964 Civil Rights Act.[72]

Nancy Gore found her métier in the early days of the Kennedy administration. The fresh appeal of the Kennedy campaign and the president's call to public service inspired many young people to come to Washington. There had never been such an influx since the first hundred days of the Roosevelt administration in 1933. Nowhere was youthful enthusiasm and idealism more obvious than in the newly created Peace Corps under Sergeant Shriver. Indeed one of his assistants claimed the Peace Corps was "probably even more exciting and innovative than anything in the New Deal." In the spring of 1961, it was *the* fashionable place for young idealists to work. Nancy Gore, alongside Sally Bowles, daughter of Under Secretary of State Chester Bowles, was in at the start. In March 1961 Nancy was one of only twelve staff members helping to set up the organization. When quizzed by David Halberstam, neither Nancy nor Sally knew whether they were actually on the payroll or, if they were, what they were being paid. Nancy told Halberstam that she had signed up to work for the corps because it was the "first new idea of the New Frontier. It's one of the few original things that has happened in a long time, and it's one thing that I can participate in, something that I can contribute to." She flourished in what Shriver's biographer described as the continuing atmosphere of "the anything-is-possible creative anarchy—a mixture of idealism, naiveté, and brilliance." (One historian described the administrative setup of the Peace Corps as "an antibureaucratic bureaucracy.")

She seemed to be a law unto herself in terms of time-keeping and long lunches, and she floated through the office seemingly independent of any hierarchy or organizational chart. But her political nous was soon regarded as indispensable. She became assistant to Bill Moyers, the young assistant director of the Peace Corps, with responsibility for special projects. As the chronicler of the Peace Corps, Coates Redmon, recalled, she was "the resident Scarlett O'Hara and female political sage." Young assistant directors like Moyers and William Haddad found that they could turn to Nancy for impeccable political advice on how to steer Peace Corps projects through the Washington journalistic and political minefields. She took a leave of absence to run her father's reelection campaign in 1964.[73]

In 1966 Nancy married Frank Hunger, an air force veteran and Mississippi lawyer who had been captivated by her from the time he first met her, when she was an undergraduate at Vanderbilt. They settled in Greenville, Mississippi, a relatively liberal enclave in the Magnolia State, where the legendary Pulitzer Prize–winning Hodding Carter published the *Delta Democrat Times*. Indeed when Frank and Nancy first moved there, they lived in the Carters' old house and then moved in next door to Hodding Carter III.

Frank Hunger had grown up in Winona, Mississippi, and attended the University of Mississippi as an undergraduate and for one year of law school. It was during that year that an ugly mob rioted over James Meredith's admission to the university. Hunger may well have thought of Greenville as a progressive oasis in the Magnolia State, but he and Nancy discovered that it was a "conservative with a small c town," recalled neighbor Hodding Carter III. Frank built up a career as a successful corporate litigator with Lake Tindall, Greenville's leading law firm. Mississippi Democratic politics were complex as the state's politicians wrestled with the ramifications of a dramatically increased African American electorate after the 1965 Voting Rights Act. Nancy could not get too involved in those state politics for fear of alienating her husband's clients. The Hungers' ability to blend in was summed up by a conservative neighbor who approvingly told the FBI who were vetting Nancy's father in 1977 that Frank and Nancy were "excellent neighbors, maintain their lawn and property in meticulous manner . . . jog regularly. They are good American citizens."

But, as in Washington, Nancy threw herself into various projects, even though she usually did not take up a formal or official role. It was no coincidence that, with her Peace Corps background, she advised the controversial Head Start program of the Office of Economic Opportunity in the state. She remained, Carter remembered, a Pied Piper who had a remarkable ability to talk people into doing things. She was also unafraid to tell him and others that they were, in his words, "full of shit." She may have missed Washington, but she never publicly said so. She also yearned for the farm in Carthage. Nancy never lost the political bug. She came back to Tennessee to run her father's final campaign in 1970 and, later, to help her brother, Al, whom she adored, in his congressional races. In 1982 she was diagnosed with lung cancer. Frank Hunger took her to Nashville for treatment in the painful final stages. As the lung cancer took hold, she returned to the family farm to die in 1984, just before Al was elected to the Senate. The Hungers were childless, and Frank continued to be devoted to Al Gore's four children and to consider Al a brother. He served in the Justice Department in the Clinton administration and was Al's closest adviser and constant companion during his 2000 presidential bid. Ralph Thompson, an air force friend of Frank's and later U.S. appellate court judge, once had dinner with Pauline and Albert Gore. He remarked that they were lucky to have Hunger for a son-in-law. "Ralph," Pauline Gore replied, "Frank is our son."[74]

⌒

WHAT IN RETROSPECT seemed like golden days for the Gore family were abruptly ended when the news of President Kennedy's death came through on 22 November 1963. Albert Gore was deeply distressed. He quietly went home to his apartment and consoled himself with the family. There was real personal grief, but apart from the shock, Gore was soon contemplating the previously unthinkable: the need to deal with LBJ. Gore had thought he would never have to worry about Lyndon Johnson again, once LBJ had been marginalized as vice president. He now had to confront the reality that his old nemesis would be in the White House. Having failed to persuade his friend John Kennedy over Vietnam, Gore would now find himself debating Vietnam with a very different inhabitant of the White House.

CHAPTER 7

Race and War:
Albert Gore and Lyndon Johnson

A FEW DAYS AFTER LYNDON JOHNSON was sworn in as president, Albert Gore received a call from Johnson. Gore asked Jack Robinson, the young man from Carthage who served as an assistant in his Senate office from 1956 to 1964, to drive him over to the White House. Robinson remembered that it was not "Lyndon this time, it's the President." Robinson waited, and the meeting was short. Robinson asked Gore what happened:

> [Gore replied:] "Well, the president said, 'Albert, you know we're both old school teachers, and what I would like to do is to take the eraser and wipe the slate clean.'" And I said, "What did you say?" [Gore] said, "Mr. President, I agree." He was so serious, you know. Well it wasn't two weeks that each was snipping the other again.[1]

As Johnson moved to take control of the presidency, ensure a sense of national unity, and position himself for election in his own right in 1964, two of the major items of unfinished business offered the chance for Johnson to continue the Kennedy legacy, display his legislative mastery, and establish his liberal credentials. On neither of these issues—tax cuts and civil rights—however, did he receive any assistance from Albert Gore.

Johnson was infuriated by Gore's intransigence on tax cuts but resigned to Gore's inaction on civil rights. At the same time Gore supported the rest of Johnson's domestic program enthusiastically. In particular he carried the ball for Medicare in the Senate Finance Committee. Meanwhile, Vietnam was largely on the back burner in 1964. When, however, Johnson used an apparent North Vietnamese attack on American cruisers in the Gulf of Tonkin to seek a congressional resolution in favor of military action, Gore, like the vast majority of the senators, backed the president—a move he later bitterly regretted. Involved in a tough reelection battle himself, Gore praised a president who had acted with restraint, in contrast to the hawkish Barry Goldwater.

Safely reelected, Gore became a fervent supporter of LBJ's Great Society legislation. He was also now free to support the president on civil rights. But the early rapprochement on Vietnam did not last. Gore's conviction that the war was unwinnable surfaced early. His prominence among the dissenters on the Senate Foreign Relations Committee made him a highly visible opponent of the war. The war came to dominate Gore's relationship with the president and exposed the underlying tension between them.

～

KENNEDY'S TAX CUT had been stalled in the Senate Finance Committee. Kennedy had worked hard to sell the tax cut to the business community, but a tax cut at a time of large budget deficits was still anathema to pay-as-you-go fiscal conservatives like Harry Byrd, the veteran chair of the Finance Committee. Albert Gore opposed it from the opposite direction. He did not want to cut government spending and reward the rich at the expense of ordinary Americans. He was not convinced that the tax cut would produce the economic growth that its sponsors championed.

For Johnson the tax cut was the first step in maintaining continuity with his predecessor's program. He was convinced of its economic validity by Walter Heller, the chair of the Council of Economic Advisers. The promised economic growth would be crucial in the 1964 elections. The challenging legislative environment gave him the opportunity to develop his reputation as a master legislator, able to deliver what his predecessor could not.

Gore was unrepentant about the tax cut. As he told a reporter, the bill failed in not providing the stimulus to consumer demand, which is what he thought the economy needed. Instead, he claimed, "The principal stimulus will go where it is not needed—greater corporate profits, larger cash reserves, more investment savings and more automation. All of those are at record highs." He regarded the tax-cut bill as "one of the worst and most dangerous bills to receive serious consideration by the Congress in a long time." It was "unconscionable" and "utterly unsound." He summed up his opposition to Walter Lippmann: Society's pressing needs were in the public sector—"education, health, transportation, employment, highways, streets, community facilities, etc." Because governmental revenue would be reduced as a percentage of gross national product, it would "permanently impair the capacity of the government to meet these needs." Gore promised to fight this battle, however lonely: "I am going to shout these truths from the house tops for the next two months."[2]

As an advocate of progressive taxation, he also despaired that the bill would accelerate reversal of the trend toward a more equitable distribution of national income, which began in the 1930s. The result in due course, he feared, would be "another gigantic depression, social and political upheaval, or drastically stepped-up direct Government action in many economic areas where Government ought not to tread." In vain he attempted to raise the personal income tax exemption from $600 to $1,000.[3]

Johnson was assured by his advisers by contrast that the boost to consumer demand would be massive: "This is the largest extra tax stimulus to consumer demand, the largest single boost in take home pay in U.S. history. And this will be to every wage and salary earner in the nation. Retailers in every city and hamlet will feel the impact of this mass of extra purchasing power pouring into their cash registers."[4]

Gore was unmoved by those arguments. It was a lonely battle that pitted him against Johnson and his closest advisers. From the day he took office, Johnson tried to move the tax cut forward and chivvied his friends, particularly George Smathers of Florida, to have a showdown with Gore. Gore's amendments, many of which Treasury Secretary Douglas Dillon considered dreadful, were what was holding up the bill. Smathers in particular was anxious to curry favor and denigrate Gore, and LBJ was always keen to egg him on. Smathers challenged Gore to a fistfight and, in his descriptions of his confrontations with Gore, gloated that he had poured cold water on Gore's boasts of effectively derailing the bill. He reminded Gore that his earlier bravado and filibusters had come to nothing. "Gore was just making trouble" was the constant refrain. Johnson and his informants worried that Gore would team up with John Williams of Delaware and secure Republican support for his amendments. LBJ was even more upset when Gore called for a debate on the scandals involving former secretary to the Senate Bobby Baker. Neither LBJ nor any of the Senate leadership wanted close scrutiny of Baker's activities. Johnson reached out to many people in his efforts to move the bill forward—Harry Byrd, Secretary Dillon, Smathers, Clinton Anderson, Eugene McCarthy, and Mike Mansfield. He encouraged the press to "put a little heat" on Gore for filibustering. The one person he did not try to reach out to as he worked the phones was Gore himself. As he told McCarthy, "You can't get Gore."[5]

The Kennedy–Johnson tax cut has been celebrated by liberals as a stunning success—and praised retrospectively by conservatives today. They point to the unprecedented economic growth that followed the cut. Gore never repented of his opposition to the tax cut, however. Subsequent prosperity did not change his views. Instead he blamed the tax cut for inflation. The cost of the Vietnam War gave added credibility to his arguments. He argued that war spending meant the government should raise taxes in 1966, at a time when Johnson was reluctant publicly to acknowledge the true cost of the war. Indeed the cost of the war and the inflationary pressures on the economy confirmed Gore's belief that taxes should never have been cut in the first place. Gore continued to hound Dillon and his successor, Henry Fowler, as Andrew Mellon–style Republican advocates of tax cuts and tight money. High interest rates threatened to destroy the reputation of the Democratic Party as the "people's party." The administration's record in fiscal affairs was an unenviable one, Gore argued. He reminded his constituents in 1967 that he had opposed the tax cut in 1964, and that he now similarly opposed restoration of the investment credit: "I have always been one who wanted to pay some respectable heed to the principle of pay as you go and particularly in times of maximum prosperity such as now." Instead of restoring the investment credit, he maintained that a tax increase was absolutely necessary to meet the rising costs of a very costly war. He claimed the high ground: "From an economic standpoint, taxes should have been raised a year ago, and I so recommended. The fact that this was not done last year increases the need for action now from a budgetary standpoint." Why should only those in military service be forced to sacrifice for the war effort?[6]

✍

GETTING THE TAX cut passed enabled Johnson to demonstrate his legislative mastery by enacting a major part of Kennedy's program that had been stalemated in Congress. The other major Kennedy legislation that was stymied in November 1963 was the civil rights bill. Enacting that legislation would serve as the most fitting memorial to the dead president, said Johnson. It would also establish his own liberal credentials in the eyes of skeptical Northern Democrats. Albert Gore had actively opposed the president on the tax cut, LBJ's first-priority issue. On the second, Gore could be of little help to Johnson: He was largely irrelevant in the struggle that secured the landmark 1964 Civil Rights Act.

As Southern moderates in the 1950s, Gore and Johnson had had very similar ideas on racial change in the South. Neither had signed the Southern Manifesto: Neither wanted to stir up constituency passions by raising what they saw as an unnecessarily sectional issue that would divide the party. But both had national political ambitions, which meant that they could not sidestep civil rights as an issue indefinitely. When LBJ worked to secure the passage of the Civil Rights Act in 1957 (and indeed again in 1960), Johnson's tactics and Gore's needs meshed perfectly. To prevent a Southern filibuster, which would have killed the bill, Johnson worked to secure concessions from Northern and Western Democrats to make the bill moderate enough for Southern conservatives to keep their powder dry for more threatening legislation in the future. The concessions Johnson won enabled Gore to vote for the bill. He could justify his votes to his constituents in terms of positive support for a voting-rights bill. At the same time he could note that he had voted with the Southern bloc on the matters Southerners had regarded as particularly threatening. When the Kennedy civil rights proposals came forward, Gore hoped—and at the time of Kennedy's death could reasonably expect—that amendments to the bill would be sufficient to enable him to vote for it in the end.

But whereas in 1957 Johnson knew he had to compromise to pass the legislation, in 1964 he knew he could not afford to weaken the civil rights bill in any way. If he was to secure the presidential nomination in his own right, Johnson had to win over skeptical Northern liberal Democrats who assumed that Johnson was a wheeler-dealer conservative Southerner. Even more important, in 1964 Johnson knew that he could not prevent a Southern filibuster by making the bill less objectionable. A bill to outlaw segregation in public accommodations, cut off funds to state government agencies that perpetuated segregation, and end employment discrimination was precisely the sort of apocalyptic and coercive legislation that Southerners had preserved the filibuster to defeat. Thus for Johnson to get the necessary votes to close off debate and defeat the filibuster, the president needed Republican votes. His dependence on GOP support meant that he flattered and cajoled the Republican leadership, notably Everett Dirksen. Above all it meant that he had to persuade Republicans that he would not compromise. Having been outmaneuvered on civil rights by Johnson as majority leader, the Republican leaders would give their votes to Johnson as president only so long as they were convinced that he would not make last-minute concessions to the Southerners and leave the Republicans high and dry. Johnson had to convince both Northern Democrats and Republicans that he was in the fight to win, that he intended to break the Southern filibuster, and that he would fight for the strongest possible legislation.[7]

Gore therefore could not expect the face-saving compromises that would enable him to go back to his constituents, as he had in 1957, to claim that the bill had been softened to the extent that he could support it. Gore simply was not a factor for the president and Hubert Humphrey, who was leading the fight for the bill in the Senate, as they sought to secure enough votes for cloture and break the filibuster. Johnson and Humphrey knew that Gore would not be part of the teams of Southern senators organized to prolong debates on the Senate floor. But there was no incentive for them to win Gore over. It was the Republicans, not Southern moderates like Gore, whom Johnson needed in the summer of 1964. There were those who thought that Gore was a Southerner who might have been persuaded "to do a Vandenberg" and move over to support a cloture vote to end the filibuster and to support the bill, just as isolationst Republican Arthur Vandenberg had moved over to support the Truman Doctrine in 1947. There is no evidence that Johnson reached out to Gore. Indeed Johnson made few attempts to win over individual senators that summer. Instead he kept himself meticulously informed about the Mansfield–Humphrey strategy for bringing the bill to the Senate floor but did not involve himself individually with senators, except for Republican minority leader Dirksen. Stephen Horn, minority whip Thomas Kuchel's assistant, kept very detailed minutes of the bipartisan daily strategy meetings of the staffers of the Senate leadership. Gore is clearly identified in the "no" camp in vote tallies for possible cloture votes. There is no evidence to suggest that the strategy team thought he could be tempted over to the civil rights side. If he voted for the bill, so much the better, but if he did not, it would not affect the final outcome, which they struggled so hard to achieve.[8]

What would Gore do? His mail ran overwhelmingly against the legislation. Constituents mostly asserted that the sections desegregating public accommodations were gross assaults on private property rights and would impose great burdens on businesses. Others posted dire warnings that the legislation would give rise to communism, black violence, and intermarriage. Unlike the case in 1956, when many correspondents praised his stand against the Southern Manifesto, few encouraged Gore to vote for the 1964 bill.

At first Gore expressed the hope that the bill would be amended, as the 1957 and 1960 bills had been, so that he could support it. He claimed that he saw the need for legislation to end segregation and discrimination in public accommodations. He touted Tennessee's progress in race relations as "a remarkable story of cooperation and good will and a minimum of federal intervention." But he strongly attacked the proposals to eliminate job discrimination. He labeled these a new "FEPC," the Fair Employmernt Practices Committee which he had so vehemently denounced in 1949 and which had served as the lightning rod for Southern segregationist criticism of federal government tyranny.[9]

Gore above all focused on what he saw as the arbitrary power of the attorney general specified in the bill and, particularly on Title VI, which provided for the elimination of federal funds to state and local programs that discriminated. Gore complained that there were no guidelines, no standards, by which local school boards, for example, could be judged. Instead, power appeared to reside solely with unelected and unaccountable bureaucrats. He feared that a school district desegregating under court order, for example, would still find itself punished by the loss of federal funds if administrators, not the court, deemed its compliance insufficient. He feared that token school desegregation, which white Tennesseans appeared to accept, would fall afoul of zealous bureaucrats, and that he would find it even harder to contain white anger. According to Clarence Mitchell of the Leadership Conference on Civil Rights, Gore worried that all the funds for a state would be cut off if some programs in the state were not in compliance. The Justice Department's Burke Marshall believed Gore was simply wrong. But no one felt the need to alleviate Gore's concerns. His amendment to strike Title VI from the bill failed easily. Then, on the morning of the final vote, Gore received unanimous consent to introduce a motion to recommit the whole bill to the Judiciary Committee on the grounds that Title VI was too onerous and needed further legal scrutiny. Although the motion was overwhelmingly defeated 74 votes to 25, the amendment infuriated Hubert Humphrey, the bill's manager. According to Humphrey aide John G. Stewart, Humphrey regarded Gore's move as "the highest breach of senatorial ethics." Gore had gone behind the floor leaders' backs the night before to secure unanimous consent without informing Humphrey.[10]

Gore voted against the final measure. There is little doubt that he was aware of the challenge he faced in his own Senate race and the disaffection of white supporters in Tennessee. In the past the presence of Estes Kefauver alongside Gore in the Senate had given him a measure of protection: Kefauver was a lightning rod for segregationist criticism. Kefauver was no longer there. Herbert S. Walters, appointed to Kefauver's seat, was a state party warhorse who routinely voted with the other Southerners against the bill. On the other hand, Gore could have looked close to home for reasons to back the bill. His Senate friends, Mike Monroney and Ralph Yarborough, voted for it. In his own state Gore knew that two young congressmen, Ross Bass and Richard Fulton, voted for the bill.[11]

Gore, as was his custom, took his own counsel. He undoubtedly was aware that he faced strong Republican opposition and that there was the danger of a white backlash in the state. His advisers were certainly aware of intense white hostility to civil rights in the western part of the state. Some observers thought his stance on the bill was a "shoddy" attempt to get the best of both worlds—opposing the bill without threatening its final passage. But it may not have been just political calculation that dictated his vote. A Southern moderate of Gore's generation was still much more attuned to the alarms of white constituents than to the impatient demands of a new generation of African Americans. His pattern of behavior was not uncommon among Southern moderate congressmen. Jim Wright in Texas and Dante Fascell in Florida followed the same path—refusing to sign the Southern Manifesto, voting for the 1957 bill, but coming out against the 1964 bill. Endowing the right to vote was one thing; but dictating to local school districts was another, and imposing restrictions on how businessmen ran their daily affairs was yet another entirely different matter.[12]

⸙

THE TAX CUT and civil rights were crucial to Johnson, but so were his "war on poverty" and the raft of domestic reform programs he tried to put through in 1964. Gore was an enthusiastic supporter of the president on these issues. So many of these measures represented unfinished business of the New Deal. Many were also underpinned by the shared vision of Gore and Johnson that the federal government was the solution to the South's problems. Gore had the most liberal record of any Southern senator in this session of Congress.[13]

It was on Medicare—health insurance for the elderly—that Gore made his most important contribution to the effort to carry forward the administration's program in 1964. He had enthusiastically supported health insurance from the time Truman proposed it under the Fair Deal. When Congress had recognized the problem of crippling health costs for the elderly in a limited way with the passage of the Kerr–Mills Act of 1960, Gore had introduced his own bill to cover hospital costs for individuals sixty-five and over. As far as Gore was concerned, the Kerr–Mills program, which provided matching funds for state programs, was essentially a means-tested welfare program—

and only wealthy states could afford to take full advantage. He preferred the approach based on social insurance, where the contributor had an entitlement to health care.[14]

After Kennedy called for a Medicare program, Gore had supported the efforts of his old atomic-energy ally, Clinton Anderson of New Mexico, to provide hospital insurance for people over sixty. Despite their defeat in the Senate Finance Committee in 1962, they were optimistic that the tide had turned for Anderson's bill in 1964. But the House Ways and Means Committee would only support increases in old-age benefits. The increase in payroll tax to fund those benefits would preclude any Medicare insurance. Gore, leading the fight for the Anderson bill because his ally was ill, was defeated in the Finance Committee but did persuade the full Senate to add a Medicare rider to the Social Security amendments in September. Francis Valeo, Mansfield's Majority Secretary, was no friend of Gore but he saw Gore's Medicare amendment as a crucial first step in the enactment of Medicare. "In this casual way," he concluded, "without fanfare, a beginning was made on the federally sponsored health insurance program of the United States." Although LBJ twisted arms to get Senate passage in the hope of getting Medicare before Congress adjourned and Mansfield kept the Senate in session to achieve that, Wilbur Mills, the House Ways and Means chair, remained an implacable opponent. Outnumbered on the conference committee, Gore, like Johnson, had to be satisfied with an assurance from Mills that he would make Medicare the number 1 priority of his committee in the new Congress in 1965.[15]

෴

GORE'S VIEW THAT the war in Vietnam was unwinnable and that the United States should withdraw its troops was already clearly established by the end of 1963. But Gore's pessimism was not very different from Johnson's own pessimism about the deteriorating situation in South Vietnam when he took office. Old political allies of the president in the Senate and in the South were equally gloomy about the prospect of American involvement in a ground war in Asia. As one regime succeeded another in South Vietnam, the United States looked in vain to find a government that was popular, anticommunist, and capable and willing to fight the Viet Cong. Nothing in 1964 changed Gore's mind about the futility of the American military effort.[16]

To the dismay of some of his advisers, Johnson was determined to put Vietnam on the back burner for the election year of 1964. But he did agree to the drafting of a congressional resolution that would, if necessary, give the president authorization to engage militarily in Vietnam. When North Viet-namese torpedo boats attacked two American destroyers in the Tonkin Gulf, Johnson launched retaliatory air strikes on North Vietnam. He then activated the draft resolution and asked Congress for the authority to use all means necessary to defend American armed forces and to take all necessary steps, including the use of armed force, to defend countries under the Southeast Asia Collective Defense Treaty. He assured both the American people and the Russians that he sought no wider war. The chairman of the Senate Foreign Relations Committee, J. William Fulbright, was briefed about the North Vietnamese attacks, and he introduced the resolution in the Senate. The resolution passed with only two dissenting voices, Ernest Gruening and Wayne Morse. There was no opposition in the House.[17]

A roll call of future "doves," including Gore, voted for the Tonkin Gulf resolution. Later Senate Foreign Relations Committee hearings exposed the very real doubts as to whether any North Vietnamese attack had taken place. The hearings demonstrated that the reason the two American destroyers were in the Gulf was to support covert South Vietnamese raids on the North. It was this evidence that convinced Gore that he had been misled by the president. He complained that every time he and other Vietnam dissenters went to see the president, Johnson would pull the resolution out of his pocket and remind them that they had voted for it. But in the summer of 1964, Gore believed that Johnson was a force for restraint against the military. Gore may have been misled by Johnson and his advisers, but he also faced the possibility of the trigger-happy Barry Goldwater in the White House and a surprisingly strong right-wing Republican challenge to his own reelection in Tennessee. Gore, like Fulbright, was only too keen to be overpersuaded. In his speech in the Senate on the resolution, Gore acknowledged that he had previously expressed deep concern about U.S. policy in executive sessions of the Foreign Relations Committee. But now whatever doubts had to be "water over the dam" "when U.S. forces have been repeatedly attacked on the high seas." Freedom of the seas must be preserved; aggression against American forces must be repulsed. He reiterated these themes and his faith in Johnson's restraint throughout the fall.[18]

↩

IN 1964 ALBERT GORE faced only nominal opposition in the Democratic primary. A disbarred lawyer, a veteran politician who had served in the Browning administration, and a Nashville lawyer who blithely announced that he would not do any handshaking tours around the state ran against him. Gore relied on his daughter, Nancy, to do whatever campaigning there was to be done.[19]

But for the first time in his career, Gore had to worry about a Republican threat in the general election. In 1952 and 1958 Republicans had mounted only token campaigns against him, but 1964 promised to be different. Tennessee had voted Republican in three successive presidential elections. Now there was evidence of local GOP strength to match that national electoral performance. In 1962 William E. Brock, Jr., of Chattanooga, had won the Third District congressional seat: the first time Republicans had managed to break out beyond the east Tennessee mountain First and Second districts. At the other end of the state, Robert James in Shelby County had come within 1,200 votes of unseating veteran Memphis congressman Cliff Davis. James's campaign manager, Dan Kuykendall, planned to challenge Gore for the Senate seat.[20]

Kuykendall was a young businessman who had served as a B-29 pilot in the war. He had moved to Memphis from Texas in 1955 to become manager of Procter & Gamble's regional office. Like so many young businessmen in the South, he chafed at the control of local politics by old-style Democrats. But Kuykendall was also enthused by the aggressively conservative candidate for the Republican presidential nomination, Arizona senator Barry Goldwater. Goldwater, another air force veteran, had made his reputation representing the pro-growth businessmen who took control of Phoenix after World War II and implemented pro-business, free-market, anti-statist, anti-union, and anti-communist policies. Goldwater also had a Southern strategy. A passionate advocate of states' rights, he had voted against the 1964 Civil Rights Act. He and his advisers, when they took control of the GOP at the San Francisco convention that summer, planned to "go hunting where the ducks are" to appeal to segregationists in the South.[21]

Gore had been alarmed by Goldwater's potential appeal to white Democrats in Tennessee from the start. He was agitated, according to John Seigenthaler, as early as November 1963. By the summer of 1964, there was much speculation about a white backlash to Johnson's civil rights policies in Tennessee and the whole South. Liberals looked to the Tennessee primaries that summer for comfort. In the race for Estes Kefauver's old seat, Congressman Ross Bass had upset Governor Frank Clement and the state political organization by more than 100,000 votes. Bass had voted for the Civil Rights Act, and he was rewarded by substantial African American support in Shelby County and Memphis. In Shelby, African American votes were thought to have been decisive in the victory of George Grider over incumbent and former Crump loyalist Cliff Davis. They had helped another congressman who had voted for the act, Richard Fulton, win renomination in Nashville. But those primaries had also opened up bitter divisions in the state party. There was a real fear that disgruntled conservative Democrats would either stay at home or vote for Goldwater-inspired Republicans. A *Wall Street Journal* poll in August showed Goldwater twenty points ahead in Tennessee.[22]

This division was a particular threat to Gore. Gore had never worked to build up a political organization of his own. Gore's office staff in Washington was always small. In the early sixties his young aide Jack Robinson would try to arrange for Gore to visit every county when he went home in the summer. But the senator usually could be persuaded to leave the farm to make only a small number of these fence-mending visits. In early August 1964 Gore claimed to be "always running," but no campaign plans had been laid. In any case he would have to shuttle back and forth from Washington until the congressional term ended on October 3. Finally, it was not clear that he would get the African American support that Bass and Grider had enjoyed. Despite Gore's record of racial moderation, African American leaders found it difficult to forgive Gore for his vote against the 1964 bill. The *Tennessean* and the local NAACP had condemned his vote. Stickers exhorting "Ignore Gore in 1964" began to appear in black communities. Crusading black lawyer (and Republican) Z. Alexander Looby never forgave Gore and refused to vote for him even in 1970. In the primary Gore had run way behind Bass and Fulton in African American wards in Nashville and behind Bass and Grider in Shelby. Shelby black leaders pointedly endorsed Bass and Grider for the general election but refused to endorse Gore.[23]

Kuykendall took to the campaign trail with a vengeance. Little known outside western Tennessee, he needed to be seen all across the state. In fifteen months Kuykendall crisscrossed the state 116 times. He was greatly helped by the fact that the well-connected Howard H. Baker, Jr., the ambitious and attractive son of the former east Tennessee Republican congressman, was running against Ross Bass for the other Senate seat. The two men coordinated their campaigns and regularly appeared together. Visitors had little doubt that Tennessee was now a two-party state when they looked at the billboards and TV advertising.[24]

Kuykendall firmly echoed the Goldwater campaign. He lambasted Gore for his vitriolic anti-business stance, which he argued deterred business from investing in Tennessee. The state, he said, needed jobs, but a manufacturer who produced televisions for Sears, Roebuck had located its plant in Arkansas, not Tennessee, because of the Gore tax proposals' effect on employee retirement plans. A steel plant was not going to come to Memphis because of Gore's attempt to fix steel prices.[25]

Gore's support of free trade and foreign aid cost Tennessee jobs, charged Kuykendall. "We need," he proclaimed, "a man who thinks of Tennessee's poverty before Australia's and of the interests of the people of Memphis before those of the people of South Africa." He would not vote, as Gore did, to "give away six million yards of textile business to Pakistan" at the expense of jobs in the United States." Poverty programs would not end poverty; new jobs would. Kuykendall called for better job training and restraints on unions, and he promised to appoint an aide to be solely responsible for attracting industry to the state. Furthermore, he charged, Gore was absent from too many committee meetings, had failed to protect cotton and cattle farmers, and had sacrificed the elderly by insisting on putting Medicare on the statute books instead of accepting pension increases for seniors.[26]

Kuykendall's racial appeal was careful. It was linked first to criticism of the power-grabbing federal government: "a government which has now told a private businessman that he cannot use his property as he wishes [according to the Civil Rights Act]." But the racial appeal also linked up with a call for law and order. The law needed to be maintained against rioters and demonstrators. Kuykendall joined Goldwater in hammering away at the breakdown in morality in Washington as evidenced by the Bobby Baker scandal and the arrest of Johnson's chief of staff, Walter Jenkins, on a morals charge. Gore, charged Kuykendall, had "four times voted against investigating Bobby Baker and calling Walter Jenkins as a witness. What really goes on when they turn the lights out at the White House?" But Kuykendall also latched on to the Supreme Court ruling against school prayer to turn the moral breakdown into a religious crisis. The moral breakdown in this country was a result of "a lack of faith in God." There had been a "frontal attack on Almighty God," "a vicious attack on the idea of ours being one nation under God."[27]

Finally, America had been appeasing communism in Berlin, Cuba, South Vietnam, Africa, and Indonesia. Gore, he said, was preaching "defeatism in Vietnam."[28]

By the start of October, the *Wall Street Journal* was reporting that the Tennessee Senate races were "in reach" of the Republicans. Goldwater spoke to enthusiastic audiences in Memphis and eastern Tennessee. Vice-presidential candidate William Miller also came to the state. But the link to Goldwater was a problem for Kuykendall. As he attempted to craft his campaign against Gore in western Tennessee, his attempts to condemn Gore for failing to defend cotton growers and cattle farmers were undermined by Goldwater's unapologetic opposition to farm subsidies. Kuykendall had a problem in casting himself as a defender of farmers when Gore had a long and sustained record of support for price controls and farm programs and impeccable credentials as a cattle farmer himself. Journalists reported that farmers were skeptical of businessman Kuykendall's efforts to identify with their plight on the campaign trail.[29]

An even greater handicap was Goldwater's implacable determination to sell off the TVA. Both Kuykendall and Howard Baker, Jr. emphasized their personal support for the TVA; it would have been politically suicidal in Tennessee to have done otherwise. The TVA was simply too important to east Tennessee: Baker's father had been a passionate supporter of the TVA in Congress. The two Republican hopefuls trusted that Goldwater would soften his stance on Tennessee's favorite federal program when he visited the state. Even at his most optimistic, Kuykendall publicly admitted that Goldwater's hostility to the TVA was costing the GOP at least 50,000 votes. Before Goldwater was due to speak in Tennessee, Baker wrote to the candidate's campaign team with draft paragraphs of how Goldwater might talk about the TVA during his campaign stops. Baker heard nothing back from Goldwater's staff. He and Kuykendall had to sit in impotent silence as they heard their presidential candidate in Memphis and Kingsport stand by his commitment to sell off the authority. At that point Baker knew that he and his fellow Republicans had lost the election.[30]

There is no indication that Gore was complacent about his prospects. He was acutely aware of Goldwater's appeal among business conservatives and segregationists in the state. Gore could not rely on the state party organization. The Clement–Ellington faction was smarting from the defeat inflicted on the governor by Ross Bass. It was not clear that the state employees who Bass claimed were "shaken down" by the Clement administration would be prepared to work for a Bass victory. Bass himself showed no sign of wanting to cooperate either with the defeated faction or with Gore. He thought his primary victory meant that he could control the party apparatus in the campaign. Would discontented African Americans turn out in large numbers for Gore, a man who had voted against the 1964 Civil Rights Act?[31]

Lyndon Johnson and Barry Goldwater between them largely solved these problems for Gore. Johnson was effectively his own campaign manager. He was desperate to win as many votes as possible in the South, and to sidetrack the white backlash that he, more than most, knew was there. His closest friend in Tennessee was Buford Ellington, the former governor, and the Johnson team inevitably turned to him and Governor Clement, not Ross Bass, to run the campaign in Tennessee. However much Ellington and the state party may have disliked Bass, they knew they had to deliver the state for LBJ: After 1960 Ellington could not afford to have another president disappointed by Tennessee's national vote. In turn Bass knew that he needed to cling to Johnson's coattails to offset local bitterness against him; he also knew that he needed Gore's supporters as much as Gore needed his. Gore also knew that he needed Johnson's popularity among both whites and blacks in Tennessee to counter the Goldwater threat. Johnson threw national resources into the state—he spoke there twice to huge crowds, and cabinet secretaries visited as well. Bass and Gore basked in the limelight as the president told Tennessee voters that he needed both of them in Washington. In Chattanooga and Memphis LBJ praised Gore "as his lifelong friend and co-worker." Johnson's appeal and the threat of Goldwater reunited African American leaders with Gore. They may have been annoyed with the senator, but Goldwater's anti–civil rights stance thoroughly alienated even traditional African American Republican leaders like G. W. Lee in Memphis and Looby in Nashville. Civil rights leaders like Benjamin Hooks switched to the Democrats. African American leaders, and African-American voters, overwhelmingly voted a straight Democratic ticket. As A. W. Willis, a young African American elected to the state legislature, said, "Senator Gore stood for a philosophy the Negro felt he could live with," and this outweighed his stand on civil rights.[32]

Once he was back in the state full-time a month before the election, Gore lost no time in mounting his usual punishing campaign schedule. At every opportunity he reminded his listeners how much their county had benefited from federal programs. In Athens he told his audience that McMinn County had received $4.3 million during the Kennedy–Johnson years, including grants and loans for water projects, schools, and urban renewal. "You would not have received this help without a Democratic President or Congress." Gore made a point of never mentioning his Senate opponent by name. But he hammered away at Goldwater. Goldwater's election, he repeated, would take away all those federal benefits. In western Tennessee in particular, he predicted a drastic cut in cotton farmers' income if the Republicans won. He promised an extension of the Great Society if the Democrats won, including a poverty program for Appalachia and Medicare, whereas Goldwater, he warned, would make Social Security voluntary. Johnson was the most effective domestic-affairs president Gore had served with during his quarter of a century in Washington.[33]

All over the state Gore remorselessly emphasized the threat to the TVA posed by a Goldwater election. If the TVA was sold, Gore warned, power rates would double. In early October he claimed that the status of the TVA was "the most frequently asked question" during the campaign. When Johnson visited the state, he, unlike Goldwater, said what his local candidates wanted him to say: He vowed never to sell the TVA.[34]

But one issue transcended even this in Gore's invocation of the dangers of a Goldwater victory. In the perilous world of 1964, Gore said that America needed a safe president: "Barry Goldwater isn't. Lyndon B. Johnson is." He conjured up the vision of "some NATO commander, instead of the President" unloosing atomic bombs. Gore cited the Gulf of Tonkin as an example of Johnson reacting immediately with both firmness and restraint. He lectured his audiences (in the manner of a professor, as one journalist noted), "The over-riding issue today is the preservation of peace. The president of the U. S. must have patience, courage and a sense of responsibility in connection with the awesome power at his disposal." The sense of crisis was dramatically increased when the news came that Khrushchev had been ousted in Moscow and the Chinese had detonated a nuclear weapon.[35]

Gore won reelection with 53.6 percent of the vote. The national Democratic landslide suggested that the domestic reform measures Gore had long fought for, like Medicare, federal aid to education, and Appalachian development, would now come to fruition. But pleasure had to be tempered by foreboding. LBJ's victory in Tennessee was very much an exception to the state's Republican trend in presidential elections. His win, Jimmy Carter's in 1976, and Bill Clinton's in 1992 and 1996 would be the only Democratic victories in the state in the seventeen presidential elections from 1952 to 2016. The Democrats won by 126,000 votes. That margin of victory could be accounted for by an estimated 150,000 African American votes. What one newspaperman described as the "mammoth" black vote alarmed Republicans. As Dan Kuykendall ruefully mused, "I don't know what the party can do about this bloc vote. I don't think the Republican Party will ever be a mass appeal party for the Negro." But Republicans also saw the opportunity for the future. They had failed to win the expected votes in eastern Tennessee because of the issue of the TVA. Everywhere they believed that the peace issue and the perceived threat Goldwater posed harmed them. The basic Republican lesson was clear: The Democrats had failed to get a majority of the white vote and would never do so again in a presidential election in Tennessee. A Republican candidate without the crippling handicaps that Goldwater possessed could attract enough whites to win, and the party could afford to ignore the African American vote.[36]

For Gore, the future was also troubling. In 1952 and 1958 Gore had not had to worry about Republican opposition. He overwhelmed the token opposition with almost 80 percent of the general election votes. Now he not only had eked out a narrow majority but had, like Ross Bass, run behind President Johnson: the first time in modern Tennessee that the Democratic candidate for the Senate had run behind the party's candidate for president. If the president did not remain popular, how would Gore fare? The senator had been saved by African American votes. He had appeared to have been spared the worst effects of a white backlash—but could his immunity last if African Americans became more demanding? What would happen if Republicans nominated a candidate without the ideological baggage of a Goldwater? The splits in the Democratic Party in the state boded ill for someone who needed a united party organization to offset his own lack of a political organization.

THE LEGENDARY 89TH CONGRESS was the most far-reaching session of the sixteen of Gore's congressional career, and Gore delighted in being a foot soldier in the drive to enact Johnson's Great Society. There were few areas of American life that were not touched by the legislation of 1965–66: education, urban poverty, rural development including Appalachia, agriculture, civil rights, immigration, health insurance, consumer protection, and the environment. Some of the measures were incremental reforms simply adding on to, or updating, measures launched in the 1930s—for example, farm price supports. Some were unfinished business of the New Deal or the Fair Deal: health insurance, federal aid to education, civil rights, measures to tackle urban poverty. Some broke new ground: consumer and environmental protection and a national immigration act that redressed the discrimination of the 1921 and 1924 acts but also had the unintended consequence of sparking a third new wave of mass immigration from the third world. Gore and his friend Ralph Yarborough were the two Southerners most committed to Johnson's domestic reforms in the Senate. They were comfortably the most liberal Southern senators, according to Michael Foley's analysis of the votes of all senators on civil rights, social security, poverty programs, housing and urban affairs, education, consumer protection, congressional reform, and foreign aid.[37]

Two measures gave Gore perhaps the greatest satisfaction, because they were issues he had championed since the 1940s. He had little to do with the passage of federal aid for education, a measure that had been promoted originally by Harry Truman. Many Southerners had recognized that the South needed federal aid for its students, schools, and universities more than any region in the country. Before civil rights was a national issue, a conservative like Pat Harrison of Mississippi favored federal aid because his state was too poor to fund a decent school system. But after the World War II, conservative Southerners feared that federal aid to schools would be a wedge for federal interference in race relations. Kennedy's attempt to secure federal aid had foundered on the issue of aid to parochial schools. The Johnson administration proposal allocated funds to students, not schools, and the criteria drew on the precedent of federal aid to school districts that had been impacted by defense installations. Under the Elementary and Secondary Education Act of 1965, aid went to districts that had been impacted by poverty. Since the South was still the poorest region in the country, it stood to benefit disproportionately. Once the Civil Rights Act had passed, the lure of federal dollars proved irresistible to the South. Later that year Congress also sought to help higher education. Gore had always supported federal aid, given both his understanding of the region's needs and his own struggles to get an education. When Johnson signed the Higher Education Act at his old college at San Marcos, now Texas State, Gore could not avoid thinking of his time at Middle Tennessee.[38]

The battle for Medicare in 1965 was largely centered in long-winded hearings in the Ways and Means Committee of Wilbur Mills and the debate in the House of Representatives. Republicans and the national medical organizations came up with Eldercare, a more generous version of Kerr–Mills, in an effort to head off establishment of Medicare. But after three months Mills finally secured passage of the administration's bill. Passage in the Senate, even the Senate Finance Committee, was much smoother. Whatever politicians were hearing from organized medicine, they knew that Medicare was popular. Gore helped build support for the bill, and he accompanied Johnson to Independence, Missouri, so that Johnson could sign it in the presence of former president Harry S. Truman, who had called for that legislation in February 1952.[39]

It was not just on social-welfare measures that Gore backed Johnson. Now safely reelected, he also supported the president on civil rights.

Immediately after passage of the 1964 Civil Rights Act, Gore kept his eye on the implementation of Title VI. In August 1964 an assistant secretary at Health Education and Welfare had gone to Memphis, emphasized the fund's cut-off provision, and stressed how quickly it would be applied to enforce school desegregation. Gore put pressure on the secretary of HEW, Anthony Celebrezze, to disown that statement. Celebrezze made reassuring noises about the expectation that most compliance with school desegregation in the South would be voluntary.[40]

As it turned out compliance with the 1964 act turned out to be largely uncontroversial in Tennessee, and token compliance with school desegregation continued peacefully across the state. At this point only a small number of African Americans were attending previously white schools. With the 1964 election out of the way, Gore did not need to be so defensive. He was in a position to act more freely on civil rights. The violence at Selma in March 1965 and the proposals for voting-rights legislation were much easier for Gore to support than the 1964 act had been.

In March 1965 the Southern Christian Leadership Conference (SCLC) attempt to register voters in Dallas County, Alabama, and to secure national voting-rights legislation was brutally interrupted by Alabama state troopers with tear gas and nightsticks on the Edmund Pettus Bridge outside Selma. National outrage at this violence and at the murder of a Northern white Unitarian minister (in Selma to express solidarity with the civil rights campaign) gave Lyndon Johnson the opportunity to address Congress and call for the voting-rights legislation his Justice Department had been working on since January.

Many of Gore's constituents blamed Martin Luther King, Jr. and the protesters for the violence and feared that Johnson's 1965 voting-rights bill would create a "watered down replica of the Russian monstrosity." By contrast Gore found Johnson's address to Congress "inspiring" and from the start indicated that he would support the Voting Rights Act. "Freedom of the ballot box is the very essence of democracy," he proclaimed. It was a relatively easy step for a man who had supported the 1957 Civil Rights Act as a voting-rights measure. Gore went further. As someone who had supported anti–poll tax legislation in 1942, he supported Ted Kennedy's efforts to add the abolition of the poll tax in state elections to the bill. Gore received a modicum of support from newspapers and constituents appalled by the vivid televised footage of Bloody Sunday. Southern historian Bruce Clayton wrote Gore from Bristol, Tennessee, that the "moral and constitutional issue is clear: we Americans must act if we believe in democracy."[41]

White disillusionment in western Tennessee grew over the next five years, and it was reflected in Gore's constituent letters. The specter of communism loomed large. "The Communists are our most deadly enemies, our boys died by the 1000s in Korea and now over 400 in South Vietnam so far—why let these boys down by letting these Communist agitators create chaotic conditions as exist in Selma today?" A repeated refrain was the double standard applied to whites and to civil rights protesters. King was a lawbreaker "who violates any law he wishes, according to his conscience, while no one else is allowed to." Welfare mothers also loomed large. Is it right, asked one constituent, "for us to be taxed to support the negs to raise bastards? Negro preacher's daughter down here has six bastards. And the U.S. News shows that Washington is full of bastards."[42]

Gore was unmoved by the white backlash. When Johnson called for fair housing legislation in 1966 to eliminate discrimination in home sales and rentals, real estate interests deluged Gore with mail opposing the bill. Progress in the Senate was painfully slow, but Gore did support the civil rights caucus, marshaled by Walter Mondale, in two unsuccessful attempts at cloture. Gore was still, however, a loose cannon. When Philip Hart and Hubert Humphrey got Everett Dirksen on their side, Mondale assumed the Republican votes would guarantee that the Southern filibuster would be defeated. But Mondale then lost Gore on the next cloture vote. Gore told a surprised Mondale that he had not had enough time to read the amendments that had been made to ensure Dirksen's support. "I'm not voting for cloture," Gore told Mondale. "I don't know what's in this bill." Gore's defection on one cloture vote did not stop the Senate, including Gore, from passing the bill on the day King was assassinated, on 4 April 1968. The House passed the bill shortly afterward.[43]

Some Tennesseans, like Gore, lamented King's assassination and were ashamed that it had taken place in their state. Other angry whites believed that King got what he deserved and thought it somehow dreadfully unfair that King had gotten himself killed in Memphis, which did not deserve national opprobrium.[44]

༄

GORE'S DEFIANT REACTION to Mondale highlighted his independent
streak. He did not mind going it alone. Campaign finance, about which
Gore had clashed with Johnson back in 1956, became a prominent issue ten
years later. Campaign costs had escalated as a result of television and the
zeal of political action committees, a process documented by the Citizens
Research Foundation headed by Herbert Alexander, who had worked for
Alexander Heard during Gore's 1956 investigation. In 1964 Gore and Heard
had appeared on the ABC TV program *The Price of Politics*. Gore said
that, to avoid having politics become the reserve of the rich and the special
interests, the government should fund party organizations and campaigns. In
May 1966 Johnson called on Congress to extend the spending disclosure for
federal elections to primary and state elections. Russell Long countered by
proposing federal funding of presidential elections. A presidential campaign
fund would be established either by direct federal subsidy or a tax check-off
on individual tax returns. While Republican John Williams denounced the
proposal as too expensive, Gore complained that it would cripple third parties
and that, without overall limits on campaign spending, it would simply be
an irresponsible gift to the established parties. When Congress passed the
law, Gore extended the discussion of technicalities of the implementation of
the funding mechanism to the extent that the fund was made inoperative.
Gore managed to alienate everybody: president, Long, conservatives, and
reformers.[45]

The halcyon days of 1965 saw Gore heavily involved in detailed lawmak-
ing in committees; he was invited to meetings at the White House, he received pens from a grateful president when bills were signed into law, and
he got warm notes of thanks for his efforts and cooperation from aides close
to Johnson, including Jack Valenti and Larry O'Brien. But the last friendly
gesture from the president came on 17 June 1966, when Johnson sent a signed
photograph to Gore on the occasion of the passage of a crop disaster bill.[46]

༄

WHAT HAD GONE wrong was Vietnam.

Gore had voted for the Tonkin Gulf resolution because he wanted to believe that Johnson was a force for restraint and that LBJ did not want a wider
war. Johnson's advisers, however, had developed plans for bombing North
Vietnam and the deployment of ground troops in the south. They despaired
of getting the president to make decisions before the election, but they lost no

time after November 1964 in expressing the gravity of the situation to Johnson. They presented the president with stark alternatives couched in terms of honoring commitments and establishing continuity with Kennedy foreign policy, arguments LBJ found difficult to resist. The rationale subtly changed. The argument, at first, was that American military involvement would have to wait until the South Vietnamese government was strong enough to work for a negotiated settlement. Then the compelling argument developed that the Americans had to intervene to strengthen the South Vietnamese regime so that a negotiated settlement could be contemplated. American resolve would bring North Vietnam to the conference table. In February 1965 a Viet Cong attack on a base at Pleiku prompted the massive retaliatory bombing of the north and the deployment of marines to South Vietnam. The bombing failed to convince North Vietnam of the need to negotiate, and the situation on the ground deteriorated. In June 1965 Johnson committed the first of what would be a steadily escalating number of ground troops to Vietnam—175,000 initially.[47]

On Vietnam Gore largely walked in lockstep with the chair of the Senate Foreign Relations Committee, J. William Fulbright of Arkansas. When Fulbright was elected to the House of Representatives in 1942, one of the first people he made contact with, on the recommendation of a mutual friend, was Albert Gore. They had much in common. Memphis was a newspaper hub for both of them, covering the "black belts" of the Arkansas Delta and west Tennessee. They made sure to entertain *Memphis Commercial Appeal* editor Frank Ahlgren when he visited Washington. The Arkansas delegation supported Gore's vice-presidential bid in 1956.

Fulbright, like Gore, was a racial moderate, but he was more conservative on civil rights. He shared many of the sensibilities of Delta planters and sought to preempt any electoral challenge from Orval Faubus. Where Gore advocated for public power, Fulbright had close ties with the oil and gas interests in his state and was supported by Witt Stephens and the Arkansas Power and Light Company. Fulbright and his wife enjoyed the social scene in Washington, which Gore largely avoided. Fulbright enjoyed duck-hunting with conservative segregationists such as Faubus or Allen Ellender of Louisiana. Gore rarely joined them. The cerebral Fulbright easily fit in with the Senate "club," whereas Gore was always viewed with some suspicion.[48]

It was not surprising that Lyndon Johnson and Fulbright had worked closely together in the past. When Johnson was majority leader, Fulbright gave intellectual credibility to Johnson's foreign policy credentials. LBJ relied on Fulbright's judgments and gladly used his critique of Eisenhower's foreign policy. Fulbright in turn had little trouble with Johnson's closeness to oil and gas interests. The close relationship continued when LBJ was vice president, and Johnson invariably turned to Fulbright for advice in his first eighteen months in the White House. Fulbright drew on his vast foreign affairs experience and reputation to lead the drive for the passage of the Tonkin Gulf resolution. When Fulbright started to warn against the imperialist tendencies in American foreign policy, he was initially identifying a national arrogance, not targeting Johnson.

Whereas Gore had long been vocal in his criticism of American policy in Vietnam, Fulbright, whose overriding concern was with American–Soviet relations, was much more reticent. Fulbright had been excluded from the planning to escalate the conflict from the 1964 election through to February 1965. But while Fulbright was uneasy about the bombing and the commitment of troops, he publicly proclaimed what he wanted to believe: that Johnson was a force for restraint in the administration and the troops were mainly designed to stabilize the situation until South Vietnam was strong enough to start negotiations. He was appalled to realize at a meeting in the White House that Johnson was settling in for a long haul of seven to eight years and might be looking for a battlefield victory. Johnson kept his decision-making on foreign policy tightly controlled within a small group of advisers—McGeorge Bundy, Dean Rusk, and Robert McNamara. He tended to inform Fulbright rather than consult him. Nevertheless, Fulbright's doubts about the Vietnamese venture surfaced only when Johnson authorized intervention in the Dominican Republic in 1965. Fulbright was angered that the president had lied to him about the nature of the communist threat and the danger to American lives on the island. He spoke out about the duplicity that led to false stories about that threat and the imminent danger it posed. It was at this point that Fulbright decided to immerse himself in the Vietnam issue and to read up on Chinese history.[49]

Gore's concerns predated Fulbright's. Gore had already called for a negotiated settlement in Vietnam in a December 1964 speech in Miami. He took credit for being the first senator to do so. He followed up that call in January 1965. There needed to be a face-saving way to disengage, otherwise the United States risked war with China. LBJ responded by simply telling him, testily, that he looked good on TV. But in executive sessions of the Foreign Relations Committee in January 1965, both Gore and Fulbright expressed the need for negotiations, because military action was failing to generate the necessary political stability. Gore was identified by an assistant to William Bundy as part of a Senate "group of fairly junior liberals growing in size and boldness who advocate finding a way to withdraw honorably and under the protection of international safeguards as the first order of business."[50]

Gore's alarms, however, were greater than Fulbright's. Gore's doctor, Gordon Petty, recalled that in March 1965 he called Gore to talk about Medicare. When they finished their discussion, he asked Gore what he was doing and when he was coming back to Carthage. In about twenty minutes, he would be home, Gore replied. Petty asked him if he would be interested in going to the Vanderbilt basketball game that night. When Petty picked Gore up later, he told Petty, "I've had my mind so torn up by problems of state lately and probably you're having the same problem with problems of medicine. Let's forget it all tonight and just let it all hang out and just relax and let our hair down and have a good time." But twenty miles down the road, all Gore had done was grunt and answer monosyllabically. It was obvious that his mind was on something else. When Petty challenged Gore, Gore poured out his troubles.

> "Well something has developed that I just can't get out of my mind. The President is about to commit the fighting troops in Vietnam." He says, "It is one of the worst mistakes that the United States has ever been involved in. We have no business there. The French fought in Vietnam for twenty years and finally they gave up and went home and now we are getting sucked into the same problem." And he said, "We have no business there, heretofore we've had manufacturers selling equipment, military equipment over there and just advisors over there to advise them how to use it." But he said, "Now the President is about to commit fighting troops." He said, "It will go down in history as one of the worst mistakes our country has ever made." He said, "I called the President this morning from my office in Washington and discussed it with him quite a while and he's committed to do it." He said, "Before I left up there to come here I called him and talked to him again and went over to the White House and talked to him and tried to talk him out of it." He says, "Then after I got home to Carthage I called him again and talked to him again about it. There's no changing him. He's going to commit fighting troops. It's a mistake." Says, "We'll lose a lot of good American boys. It'll cost a whole lot. We will fight a war that can't be won." And he said, "It will just drag on, and on, and on and just be a mess."[51]

Gore tried to find reasons to believe that Johnson was a force for restraint. He supported the portions of Johnson's speech at Johns Hopkins on 7 April that called for unconditional negotiations. He continued in June 1965 to think Johnson was restricting escalation. When Johnson made his 28 July announcement of the full-scale commitment of ground troops, however, Gore lamented that the president was following a policy that had not "worked well in any respect since 1954." The war was unwinnable "except at a cost which far outweighs the fruits of victory." The war might escalate into a major power confrontation and even a nuclear holocaust. But he professed to be pleased that the president emphasized negotiations and did not seem to envisage a major ground war.[52]

As Fulbright became more and more exercised by American involvement in Vietnam at the end of 1965, he and Gore moved even closer together. Fulbright was increasingly convinced that the administration was no longer a force for restraint and that Johnson and his advisers were pursuing a strategy that would inevitably escalate the conflict. Behind closed doors Mansfield gave the committee a grim report about the state of the war on the ground after an inspection visit to Vietnam.

Gore and the other more vocal critics of the war on the committee, Frank Church and Wayne Morse, were pressing for public hearings to educate the American people about the war. But when Fulbright reluctantly proposed hearings on 11 January 1966, he allowed Mansfield and Bourke Hickenlooper to block the move.[53]

Over the next three weeks, Fulbright became convinced that there was no prospect of containing the war: The administration had made an open-ended commitment that left no room for any negotiated settlement short of total victory. He was furious at the "charade" of apparent consultation at a meeting he was invited to at the White House on 25 January 1966, when it became clear to him that the administration did not even contemplate extending the bombing halt. Dean Rusk's closed-door testimony in support of a supplemental appropriation for the war confirmed the president's unbending commitment to the current military strategy. When the request was made in public hearings on 28 January, Gore was anxious that Rusk not interpret support for a supplemental appropriation as an endorsement of the war. He would always, he said, support forces who were in Vietnam not of their own choice but at the orders of the government. He reminded Rusk that he had opposed American intervention since 1954. He questioned whether the Tonkin Gulf resolution could be treated as a declaration of war, and he argued that Vietnam was diverting attention from more critical relations with China and the Soviet Union.[54]

Fulbright despaired when the bombing of North Vietnam resumed on 31 January. But what really alarmed Fulbright was a speech that John Stennis, chair of the Armed Services Committee, had given in Mississippi on 27 January. In this speech the Mississippi senator seemed to advocate an unrestrained war. Stennis appeared to view with equanimity the use of nuclear weapons if unleashing the U.S. military led to Chinese intervention. The prospect of a nuclear confrontation with China scared Fulbright, as it had always troubled Gore since the Korean War. Gore worried that Johnson could not stand up to Stennis and the military. As he lamented at a small meeting of antiwar senators, Johnson was "a desperate man who was likely to get us into war with China, and we've got to prevent it. We all like the President, but we've got to stop him."[55]

On 3 February, Fulbright therefore agreed to the proposals from Gore, Church, and Morse that there should be public televised hearings about the war. Gore argued that meetings with Rusk and McNamara had been futile, and that it was now time to go over the head of the president "to the American people and reach him by way of the people." Gore played a prominent role in the hearings. No one was more forensic in their questioning of administration spokesmen or more receptive to the arguments of critics of the war like George Kennan and James Gavin. Gore, unlike Wayne Morse, was more restrained in his questioning of Secretary of State Rusk and General Maxwell Taylor. He went out of his way to praise them as great public servants while never letting up in his critical questioning. He reiterated the point that there was no chance of a negotiated settlement if the demand was for North Vietnam to surrender unconditionally. He was particularly alarmed that neither Taylor nor Rusk could define an upper limit on the size of U.S. forces. The prospect of unrestricted escalation confirmed his worst fear: a nuclear war with China. Gore strongly believed that the hearings, which infuriated Johnson, had a positive educational impact. He claimed that mail across the nation was 25 to 1 in favor of the hearings, and he quoted a reporter's wife who said, "You have an unclean house, but an informed wife." The Southern historian C. Vann Woodward, watching from Yale, memorably captured Gore's impact on Northern intellectual and academic audiences: "Anyone who has seen him on the TV screen interrogating a witness will never forget those unblinking, hypnotic eyes and frozen accusatory features, and will have known at a glance there was no Southern good-old-boyism in him."[56]

The Foreign Relations Committee hearings made Gore's break with the president—as it did for Fulbright and Church—increasingly bitter. Other Foreign Relations Committee critics of the war, including Stuart Symington, Mike Mansfield, George Aiken, and even Wayne Morse, kept their lines of communications open to the White House and even provided intelligence to Johnson on how the committee was shaping up. Gore refused to do so and moved to distance himself from other administration foreign policies. He led the effort to force Secretary of State Rusk to testify before the committee, refused to support the Punta del Este resolution backing the president's diplomacy in Latin America, and became an unreliable supporter on foreign aid because of his fear that it would be used to sustain unpopular right-wing military governments. No one was more vociferous in demanding that Secretary Rusk be forced to testify in public before the Foreign Relations Committee in 1967. But Gore went about his opposition in his own way also. He never voted against appropriations for the war. He argued that the troops in the field had to be supported. Similarly, he disliked antiwar demonstrations and student protests.[57]

Gore's underlying position was unmoved. He was convinced that the war would prove to be "an historical, tragic mistake." No military victory was possible "unless one imagines that he can throw gravel into the Mississippi until it is successfully dammed," and no political victory was likely given the nature of the war they were fighting and its inevitable effect on the civilian Vietnamese population. "Perhaps even more importantly in this regard, it has been, and is now becoming even more so, white man against yellow man. Racism is big in this equation, so is religion, so is anti-colonialism." He later said, "[No matter] how pure our motives, the United States cannot master the revolutionary, nationalistic tide that is sweeping the world." Two mistakes had been made, he believed. Vietnam had become an American war; bombing was ineffective because "the strength and manpower of the Vietcong is still predominantly indigenous to South Vietnam." Military victory could be achieved only "at tremendous cost which is out of proportion to the vital interests of this country" and at the risk of a war with China that might well lead to nuclear war. Gore feared war with China. His awareness of the dangers of escalation in Vietnam went back to his 1951 fears in Korea about endlessly swapping lives with the Chinese, and the possibility of a nuclear holocaust. He worried now that bombing close to the Chinese border—or worse, bombing enemy sanctuaries inside China—would lead to a war with China. It would be impossible to contain China with conventional forces. Escalation to a nuclear conflict would be almost inevitable. He also worried that the war would free up the Soviets to wreak havoc in Africa and Latin America and perhaps heal the Sino–Soviet split. But the war also threatened better relations with the Soviets. As someone who had taken a keen interest in Europe and in Soviet relations, perhaps influenced by his friendship with Armand Hammer, Gore saw Vietnam threatening the improvement of relations with the Soviets, which he took to be crucial to future world security and far more important to America's national interest than Vietnam.[58]

In 1967 Gore became convinced that the administration's terms for negotiations were impossibly severe and an excuse for further military action. In October 1967 he called for the neutralization of Southeast Asia. Only that goal had the prospect of moving negotiations forward. The administration could not claim that "we are in mortal peril in Vietnam" and then claim to negotiate. Neither U.S. security nor vital interests were in fact at stake, he believed. The *New York Times* commented that, apart from Wayne Morse and Ernest Gruening, "no other Senator until now has gone as far as Senator Gore did today in urging that the United States should get out of Vietnam."[59]

Johnson finally conceded that his massive military effort had simply created a stalemate and that more troops would not win the war. He announced on 31 March 1968 that he would not seek reelection so that he could pursue peace negotiations in an unfettered way. Talks shortly began in Paris. Gore praised Johnson's decision as "the greatest contribution he could have made toward unity and possible peace in Vietnam." Negotiations would be impossible if he were still a candidate. "If these steps were taken by a presidential candidate, they would be politically misunderstood and subject to change and question. The President will now be able to work without the political inhibitions that would be necessary for a successful political campaign for reelection."[60]

As the summer wore on, however, Gore had increasing doubts about how realistic the administration's negotiating stance was going to be. If Johnson continued to insist that North Vietnam and the Viet Cong give up their military goals, there was little to negotiate. Gore worried that Hubert Humphrey would be unable to disassociate himself from the Johnson position. He expressed his admiration for Eugene McCarthy, whom his son, Al, enthusiastically supported. He had great faith in Robert Kennedy, who had announced his candidacy for president on 16 March 1968. On 21 March Kennedy spoke to a crowd of ten thousand at Vanderbilt University in Nashville. Harold Vanderbilt, who had been chair of the board of trustees since 1955, telegrammed his apologies because of ill health but added, "I too oppose the Vietnam War." Gore did not attend, but after the speech many of his allies met Kennedy at John Seigenthaler's house. From the start the Kennedy team recognized that Governor Ellington had tight control of the Tennessee delegation to the national convention. After LBJ announced he would not be running, the team looked for individuals they might pick off from the delegation, but they ruefully acknowledged that they had lost any chance of winning over the Tennessee delegation when long-time Kennedy friend John Jay Hooker had been defeated for the governorship in 1966. They toyed with the idea of a lawsuit attacking the unit rule: "We could get an excellent three judge court in Nashville and it would infuriate Ellington which is all the more reason why the idea is appealing." But they did not pursue the idea and, as in North Carolina and Alabama, they did not even send campaign materials to Tennessee.[61]

After Robert Kennedy's assassination, Gore went to the Chicago Democratic convention ready to support the last-minute attempt to draft Edward Kennedy. He was bitterly disappointed that Ted Kennedy would not let his name go forward. In a draft of his convention speech in favor of the peace plank on the Democratic platform, Gore wrote: "Only a few hours ago, I thought it possible to coalesce forces and to call to duty one who could rekindle for America and for a yearning world the idealism and the flame of youthful hope that was lost five years ago. But this is not to be."[62]

Gore spoke passionately for the peace plank at the Chicago convention. He worked through his speech with his son, Al. He pulled no punches. Democrats had "voted for our distinguished leader, President Lyndon B. Johnson, but they got the policies of Senator Goldwater." The consequences had been dire. "What harvest do we reap from our gallant sacrifice? An erosion of the moral and spiritual base of American leadership, entanglement with the corrupt political leadership in Saigon, disillusionment, despair here at home and a disastrous postponement of imperative programs to improve our social ills." His speech was wildly applauded by the New York and California delegations and studiously ignored by the Tennessee delegation. The delegation was bound by the unit rule to vote for Governor Ellington as a favorite son. But it was clear that the favorite son candidacy was a move designed to provide support for Hubert Humphrey. Gore voted for George McGovern rather than Eugene McCarthy. He admired both men but thought that McGovern was more responsible and acceptable to more people than McCarthy.[63]

Gore did not sit out the 1968 election, but his campaigning for his old friend Hubert Humphrey was rather token. He was at home in Carthage when Johnson announced the bombing halt that Humphrey had wanted. Gore was pleased: The halt was "what I've advocated for many months. I hope it leads to a ceasefire and peace." He added, "No negotiations would be possible without it."[64]

Gore's stance on Vietnam was a lonely one in Tennessee and the South. The South was a region where a large majority of white voters supported the war, had little truck with a limited war, and wanted the United States to go all out for victory. More than a quarter of the casualties in the war came from the South. Gore and Fulbright were the only Southern senators to dissent on the war. While Johnson was president the dissenters were a relatively small, unorganized group; apart from veterans Wayne Morse and Ernest Gruening, Gore and Fulbright found themselves working with younger, more recently elected senators like Frank Church, George McGovern, and Eugene McCarthy. Gore was a lone vote in the Tennessee delegation at the Chicago convention. He recalled that the war was an issue even more intractable than civil rights or abortion. It was the one issue that caused long-time friends and acquaintances to cross the road rather than meet him or shake his hand. But Gore was always convinced that he had been right. When Lyndon Johnson rehashed his Vietnam decisions over and over and replayed them in his mind, he would muse that perhaps he should have paid more attention to his old friend William Fulbright and not broken with him. He never mused that he should have paid more attention to Albert Gore.[65]

〜

DESPITE THE BREAK between Gore and Johnson, Gore found himself helping the administration twice in 1968.

When Earl Warren told Johnson that he wished to retire from the Supreme Court, Johnson saw the opportunity to recommend the appointment of his old friend and confidant Abe Fortas as chief justice. Gore had known and admired the Memphis-born lawyer Fortas since the New Deal. He willingly took up the baton of leading the Senate campaign for Fortas's confirmation. On the day of Johnson's announcement of his choice, Gore took to the floor of the Senate to commend Fortas's selection "with pride." He was confident that Fortas "will make an indelible record as Chief Justice."[66]

Strom Thurmond and other Southerners were determined to thwart Fortas's nomination. Robert Griffin of Michigan led like-minded Republicans who did not want to see the liberalism of the Warren court perpetuated by the lame-duck appointment of a chief justice who was a "crony" of Johnson.

They hoped to delay confirmation so that Richard Nixon would choose the next chief justice. When Gore presented this "distinguished son" of Tennessee to the Senate Judiciary hearing on its second day, there had already been a day of testimony from Griffin and from hostile right-wing opponents. In an attempt to put Fortas's appearance in a positive light, Gore noted that Fortas was the first sitting justice (not a recess appointment) to appear before the committee and that he was the first nominee for chief justice to appear. It was ironic that the Johnson administration had to rely on Gore and Ralph Yarborough, friends who were at odds with the administration, to present their nominees to the committee. Yarborough had introduced Homer Thornberry from Texas, the nominee who would take Fortas's place when he became chief justice. Thurmond and his fellow conservatives were not deterred: The hearings dragged on as evidence focused on Fortas's relationship with the president and the effect of the court's decisions on obscenity laws which, critics claimed, had unleashed a flood of pornography. In September Republicans filibustered Fortas's nomination in the Senate, determined to keep the choice of chief justice for the incoming president. Gore, identified as the "principal sponsor" of the nomination, concluded sadly on 1 October that although Fortas's qualifications to be chief justice were "unexcelled by any Chief Justice in the history of our country", Fortas was being made a scapegoat for the liberal Warren Court by those who wish to curb the court. "This is not the Senate's finest hour," intoned Gore. Efforts to end the filibuster failed, and Fortas withdrew his name from consideration as chief justice.[67]

In the summer of 1968, the United States signed the Nuclear Nonproliferation Treaty (hastened by China's acquisition of a hydrogen bomb). In September Gore was the main figure pushing to get the NPT out of the Foreign Relations Committee and on to the floor of the Senate. As the *Washington Post* noted, Gore had other things (the Fortas nomination) on his mind, yet he persisted with the NPT effort. It was, said the *Post*, "an act of statesmanship such as you don't witness very often in the Senate—certainly not in September of 1968." Gore, the *Post* concluded, "deserves a full measure of praise."[68]

The NPT failed because in the end its advocates feared that the Soviet invasion of Czechoslovakia and suspicions of the Soviets would lessen support for the Treaty on the Senate floor. Gore was concerned that the Soviet invasion and America's Vietnam involvement would reverse the lessening of east–west tensions with Russia. He feared America would slip back into isolationism and hard-line anti-communism. He explained his concerns in a meeting with Soviet premier Alexei N. Kosygin in Moscow after the November presidential election. He had joined Foreign Relations colleague Claiborne Pell from Rhode Island on a visit to Prague and Moscow. There was little doubt that their antiwar credentials and their votes against the deployment of an antiballistic missile (ABM) system led them to be favorably received in Moscow. Gore praised the vast improvements in housing and schools in Moscow and cited his own record as a supporter of infrastructure development in the South. On the key issues Gore left Kosygin in no doubt of the shock and dismay that Americans had felt at the Czech invasion and noted it was impossible for President Johnson to initiate missile-reduction talks in that climate. Gore argued that it was still possible to resume progress toward detente provided there were no more "kindred events"—that is, Soviet intervention elsewhere in Europe. After all the United States and the Soviets had a greater mutual interest in controlling arms expenditures than at any other time. Kosygin mounted the standard defense of the Soviet actions in Czechoslovakia, chided America for its policies in Vietnam and its stationing of troops overseas, and blamed the United States for the lack of progress in the Paris peace talks. But Gore was able to bring back to Washington two key insights: that Kosygin did not see Vietnam as a barrier to making progress on nuclear disarmament, and that he had been alarmed by Nixon's campaign rhetoric about only negotiating from a position of military superiority. Gore had stressed that a change in administration did not mean a change in policy in the United States. He noted that Kosygin had expressed pleasure in the tone of telegrams received from Nixon the week before.[69]

The antiwar and anti-ABM stances of Gore and Pell probably eased their way to a meeting with Kosygin. It probably also helped that Gore was a friend and business partner of Armand Hammer. Hammer, whose father, Julius, was one of the founders of the American Communist Party, originally made his money from his trading links in the Soviet Union in the 1920s. He made pharmaceuticals available to the Soviets, won concessions for the provision of stationery supplies, and facilitated exports and imports from a country that did not have diplomatic relations with the United States. He aroused the suspicions of J. Edgar Hoover, which never abated. He invested in oil and would eventually become chair and CEO of Occidental Petroleum. Like Bernard Baruch, Hammer was always on the lookout for young, potentially influential politicians to support. He was renowned as a collector of fine art, but also of purebred cattle.[70]

Whatever Hammer's motives may have been, a shared interest in cattle led to a friendship with Gore. This friendship started at a time when Gore had little influence over Hammer's main business concerns and his interests in the USSR. Gore was scarcely in a position to help Hammer further the interests of the Soviet Union, in whose service, some historians maintain, Hammer continued to serve after his early business career in Russia. The friendship reaped rewards for Gore largely in his business career *after* he left office. Yet there were accusations that Hammer, allegedly a Soviet agent, was buying influence with Gore. Critics said buyers at the Gore cattle sales sometimes paid over the market price to boost the senator's finances. If they did, they made no noticeable impact on Gore's finances while he was in the Senate. Corrupt relationships are usually demonstrated by large sums of cash flowing from the influence-seeker to the politician. It is counterintuitive to believe there was a corrupt relationship when Gore scrupulously presented modest feed bills and wrote personal reimbursement checks to Hammer. Gore's 1968 trip and Hammer's visit to the Soviet Union in 1961 did highlight the fact that each could facilitate the other's access to Soviet officialdom. There is no doubt that Hammer and Gore shared similar and consistent views about the desirability of easing tensions with the Soviets.[71]

⸏

GORE MIGHT HAVE stressed the continuity of policy between presidents, but he was not optimistic about a Nixon presidency. Gore had been cautious when LBJ became president. But, despite his opposition to signature measures of the Johnson administration—the tax cut and the 1964 Civil Rights Act—he had shared the optimism of the Great Society that the expertise of the federal government could solve the nation's social ills. Vietnam left Gore dispirited and cast off from the administration. When Johnson left office the prospects for Vietnam looked bleak, despite the Paris peace talks efforts. Now Gore once again would find himself going head-to-head with a president—this time one whose views about social programs and the South differed greatly from those of LBJ and Gore.

CHAPTER 8

The Struggle for a Conservative Majority

ANY DEMOCRAT WHO had been in Congress in 1947 and had been mentored by Sam Rayburn was taught to be suspicious of newly elected President Richard Nixon. Albert Gore was no exception. At the start of the new administration in 1969, Gore took some heart from the fact that Nixon appeared to rule out total military victory in Vietnam. Perhaps a new Republican president could extricate America from Vietnam in the same way Eisenhower had extricated the country from Korea? But Gore was soon disillusioned by the Nixon policy of Vietnamization. Like many Democratic dissenters on the war, Gore became more strident in his opposition with a Republican in the White House.[1]

But Vietnam was only part of a wider ideological and political battle for the future of America. Nixon, who had narrowly beaten Hubert Humphrey in 1968, aimed to create a new conservative ideological majority. Nixon and his advisers crafted an appeal that was based on patriotism and law and order. These goals involved peace with honor in Vietnam, an antiballistic missile (ABM) system to protect America's first-strike capability, social conservatism, and a robust policy toward criminals and protesters, including rioting African Americans and student activists. Presidential speechwriter Pat Buchanan summed up the strategy—to use the racial issues to split the electorate: "This is a potential throw of the dice that could bring the media on our heads, and cut the Democratic Party and country in half; my view is that we would have far the larger half."[2]

⟿

FOR THE NATIONAL conservative project, the South was indispensable. To secure the party nomination in 1968, Nixon had come to an agreement with Strom Thurmond, the Republican senator from South Carolina. In return for Thurmond's support, Nixon would rein in zealous bureaucrats on school desegregation, take Thurmond's aide Harry Dent into the White House to oversee the distribution of patronage and party development in the South, and appoint strict constructionists to the Supreme Court. In the 1968 election itself, in a state like Tennessee, Nixon and Wallace had split the white vote, with middle- to upper-income voters going to the Republicans and lower-income whites to Wallace. The purpose of the Southern strategy in Nixon's first term was to win over those Wallace voters to the Republicans. Patriotism and law and order were the keys to winning these voters, as it was to winning over working-class ethnics and Catholics in the North. In both cases the makeup of the Supreme Court was crucial. The issues at the core of Nixon's conservative strategy—race relations and the pace of desegregation, law and order and the treatment of criminals and dissidents, the protection of traditional moral values—all revolved around issues that would ultimately be decided in the courts. The appointment of judges, particularly Supreme Court justices, would be a vital battleground.[3]

The court, conservatives believed, had coddled criminals, undermined respect for traditional morality, and imposed unwarranted racial change on the South. Because of LBJ's failure to get Abe Fortas confirmed as chief justice in 1968, Nixon was going to be in a position to replace his old nemesis, Earl Warren. Behind the scenes Nixon had encouraged conservatives in the Senate in 1968 to oppose Fortas precisely to give himself the chance to appoint his own chief justice. But Nixon and Attorney General John Mitchell also saw an even greater opportunity. They could appoint another strict constructionist to the court if they could force Fortas off the Supreme Court altogether. A determined *Life* magazine reporter uncovered a retainer that Fortas had received from the Wolfson Foundation, headed by financier Louis Wolfson, who was under indictment. The reporter alerted Will Wilson, head of the criminal division of the Justice Department, who "wanted Fortas off the court." Wilson in turn briefed J. Edgar Hoover, Nixon, and Mitchell. They put pressure on Wolfson, found documentary evidence of Fortas's arrangements, put the material before Earl Warren, and stirred up the press. Fortas had no alternative but to resign.[4]

Gore had enthusiastically led the fight to secure Fortas's confirmation as chief justice in 1968. He did not now rush to judgment against him in 1969. But when the revelations came out, he admitted that things did not look good. He stated, "In my view, members of the Supreme Court should be most circumspect in their conduct and as nearly like Caesar's wife as possible." He continued to refer to Fortas as one of the ablest lawyers he knew. He justified his 1968 support of Fortas by saying that he had not been aware of some of the facts that had subsequently come out. But he was also suspicious of the way in which Fortas had been hounded out. He called for a congressional investigation to determine if Republicans had used information that they had not shared with the public to make Fortas resign.[5]

When Fortas was forced out, Gore found it easy to support Nixon's nominee, Warren Burger, for the chief justiceship. To replace Fortas, Gore supported Howard Baker's endorsement of U.S. District Court Judge William E. Miller of Nashville. But Nixon appointed Clement Haynsworth of Greenville, South Carolina, whom Eisenhower had appointed to the Fourth Circuit Court in 1957. Civil rights groups and labor unions protested his conservative rulings, but the press assumed Gore was going to support Haynsworth. Journalists knew Gore firmly believed that any president's nominee to the federal court should normally be confirmed.[6]

Allegations that Haynsworth held stock in a company whose case he heard gave the opposition the chance to turn the debate into one not just of liberal opposition to his rulings but of accusations of conflict of interest. Joe Hatcher of the *Tennessean* put the argument with characteristic vigor: "It's turning out that Judge Clement F. Haynsworth Jr. has more conflicts of interest than a country dog has fleas. Compared with the rather shadowy conflicts of interest which caused Justice Abe Fortas' resignation from the court, the charges against Judge Haynsworth are specific, dated, collar-marked, and clearly documented." There was little doubt that many Democrats had not forgotten the Republican drive against Fortas and welcomed the chance for revenge.[7]

One of Gore's supporters lamented that "you are going out on the wrong limb in almost everything." If he voted to confirm Haynsworth, he argued, it would go some way toward compensating for his fight for Fortas, his stance on Vietnam and the ABM, and his support of Ted Kennedy for majority whip. His constituent letters left Gore in no doubt about what was at stake. Wrote one Oak Ridge constituent: "If you have one inch of soul left unsold, if you have one micron of self-respect left, if somewhere in the darkest corner of the coal bin of your psyche you have remaining to you one shining golden thread of nobility, of fairness, of justice, then you will vote for the confirmation of Judge Haynsworth."[8]

Right up to the last minute, the White House expected that Gore would vote for Haynsworth. If he and John Sherman Cooper of Kentucky did so, the White House believed it had forty-seven votes, and that three senators—Robert Packwood (R-Oregon), Thomas Dodd (D-Connecticut), and Alan Bible (D-Nevada)—had then agreed to vote to confirm. But Gore disappointed both the White House and many of his constituents by voting against Haynsworth, as did Cooper. Packwood, Bible, and Dodd were free therefore to vote against the judge—and Haynsworth was defeated 55 to 45, the first defeat of a Supreme Court nomination since Judge John J. Parker in 1930.[9]

For Gore his vote was simply based on judicial ethics. "It would be an unwise precedent," he wrote, "to place on the Court a judge who had sat on cases involving a company in which he owns stock." It was a measure of the incompetence of the pro-Haynsworth forces that the only pressure they could think to bring to bear on Gore was the prospect of moving a vacant Sixth Circuit judgeship from Michigan to Tennessee or to get Tennessee bankers to lobby Gore. To Gore's opponents in Tennessee, he had betrayed his state and region. They promised him swift electoral retribution:

> Your vote against Judge Haynsworth marks you as a gutless coward who has sold his soul to the corrupt union bosses and the black militants. It's little comfort to know that you'll get your "reward" someday.
>
> I just want you to know that I'm going to do everything in my power to see that you're rewarded NEXT YEAR. I'm going to work tirelessly for Bill Brock starting NOW and I'm going to give what money I can to his campaign. And remember, there are thousands more Tennesseans like me.
>
> We want to rid this nation's government and the Union-owned Senate of our long haired, vacuous, arrogant, anti-American disgraceful Senator.
>
> You make me sick.
>
> p.s.: And don't waste my hard-earned tax dollars, which you so love to redistribute to the lazy, by having your staff send me one of your innocuous form letters.[10]

After Haynsworth was defeated, Nixon nominated Harrold Carswell, a Florida judge, to the Supreme Court. No one thought the Senate would defeat a second Supreme Court nomination. Even the *Tennessean* assumed there would be little opposition. Surely after the Haynsworth embarrassment the administration would have done its homework in screening the candidate and examining his personal financial holdings. After the reaction to his vote against Haynsworth, Gore was very anxious to support a Southerner for the court if at all possible. Labor and black organizations urged him to vote against Carswell, but Gore made it clear in early March 1970 that he saw no reason to oppose the nomination.[11]

Opponents lamented Carswell's mediocrity, lawyers cast doubts on his qualifications, and liberals uncovered ancient segregationist speeches. Even Fritz Hollings of South Carolina, who had championed Haynsworth, lamented that "Carswell can't even carry Haynsworth's law books." But still Gore kept his own counsel. What tipped the balance for Gore was what he considered to be Carswell's deliberate misstatements and faulty memory in his sworn testimony before the Judiciary Committee. Nevertheless, Gore was still inclined to support Carswell, and his staff did not know how he intended to vote. He finally made his mind up the night before the vote, when he read the entire record. The next day he voted to recommit the nomination to the Judiciary Committee and then voted against Carswell. The Florida judge was denied confirmation by 51 votes to 45.[12]

Liberals recognized that it was a politically difficult vote for Gore. Senator Thomas F. Eagleton (D-Missouri) had not "written a 'love letter' since entering the Senate," but Gore's vote made him "prouder than ever to be a member of the Senate by reason of the courage you displayed yesterday." Birch Bayh of Indiana, one of Carswell's opponents on the Judiciary Committee, recognized that, as difficult as it was for each member of the Senate, "your position was particularly trying." As his handwritten note at the bottom of the letter exclaimed, "Albert—We couldn't have done this without you!" Ted Kennedy, who had led the fight against Carswell on the Judiciary Committee, later recalled the "two very hard decisions" that Gore had made on the Supreme Court nominations: "Gore was just terrific on both of these."[13]

National civil rights leaders like Whitney Young and Ralph Abernathy praised his vote. For black organizations in Tennessee, Gore's vote seemed to erase the memory of his vote against the 1964 Civil Rights Act. The Tennessee Voters Council, the conference of state branches of the NAACP, and the Memphis branch of the NAACP hastened to congratulate him.[14]

Nixon argued that the Carswell vote showed that it was impossible to get a Southern strict constructionist confirmed as a Supreme Court justice and therefore hastened to nominate Harry Blackmun of Minnesota, whom Gore voted to confirm. In vain an exasperated Gore noted that Nixon could easily have found a distinguished Southern judge who would have been confirmed with little opposition. When Gore was accused of disloyalty to the region, he argued that "to suggest that Mr. Carswell was the best the South could offer is, in my mind, a greater insult to the South." But Gore knew how effective the Nixon argument was among Tennessee voters. As Wade Brown from Memphis told him, "You, I'm afraid, are out of tune with the political tone of the State of Tennessee. Pity!!" In an argument that gained increasing currency as the summer wore on, Brown concluded, "Your behavior smacks as someone who thinks he was put in congress by the Northern Liberal Establishment (and an assist from the 'great' intellectual from Arkansas)." Gore had made much of Carswell's lapse of memory. Would Gore, Brown wondered, be "so firm and resolute when your fellow liberal, Senator Kennedy, steps forward in 1972?"[15]

～

ON VIETNAM, AS with the Supreme Court nominations—where Gore had been reluctant initially to oppose the president—Gore was inclined to take some heart from the early moves of the Nixon administration. The president appeared to rule out total military victory in Vietnam, and he boasted of troop withdrawals. "Peace with honor" in the Nixon formulation meant increasing military pressure on North Vietnam, primarily through bombing, to persuade Hanoi to negotiate meaningfully in Paris. At the same time, the administration argued, increasing the size and capability of the South Vietnamese army would enable the Vietnamization of the war and the gradual withdrawal of American troops. As late as May 1969, Gore seemed to be giving the president the benefit of the doubt. He believed, for example, that Nixon was prepared to accept a coalition government in Vietnam. By June, however, those initial hopes had largely disappeared. Gore feared that Nixon's policies were simply a continuation of the old Johnson–Rusk line. The Midway conference in June seemed to tie Nixon to the Thieu regime even more. Gore feared that the policy was simply a way of buying time to secure military victory. Strengthening the South's army, the Army of the Republic of Vietnam (AVRN) was a chimera: "too many of the South Vietnamese have no stomach for the fight and no sense of identity with the ruling clique." The United States was in a hopeless quest to "stem the revolutionary, nationalist tide" across the world. Ideologically the United States might prefer a democratic regime in South Vietnam, but for Gore there were no national security grounds for staying in South Vietnam. Gore still hoped against hope that the administration's rhetoric was a cover for behind-the-scenes realistic negotiation, but he increasingly doubted that. Gore believed that a "phased withdrawal of increments of U.S. troops" was simply a device to buy time for the administration at the negotiating table. It was a recipe for "prolonged war and indefinite involvement." There was no prospect of a negotiated settlement as long as retaining the oppressive Thieu–Ky regime was nonnegotiable. So long as the goal was a "South Korea–type client state," or, as Fulbright put it, "the puppet government in South Vietnam," there could be no settlement.[16]

Gore's stance continued to provoke passionate opposition in Tennessee. Said one constituent, "I am fed up with your representing the most extreme liberal element of this country . . . that I could VOMIT."[17]

Gore doubted the administration figures on troop withdrawal: They were "wonderland figures," he said on 31 July 1969, given that the number of American troops in Vietnam had actually increased since Nixon took office. As he began to despair of any change of policy, his own rhetoric became harsher and more emotional. He deplored the continued loss of life in a futile cause: "This war must end. It must end because it is immoral and because it is wrong. It must end too, because it threatens to destroy us."[18]

Gore's focus on the loss of life became even more strident when the president gave his "Silent Majority" speech on 3 November 1969. Nixon focused on the maintenance of American will, the refusal of Hanoi to negotiate, the strengthening of South Vietnam, the Vietnamization of the war, and the gradual withdrawal of American troops. Nixon cast the alternative policy as simply "precipitate withdrawal" and defeat. Gore reacted with dismay. The president had abandoned the search for a political settlement and was still looking for an elusive military victory. That victory would be impossible with the current regime in Saigon, argued Gore: "Saigon is our albatross." He felt that having Thieu in power would only lengthen the war: "Until the United States shows to the other side that it is no longer wedded to the Thieu government and uses its influence to bring a representative government to power, I fear the killing will go on." Maintaining "the existing corrupt regime in Saigon" was, wrote Gore, a major point on which he differed with the Nixon administration. When challenged by Senator Bob Dole—"Is the Senator suggesting that we topple the government in Saigon?"—Gore replied that the Saigon regime should be broadened to involve various groups including the communist Viet Cong, Buddhists, and other "diverse elements." He now focused even more on the loss of life. Forty-six thousand Americans had been killed by November 1969, a year after Nixon's election. Gore inserted the casualty figures each week in the *Congressional Record*.[19]

Gore fully supported moves to restore congressional prerogatives in for-eign policy-making. He supported Fulbright's National Commitments Reso-lution, which would have required that any commitment of American troops abroad would need the specific authorization of both the executive and legis-lative branches by means of a treaty, statute, or concurrent resolution of both houses. It was a belated nonbinding attempt to prevent another open-ended commitment such as the Gulf of Tonkin resolution. In December 1969 Gore next supported the move by John Sherman Cooper and Frank Church to pro-hibit U.S. combat intervention in Laos and Thailand, although the move did not halt the administration's secret air war in Laos. As evidence of the admin-istration's build-up in Laos in February 1970 grew, Gore supported the reser-vations of Cooper and Church, together with Mike Mansfield, Stuart Syming-ton, and Mac Mathias, about this further defiance of the Geneva Accords. He believed that there was a coverup of U.S. involvement in Laos and threatened to release secret Foreign Relations Committee testimony that would confirm that activity.[20]

These relatively austere, Congress-oriented, discussions were suddenly made explosive by Nixon's address to the American people on 1 May 1970. When a military coup under Lon Nol overthrew Prince Sihanouk, Cooper and Church were preparing to ban U.S. combat troops in Cambodia. Un-known to them, Nixon planned to send U.S. troops into Cambodia in sup-port of South Vietnamese forces to bolster the Lon Nol regime and destroy the Viet Cong sanctuaries there. Nixon saw this move as a message to both Hanoi and the U.S. Senate that the president could not be pushed round by either of them. When the president went on television to announce the inva-sion on 30 April, Gore was outraged. He saw duplicity by the administration: The move was at odds with recent assurances by the president and testimony by Secretary of State William Rogers, as late as 27 April, to the Senate For-eign Relations Committee. He talked of an impending constitutional crisis. He challenged the whole premise of the invasion: that the destruction of the sanctuaries would end the Viet Cong insurgency. After all, he said, the enemy sanctuary extended from the Cambodian border to "all of Asia behind it." At a meeting with the president on 5 May, he ridiculed Nixon's offer to restrict the incursion by American troops to just twenty miles without Congressional approval. What was the difference in principle, asked Gore, between invading twenty miles or thirty miles? Why not fifty? The whole operation was fun-damentally flawed: the invasion of a small sovereign state without authority from Congress. "Yet you now," he lectured the president, "promise the invasion will not go deeper than 20 miles unless Congress approves. What is the principle; where is the logic?" Nixon replied that Cambodia was not sovereign territory; the enemy completely dominated it. He then turned to another congressman.[21]

The Cambodian invasion unleashed protests across the country, violent confrontations on campuses, and a mass student protest in Washington. Even in Tennessee three thousand University of Tennessee students rallied against the war and held a three-day strike, though in Nashville prowar rallies on the Vanderbilt campus equaled the antiwar protests. Gore moved to support moves to rescind the Gulf of Tonkin resolution and to pass another Cooper–Church amendment. The amendment to the Foreign Military Sales Act, which forbade funding for U.S. troops in Cambodia, or for military instruction or air combat support of Cambodian forces, passed in July 1970, by which time Nixon had already withdrawn the U.S. troops.[22]

Cooper–Church was just one of a number of proposed measures designed to curb presidential power in foreign policy. The Tonkin Gulf resolution had eaten into Gore's soul. He was now instinctively nervous of a president who believed, as Nixon did, that as commander-in-chief the president had the authority to send American troops into action unilaterally, as he thought fit. He believed the Cambodian invasion was reminiscent of the original U.S. entry in Vietnam—an intervention without treaty obligations or congressional authorization. But, as befitted a Democrat of the Roosevelt–Truman era, Gore also believed in strong presidential leadership and the executive's constitutional authority to act. He favored meaningful negotiations in Paris and did not want to shackle the president so that Nixon had nothing to negotiate with. For these reasons Gore did not support the Hatfield–McGovern End the War amendment, which would have mandated the removal of all U.S. troops by the end of 1971. The proposal, he argued, "[would] have made any kind of negotiations difficult." "I thought it was an extreme use of power of the purse. I thought the only way to achieve peace in Vietnam was through a negotiated settlement with an exchange of prisoners. . . . [Otherwise] North Vietnam would wait till the time expired and then do what they wanted with prisoners and our remaining forces." A deadline for unilateral withdrawal of American troops would tie the hands of negotiators just as much as the commitment to the Thieu regime did.[23]

Similarly, Gore always voted for appropriations for the war. He did not believe that the troops should be handicapped because of a disagreement among their political masters. As a member of the Senate, he said, "I have publicly stated that servicemen who are there are there because they were ordered there and not of their own free will." Government had a responsibility "to provide them with whatever they need to accomplish their mission at minimum risk." He stressed that therefore he had "supported all appropriations requests to provide essential supplies to our troops." He also believed that effective action to stop the war ultimately had to come from Congress, not from civil disobedience. Although he was increasingly a respected figure among American students, he warned them against street demonstrations and violent protest, and would not support civil disobedience. "I believe in our system. It has worked and it is a viable order." He totally rejected and deplored disorder in protest. "Debate and reasoning dissent, yes; violence, no," he concluded. He did not support the burning of draft cards. Though the war had not been declared congressionally, that did not make the operation of a selective service system illegal: "We have had a draft through most of the so-called cold war period." He put his faith in the ultimate power of speeches and legislative remedies in Congress. Debate in Congress and televised committee hearings were what would educate both fellow members of Congress and the people at large. Gore knew that many constituents would blame the protesters, not the president. As one "tired American" wrote, she was tired of the communists who had infiltrated American universities and created unrest and riots; tired of "lawlessness and crime" and members of Congress who divided the country instead of bringing it together.[24]

It was these concerns about the proper forum for dissent and the national responsibility to men who had been drafted in fulfillment of their citizenship obligations that guided Gore's discussions with his son about the possibility of his being drafted. Al Gore was militantly against the war. Many of his contemporaries were avoiding the draft. Few of his Harvard classmates were drafted. Some were going to Canada. David Halberstam believed that Pauline Gore would have supported Al if he had done so, and that Pauline would have gone to Canada with him. Al Gore was obviously aware of his father's 1970 election campaign and what opponents would make of a draft-evading son. He did not wait to be drafted; he volunteered. As he explained, the dialogue with his peers about the war was in the Northeast. But the possession of his draft eligibility was in Carthage, Tennessee, which had a very small draft pool: "My friends there were all vulnerable to the draft without having the option to find some fancy way around it and the identity of the boys in each month's eligibility pool was known to everybody." He was aware of the political ramifications of any decision, but "the principal reason that I decided to volunteer, to go in, before I was drafted, instead of finding some way to get out of it—the main reason was the fact that my draft board was in Carthage and my life was fungible with the group of friends that I had there." He could square political considerations and his antiwar convictions. He could argue that his father's reelection would help the antiwar cause. As it happened, a distant cousin called Al in his senior year at Harvard to say that her husband had found him a place in the Alabama National Guard, a more politically comfortable way of not serving in Vietnam. If he had accepted that offer, he would have found himself in the same unit that George Bush joined. "And we would've been there together. Or rather, I would've been there," he ruefully noted.[25]

Critics of Al Gore maintain that, although unlike most children of U.S. congressmen, he did serve in the war, he received favorable treatment and a "safe" assignment in Vietnam. It is entirely possible that military commanders sought to protect a congressman's son. There is no compelling evidence that Senator Gore sought such favorable treatment for Al Gore. Although Al worked as a journalist and he was not directly involved in combat, his editor testified that Al did not lie low. He traveled out and about in search of news stories more than any other army journalists did. Service in Vietnam did not lessen Al Gore's antiwar feelings. But he did experience a "camaraderie [that] was very intense and powerful," and he came away with a much greater understanding of why the South Vietnamese, especially Roman Catholics, feared a communist takeover.[26]

Albert Gore never wavered in his belief that his course of action on Vietnam was right. He told Gene Sloan in November 1969, "If I have ever been right about anything in my entire life then I was right in opposing our involvement in the Vietnam War. I cannot claim a perfect record because I permitted myself to be misled into voting for the Tonkin Gulf resolution. I am confident that I was right in opposing escalation of the war. Indeed, except for the role that I and others played in this regard, we may well have been in war with Red China today."[27]

～

IF GORE'S INCREASINGLY strident and emotive opposition to the war irritated the White House, his harassment of the administration over the antiballistic missile system infuriated the Nixon team.

Plans for the original ABM system, Sentinel, which would throw up a defensive shield to thwart ballistic missile attacks, had been abandoned by the

Johnson administration. Sentinel had promised to defend most of the continental United States, but it brought with it practical and expensive problems. It also threatened the concept of "mutually assured destruction," which rested on the mutual understanding that both superpowers would always be able to get in a first strike. Anything that stopped one side from having a first-strike capability lessened rather than enhanced security. A scaled-down version, Safeguard, would provide some defense for major cities against a limited attack—for example, from China. Nixon called for a more fully fledged version of the ABM which would protect American intercontinental ballistic missile (ICBM) sites and expand the number of sites from two to twelve.

The Foreign Relations Committee was a center of opposition to ABM. The system, according to its opponents, was neither cost-effective not technologically capable. Rather than protect U.S. strategic capacity, it would make it more vulnerable, stimulate an arms race, and derail Strategic Arms Limitation Talks (SALT). Gore joined Fulbright, Stuart Symington, and Ted Kennedy as opponents of the scheme. They found themselves up against not only Nixon but also Democrat Henry "Scoop" Jackson and his allies on the Armed Services Committee, who took charge of the campaign for the administration's proposal.[28]

As chair of the Disarmament Subcommittee on Foreign Relations, Gore summoned David Packard, undersecretary of defense, to testify. Gore asked how many missiles were needed. As Dennis W. Brezina, later legislative assistant to Senator Gaylord Nelson, recalled, Packard came up with the usual "full media" show from the Defense Department. He gave a "very sophisticated presentation along the lines of the fact that we need all of these tens of thousands of warheads." Gore was "maybe five foot five or something" but had a "hokey-looking easel with flip pages on it." He started:

> "Well, I've got some things I want to show you, Mr. Secretary."
> Somehow they had devised a theatrical presentation where Gore
> started pointing out on this chart, which was really rough-done,
> not as well done as you see on C-SPAN on the Senate floor these
> days. But, "Here's our number of missiles." And this curve over
> time was going up and up, and then it flattened out, and then
> MIRV [Multiple Independent Targeted Reentry Vehicles] came
> in. Well, the MIRV numbers were off the top of that chart. There
> was a temporary chart on top of the main chart that his assistants
> were holding, and it showed the number of warheads going way

up. Gore got on this little three-legged stool on his tiptoes with a pointer. He upstaged Packard tremendously. He said, "I can hardly reach this high."

Gore demonstrated in this homespun way that the United States had a clear missile superiority over the Soviets. It would be "madness" to embark on building another system. Pat Buchanan lamented to Nixon that the networks had a great time "turning the entire proceedings into one giant joke." Nixon was not amused and ordered his communications director to raise hell with NBC about the coverage. Gore clearly had the knack for getting under Nixon's skin. When he cross-examined Packard's boss, Secretary of Defense Melvin Laird, Gore asked a hypothetical question about a lonely lieutenant at a Safeguard site in Wyoming. The Soviet missiles are coming over the horizon, and the young man calls the White House to ask if he should press the offensive (Minuteman) or the defensive (Safeguard) button. Fulbright's muttered aside, "Tell him to press the panic button," provoked a roar of laughter from the audience and outright fury from Laird. Later, when Laird was asked to testify again before Gore's subcommittee, he refused.[29]

Nevertheless the Nixon administration had the final legislative laugh. Although Gore and others received a barrage of tips from anti-ABM officials at the Pentagon, they failed to vote ABM down, thanks in large part to Scoop Jackson's efforts. Jackson insisted that the White House give him a free hand to secure the necessary votes in August 1969 and August 1970, and he did so, in one case by only one vote. The Armed Services Committee had defeated the Senate Foreign Relations Committee. Southern Democratic hawks, in alliance with Republicans loyal to the president, outvoted Gore, Fulbright, and Northern liberals of both parties.[30]

↬

GORE ALSO FOUND himself in opposition to the Nixon administration over tax reform.

Gore was now the third-ranking member of the Senate Finance Committee. Although he was often in a minority on a committee chaired by Russell Long, he had acquired considerable expertise on the committee which commanded respect in the Senate. Ted Kennedy recalled that, when Gore was talking on the floor of the Senate about finance, senators left their offices and came to the floor to listen to him. Gore had developed good relations with tax expert Stanley Surrey, assistant secretary of the treasury in the Johnson administration, and Internal Revenue Service commissioners Mortimer Caplin and Sheldon Cohen. He was consistently skeptical of tax reductions and was always looking to press for tax reform. The Senate Finance Committee always found its agenda largely dictated by Wilbur Mills and the House Ways and Means Committee (as the efforts to include Medicare in 1964 had shown), who initiated tax legislation. But the Senate could still make a significant contribution. Gore demonstrated that possibility in 1969 when, despite a clear defeat in the Finance Committee, his amendment to increase the personal exemption for taxpayers passed the Senate. The increase in personal exemption, though graduated and slightly reduced, survived the conference committee to go on the statute book.[31]

By 1969 the pressure for both tax reform and tax reductions had increased. Academic tax experts who had developed close ties with Wilbur Mills were increasingly worried by the number of tax breaks or deductions in the tax code, which were far more than in countries like Britain or Sweden. These deductions had come into the code partly as the result of lobbying by special interests, but primarily after World War II as a means of making a mass-based tax system acceptable. (A greater proportion of people paid income tax than in any other industrial nation.) Reformers worried that these "tax expenditures" or subsidies continued automatically from year to year. Congress liked them because they did not have to vote each year to authorize spending from general revenues. But reformers also worried that they disproportionately favored the wealthy and that they bred popular discontent with the tax regime. Johnson's secretary of the treasury had warned of a taxpayers' revolt: Citing 1967 figures, he noted that 155 taxpayers earning over $200,000 had paid no income tax. Twenty of those individuals, it subsequently became clear, were millionaires.[32]

The other pressure for tax relief was the result of mounting inflationary pressures. Not only did inflation squeeze the incomes of many Americans, it also increased their tax burden. It vaulted many into higher income tax brackets and, as the leading historian of taxation, W. Elliot Brownlee, concluded, "The price increase meant huge unlegislated increases for most individual taxpayers."[33]

The lengthy hearings of the Ways and Means Committee (the most extensive since 1958) and the careful drafting by Mills and his tax experts in 1969 led to a bill that passed the House on 7 August 1969. It proposed $9.3 billion a year in tax reductions and $6.9 billion in tax-break reforms. The bill did not eliminate tax breaks, but it tried to restrict those breaks to "legitimate" write-offs. It provided for tighter definitions of capital-gains income and tackled the problems of tax-exempt status for foundations and tax exemption on the interest from state and local bonds. Armed with the most extensive information ever marshaled on the cost of tax breaks to the budget, the committee had tackled seemingly sacrosanct write-offs to housing developers and for "hobby" farms. The most surprising testimony to the ability of Mills and his team to face down the lobbyists was that the oil-depletion allowance, which reformers for years had thought was untouchable, was reduced from 27.5 percent to 20 percent.[34]

Gore, more than most members of the Senate Finance Committee, appreciated the willingness of Mills to tackle the question of tax breaks. The bill was "excellent in many respects." He welcomed the ending of the "unlimited charitable deduction," which enabled one hundred very wealthy individuals to escape all, or almost all, federal income tax. He fought the efforts in the Senate committee to water down the House reduction in the oil-depletion allowance. He had long been a critic of the tax-exempt status of foundations. But his suspicion of tax reductions for the wealthy led him to oppose, unsuccessfully, the reduction of the maximum rate of tax to 50 percent. He noted that one of his staffers was taxed at 40 percent on $26,000 a year, whereas now his old nemesis, the chairman of US Steel, Roger Blough, would be paying only 50 percent on an income of $600,000 a year. He worried that there was little help to middle- and low-income taxpayers. He argued: "Actually, the forgotten man in this particular bill, insofar as tax rates are concerned, is the middle to lower middle income bracket taxpayers with sizeable families to support and educate." He proposed to increase the personal exemption from $600 to $1,000, introduced gradually over four years. Chairman Russell Long argued that the proposal would lose too much revenue, complicate the tax process, and lead to a presidential veto. Gore was defeated by 12 votes to 3 in committee, but he vowed to take his amendment to the Senate floor.[35]

Gore worked with Ted Kennedy, among others, on a low-income allowance that critics of his personal-exemption proposal argued would help the poor more than the exemption. But it soon became clear that the personal-exemption increase was all that Gore could get to the floor, and that the administration would be lobbying against his proposal: It would cost too much and favored large families over smaller ones. Gore retorted by charging that the administration had climbed down on all its reform initiatives, capitulating to the oil barons, to business on capital gains, and to the railroads on tax loopholes. His long speech introducing his amendment was made to a largely empty chamber, but he couched his proposal in politically compelling form. He wanted to help "tax relief to the man who needs it most—the man living in the suburbs in a little house with a big mortgage and filled with children." It was an eye-catching proposal to help the inflation-hit middle class; and, as cynics noted, perhaps one of the eyes would be on the Tennessee electorate. In an extremely rare move, the Senate supported a floor amendment to the Finance Committee report. Gore's amendment passed 53 to 38, though his proposal for the personal-exemption increase to $1,000 had been reduced to $800. It was nevertheless the first increase in the personal exemption in many years. He could take satisfaction that the amendment passed so easily despite increasingly desperate attempts by the administration to defeat it. The administration's efforts to defeat what was clearly a popular measure led to an angry outburst by Minority Leader Hugh Scott. He publicly blamed the Nixon team for failing to heed the advice of GOP leaders in the Senate. In conference, the increase in the exemption was reduced to $750. Nixon had threatened to veto the bill if it included Gore's increase in personal exemption and a 15-percent hike in Social Security, but in the end he backed down. He did not carry through on his threat. Gore could legitimately claim a triumph: a tribute to his personal standing in the Senate, Republican irritation with the administration, and the popular nature of the proposal.[36]

↜

IN THE SENATE Gore's prestige had rarely been higher. He was never going to be a member of the "Senate club." But the older generation, which never fully trusted him, was diminishing in number. Many of Gore's older Senate colleagues elected after the war and the members of the class of 1952 had died, retired, or been defeated. A younger generation of senators came to have a high regard for Gore during the 91st Congress. He and Ralph Yarborough had once again compiled the most liberal voting records among Southern senators. Gore's 1964 vote against the Civil Rights Act had now been overshadowed by his subsequent support of liberal civil rights measures. His antiwar stance, which had been divisive during the Johnson years, was now part of the Democratic Party mainstream. Fulbright, as chair of the Senate Foreign Relations Committee, relied on Gore and trusted him. Younger senators appreciated his consistency on the war issue. They appreciated his votes on the Haynsworth and Carswell nominations, which they recognized involved considerable political risk. Their support for his tax amendment testified to that respect.[37]

What gained Gore respect in the Senate and among young Northern senators was precisely what made him a target for the Nixon administration. It is clear that Gore got under the skin of both the president and his staffers. He had crossed swords with them on the war, on the ABM system, on the Supreme Court, and on taxes. The White House disliked what they saw as his intellectual arrogance, his partisan rhetoric, and his open contempt in cross-examination of administration spokesmen. They were delighted to think that his identification with Ted Kennedy and the national Democratic Party liberals would make him vulnerable in Tennessee in 1970. Gore represented an inviting target for both Nixon's national conservative project and his Southern strategy. Vice President Spiro Agnew had become the administration's attack dog for its campaign against antiwar protesters and the liberal political and media establishments. He saw himself as the plain-talking spokesman for the Silent Majority. He named Gore the administration's number 1 target in the South. He told the American Farm Bureau Federation that he relished the chance to go to Tennessee to campaign against the incumbent senator.[38]

The more Gore was respected and praised outside Tennessee, the more he was viewed with suspicion by many white voters in the state. He could not escape identification with Ted Kennedy. He had voted for Kennedy against Russell Long for majority whip in January 1969. He had defended the Massachusetts senator after the accident at Chappaquiddick. He had supported Kennedy's team in the defeat of Haynsworth and Carswell. By 1970 there were few more damning descriptors for many Tennessee and Southern voters than that of "Kennedy liberal." Could Albert Gore overcome these negative associations and translate his national prestige into local victory?[39]

CHAPTER 9

The Defeat of a Roman Senator

DURING CHRISTMAS 1968 Gore held a family war council at home in Carthage. He knew that he was in political trouble. It would be, as Al Gore recalled the discussions, "very, very difficult for him to be reelected."[1]

Albert knew that his opposition to the war, his civil rights moderation, and his support of Great Society reforms had polarized voters in Tennessee. The Democratic national convention earlier that year had seen him a lonely figure, ignored by the delegation controlled by Governor Buford Ellington. The governor, a close friend of LBJ's, represented the conservative wing of the party. He had fought a bitter and divisive battle against the wealthy, young "Kennedy man," John Jay Hooker, in 1966. His faction was gearing up for another battle against Hooker in 1970. Gore had campaigned for the segregationist Ellington for governor in the 1958 general election, when Ellington feared that a bitter primary would lead reformers in Tennessee to stay at home or defect to the Republicans. But there was no love lost between them. Ellington considered Gore arrogant and egotistical. Gore despised Ellington. He regarded him as a dolt, according to John Seigenthaler. George Barrett spoke for many in the Gore camp when he said Ellington was "a Mississippi boy that never got over it, never rose above it." In fact Ellington had come to terms with the civil rights legislation of 1964 and 1965. Working for Lyndon Johnson at the Office for Emergency Planning, Ellington had been the federal government's representative to Southern governors at civil rights flashpoints across the region. Like fellow "law and order" conservative governors Dan Moore and Bob Scott in North Carolina, and John McKeithen in Louisiana, Ellington guided the state into generally peaceful acceptance of racial change, despite race riots in Memphis and campus disturbances.[2]

Gore also knew that the Republican Party in Tennessee had been transformed. When he was first elected to the Senate in 1952, he garnered 74 percent of the general election vote. In 1958 he pushed that up to 79 percent. But in 1964 Goldwater supporter and Memphis public relations man Dan Kuykendall had polled 46.4 percent against him. Two years later Republican Howard Baker Jr. comfortably won the other Tennessee Senate seat against Frank Clement and was on his way to building up the strongest political base of any of the first generation of Southern Republican senators. In 1968 the Democratic presidential candidate, Hubert Humphrey, polled only 28 percent of the vote. Middle and western Tennessee white Democrats had switched to George Wallace. Wallace's 34 percent enabled Nixon to carry the state. Gore knew that the Republicans would mount a strong challenge in 1970. If Gore was in any doubt about the extent of anti-Democratic backlash, he had only to look at the defeat of his closest Washington friend, Oklahoma senator Mike Monroney, in November 1968. When Monroney had first been elected to the Senate in 1950, Oklahoma was still a one-party state. But Oklahomans voted for Eisenhower in 1952 and 1956, and for Nixon in 1960. They elected their first Republican governor, Henry Bellmon, in 1962, and reelected him in 1966. When Bellmon challenged Monroney in 1968, Monroney found that thirty years of service in Washington—he had been elected to Congress in 1938 at the same time as Gore—were not enough to retain his seat.[3]

Gore also knew that he was perceived as being too aloof. One pollster reported that "he is frequently criticized on the basis of being out of touch with the state, a 'politician' who appears on the scene a few months before election time to take popular stands on controversial issues—and once elected is seldom seen or heard from by his constituents." Said one voter, "He's a politician. Until six months before the election we never hear from him, then you start getting mail, films, and so on."[4]

Gore was under no illusions. He recognized that the odds were stacked against him, but the issues he was fighting for seemed too important for him to back down. So he and the family decided that Christmas that he would run again in 1970, and from then on he ran to win—and believed he could.

But the family considered steps to shore up his position. Albert suggested that it might be a good idea to move his home to Memphis. A Memphis base might bolster his chances of hanging on to western Tennessee. If he maintained his hold on middle Tennessee at the same time, he could offset the Republican majorities in the eastern part of the state. The family saw no merit in that, and Gore dropped the idea. But at the meeting he decided that he had to increase his visibility in the state.

His family immediately reorganized his calendar. For the next two years, his weekly schedule usually placed him in Nashville on Friday afternoons to catch the chance to be on the local newscast that night; in Knoxville and Chattanooga on Saturday to get TV exposure there; in Memphis on Sunday for similar television coverage; and in his Memphis office Monday morning for constituency work. Gore followed this schedule, and he did get back to the state very frequently. Indeed in 1967 and 1968, he had been back to the state at some point in forty-three weeks of each year. But how much effective fence-mending he did on these visits was open to question. Jim Sasser noted that Gore would go to Memphis and say he was campaigning, but nobody knew he was there. "I don't know what he would do, but I don't think he made any real—maybe he'd go into his office in Memphis or something like that, but you've got to get out and get on the television and go to a church or do something. I don't think he did much of that. He would just be there."[5]

⌒

FUTURE TENNESSEE REPUBLICAN governor, secretary of education, and U.S. senator Lamar Alexander was a law clerk with the Fourth Circuit Court of Appeals in 1966, along with Frank Hunger, who was to marry Nancy Gore. As Hunger recalls: it was "just before we left to go our separate ways. He and I were sitting back in the library of the Court of Appeals and I asked him what he was gonna do. And he told me he was gonna go back to Tennessee and work with the party. He said Howard Baker. I said 'Lamar, you're out of your mind! You're gonna be working for a Republican. You're never gonna get anywhere politically.'"[6]

In fact Howard Baker's victory over Governor Frank Clement in 1966 had confirmed that Tennessee had become a two-party state. Baker had run against Ross Bass in a close but unsuccessful race for Estes Kefauver's old seat in 1964. In 1966 Bass had been defeated, in a ferocious Democratic primary battle, by the incumbent governor, Frank Clement. Baker in turn defeated Clement, but not just because of the Democrats' internecine disputes. Baker had polled 47 percent against Ross Bass in 1964. Two years later he defeated Clement by more than a hundred thousand votes. Baker joined Texan John Tower as one of only two Republicans in the Senate from the South.

Traditionally the Republican Party in Tennessee had been restricted to its historic base in the eastern mountains. From 1951 till his death in 1964, Howard Baker's father had held one of the two Republican seats that the party routinely won in the east. Gore and Howard Baker, Sr. got along well and cooperated on TVA and atomic-energy issues. When Howard, Jr. married Everett Dirksen's daughter, Gore wrote a personal note of congratulations.[7]

But four developments changed the Democratic domination of the state. First, in presidential elections Republicans appealed to white, middle-class professionals and businessmen across the state. Eisenhower carried the state in 1952 and 1956; Nixon, in 1960. Second, under Barry Goldwater the GOP aimed "to go hunting where the ducks are" by appealing to old-style segregationists, particularly in western Tennessee, who were alienated by the civil rights stance of the national Democratic Party. That campaign in Tennessee boomeranged against the Republicans in the 1964 presidential elections—and, Baker always felt, against his own campaign—but it enabled Dan Kuykendall to run Gore close in the Senate race. Third, Baker showed how to win a race for statewide office. He appealed to his traditional eastern Tennessee base but also reached out with a fiscally conservative message to business and professional urban voters, winning a majority of white votes; with a moderate civil rights record, he also reached out to African Americans, winning 15 to 20 percent of the black vote. Baker, with Lamar Alexander at his side, then set about building up an organization that would enable him to buck the trend of one-term Republican senators in the modern South.[8]

Fourth, Richard Nixon was pursuing a Southern strategy to pave the way for his reelection in 1972. Despite an unpopular war and a bitterly divided Democratic Party, Nixon had only narrowly defeated Hubert Humphrey in 1968. In the South he had won the support of middle-income white voters, while George Wallace had won lower-income white support and Hubert Humphrey had won the backing of minority voters. If Nixon could win over those Wallace backers in 1972, he could sweep the South with an overwhelming white vote. The gospel for the administration was the work of political analyst Kevin Phillips, whose book *The Emerging Republican Majority* laid out a strategy for Republican national success based on picking up white Southern support. White House aides were made to read Phillips alongside Richard Scammon and Ben Wattenberg's *The Real Majority*, which tried to remind Democrats that the majority of Americans were "unyoung, unpoor, and unblack." Policies and political strategies of the Nixon administration were assessed by the degree to which they furthered the ideas in these books. The Southern strategy was based on an appeal to racial conservatism (a go-slow approach on school desegregation and opposition to busing) together with an appeal to regional pride (the appointment of Southerners to the Supreme Court), an appeal to law and order (against both urban crime and campus protest), and an appeal to traditional values (patriotism and conservative morality).[9]

From Nixon's perspective, as Robert Mason has shown, the strategy was not so much a partisan policy as a personal and ideological one. Nixon was concerned to build a national conservative majority and to secure reelection. He was not interested in building up the Republican Party in states like Mississippi, where veteran Democratic senators James Eastland and John Stennis were reliable supporters of a conservative Republican president. He had no desire to unseat John Sparkman in Alabama, who promised to be a sound chair of the Senate Banking Committee. He was quite cold-blooded in leaving local Republicans to fend for themselves in those states. But Tennessee was a different case. In the first place, he knew that he had won the state in 1968 only by virtue of the Wallace vote. He needed those votes to win in 1972. Above all Nixon wanted to get rid of Gore. Along with Ralph Yarborough and William Fulbright, Gore was one of the senators who could be identified by the administration as a "radical liberal"—a liberal whose relentless and superior criticism of the administration's Vietnam policy infuriated Nixon as much as it had Johnson. Gore's increasingly scornful attacks on Nixon's Vietnam policy, so Nixon believed, hurt Nixon's chances of securing an honorable settlement in Vietnam, since it encouraged the North Vietnamese to stand firm. In addition, of course, Gore had helped thwart the administration's Supreme Court ambitions.[10]

Harry Dent, Strom Thurmond's former aide, was the point man for the administration in the South. He kept a close eye on Tennessee and worried whether the best candidate would emerge as the party choice. He was dismayed by a special congressional election in western Tennessee when a well-financed businessman from Memphis failed to pick up the rural and small-town Wallaceite votes that were there to be taken. As Johns Sears pointed out to Nixon, candidates had to recognize that in many areas "the populace is outwardly conservative but Populist in reality." Instead the Republicans in this case had spent most of their money in urban centers, had ignored rural newspapers, and were defeated by a Democrat long-time chair of the Agriculture Stabilization and Conservation State Committee (Ed Jones). The Republicans, said Sears, should have chosen a small-town mayor to counter someone so well connected to farmers.[11]

The administration engaged at least in some wishful thinking that Democrat Buford Ellington might be persuaded to run against Gore. After all, as Dent commented, Ellington sounded like a Republican and ought to become one. Dent worried that Maxey Jarman, a wealthy Nashville businessman, would win the gubernatorial nomination, alienate former Wallace supporters, and bring no real strength to the ticket. Lamar Alexander memorably warned Dent that Jarman's "chances of being the nominee are close to zero because he could never win the Republican primary," since he was not from eastern Tennessee. He cautioned that "he is a big businessman, but was strong for Robert Kennedy and has supported repeal of Section 14B of the Taft–Hartley Act." He dismissively concluded, "He is 65 years old, about 5 feet 4 inches tall. Not quite the ideal candidate, but he is distinguished looking, and younger looking than he really is. A little pudgy." Dent also worried that there would be too many candidates running for the Republican nominations for both the Senate and governor who would cut each other up in the primaries.[12]

Dent was therefore pleased that, by October 1969, Congressman William E. Brock had emerged as apparently the sole Republican challenger for Gore's seat.[13] Brock, a wealthy son of the Chattanooga candy manufacturer, had been a key figure in expanding the Tennessee Republican Party out of its historic rural, mountain base in the east. Coming out of the navy, Brock was enthused by the Eisenhower presidency because of Ike's role in ending the Korean War. At the local level he was angered by his first experience as a poll watcher in Chattanooga, where he saw voter fraud at first-hand yet was unable to do anything about it. For the next four years, Brock and other likeminded Jaycees were involved in civic and local business activity. But they ran up against a complacent establishment in Chattanooga that was simply trying to attract low-wage industry to the town. Brock and his young business friends then set about organizing a Young Republican group across the state. What they found was that the old guard in the party did not welcome this new activism. They were opposed at every turn, and eastern Tennessee Republicans challenged their credentials at the Young Republicans national convention in 1961. Their success against the old guard at that convention led them to think about getting candidates elected to office. Brock and his fellow ideologues chafed at what they took to be the top-down approach of the traditional eastern leadership of the party, first under B. Carroll Reece, then under Howard Baker, Sr. East Tennessee Republicans, they argued, had been too ready to accede to Democratic dominance in the rest of the state in return for local control of patronage. Brock and his allies wanted to make the Republican Party an identifiably conservative and statewide organization. They intended to build up from the grassroots, and they aimed to win a majority of the state offices by 1970, although Brock conceded that probably a few too many beers might have fueled that ambition.[14]

Brock ran for Congress in 1962 and became the first Republican congressman to break out of the eastern Tennessee mountain redoubt by winning the Third District seat in Chattanooga and Hamilton County. Brock's achievement in Chattanooga became the model for Republican organization across the state. His campaign was based on four thousand volunteers, and he paid attention to how the AFL-CIO organized locally and how the Kefauver organization functioned. This grassroots approach was simply not needed for the old guard in east Tennessee, where the Republicans could always rely on their voters to turn out, but in the rest of the state this organizational drive was crucial. Once in office Brock also hoped to emulate the level of constituency service and attention that Kefauver was able to deliver.[15]

Brock's conservatism was unequivocal. Where Baker cringed at the Goldwater candidacy, particularly the candidate's opposition to the TVA, Brock gloried in it. He sought to prevent the party from swinging to the left in the aftermath of the Arizonan's defeat. He supported his young protégé Jack McDonald's efforts to wrest control of the Young Republicans National Federation away from former Republican National Committee chairman Hugh Scott. But, like other Southern Republicans, he latched on to Richard Nixon's candidacy in 1968 and was one of ten "surrogate" speakers for Nixon during the campaign.[16]

Brock was asked about running for the Senate in 1964 and 1966 but chose to develop his district record. The election in 1970 offered a much more promising opportunity, when his team could build on all the organizational work they had done across the state in the previous eight years. He had no love for Albert Gore. Democratic senator Estes Kefauver, also from Chattanooga, had been a friend of the Brock family. When Brock arrived in Washington in 1963, Nancy and Estes Kefauver had called to congratulate him on his victory, hosted a dinner party for him, and showed him around Washington. Brock had no such warm feelings for Gore—whom he found arrogant, pompous, and standoffish. Brock's own brand of conservatism seemed ideally suited for an attack on the liberal senator.[17]

In May 1969, when Brock's pollsters surveyed his prospects for statewide election in Tennessee in 1970, they identified only one possible Republican rival for the senatorial nomination, Memphis congressman Dan Kuykendall. The pollsters argued that Brock's ability to raise funds was more important than Kuykendall's name recognition across the state, and they believed that an early indication by Brock that he would seek the Senate seat would pre-empt the Kuykendall candidacy. In fact Brock had met Kuykendall, and they agreed to test the waters in the state for six months to find out who was likely to be the strongest candidate. After six months the polls showed Brock clear-ly ahead, and Kuykendall recognized that Brock had an organization right across the state, while his own strength was largely confined to the Memphis area. Brock was also supported by James Quillen, GOP congressman from the First District and a force of nature in east Tennessee politics. The White House may not have anointed Brock, but his former administrative assistant, Bill Timmons, was working for Nixon's congressional liaison team, headed by Bryce Harlow. In November 1969 Timmons would take over from Harlow. Brock had already acquired the services of Ken Rietz, of Treleaven Associ-ates, who had run Nixon's media campaign in 1968. Harry Dent undoubtedly favored Brock and was pleased that Kuykendall had agreed to stand down. He had been, Dent told Nixon, "a good sport" who merited some personal flat-tery from the president. As early as October 1969, the White House and Rietz agreed that grant announcements, patronage appointments, and presidential visits would be carefully coordinated to aid the Brock campaign. Brock's path to the Republican nomination appeared to have been smoothed, and he was running with every sign of White House backing.[18]

From the start, Brock's pollsters and advisers identified three main issues of public concern: support for law and order, particularly in regard to student unrest; opposition to increased welfare support for those who did not make any effort to support themselves, especially African Americans; and opposi-tion to the interference of the federal government and the Supreme Court in local affairs.[19]

With Kuykendall out of the running, Brock and his aides did not an-ticipate a Republican opponent in the 1970 primary, and could not have predicted that the opponent who would emerge would be popular country singer and veteran of eighty cowboy movies Tex Ritter. Journalists believed, and Ritter later confirmed, that he had been put up to run by members of Howard Baker's staff. Baker himself announced a policy of strict neutrality in both senatorial and gubernatorial primaries, but later conceded that, al-though he was not involved at all, some members of his staff backed Ritter. As Lamar Alexander recalls, there was inevitably some personal rivalry between Brock and Baker, two attractive and popular young politicians. They clearly represented two wings of the Tennessee Republican Party: Baker for the east Tennessee old guard, Brock for the Young Republicans. Whatever Howard Baker's official stance, it was not surprising that some Baker people backed Ritter.[20]

Ritter's campaign against Brock previewed Gore's campaign against his challenger. Ritter argued that Brock was too conservative to defeat Gore, and that a candidate from the mainstream was needed to pick up dissident Democrat voters. Ritter vowed that, unlike Brock, he would not "have my picture made with prominent members of the John Birch society." He castigated Brock as the "against" man, the negative congressman who was lukewarm on the TVA, who had voted against federal programs that funded local hospitals and against funds for the Appalachian Regional Commission. Ritter criticized Brock's votes for the ABM system and the supersonic jet project. He dismissed Brock's advocacy for a constitutional amendment against busing as impractical. He pointedly refused to attend a Billy Graham Crusade in Knoxville. He maintained he did not want to "use the crusade for political gain." Both Brock and President Nixon attended. In highlighting Brock's negative votes on issues affecting Tennessee and distancing himself from too blatant a religious and cultural conservatism, Ritter's campaign closely resembled Gore's later attacks on Brock.[21]

Ritter was no mere singer. He was a political science major from the University of Texas and had studied law at Northwestern. He was probably the most scholarly country singer ever, learning about country and folk music from the Western historian J. Frank Dobie and the folklorist John A. Lomax, in Austin. As a movie star whose fame was cemented by singing "Do Not Forsake Me, O My Darling" in *High Noon*, Ritter was still singing in medicine shows and tent revivals in small towns across the South throughout the 1950s. But the crowds did not necessarily come out in 1970 to hear Ritter speak. It was the country stars who appeared on the campaign trail with Ritter who attracted the crowds. His bandwagon around Tennessee brought a galaxy of stars to warm up the audience—including Roy Acuff, Ernest Tubb, Loretta Lynn, Dolly Parton, and Porter Waggoner. Brock himself was surprised to discover that Johnny Cash, who had promised to endorse Brock, also endorsed Ritter. And after his own speech, Ritter himself would usually sing the "Boll Weevil" song and "Do Not Forsake Me, O My Darling." However, just like Roy Acuff in 1948, Ritter attracted the audiences but not their votes. He polled just over 54,000 votes in the primary, while Brock piled up more than 175,000 votes.[22]

~~⌐~~

THE RITTER-BROCK BATTLE showed that the threat to Gore was formidable. The Republicans had their largest ever primary vote. But Gore had also faced an unexpectedly serious challenge in the Democratic primary.

Gore had not expected significant opposition in the primary, though there were warning signs from Texas. In May 1970 one of Gore's close friends in the Senate, and fellow enemy of LBJ, Ralph Yarborough, was beaten by conservative Lloyd Bentsen. The Texas primary was a race that foreshadowed the Gore battle. Bentsen waged a very expensive campaign that climaxed with a barrage of TV ads linking Yarborough and his opposition to the Vietnam War to crime, looting, and burning. Bentsen also hammered away at Yarborough's anti-Southern votes against Nixon's Supreme Court nominees, his support of "forced busing," and his opposition to voluntary prayer in school. But Yarborough also suffered from the decline of his aging organization. As one liberal activist warned him a year before the campaign, as many as two hundred stalwart local organizers had died since Yarborough's last campaign in 1964. He lamented that he had "talked to Ralph and said we have got to put somebody in Texas to organize because the organization is flat dead and you don't have anything left. You've got to go out and find new people to take over the campaign managers jobs in those counties where you no longer have somebody." Like Gore the same year, Yarborough had failed to rejuvenate his organization.[23]

For a long time it looked as if Gore's hopes of merely token primary opposition were justified. Major Democrats in the state were reported to be considering a Gore challenge—Buford Ellington, Ray Blanton—but none materialized. As late as March there was no opposition at all. Then two political unknowns, Stanford Andress and retired Admiral Herman Frey, announced their intentions to run. Between them they would receive less than 4 percent of the Democratic primary vote. Andress was a travel agency executive and former detective from Madison who identified himself very clearly with George Wallace. Frey campaigned on a platform of "Go in to win or get out" in Vietnam and promised to protect the interests of the state's many military facilities.[24]

But at the last minute Buford Ellington's press secretary, Hudley Crockett, entered the race. Crockett was not in the race at Ellington's behest—otherwise he would not have announced at the last minute, and he would have had significant financial backing. He did not have the money to produce TV ads, but he did produce an effective alternative: a live "Crockett Report," where the former TV newscaster, well known to middle Tennessee viewers, delivered half an hour of unscripted and unrehearsed talk straight to the camera. He harried Gore as out of touch with the views of Tennessee voters and particularly assailed his stance on Vietnam. Crockett attracted young businessmen and politicos about his age. He was supported by businessmen who had been involved in the industrial development drives by governors Clement and Ellington. He was endorsed not merely by the conservative *Nashville Banner* but also by the *Memphis Commercial Appeal*, which had previously always backed Gore. Crockett tapped into the latent hostility to Gore among moderate and conservative state legislators and local politicians. They felt patronized by the senator. They knew that many of their constituents were uneasy with what they saw as the unrepresentative liberal views of an arrogant and unresponsive senator. Crockett's campaign manager was Eddie Evins, nephew of the powerful veteran congressman Joe Evins, who represented Gore's old congressional district. (Ellington had been Evins's first campaign manager.) Crockett was also supported by future congressmen Bart Gordon and John Tanner.[25]

Crockett's campaign previewed almost all the main themes that Brock would pursue against Gore in the general election. Republicans in Chattanooga indeed complained that he "out-brocked Brock." He argued that Gore was out of touch with Tennessee voters, that he failed to represent Tennessee's interests in Washington. He found confirmation for this charge in Gore's decision to hire Charles Guggenheim to come to Tennessee to prepare his TV commercials and in fundraising dinners organized by liberals in Washington for Gore. Guggenheim was, according to Crockett, a "high-powered out-of-state image maker obviously paid by powerful out-of-state friends to try to build a new image for an out-of-touch candidate." He criticized Gore and the Foreign Relations Committee for opposing Nixon's Vietnam policy and lambasted the senator for his votes against the nomination of Southerners Clement Haynsworth and Harrold Carswell to the Supreme Court. Crockett supported Nixon's and Brock's plans for revenue-sharing and fervently opposed gun control. These were all issues that would loom large in Brock's campaign against Gore.[26]

Gore's campaign manager hoped for a majority of one hundred thousand voters in the primary, which would give Gore momentum for the general election. Instead Gore won by fewer than thirty-two thousand votes, and Crockett won more than 45 percent of the vote. The results did not bode well for the November election. As the *Tennessean* noted, Crockett's votes "picked up steadily as he moved westward across the state into the counties that supported George Wallace in 1968." The *Chattanooga News* made the same calculation: Crockett "ran ahead of Gore in those areas carried by George Wallace in the 1968 presidential election." Gore won Alabama border counties, but as R. W. Apple observed in the *New York Times*, "Over rural west Tennessee—in backwater counties like Lauderdale, Dyer, and Tipton, where the race issue is central—Mr. Crockett matched or bettered Mr. Wallace's vote." Crockett carried Shelby County and the four western congressional districts. If the Wallace vote was to be the key in November, then it appeared that Gore had a mountain to climb.[27]

⤺

BROCK'S STRATEGISTS WERE in no doubt that the Wallace voter was "the deciding political force in Tennessee." As they saw it, the "indications are that the Wallace people would support Brock and actively vote for him against Gore. They should not be courted but great pains should be taken to see that they are not offended." What the candidate needed to do in the campaign against Gore was to draw a stark contrast "between political philosophies, as shown in the voting records. Brock is a Nixon conservative. Gore is a Kennedy liberal." Not only was the strategy to target Wallace voters in line with Nixon's Southern strategy, but Brock's campaign could also be sold to the White House as "a testing ground of Nixon-Kennedy strength as well as Brock-Gore."[28]

Brock's strategists laid out a timetable in May 1969 that they followed with great precision. It set out target dates for fundraising, appointment of county chairmen, and door-to-door canvassing, all culminating in a phase 3 media blitz in October 1970. The campaign ran with military precision, with carefully staged events and a meticulous timetable that made sure the candidate had time to freshen up between 4 and 6 P.M. and always to be in bed by 11, so he could look his best on television. Journalists were transported by plane, their motel rooms were booked, and they were kept fully briefed on the candidate's schedule. Larry Daughtrey described this new brand of campaigning in April 1970:

> Brock's first day left no doubts that the message will be delivered
> by a tautly-managed and efficient organization. His itinerary
> was charted out, in writing, to the minute, and there was a time-
> table for applause by the mini-skirted girls at each rally. . . . All

the little touches of polish were there: a short, patriotic speech, a little (but not too much) time for handshaking, different colored buttons to distinguish between party, press, and security, a device heretofore limited to presidential campaigns. "Broadcast media" representatives were given a Nashville telephone number they can call to get a tape-recorded comment from the candidate daily.[29]

Crucial to Brock's campaign were a series of carefully crafted TV ads. The scene was set for the ads by a billboard campaign bearing the slogan "Bill Brock Believes." When asked by journalists what that meant and what he believed in, Brock replied, "Well that was just for name identification. You'll see it change when we get closer to election." And it did change, to "Bill Brock believes in the things we believe in." That was the mantra of the TV ads produced by Harry Treleaven. Nixon's media manager had faith in thirty- to sixty-second spot ads. Spending on these spot ads doubled nationally between 1964 and 1968. Even a sixty-second spot was thought to be too long by some political consultants—they could become refrigerator-visiting time. The spot ads focused on just the issues the Southern strategy aimed to exploit: busing, support for the president on the war, control of government spending to curb inflation, appointment of judges who would put criminals in jail, a Supreme Court that would not tie the hands of the police, opposition to gun control, stronger drug laws and enforcement, and the expulsion of violent student protesters. The thirty- to sixty-second slots showed Brock talking to ordinary Tennesseans: a parent, a veteran, a pensioner, a farmer, hunters, constituents who had been helped, disaffected Democrats, the wife of a POW, a textile worker, a young man. The message was that, unlike Gore, Brock listened and took local issues seriously. The implication of course was that Gore did not believe in what Tennesseans believed in. Indeed, some in the Gore camp were convinced that the subliminal message of the first billboards was that Gore was not a religious believer, whereas Brock was.[30]

Brock appealed to Tennesseans to support their president, not to "handcuff" him in foreign policy. He defended the Cambodia invasion. He accused Gore and the other senators of undercutting the president's peace efforts by trying to set a timetable for withdrawal. Gore was betraying American soldiers who were sacrificing their lives for their country. His antiwar statements were being used to brainwash American POWs in Vietnam. In return Nixon came to east Tennessee to speak to huge crowds in Johnson City and to appeal for Brock's election to support him in his efforts to secure a peace that would discourage, not encourage, aggressors.[31]

James Stahlman, editor of the *Nashville Banner*, was ecstatic about Nixon's visit on 20 October. The president, he reported to Harry Dent, did a "bang-up job, as in old-time pro form. He is best as a slugger, and he was tops yesterday." He believed that Nixon had guaranteed the Republicans a 150,000-vote majority in the first three congressional districts which would see both the gubernatorial candidate, Winfield Dunn, and Brock safely home. Stahlman told Nixon that he was "praying for success in your efforts to bring peace, economic stability, law and order, respect for our Flag, unity of our people and genuine love of this great country of ours. We are certain that with God's help, you will prevail." Stahlman's only regret was that Brock did not have "the fervor, the campaign vigor and the flashing attractive personality of Winfield Dunn." Stahlman's praise would have been music to Harry Dent's ears; Dent had been pushing for a presidential visit to what he considered to be one of the top five GOP target seats in the nation. In fact Nixon visited Tennessee twice, also going to a Billy Graham rally in Knoxville. The Graham rally took place at the massive University of Tennessee football stadium—perhaps appropriate given that Dent believed football was a "religio-social pastime in the South." (He was always looking to get the president to attend a big SEC game in the region.) Nixon took a keen interest in Tennessee politics and had no illusions about them. "Tough politics down there," he told Lamar Alexander in August 1970: "Tennessee and Indiana are the two states with the nut-cuttingest politics in the United States."[32]

Nixon's visit highlighted the close interest the administration took in the campaign. During the Watergate hearings it became clear that $200,000 had been funneled illegally to the Brock campaign through Operation Town-house. These campaign contributions represented one portion of the funds that enabled the campaign to spend $1.25 million—an unprecedented sum—for a Southern race. By contrast Gore spent $500,000, still five times more than he'd spent in 1958 or 1964. Operation Townhouse had been devised by Commerce Secretary Maurice Stans, the master fundraiser of the Nixon administration, to bypass the Republican National Committee and secretly channel money to candidates loyal to Nixon rather than to the Eastern party establishment. The fund was maintained by Jack Gleason, Stans's subordinate at Commerce. It is unlikely that Brock knew of the illegal contributions. After the election Brock said, "I have no idea where the money came from and I don't want to know." His finance chair admitted, "There was very little in the way of records and I imagine most of them have already been flushed." It is more likely that Harry Dent had a shrewd idea of where the money was coming from. In 1974 Dent, along with Gleason and Herbert Kalmbach, pleaded guilty to misdemeanor charges for failing to follow federal disclosure requirements. The judge described Dent as "more of a victim than a perpetrator" and placed him on one month's unsupervised probation. Dent continued to protest bitterly that he had pleaded guilty only because he was sure he would not receive a fair trial in Washington in the post-Watergate era.[33]

But the White House did not merely arrange money to go to the campaign. There was detailed advice on tactics. In September the White House chief of staff, H. R. Haldeman, instructed: "It is imperative that our candidates call upon their opponent to repudiate what some of the leaders of the Radiclib have said—not just what the opponent himself has said. . . . In other words, Brock should call on Gore to repudiate specific statements made by McGovern, Hubert or Teddy." He had specific suggestions as to how Gore could be presented as distant from Tennessee. "Albert Gore can be expected to campaign against Brock with a never-ending stream of folksy gibes and populist economics, but Gore's cocktail party liberalism offers a chance to rebut his folksy image." Haldeman suggested that someone research the society pages of the *Washington Post* from 1965 and compile a complete list of parties Gore attended, the menus—"the Frenchier the better"—and the "society types and northern liberals" who were also there. Haldeman believed that the involvement of country-music people in the Brock campaign could help offset the image of Brock as a country-club type.[34]

The self-appointed administration spokesman for the Silent Majority against the liberal media, effete intellectuals, and radical liberals in Congress was Vice President Spiro T. Agnew. For Agnew, Gore was a perfect target, and he and his staff itched to come down to Tennessee. But the last thing Brock wanted was Agnew coming in and talking about "nattering nabobs." As Brock recalled, "I didn't need the conservative vote to be drummed up. I had 'em I really did. And I did not know . . . I did not need to . . . be . . . creating the sense of being extreme in any sense of the word. I already was challenged enough. Gore was saying plenty of that." Agnew's people kept insisting that he be scheduled. Eventually the Brock campaign arranged for a POW rally in Memphis. Everybody was in favor of getting the POWs back, and the campaign staff thought that, if Agnew stayed with that theme, damage could be limited. Gore upstaged the vice president a little, as Pat Buchanan later wryly acknowledged, by appearing at the bottom of the aircraft steps when Agnew landed in Memphis to welcome him to Tennessee. But Brock felt that, on the whole, the damage-limitation exercise worked. Agnew mainly kept to his brief and then drove home the point that Gore did not represent Tennessee views and values. Gore was a "radical liberal," to "all intents and purposes the Southern regional chairman of the eastern liberal establishment," who seems to think that "Tennessee is located somewhere between the *New York Times* and the *Greenwich Village Voice*." Brock breathed a sigh of relief until he received a bill for the damage Agnew's party had caused to the hotel where they had stayed. Staff members had knocked down walls between rooms rather than go out into the corridors to get to others' rooms. In addition polls in the Memphis area showed Brock's support falling seven points after the Agnew visit. It was no wonder that Brock unhesitatingly told visiting journalist Richard Harris that he would not be inviting Agnew to return.[35]

On *Face the Nation* in October, Brock asserted that Gore "has refused to stand up for the South and for Tennessee." The appeal to regional interest and racial conservatism was highlighted by Brock's attack on Gore's votes against Nixon's two Southern Supreme Court nominees, Clement Haynsworth and Harrold Carswell. Gore's stance on Vietnam, to Brock supporters, encapsulated a worldview that was alien to Tennessee. They were attacking "Gore's record of unSouthernism and unpatriotism." Henry Loeb, the mayor of Memphis and a bitter opponent of Gore, summed up this view: "The basic immorality is not backing our fighting men in Vietnam, and in not winning the war, and I mean it. From that immorality, we go to rationalization on smut and pornography, turning away from prayer etc."

As the *Tennessean* reporters described Brock's early campaign, he "hits the 'new left' in the Senate and terrifies people with threats of pornography and dope in high schools in Tennessee." Brock kept hammering away. "The robbing and the riots and the vandalism and the muggings go on," he said. "This tidal wave of crime and violence" had to be stopped. This approach was entirely in line with the White House and the vice president's strategy. White House speechwriter William Safire wanted to emphasize that "the President needs affirmative men with moral values and a streak of practicality to overcome the drug culture, the despair, the defeatism of the minority who form the dropout society. Hit the subtle drug peddling in some pop music and movies; hold the line against smut, especially the young; stress the point that licentiousness destroys liberty." Toward the end of the campaign, Brock simply summed up these appeals to traditional racial and social values. The election gave Tennesseans the "opportunity to vote against violence and permissiveness, for a balanced Supreme Court, against forced busing and for the President's policy for a lasting peace in Vietnam."[36]

       ↬

HOW WOULD ALBERT GORE respond to this assault?

    The evidence of Gore's unpopularity in the state Democratic party made it crucial that he mend fences quickly with other sections of the party. The day after the primary election, he met Ellington and Hooker to try to unify the Democratic Party in advance of the November general election. He was slower to reach out to Crockett. He did not mention Crockett when he declared victory on the Thursday night of the election results and did not ask for support from Crockett's supporters. It was not until Saturday morning that Pauline telephoned Crockett to ask if he would take a call from Gore. "Hudley, Al Gore, we're in trouble," said the senator. Crockett replied, "Who the hell is 'we'?" Crockett did finally endorse Gore and persuaded most of his campaign managers to endorse Gore as well, which many did, albeit reluctantly. It still rankles Crockett that Gore never publicly asked his supporters for their vote.[37]

    There was an initial air of fatalism about the Gore campaign. Gore himself seemed reluctant at first to make the effort. At one point on a Saturday afternoon, MTSU professor Norman Ferris went over to a bookstore at Mercury Plaza, one of the two biggest shopping centers in Murfreesboro, which was full of people everywhere. Gore was in the bookstore, "sitting in the back at a table and a few people would wander in and maybe somebody would buy his book *The Eye of the Storm* and he would sign it and I said, 'Senator, all those people out there. Why don't you go out and shake some hands and be visible?' This was not long before the election. He said, something like, 'Well if they don't know what I stand for by now, it seems a little late.'"[38]

    Despite the fundraising efforts of Ted Kennedy and Gore's Washington allies, the campaign did not have the resources to compete with Brock's spending. One solution was for the Gore and Hooker camps to cooperate. The two Democratic standard-bearers both represented the liberal wing of the party. They had both been strong Kennedy men. Hooker's campaign treasurer was Gil Merritt, Gore's protégé and also Hooker's brother-in-law. Al Barkan, director of the AFL-CIO Committee on Political Education, was vitally interested in Gore retaining a critical liberal seat in the Senate. He went down to Nashville to try and get the two teams to cooperate. The AFL-CIO, he promised, was willing to put a large sum of money into the campaign, but only on condition the two campaigns merged. Gore was very interested: He knew that the AFL-CIO money and the Hooker organization might compensate for his own lack of organization. He was cautious only because he feared being tainted by Hooker's collapsed Minnie Pearl chicken franchise. The Hooker team was leery of the impact of Gore's alleged radicalism and his stance on the war. They thought they did not need his help. In fact, a merged campaign, with Gore's stump-speaking attracting the crowds and AFL-CIO money funding the logistics, would have greatly strengthened both candidates. As it happened Hooker's campaign floundered: The constant barrage from the *Nashville Banner*, which attacked his financial problems and rehashed allegations of mental instability, took its toll. Too late did Hooker's team realize they needed Gore more than he needed them.[39]

Hooker's campaign for governor exacerbated Democrat disunity. Governor Ellington hated Hooker from the 1966 campaign. When Hooker came into Ellington's office after the 1970 primary, he put his feet on the desk and said, "I'm gonna like this place." Ellington made no secret of his contempt. Ellington's abandonment of Hooker was not made public, but many Democratic state officeholders were quite clear in their endorsement of Hooker's Republican opponent, Winfield Dunn. Lamar Alexander, serving as Dunn's campaign manager, was helped by a steady stream of Democratic stalwarts. The Ellington team may not have abandoned Gore quite so emphatically, but there is little doubt that they did not support Gore in the way a Democratic candidate for the Senate might have expected.[40]

As before, Gore's campaign was personalized. Nancy Gore Hunger came back from Greenville, Mississippi, to run her father's campaign. An instinctive politician like her mother, she had a wonderful ability to remember and communicate with campaign workers but had no taste for raising money. The trio Gore had relied on in the past, Harry Phillips, Frank Winslow, and Bailey Brown, were now far removed from local grassroots politics. Martha Ragland had been running campaigns for almost twenty-two years. Norman Ferris recalled that in Rutherford County Gore relied on his old local organizers, now elderly ladies who did little, but would not let young people get involved in the campaign. Gore's reliance on a skeletal organization that no longer existed at the local level was reminiscent of the Yarborough campaign in Texas, or even McKellar's last campaign when Gore himself was the young challenger. Gore's county organization was no match for the county-by-county teams that Brock had spent years assembling for the Republican Party.[41]

Vital posts were filled very late. Gene Graham came down from teaching journalism at the University of Illinois and stayed on to serve as the much-needed consultant to support the young volunteer press secretary, Thomas Gillem. There was no campaign manager for Nashville and Davidson County, an area vital to Gore's success and where he had faltered in the primary. Jim Sasser was about to scale down his political involvement in favor of his law practice. His wife was an old college friend of Nancy Gore Hunger. First Nancy telephoned, then Pauline. Sasser turned them both down. Finally the senator phoned, and Sasser gave in. But he then found himself on his own. "I mean, I had no money. I said, 'What do we do about money?' [Gore] 'You'll have to raise that.' 'Well what do we do about headquarters?' [Gore] 'You'll have to get one.' So I was just totally on my own." It was an entirely amateur campaign, shunned by the professional politicians who were only interested in the governor's race, where the patronage lay. Two McCarthy volunteers taught the Sassers about door-to-door canvassing. Students from the Vanderbilt Divinity School were able to help in the campaign because the school responded to their pleas by establishing a formal reading week without classes to let the students help with the campaign. A future dean of the divinity school recalled that they could not stomach the "syrupy pietism" of the Brock campaign. They set up the first phone bank in a Tennessee campaign and a completely volunteer get-out-the-vote car operation on polling day. They were rewarded in Davidson County by Gore's highest percentage of votes in the state.[42]

The one concession Gore made to modern campaigning was the use of TV advertising. In his day Gore had been a pioneer in the use of both television and radio, but he had used them in a didactic way, to inform and persuade constituents. He regarded the new type of spot ads as an "abomination," which he hated. But he knew that political campaigns had changed, and he made a concession to the new techniques by employing Charles Guggenheim to make six TV advertisements for him. Guggenheim was the favorite filmmaker of the Kennedys. He had worked on Bobby's Senate campaign in 1964, and in 1968 he made a documentary, *Robert Kennedy Remembered*, which he produced in the six weeks after Bobby's assassination. It was this film that brought the 1968 Chicago convention to a standstill. Guggenheim's style was about as far removed from the "slash and burn" technique of Harry Treleaven as could be. He used cinéma vérité techniques and would follow a candidate for two days; he then spent two weeks editing the hours of footage into the final product. As Ted Kennedy recalled, his brothers "just absolutely relaxed and [had] confidence in him . . . and great confidence in his taste and judgment, his artistry." Guggenheim "was just sort of able to catch them [my brothers] in a very, very special ways that others didn't." Guggenheim worked almost exclusively for Democrats; Treleaven, for Republicans. In 1970 they were campaigning head-to-head in two states: Michigan and Tennessee.[43]

Guggenheim made some memorable ads for Gore. They stressed that Gore grew up in Smith County and still held to the principles he had learned in the hill country of Tennessee. One showed Gore playing checkers with an old-timer in a county courthouse square. Gore joked that the man beat him because he had been practicing while Gore was in Washington protecting his Medicare. Another old man approaches and reminds Gore that he had voted for him six years previously and promised to do it again if he lived. "Here I am, Albert," he comes to tell the senator. Another featured Albert and Al riding horses on the farm. Yet another featured Gore telling his uniformed soldier son, Al, to love his country. There was no doubt the ads were beautifully shot. How effective they were divided observers at the time.[44]

For the most part the campaign revolved around Gore's personal campaigning on the stump. But the schedules were chaotic; there were no advance men, and little provision for the press. Turning up often without warning, Gore frequently only met small groups of largely older voters. One Democratic county chairman lamented that he did not know Gore was coming. It would have been so much better if he had come a few nights before, when they had a crowd of a thousand. But once Gore finally got involved, he campaigned furiously, from dawn to dusk, at factory gates, stockyards, and courthouse squares. He campaigned with a flesh-and-blood fervor that made Brock seem like an invisible candidate manipulated by image-makers. Gore had not lost his liberal evangelical zeal in 1970. Republican gubernatorial candidate Winfield Dunn had never heard Gore make a campaign speech before. But at a husting of all the candidates for statewide office, Gore's eloquence reminded Dunn of the Mississippi orators of his boyhood:

> His voice was strident from the beginning, his Tennessee twang
> was crisp and generous, his conviction was clear that his reelection
> to the Senate was pivotal in terms of the economic and military
> security of the nation, his guardianship of the rights and benefits
> of the working man was irreplaceable, and his statement was
> emphatic that the mothers, babies, and veterans of the state of
> Tennessee would be in some kind of jeopardy were he not sent back

to Washington. His delivery overall exposed an evangelical zeal
that was unmatched by any other speaker that evening. And at the
conclusion, his shirt was soaking wet from perspiration.

Tom Wicker of the *New York Times*, who heard Gore stir up students at
the University of Tennessee, thought Gore was "one of the best stump orators
in the country."[45]

David Broder came down from Washington to observe the campaign
and concluded that it was really a test of two different styles and theories of
campaigning. Broder argued:

> Gore was campaigning in the way that he had always campaigned,
> which was personal appearances, very folksy, talking to people
> directly. Brock ran what was one of really the first modern media
> campaigns. And as I watched it, the impression that I had was that
> Gore could not understand really what was happening to him and
> he couldn't figure out, sort of, what the dynamic was and even
> though his own people made beautiful commercials, as you've seen
> in that campaign—the white horse which became sort of a classic
> thing. So I think it was something done for him, but not really
> representing anything in which he was personally invested. And
> he'd go around and, you know, still very much in the old-fashioned,
> have these kind of conversations with, with voters believing that,
> you know, that was still how you communicated with the State that
> he had come to know very well over a long period of time.

But despite the changes in campaigning techniques, the contest was, as
Brock proclaimed, "a battle of basic philosophies." Gore agreed. Brock, he argued, was appealing to "the prejudices, the provincialism, the narrowness of
the people." Gore was appealing "to the best, rather than the basest in men."
Queried a quarter of a century later about the negative campaigning, Brock,
after noting how tame the campaign was compared to later campaigns, defended himself: "We were just trying to say these are two radically different
positions."[46]

The voters Gore was targeting in these conversations were the same
voters Brock was concentrating on, the Wallace voters. He believed that he
could appeal to their populist instincts on pocketbook issues. He hoped to
win their support by stressing economic issues, not racial or social ones. He

called the roll on all Brock's votes against programs that benefited Tennessee and stressed, in contrast, what he had done throughout his career for low-income voters. Surprisingly and dramatically, Gore started to claw back, so that by mid-October polls for both Brock and Hooker suggested that his bid to reclaim the Wallace voters was succeeding. The White House worried that Brock's unabashed economic conservatism laid him open to this Gore surge.[47]

↬

BROCK NEVER DOUBTED that he would win. One reason for his confidence lay in a media blitz for the end of the campaign that Ken Rietz and his team had planned since May 1969. But Brock also had a new issue with which to appeal to Tennessee voters' traditional cultural values.

The opportunity arose on 13 October, when Howard Baker tacked on a rider to the Equal Rights Amendment in the Senate that allowed voluntary prayer in public buildings. The rider was one that Baker and his father-in-law, Everett Dirksen, had routinely tried to pass ever since Baker had been in the Senate. It passed after a perfunctory debate; Gore voted against it without any impact, and the sponsors of the ERA withdrew the amendment, knowing the Senate would not pass it in that form. Brock latched on to this vote with alacrity. He announced that "I have and will continue to support school prayer. In contrast Albert Gore has gone on record against school prayer on three separate occasions." Three days later a full-page ad appeared in the *Banner* announcing, "Albert Gore Has Taken Position Against School Prayer Three Times." Many ministers asserted the importance of the division of church and state, and the Baptist Gore was shocked at the injection of the religious issue into the campaign. But for Brock the issue—a complex one to rebut so late in the campaign—was a perfect fit for the campaign to appeal to traditional cultural values.[48]

Brock had no TV ads prepared on prayer in school, but he compensated with newspaper ads and leaflets. It had an immediate impact. Jim Sasser remembered that "we were picking up the school prayer issue on the phone banks. They would say, 'Is Senator Gore really opposed to prayer in school?' So I think that's the issue that hurt him the most, but also we didn't quite understand the gun control issue, and I don't think that the gun control issue was as strong then because the NRA was not as strong and as technically proficient as they are now." Gene Graham agreed. He told Richard Harris, "What's hurting us most is this voluntary prayer stuff." Gore was genuinely puzzled by the issue and how to respond. As a Baptist he pronounced his profound belief in separation of church and state. Indeed the Southern Baptist Convention itself had endorsed the school prayer decision in 1962 precisely because of the belief in the separation of church and state. For Gore, as for so many politicians of his generation, religion was a private and understated issue. He had been "saved" at the age of twelve, but he had what his son described as an "enlightenment" attitude to religion. He went to the Baptist church in Carthage one week, then to his wife's Church of Christ the next. In Washington he rarely went to church. Both he and Pauline had seen the damaging effects that came from the injection of religion into politics. They had seen the devastating effect of anti-Catholicism in 1928 and 1960. In his final TV broadcast, Gore stressed his church attendance (as well as his enjoyment of hunting) and his Baptist belief in the separation of church and state, but the momentum Gore had generated had been lost.[49]

Instead his rise in the polls was halted by the media blitz the Brock team had always planned for the final ten days. As Kenneth Rietz told David Broder of the *Washington Post*: "We had 18 per cent undecided in our polls—mostly Wallaceites who were anti-Gore but not pro-Brock or pro-Republican. . . . Now we're really going after the undecided with the four big issues we've saved for the last ten days—prayer, busing, gun control, and the judges."

On each issue the TV and press ads relentlessly put over the message that Gore was at odds with the people of Tennessee. As Gene Graham bitterly observed, "Make it read from right to left—John T. Scopes, race, race, and race."[50]

Brock's strategy worked. In the battle for Wallace votes, Gore's economic appeal made headway in middle Tennessee but not enough to offset the wholesale defection of Wallace voters in the west. Whereas in Nashville Gore retained the support of nearly 60 percent of the low-income white voters, in Memphis he won only 27.3 percent. In the state as a whole, Brock won by 52.1 percent to 47.9 percent. Observers across the state felt that Gore had done well to give Brock such a close race, given his unpopularity and his chaotic campaign. They agreed that Gore had been coming up fast and looked as if he might catch Brock, but the last two weeks of the campaign saw that rise in the polls thwarted. Brock, concluded R. W. Apple for the *New York Times*, was selling the social issue better than Gore was selling the economic issue.[51]

↩

ON ELECTION NIGHT at the Hermitage, a despondent Gore attempted to rouse his supporters by proclaiming that "the truth shall rise again."

Across town, James Stahlman, editor of the *Nashville Banner*, was exultant. He fired one telegram off to Nixon at San Clemente: "WE GOT 'EM BOTH, ONE WITH EACH BARREL." Stahlman actually derived greater satisfaction from John Jay Hooker's defeat in the governor's race. Stahlman had waged a relentless campaign against Hooker as a man psychologically and morally unfit for office. But he knew that the man he telegrammed the next day was interested only in the Gore race. He wired Lyndon Johnson, "THANK GOD, WE HELPED GET RID OF ONE OF YOUR ARCH ENEMIES. NO ACKNOWLEDGEMENT NECESSARY."[52]

The response of liberals across the nation was different. In the Midwest, just before the election, a liberal Democrat had said that if Gore lost, "a little bit of steel will go out of all of our backbones." Immediately after the election presidential candidate George McGovern, no doubt aware of the election's implications for 1972, told Gore how grievously distraught he felt over his defeat. "No Senate race, it seems to me, was as important as yours." He tried to console Gore: "You can, however, draw the deep satisfaction that comes from knowing that you were a statesman at a time when this country desperately needed statesmanship. In that sense no one has really defeated you." Jonathan Daniels, the veteran North Carolina liberal newspaperman, understood the significance of the election. His old iconoclastic soulmate, Thad Stem Jr., wrote to Daniels, "As old and as feeble as I am, I'd walk from here [Oxford, NC] to Tennessee, backwards, if Albert Gore could whip Brock, the chocolate candy scion." When Gore was defeated Daniels, who had been FDR's and Truman's press secretary, replied that Gore's defeat left him "sick."[53]

Yet Gore was the only major prize for the Republican Southern strategy in 1970. Matthew Lassiter concluded that "the midterm elections of 1970 must be viewed as a smashing defeat for the Southern Strategy promoted by Kevin Phillips and orchestrated by the White House." Given that regional failure, why did Brock succeed while Republicans in other Southern states did not?[54]

Elsewhere in 1970 Republican candidates appealing to the segregationist vote lost. In South Carolina Albert Watson's incendiary rhetoric about court-ordered busing appeared to incite a mob in Lamar to attack and overturn a school bus, but Democratic lieutenant governor John C. West still triumphed in the election. Strom Thurmond ruefully acknowledged that GOP tactics exploiting racial politics had failed. A confidant of the victorious West saw Thurmond put his arm round Watson on election night and observe, "Well, Albert, this proves we can't win elections any more by cussin' Nigras." John West had picked up suburban white votes that had been expected to go to the

GOP. Similarly Jimmy Carter, Reubin Askew, and Dale Bumpers in Georgia, Florida, and Arkansas, respectively, put together biracial, cross-class alliances of affluent whites committed to economic growth and racial moderation and African Americans. As Randy Sanders has shown, successful Democrats in 1970 campaigned for the governorships as new faces who, in a rather fuzzy and indeterminate way, were racial moderates. Gore was neither fuzzy nor a new face. He was unlikely to appeal to affluent whites because of business opposition to his economic policies. In addition, candidates for state governor were not encumbered by the need to have clear policy stances on either the war or Supreme Court candidates. An antiwar Senator Gore, by contrast, was an easy target, having established a clear record on these two key issues. William Brock himself identified Gore's "position on the Supreme Court nominees and RN's VN policies as major factors" in his victory.[55]

Local factors clearly played a part. The unexpected strength of Republican gubernatorial candidate Winfield Dunn from Memphis helped Brock in western Tennessee in a way that a Nashville candidate like Maxey Jarman could not have done. Gore claimed that Dunn won it for Brock. Lamar Alexander recalled how the Brock team scorned the Dunn campaign in August 1970. After all, Brock had been organizing for two years, had a substantial war chest, and had engaged Ken Rietz as a campaign manager. By contrast Dunn had no money and no advertising agency. While the Brock campaign may have helped Dunn organizationally, there was no doubt that Dunn, a fresh face in Tennessee politics, brought an excitement and momentum to the GOP campaign that had previously been lacking. Equally, the imploding gubernatorial candidacy of Democrat John J. Hooker harmed Gore. The failure to merge campaigns hurt Gore in particular, because he needed the infrastructure of the Hooker team to compensate for his own lack of organization. He especially needed the support of the professional politicians in west Tennessee. The failure to merge also significantly reduced the amount of financial backing from the national AFL-CIO, which would have provided far greater financial support if the campaigns had been unified. By contrast the Brock campaign had the benefit of large sums of money delivered by the Committee to Re-Elect the President.[56]

The particular circumstances of Howard Baker's rider, which made the school prayer issue a salient one, was also important. It was an early foretaste of what the religious right could do for Southern Republicans. As Gore's Davidson County campaign director, Jim Sasser, recalled, "That amendment put Brock over the top."[57]

Gore also paid the price of being away too long. No one can reflect on this more vividly than Jim Sasser, who was himself defeated in 1994, when he was confidently expected to win a fourth Senate term and become majority leader: "I mean when you spend eighteen years in the Senate as Gore did and I did, you get out of touch without knowing it and as you progress in the Senate, as your responsibilities get heavier, you just can't attend to as much of the fence mending and massaging of egos as you could when you had more time. But having said that, Senator Gore was not any good at that anyway." Hudley Crockett and William Brock effectively persuaded the voters of Tennessee that Gore's worldview now differed in so many ways from the worldview of the ordinary Tennessean. Gore may have paid the price for being complacent, but he also paid the price for his open-mindedness and expanded horizons.[58]

That most astute observer of Southern politics, Claude Sitton, had covered Gore's 1958 campaign for the *New York Times*. He subsequently covered the civil rights movement and then supervised the remarkable group of *Times* reporters who provided matchless coverage of the movement. In 1970 he was observing the South from Raleigh, North Carolina, where he was editor of the *News and Observer*. After the 1970 elections he wrote an epitaph for the politics of race and Nixon's Southern strategy. The headline ran: "Southern Voter Spurned Race." Sitton wrote, "The South turned its face to the future Tuesday and walked away from the wreckage of Mr. Nixon's southern strategy. The keystone of that strategy was the racial issue." That issue had taken many white Southerners into the GOP, "but election returns in state after state show that race alone no longer has the power to keep them there."[59]

It seemed different in Tennessee. For Gore's supporters and old friends, the politics of race, as Gene Graham had observed, were crucial. David Halberstam, who had cut his journalistic teeth in Mississippi campaigns in the 1950s, thought Brock's campaign was as shabby a racist campaign as any he had covered. Gore's chief of staff, Bill Allen, said categorically that the race issue was the biggest one in the campaign. David Broder saw it in a more complex light: "The cultural issues were very clear and the contrast in the way in which they were attempting to communicate their messages to the voters was very clear. That sticks out in my mind much more than the racial component." Religion, as well as race, were now part and parcel of Southern politics, as they would be in the future.[60]

Unlike Albert Watson in South Carolina, Brock did not run a crude, race-baiting campaign. Brock had supported desegregation in Chattanooga. Nevertheless, he was appealing to a white backlash against the federal government in which race was intimately involved as part of the defense of traditional local values, whether on prayer, guns, or busing. The result, as elsewhere, was the creation of a lily-white Republican Party that may not have been racist, but which had no electoral incentive to attend to the needs of African Americans. The trajectory of white backlash had a different path in Tennessee when compared to the Deep South. The Deep South states that had been at the center of the defiance of racial change in the 1950s were now the sites of the New South successes in 1970. On the one hand there had been a dramatic increase in black voting in those states. On the other, economic leaders had mobilized to mediate what they now recognized as inevitable desegregation. New South racial moderates could triumph there.

In states like Tennessee and North Carolina, which had practiced token compliance in the 1950s, the post-1965 rise in black voting was less dramatic and less important. Equally, the timing of white backlash was different. Token compliance in the late 1950s and early 1960s had implicitly promised white voters in the black belts of west Tennessee and eastern North Carolina that they would be spared desegregation. By the late 1960s it was clear that they would not be spared. Voters in west Tennessee responded by defeating Albert Gore. Two years later, in eastern North Carolina, whites would elect Jesse Helms.

Epilogue

"THE TRUTH SHALL RISE AGAIN," Albert Gore told his disconsolate supporters on election night in 1970 at the Hermitage Hotel in Nashville. But there was both sadness and bitterness for Albert Gore after his defeat. Rejected by the people he had served for thirty-two years, defeated in what he considered to be a scurrilous and unfair campaign, Gore's gloom was lifted only by his son, who told him to be proud of those thirty-two years. It was still a depressing Christmas. Not only were Albert Gore's days in the Senate chamber coming to an end, but Al was set to leave for Vietnam on 29 December.

After a holiday in the Florida sun, Gore started to look to the future. Events moved rapidly. He shipped all his political papers to his old college, Middle Tennessee State University, in Murfreesboro. He signed a book contract with Viking, and then on 5 February 1971, he gave the first of eight public-policy workshops at Vanderbilt University's department of political science. He admitted "that private life has proven to be a fulltime endeavor already." He had more engagements than he could fill—lectures all over the country, starting with an address to the Young Democrats in St. Louis.[1]

Gore told the Vanderbilt students that "the biggest mistake of my 32 years in Congress was approving the Gulf of Tonkin Resolution." He lamented the loss of independence of the regulatory commissions in Washington, whose influence was much greater than that of elected officials. "This policy of presidential domination, which began during the Johnson administration, is regrettable because these agencies were set up to look after the public interest with little interference from the President or Congress." In foreign policy he was saddened by "an affinity for military dictators—we seem to prefer them to all other forms of government in the past few years. . . . The degree to which we are identified with reactionary governments is eroding our influence around the world." On the domestic front he took heart from the fact that, while he had been beaten in Tennessee, Democrats in other Southern states had won. He took heart in the wins of the younger generation: Reubin Askew, John West, Dale Bumpers, and Jimmy Carter. He professed a tentative hope that the Democrats could carry the South in 1972.[2]

The lingering taste of defeat informed Gore's assessment of Southern Republicans. He was unapologetic in his distaste for the new Republican politics both locally and nationally. The Republicans, he said, "seek to exploit racial prejudice." The new politics of the right were "diabolical." He accused Republican candidates of "surveying people to assess their fears, hates, prejudices," and then spending vast sums of money to "tailor campaigns to exploit the worst, not the best, in politics."[3]

In these lectures Gore imparted to the students his understanding of the twentieth-century South and the impact of racial politics in dividing low-income whites and African Americans. It was this analysis that informed his autobiography, *Let the Glory Out: My South and Its Politics*, which appeared in 1972. The book was more than the story of Gore's life in Washington. It was a history of the modern South. The optimism about the future that came through in his lectures was reflected in his belief that Wallace's low-income whites would come to renounce the racism and recognize their common class interests with African Americans. That emphasis reflected Gore's own worldview, but it was also informed by the two historians he brought in to help him write his book. Dewey Grantham was one of the most distinguished historians of progressive reform in the modern South. He had been teaching at Vanderbilt since 1952. Gore's younger collaborator, Hugh Davis Graham, was the son of a leading Presbyterian minister in Nashville. Hugh's father was a diehard segregationist, but his sons were part of the younger generation that looked to Kefauver and Gore as their role models in the 1950s. Hugh's eldest brother, Fred, roomed in Nashville with David Halberstam. They were part of a remarkable group of young reporters who would go off to work for the *New York Times*, a cohort that included Hedrick Smith, Tom Wicker, and Bill Kovach. Fred became legal correspondent for the *Times* and then for CBS, before finally becoming managing executive of Court TV. Middle brother Otis became a distinguished historian of planning programs of the New Deal and modern immigration policy. Hugh was at Johns Hopkins when he worked on Gore's memoir. He was already writing, with Numan V. Bartley, a landmark study, *Southern Politics and the Second Reconstruction*. Bartley and Graham identified the new, post-1965 cross-class alliance of upper-income whites and

African Americans that propelled New South governors into office at the same time Gore was defeated.

Gore's book merited a respectful review by the great Southern historian C. Vann Woodward. Woodward had been almost the first historian to take Southern populists seriously and had identified the racial fault line that had brought them down. No one was better placed to assess the play of racial and class forces in Gore's career. Woodward praised Gore for building a "career on a platform to the left of any elected politician south of him and of most of those to the north." Woodward read the lessons of the 1972 elections differently from Gore. He believed that Gore's optimism about the return of Wallace voters to the Democratic fold may have been premature. He noted approvingly that Gore hoped for a revival of a progressive populist Democratic party, but he injected a note of caution: "Out of all this social upheaval is likely to come a number of surprises that will upset old stereotypes about the politics of the South. They need not, of course, all be pleasant surprises."[4]

Godfrey Hodgson, who has written astutely about the liberal postwar consensus in the United States, had been a young Washington correspondent for the London *Observer* in the 1960s. He reviewed Gore's book for the *Washington Post*. Hodgson took heart from Gore's optimism. He thought that, by concentrating on race, Southern Republicans were building "their house on an eroding issue." He applauded Gore's interest in Southern history and his wide reading in it. He celebrated the fact that Gore's reading of the South was "not of the sentimental remember-Shiloh variety which is standard equipment among many Southerners of the lawyer class." Why had the admirable Gore not been more successful in politics? First he was not a "clubbable" man, not willing enough to "go along." Second, Hodgson thought it unsurprising that, however cogent Gore's arguments were, both JFK and LBJ must have wished that he were not so relentless in making them.[5]

For William Fulbright, his continued disappointment over Gore's 1970 defeat was exacerbated by reading Gore's "fine book." The book reminded him of what a tragedy it was that Gore had been defeated at the height of his powers. It gave Fulbright pause for thought about the future of the democratic system if people like Gore were not retained in positions of influence. Fulbright clearly missed Gore on the Foreign Relations Committee. He had left a "gaping hole" at a time when, Fulbright lamented, the Armed Services Committee seemed even more dominant than when Gore had been on Capitol Hill.[6]

∽

THE BOOK, HOWEVER, was not the forerunner of a life in academe or on the lecture circuit. Instead, Gore started a career in law and business. In 1974 he confidentially told journalist Jack Bass that he was having "fantastic success in the business world." He was excited: It was "challenging and rejuvenating . . . . to start a different career in law business at a time when most men are pushing to retire." He was unapologetic about his success: "Since the voters of Tennessee have chosen to send me out to pasture, I intend to graze in the tall grass." Albert and Pauline had set out to practice law in Washington together—the first time they had practiced as lawyers together. Like most senators who set up practice in Washington, they found clients were not hard to come by. In Gore's case a particularly important client was Armand Hammer, his old cattle-raising business partner. Gore was retained by the Island Creek Coal Company, a subsidiary of Occidental Petroleum. Soon the Island Creek chairman disagreed with Gore's legal advice, and Gore was summoned to explain himself to the Occidental board in California. He went into the meeting as a lawyer whose expertise was being questioned. He left the meeting as chair of the coal company.[7]

Island Creek was the third-largest coal company in the world. Gore was paid at least $175,000 a year and was no mere figurehead. He relocated the company's headquarters from Cleveland, Ohio, to Lexington, Kentucky, within two hundred miles of Carthage. He installed his former administrative assistant, Bill Allen, as his representative there. Stonie Barker, CEO of Island Creek, was the son of a miner and had dug coal at Island Creek to pay his way through college at Virginia Tech. He then worked his way up through the company. His mining background went a long way toward explaining his success in settling the company's sometimes violent labor disputes with the United Mine Workers. He would succeed Gore as chair in 1983. Gore had an apartment in Lexington and was there most weeks; twice a month he went to Los Angeles for Occidental Board meetings. He became an executive vice president of Occidental. Senior executives at both Island Creek and Occidental credited Gore with the renegotiation of coal contracts with public utilities—contracts that had been previously disadvantageous to Island Creek. They also noted how heavily involved he was in negotiations with Japan and governments in Eastern Europe, especially. They believed he was able to get Island Creek meetings with the most influential foreign leaders because of his status and previous contacts.[8]

Island Creek used a particular technique for deep mining that could be transferred overseas to countries and companies that wanted to exploit diffi-cult-to-mine reserves. Gore's abilities were particularly important in negotiat-ing for the company to build mines in Romania and China. A series of agree-ments with Romania provided for a joint venture to construct a coal mine in Virginia that would export high-grade metallurgical coal for the expanding Romanian steel industry. These agreements also focused on the long-term de-velopment of mines in Romania. Gore never lost his excitement about this part of his life. When I met Albert Gore in 1990, he was very happy to talk about the Southern Manifesto and about Vietnam, but he was really most enthusiastic when he talked about his time at Island Creek. He had retired by then and had become life president, but he was anxious to talk about his visit to Romania, where he had dealt one on one with Nicolae Ceausescu, and about his negotiations with the Chinese leadership in Beijing. In 1982, after five meetings with Deng Xiaoping, Gore and Island Creek signed a contract to build a mine in Shanxi province.[9]

Gore's links with the coal company and with Hammer came under par-ticularly close scrutiny when Al Gore became a national political candidate. Was there not a contradiction between Gore, Sr.'s political career and a career with a subsidiary of the giant Occidental Petroleum, which seemed to exploit the environment rather than sustain it? Island Creek's strip mining aroused attention at the very time that Gore's son, Al, was campaigning for more en-vironmental regulation. The company received numerous citations for violat-ing Environmental Protection Agency regulations. But Albert Gore, Sr. was undoubtedly an environmentalist. He had campaigned for conservation of water resources. He championed clean air and supported consumer-protec-tion legislation in the Great Society. He supported the close to three hundred conservation, beautification, and environmental measures that the Johnson administration had passed between 1963 and 1968.[10]

But the environmental movement had changed in the 1960s. Environ-mentalists of Gore's generation, particularly in the South, saw conservation as the wise use of resources, and they had faith in economic growth and prog-ress. The new generation of environmentalists were more concerned with quality of life issues: They emphasized the dangers of economic growth; they were skeptical of nuclear power; they fought pollution and campaigned to preserve natural places of beauty from economic development. The TVA, with its commitment to nuclear power and its continuing efforts to construct dams, was one of their targets. Gore understood and was sympathetic to many of these concerns. Pauline Gore had read Rachel Carson's *Silent Spring* in 1962 and insisted that all members of the family read it. In 1970 Albert wrote of the danger that the whole earth's climate might change. But for Gore economic growth for the poorest region in the country was more important than some environmental concerns. Preservation of an unblemished landscape was a noble goal, he argued, but the "noblest goal was to provide man with the basic stuff of his existence." "Ecology," he wrote, "is tied to economics. . . . Before we can recreate, we must create."[11]

Whereas environmentalists talked of restricting the demand for power, Gore believed that it was imperative substantially to increase the capacity for power production. To meet the needs of a fast-growing region like the South, only nuclear-fueled power stations in the short term could provide the necessary capacity. Whereas activists warned of the dangers of nuclear power, Gore remained what he always had been, as an enthusiast for the peaceful use of nuclear energy. He believed the dangers of radiation could be controlled with proper regulation. Even before he was involved with Island Creek, he could not see why activists targeted coal-fired power stations when traffic and transport of all sorts caused more pollution.[12]

The TVA epitomized the differences between Gore and the newer environmentalists. They condemned the TVA for what they saw as its single-minded obsession with electric-power—including nuclear power—production and constructing dams. Gore by contrast viewed the TVA as "one of the nation's most successful experiments in the kind of balanced ecological development." Soil conservation and water-resource development of the type the TVA promoted was the key to the region's economic growth and what Gore understood as key environmental priorities. Gore's friend Frank Smith, former Mississippi congressman, was a director of the TVA from 1962 to 1972. While he acknowledged some of the criticisms of a "cozy" TVA, Smith nevertheless despaired of the "crypto-ecologists" who refused to acknowledge the conservation work the TVA had done. Similarly, Gore lamented what he saw as the "fanaticism, righteousness and arrogance" of some environmentalists. The Gores were friendly with Wisconsin senator Gaylord Nelson and his wife, but the pioneering Earth Day that Nelson successfully initiated in 1970 did not arouse Gore's interest. Earth Day's grandiose aims—the goals of a new generation dedicated to reclaiming the planet and reversing the rush toward extinction—represented an apocalyptic vision of radical environmentalism that did not resonate with Gore.[13]

Gore's work at Island Creek therefore represented a consistent stand for the sort of Southern politician who had always been committed to economic growth and development in the region as a way of increasing the standard of living for poor Southerners of both races.

For friends of Lyndon Johnson like Harry McPherson, there was a certain wry amusement at Gore's financial success and his links to Armand Hammer in light of his stands against big business on the Senate floor . Fulbright teased Gore that he had become a "big tycoon." After meeting Hammer at a cocktail party in Washington, Fulbright noted that Hammer was riding high because he was perceived to be an intimate of the Russian leaders. Fulbright was unclear what Hammer's relationship to U.S. leaders was but noted that he had taken John Connally to the Middle East. Hammer "was a real operator," thought Fulbright, but he could see that he thought highly of Gore, and Fulbright and Hammer's wife, Frances, shared their mutual disappointment at Gore's defeat.[14]

But the charges leveled at Gore were not so much about political inconsistency as about the nature of his business relationship with Hammer. These allegations surfaced retrospectively, as bloggers attempted to discredit Al Gore in 2000. They went back to the joint cattle-buying business which, critics argued, showed that Hammer had Gore in his back pocket financially. In return Gore eased the way for Hammer to visit the Soviet Union, particularly during the early Kennedy administration. He went with Hammer to Libya to mark the agreement (the result of significant bribes by Hammer) that established Occidental's giant operation in Libya in 1968. Every Christmas the Hammers sent the Gores expensive gifts. In 1969, after Occidental took over Hooker Chemical—a takeover that Rep. Hale Boggs alleged was the result of insider trading—Gore was able to buy a thousand Hooker shares at a very advantageous price. Gore usually hosted the Hammers at presidential inaugurations.

After Gore became chair of Island Creek, the argument goes, Hammer effectively bankrolled Al Gore's political career. This argument cited the handsome salary paid to Albert Gore, including remuneration after he retired. Long-term links to Chinese interests and Al's links to Chinese-born fundraisers were traced back to Albert and Hammer's 1981 visit to China to establish a joint venture. Occidental also paid for mining rights to the zinc deposits on the Gore farms, payments that continued to benefit Al Gore throughout the 1990s. When germanium, which was much more valuable than zinc, was discovered on the plots in 1987, the Gore family benefited, after a court battle, from 4 percent of the much higher price that United Zinc, the lessee, received from the new discoveries.[15]

The idea that a cattle-buying business—in which Gore was writing checks to Hammer for a share of his feed costs—was a corrupt enterprise seems strange. From 1952 to 1968 the joint venture rarely grossed more than a thousand dollars at the end-of-year settlement. There could be no doubting Gore's genuine interest in cattle and his real pride in his herd. He started it long before he met Hammer and would continue it for twenty years after the partnership ended. Where Hammer helped was in the publicity the tycoon's presence brought to the twice-yearly auctions in Carthage, which brought Gore a hundred thousand dollars a year. The auctions of such fine cattle would always attract interest, but undoubtedly the link with Hammer brought an even more well-heeled clientele. It was alleged that buyers interested in currying favor with Hammer paid inflated prices and that sometimes the same bull was sold over and over again, with the buyers making no effort to claim their purchases. These stories smack of amused Tennesseans teasing credulous Northern journalists. These stories were then repeated by right-wing ideologues. There is no evidence to sustain the accusations.

Gore's willingness to ease Hammer's way back to the Soviet Union was entirely consistent with his concerns for lessening U.S.–Soviet tensions. Nothing in Gore's lifestyle in Washington, where he and Pauline did not even own a house, suggests that he was the beneficiary of Hammer's improper largesse. Unlike Lyndon Johnson, Gore did not make a fortune while he was in the Senate. He prospered only after he left the Senate. His salary at Island Creek was transparent and in line with the remuneration of other former politicians in roles as nonexecutive chairmen. Undoubtedly Gore's connections could help set up meetings with Romanian, Japanese, and Chinese partners. But there is no evidence the State Department and the Commerce Department did anything for Island Creek that they were not prepared to do for other American businesses.

Hammer, like Bernard Baruch, cultivated politicians regardless of party—through whom, often mistakenly, he believed he could exert influence in Washington, particularly with the White House. There was a certain irony that Hammer was convicted of making an illegal campaign contribution to the Nixon reelection campaign in 1972—a campaign that two years earlier had pumped illegal money into Tennessee to defeat Gore. There is no doubt that Gore regarded his relationship with Hammer as entirely honorable. Yet others were less certain about the perception of that relationship. When Harry McPherson was vetting Al for the vice-presidency in 1992, he asked William McSweeney about the Hammer links. McSweeney, an Occidental vice president, had served in the Lyndon Johnson White House, as had McPherson. He is said to have replied, "Let me put it this way. Pauline Gore and I spent twenty years making sure that Armand Hammer was never alone in the same room with Al Gore so I could answer this phone call."[16]

Were Gore's actions at odds with his reputation as a populist? Populists in the American tradition were never anticapitalist; they simply wanted equality of economic opportunity. Gore looked up to successful rich men who had made it on their own—Bernard Baruch, Robert Kerr, and Hammer. Texas Republican senator John Tower captured this side of Gore as a senior figure in the Senate: "Silver haired and immaculately dressed, Gore really looked the part of a senator; there was a hint of country canniness about the man, as if he had just bought up every mortgage in town." Gore was always by nature a restless entrepreneur, and that spirit never left him. In Carthage, after he stood down from regular work for Island Creek, Gore was always looking for a good local investment. There were a series of ventures: an antiques mall, a hardware store that included a gun store, a sporting goods store. He would buy buildings and renovate them. He owned some apartment houses. They were all small ventures that may or may not have made money. And there were always the cattle sales, until 1988, when he sold his prize herd when Al ran for president.[17]

But at heart he was still a farmer. When I met Albert Gore on a Saturday afternoon in December 1990, he was wearing galoshes and had been out to repair a fencepost that had blown down. He had then gone to the bank to deposit a check from one of his tenants. As Jerry Futrell, a long-time family friend who assisted the Gores in their last years, recalled:

> He really enjoyed the dirt, the foundation of the earth; he loved it;
> he loved to be out among it; he loved to deal with the birth of the
> animals and everything that was the raw nature. He just loved it;
> that's what he gained his strength by and he wanted you to be a part
> of it and he wanted to share that. He was an amazing man, but he
> was a basic individual that never forgot where he came from. He
> loved his land and he loved the grass roots of it.[18]

➾

BUT THERE WAS still a public life to lead.

In 1971 Gore became chair of the Council for a Livable World, an organization established in 1962 and devoted to decreasing the threat of nuclear weapons. He brought with him Carl Marcy from the Senate Foreign Relations Committee. The council sought to help progressive candidates for House and Senate seats and had contributed to Gore's 1970 race. One promising candidate was a long-shot challenger to incumbent Caleb Boggs in Delaware, future vice president Joe Biden. Gore told Jim Sasser that Biden reminded him very much of himself as a young man trying to get started in electoral politics. Gore recognized a "very self-assured, a little brash" candidate. Pauline Gore called Biden to Washington in 1972 to meet Albert and some concerned scientists. Afterward Gore promised to help Biden and sent out a letter to council supporters asking them "to take a hard look at the Delaware race." Gore's letter gave the Biden campaign credibility. The key thing that came out of it, recalled Biden's future chief of staff, Ted Kaufman, was that Gore "was telling people he [Biden] had a chance to win. That was what made it so special." It also unlocked a flood of small $100 to $200 contributions, accounting for a third of the money Biden raised that year.[19]

In 1975 and 1976 the U.S. Senate Select Committee to Study Governmental Operations with Respect to Intelligence Activities, chaired by Frank Church, investigated the illegal covert activities of the CIA, the National Security Agency, and the FBI which had first been highlighted by the Watergate scandal. President Ford appointed a foreign intelligence advisory board to oversee intelligence activities. Jimmy Carter replaced the board with a three-man intelligence oversight board. Thomas L. Farmer, who had experience both in the CIA and as general counsel to the U.S. Agency for International Development, chaired the board. William Scranton, former governor of Pennsylvania, and Albert Gore were the other members. Gil Kujovich, who ran the board's operation for two years under Carter, remembered that Gore was "especially important because of his familiarity with the legislative process and how it relates to the executive branch, having seen it from the other side. His presence in those issues that involve congressional dealings, for example, is especially important. But also his long experience and judgment about the process of governing has always been very useful." The board met every three weeks. These were part-time roles for busy men: only the chair, Thomas Farmer, lived in Washington, and he talked to Kujovich most days. A hostile critic argued that they rocked no boats. But the subsequent history of the board under Reagan suggests that it performed an important safeguard. Reagan's lack of interest in intelligence oversight was evidenced by his delay in appointing replacements for Farmer and his colleagues until October 1981.

Reagan's new board was undoubtedly less active than its predecessor, and Reagan may have paid the cost for that laxness in the Iran–Contra scandal.[20]

↜

BUT THE PUBLIC spotlight came not only from Albert Gore's own stature but from the rising political career of his son. After his father's defeat and his own service in Vietnam, Al Gore appeared to be shunning a political career. He enrolled in the divinity school at Vanderbilt and started work as a journalist for the *Tennessean*. But finally he also enrolled in the law school at Vanderbilt, which his father believed was a prerequisite for any political career. In 1976 the veteran congressman and chair of the House Appropriations Committee, Joe Evins, announced that he would not seek reelection for the Fourth District. The first time Albert Gore knew that his son was going to run for his old congressional seat came when Al phoned him *after* he had announced his intention to seek Evins's seat. Al wanted to campaign as his own man, and he was anxious for his father not to take to the campaign trail for him in 1976. Al was insistent that his father say nothing in the campaign. Albert Gore admitted that it was frustrating to stay on the sidelines, but he acknowledged that Al had to run without his help. He made his list of contacts available and occasionally intervened to secure key endorsements. But it was largely Pauline who was available with advice and who reached out to old Gore supporters on Al's behalf. In the last month of the campaign, Al's sister, Nancy Gore Hunger, came up from Mississippi to reactivate her network of local politicians.[21]

From the start of his time in Washington, Al Gore made a point of returning to his district every weekend. Conventional wisdom was that he wanted to avoid his father's mistake of losing touch with the people. But there was a more substantial reason for the lengths Al went to get back to the district. Joe Evins had wielded immense power in Washington and channeled huge sums to his district. There was no way Al Gore could match that as a junior congressman, and in the era of congressional reform in the House in the 1970s, no congressman could control the budget and spending items in the way men like Evins had done. To compensate, as Roy Neel, Al Gore's assistant, recalled, Gore introduced open meetings and workshops:

> So he wanted to look for a way to, not just connect with his constituents, but also a way to make government more accessible to them, the ordinary folk. And so one of the things he struck upon was doing what we called open meetings, and doing a lot of them.

And once he started it the feedback was so positive it reinforced
that and so he got on a roll, and. . . . We did them generally three
weekends inside of the month, which he would come to the state
on Friday, whenever he could after Congress adjourned, and just
hit the road and he'd plan out a circuit of up to ten in a weekend,
and have someone there to take case work and so on. The other
thing he did was a series of workshops all around the district that
were sort of unprecedented in helping people gain access to various
federal programs. They were quite remarkable programs I think.

He conducted 250 town hall meetings in his first year in office.[22]

A young staffer for Torbert McDonald recalled that Al Gore was temporarily assigned the recently deceased McDonald's office when he was first
elected in 1976. (Another McDonald staffer, Peter Knight, went on to serve Al
Gore as his chief of staff and later as U.S. president of Al Gore's Generation
Investment Management firm.) She remembered the unfailing politeness of
the young Tennessean and the effervescent presence of his wife, Tipper. She
also remembered visits from Albert Gore and felt that there was inevitably a
less relaxed atmosphere then.[23]

When Al Gore ran for the Senate in 1984, he could still call on his father's
supporters. Albert Gore could also still deliver powerful speeches. Arkansas
senator Dale Bumpers always thought of himself as a fine speaker. But he
ruefully recalled a large rally in Lexington, Kentucky, where Bumpers was
the featured speaker. Albert Gore was supposed to introduce him for seven
or eight minutes. He had never heard Gore speak before and had not realized "what a barn burning orator he was." By the time Gore had finished with
the audience, Bumpers for the first time in his life felt inadequate as a public
speaker. "On that evening I told them [the audience] publicly and I told a lot
of people since that I have never shied from the speaking circuit and I have
never felt intimidated by anybody who preceded me until that evening."[24]

Gore was immensely proud of his son's achievements. His pleasure at his
election to the Senate, however, could not compensate for the death of his
daughter, Nancy, in 1984. She had been diagnosed with lung cancer in 1982,
and she returned from Greenville, Mississippi, to Carthage to die. By common consent the most naturally gifted politician in the family, Nancy would
not be there for Al Gore's greatest campaigns and to share Gore Sr.'s pride.

Gore, if anything, was now even more ambitious for his son and anxious to help. From Christmas 1986 he tried to persuade Al to run for presi-

dent. The time was ripe, he argued, for a young, white Southerner who could win the Southern states that Reagan had won over for the Republicans. Nine Southern states planned to hold primaries on the same day in March 1988, in the hope of boosting a moderate candidate who would have a chance of winning the South for the Democrats in the November election, and therefore the presidency. A plausible Southern candidate could emerge from Super Tuesday in pole position. When Al Gore finally decided to run and called his father, Gore Sr. "yelled like a banshee." At times during the campaign, as he confided to Arthur Schlesinger, he would have liked his son to have been more progressive. With fondness in his voice he told Schlesinger that "he [Al] is not always as liberal as I would like, but he is as liberal as can be elected these days in Tennessee." He was sorry that Al was on the other side of the proponents of a nuclear freeze. But in policy terms he deferred to his son's presentation as a centrist candidate who was a hawk on foreign policy. He campaigned vigorously. Albert visited all ninety-nine counties in Iowa before Al and his staff decided to give the Iowa caucuses a miss. Lloyd Cutler recalled being stranded at Logan Airport after campaigning in New Hampshire. While Al and Cutler stood in line resignedly for a hotdog, Albert shook every hand in the terminal. The older Gore's hopes rose as the results came in on Super Tuesday, though in the end they were dampened a little by Jesse Jackson's success in the Deep South. Al Gore's press secretary, Arlie Schardt, helped Gore Sr. down from the platform at the victory party "And all of a sudden I reached up and then just then he threw his hands up in the air and then he looked down and he said 'Arlie, that boy is going to be president.'"[25]

Gore was certain that Al should use the momentum from Super Tuesday and campaign in Illinois. He had to demonstrate, his father believed, that he was a national candidate. Al Gore's staff by contrast was convinced that any effort in Illinois was a waste of rapidly diminishing resources—they had little chance of doing well when Illinois senator Paul Simon and Chicago-based Jesse Jackson were in the race. To some of Gore's aides, the father's brooding presence was inhibiting, his advice dated and irrelevant, and his constant criticism of his son belittling and humiliating. But others closer to Al did not see him as an oppressive presence. Roy Neel recalled that he did not have much effect on strategy. "He was on the road campaigning for Al, and we sent him to all kinds of places and he was really a happy warrior doing that. And, you know he was tireless. . . . And he stood in on some meetings I can recall, but he wasn't involved a great deal in the design of the campaign and the execution of it." But the pressure from the senior Gore to campaign in Illinois did perhaps overpersuade the candidate. Al followed his father's advice, not his staff's. His campaign manager believed it was the "worst mistake we made in the campaign."[26]

Al Gore's campaign limped into New York and was ended by the complex ethnic and racial politics of the Empire State. Arthur Schlesinger had a "nice chat" with Albert, who had been campaigning hard, but Schlesinger believed that Al's campaign in New York had been derailed by a disastrous decision to team up with Mayor Ed Koch, who was something of a loose cannon and who exacerbated racial tensions. Lamar Alexander recalled meeting Albert on a plane from New York after Al had been battered in the primary. Gore Sr. commented ruefully that New York City politics was no place for a country boy and an amateur. But he also confided that he had always imagined that one day Al and Lamar would run against each other for president.[27]

In 1992 Albert saw his son chosen by another Southern centrist, Bill Clinton, as a vice-presidential running mate. Pauline was said to have had doubts about Clinton's character. She also saw a provincialism in Clinton that she contrasted unfavorably with her son's wider perspective. But to Albert Gore his son's nomination was what he had devoted his life to. "We raised him for it," he said the night that the news of Clinton's choice came through from Little Rock. When Arthur Schlesinger went to the Intercontinental Hotel in New York on the eve of the convention to discuss Al's acceptance speech, he noted that the "the elder Gores could not have looked happier." Pauline and Albert almost missed that acceptance speech as the elevator bringing them up to the platform at the convention stopped short of the floor. Albert made determined efforts to climb out, but, fortunately, electricians arrived a minute before the speech was due to start to free the proud but alarmed parents. They subsequently spent seven weeks on the campaign trail—speaking especially to groups of older citizens. As Pauline Gore recalled, all Albert Gore wanted "was for someone to say go. He was in seventh heaven."[28]

꙳

BIOGRAPHERS OF THE vice president portray a father thwarted in his own quest for national office and thus investing too much in his son's career. They go further and claim that the father's overpowering presence, the family's rather formal life in Washington, and a lonely childhood were responsible for the stiff and wooden manner the vice president appeared to display in public.

Gore never lost his determination for his children to succeed. His granddaughter Karenna remembers that her grandfather was always fiercely competitive on their behalf. She once displayed her own cow in a competition. Her grandparents were there, and Albert Gore insisted that she have her photograph taken for use in the papers. Pauline, by contrast, understood why her granddaughter did not want to be photographed.[29]

When Al was born in 1948, the parents had almost given up on the possibility of another child to join ten-year-old Nancy. Al Gore spent most of his schooldays in Washington living with his parents in their apartment on the eighth floor of the Fairfax Hotel, owned by their cousin Grady Gore. But each year Al would spend three months back in Carthage, where he had many friends his own age. Yet there was also work to be done. Gore Sr. was a hard taskmaster. He laid out a schedule of chores to be done on the farm that often kept Al busy from sunup to sundown. One biographer described Al's summers in Tennessee as "character-building boot camps." His father expected a future politician to be able to plow a hillside with mules or clear a wood with a small axe. Throughout their lives the Gore parents took great pride in their son's accomplishments and lost no opportunity to tell others about him. But they, particularly Albert, had high expectations for their son and did not always express their pride directly to Al. At times they were distant parents. They were not always there to go their son's football and basketball games at St. Alban's, the relatively liberal, but elite, private school. More often than not, Al's sister, Nancy, went instead. Pauline expressed her regret to Coates Redmon, who knew Nancy in the Peace Corps and later wrote its history: "Oh that makes me feel just awful. Albert and I weren't really around enough. We traveled. We were busy. We went out a lot, which left Nancy to look after him."[30]

Al worked hard to live up to, rather than rebel against, these expectations. He respected the seriousness with which his father instructed him on policy issues and insisted on high standards of discipline. There is little sense that the Gores smothered their son. What others saw as a constraint, Al Gore recalled as a privilege. Most mornings Pauline insisted that they have almost an hour together over breakfast before Al left for school. Al Gore recalls it as an immense privilege to come down to breakfast every morning in Washington when he was growing up to listen to *two* of the most skilled and knowledgeable political operatives in the country discuss the most current events. He had huge admiration for his father's stands as a politician in Washington and enormous respect for his mother's political acumen. He always turned to her for political advice and would continue to do so after his father died.[31]

〜

ALBERT GORE HAD increasing health problems in the 1990s. In 1992 he was able to participate in Al's campaign, but in 1996 he could only make an appearance in a box at the national convention. His driving habits became notoriously erratic in Carthage. "The community," remembered Jerry Futrell, "decided to turn over the right of way to him, and when they saw him coming they just simply moved over and got out of the way." He was known to drive the wrong car home from town and to drive through all the town's red lights unabashed, despite the blue flashing lights from the police cars behind him.[32]

In 1998 Albert Gore died at his farm with his family at his bedside. Almost four thousand people came to the memorial service in the War Memorial Auditorium in Nashville, including President Bill Clinton and Hillary Clinton. They headed a fifty-member congressional and cabinet delegation. Clinton praised Gore as "the embodiment of everything public service ought to be." He said that, in the 1960s, Gore had been the role model for young Southerners like himself. Roy Neel, who was charged with organizing the memorial, had found a tape of Albert Gore playing "Soldier's Joy" on the fiddle in 1938: "then as it faded out the lights came up and the musicians were on stage and they picked it up at that point and finished it."[33]

Al Gore never spoke more eloquently than he did at the memorial service. He opened: "My father was the greatest man I ever knew in my life." He continued, "Of all the lessons he taught me as a father, the most powerful was the way he loved my mother." He recaptured his father's early rural years, his policy achievements, his courageous stances, his presence on the Senate floor, and his restless entrepreneurial spirit. Al was "proud of the choices you made. I'm proud of the road you travelled. I'm proud of your courage, your righteousness, and your truth."[34]

The casket was then taken to Carthage for the funeral, where two hundred family members and friends crowded into the tiny New Salem Missionary Baptist Church. It was the church where Gore's father had worshipped and had taken Al, and where Al had taken his children. Jesse Jackson was there, but the pallbearers were old friends: Ned McWherter, the former governor, whose mother had walked to school in Palmersville with Pauline; Jerry Futrell, the Carthage pharmacist; Gordon Petty, the Gores' doctor; Jack Robinson, Carthage boy, Gore staffer, and Nashville lawyer; and Charles Elrod, the farm operator. The service was led by Episcopalian bishop Jane Holmes Dixon, who had been a close friend of Nancy and had read the lesson at Nancy's funeral. Her sermon was punctuated by non-Episcopal "amens" from the congregation, which also joined in the second verse of "Amazing Grace," led by Jerry Futrell.[35]

Letters of condolence flooded in to the vice president. Many were dutiful expressions from Al Gore's contemporaries. But there were letters that highlighted the range and scale of Albert Gore's activities over the previous sixty years. John Kenneth Galbraith recalled working with Albert Gore on price controls during World War II. Charles Gersten remembered serving alongside Gore in Germany in 1945. Frances Zwening wrote of the inspiration Gore, Sr. had provided a teenager stuffing envelopes as a lonely Democrat in Republican east Tennessee in the 1950s. Sheldon Cohen, who had worked with Gore Sr. on tax issues for the Senate Finance Committee, and the former commissioner of the IRS, Mortimer Caplin, celebrated his mastery of tax reform. Pierre Salinger fondly remembered campaigning in California with Albert in 1964. Fellow workers at Occidental and men and women who had met Albert Gore on the campaign trail in 1988 and 1992 had vivid memories of a friendly, tireless worker with no airs and graces. Ted Kennedy reminded Pauline of what "a wonderful friend [Albert had been] to me when I arrived as a freshman Senator in 1962."[36]

In 2005 Al Gore reflected further on his father's career and expressed the hope that, in a time of anti-intellectual fundamentalism, the truth would rise again. He told his audience at Gore's old college:

> In closing I say to you all, I know in my heart that "the truth will
> rise again" and that it will rise from institutions of higher learning.
> It will rise in the minds and hearts of young people who come
> from the hills of Smith County and all over this State and all over
> this nation to places where the knowledge is kept and cared for
> and studied and researched and presented for those who want
> to open their minds and empower themselves yet again with
> the truth of our circumstances and the ability to communicate
> with one another and to say that once again all just power will be
> derived from the consent of the governed. We will give informed
> consent only because we will learn the truth; it shall set us free
> when it rises again.[37]

The father from Smith County whom Al Gore celebrated was an independent, serious-minded politician who saw the federal government as the savior of ordinary Southerners in the poorest region in the country. The

South Albert Gore grew up in was a poor, rigidly segregated region in which African Americans were economically dependent and politically powerless. The South Albert Gore spent his last years in was a booming, biracial democracy. For more than thirty years, he fought in Washington for federal programs that would benefit lower-income voters directly and also produce the economic growth that would raise their living standards through the transformation of the region's infrastructure. He supported New Deal, Fair Deal, and Great Society programs that brought undreamed-of benefits in wage levels, medical care, and education. As a champion of public works, of the TVA, of interstate highways, and of atomic energy, Gore could legitimately claim to have made a major contribution to the modernization of the South. He amply justified historian Numan V. Bartley's judgment that he was one of the few Southern independents in the 1950s—alongside Fulbright, Brooks Hays, and Frank Smith—who had "an emancipated intellect and a tendency to visualize problems in long-term perspective."[38]

Gore had no desire to initiate the collapse of segregation. At times he found it harder to respond to the impatience of African American demands than to the fears of his white constituents. His refusal to sign the Southern Manifesto and his support of the 1957 Civil Rights Act, which he had to defend against segregationist opposition in his 1958 reelection bid, came at a time when whites were essentially still dictating the timetable of racial change. The debate over *Brown* for a politician like Gore could largely be seen as a battle within the white community. With the direct-actions campaigns of the 1960s, African Americans used protest to force the pace of racial change on the federal government. Gore's careful gradualist position was largely undermined by this change.

In 1972 he sent a draft of his autobiography to his old friend Martha Ragland. She noted that in his draft he seemed always to be looking for an "alternative" to the race issue. She sternly told him that there was no alternative. Ragland, who had worked so closely with Pauline Gore in the League of Women Voters after World War II, had served on the advisory committee to the Tennessee Civil Rights Commission and on the board of the Southern Regional Council. She was chair of the Tennessee Human Rights Commission. In these roles she had direct exposure to the heightened expectations of African Americans in the late 1950s and 1960s. That personal experience was something Gore largely lacked. He remained unapologetic about his earlier caution on civil rights. But he did come to accept, earlier than most Southern politicians, that the federal government could change the region's race relations as much as it had changed the region's economy, as his votes after 1964 indicated.[39]

Gore was not always successful. He failed in his campaigns to restrict the influence of money on elections. He was usually in a minority on the Finance Committee in his efforts to make the tax system more progressive. He failed to persuade successive presidents to leave Vietnam. He was denied the chance to share the credit for the test-ban treaty, whose cause he had so eloquently championed. Gore was thoughtful, serious, and independent. Some saw that as arrogant, self-righteous, and willfully stubborn. He failed to become vice president or president.

Gore never lost his faith in the capacity of the federal government to solve the nation's and the South's problems. Gore belonged to a generation of politicians who had good reason to trust the federal government. Washington had rescued the country from the Depression. It had mobilized vast, unprecedented resources to defeat Hitler. It had then faced down the Soviet Union in the atomic age. It had managed thirty years of unprecedented economic growth. Programs like the GI Bill had benefited millions of American families and operated with a minimum of bureaucracy or corruption.

For a time Albert Gore carried both low-income white and black voters in Tennessee with him in his support for New Deal–style liberalism in the South. But in the 1960s whites in Tennessee, disillusioned by racial change and the cost of federal programs, lost their faith in the federal government as economic patron and social arbiter. Despite the electoral success of Jim Sasser and Albert's son, Al, in Tennessee, the state's politics scarcely fulfilled V. O. Key's hopes for the strengthening of the forces of liberalism. Locally and nationally faith in the capacity of the federal government to provide competent solutions has almost disappeared. The intense polarization of the electorate, a mean-spirited politics, the dominance of religious and cultural issues, the influence of vast sums of money, and the prevalence of anti-intellectual fundamentalism are all very different from the politics and policies that Albert Gore espoused. His hopes that "the truth shall rise again" seem even more distant today than they were in 1970.

PRIMARY SOURCES

MANUSCRIPT COLLECTIONS

Special Collections, University of Arkansas, Fayetteville, AR
    Papers of J. William Fulbright

Special Collections, Clemson University Library, Clemson, SC
    Papers of Harry S. Dent, Strom Thurmond

Rare Book & Manuscript Library, Columbia University Library, New York, NY
    Papers of Herbert H. Lehman

Dwight D. Eisenhower Presidential Library, Abilene, KS
    Eisenhower, Dwight D.: records as president, 1952–61
    White House Central Files
    Ann Whitman File: Legislative Meeting Series, Cabinet Series, Eisenhower Diary
        Series

Schlesinger Library, Harvard University, Cambridge, MA
    Papers of Martha Ragland

Lyndon B. Johnson Presidential Library, Austin, TX
    LBJ Congressional File
    Papers of the Democratic Leader, Box 369, Congressional File
    White House Central File

John F. Kennedy Presidential Library, Columbia Point, Boston, MA
    Pre-presidential Papers, John F. Kennedy
    Presidential Papers, White House Files
    John F Kennedy, tape of conversation with Douglas Dillon and Henry Fowler, 30
        September 1963, Audiotape 113.5
    Robert F. Kennedy, Pre-Administration Papers, 1968 Presidential Campaign
        Papers, Papers of Robert F. Kennedy

Memphis/Shelby County Public Library and Information Center, Memphis, TN
    Papers of Edward H. Crump
    Papers of Kenneth D. McKellar

Special Collections, University of Memphis Library, Memphis, TN
    Papers of Dan H. Kuykendall
    Papers of Edmund Orgill

Archives and Special Collections, Mansfield Library, University of Montana, Missoula, MT
    Papers of Mike Mansfield

Zimmerman Library, University of New Mexico, Albuquerque, NM
    Papers of Dennis Chavez
Manuscripts and Archives Division, New York Public Library, New York, NY
    Papers of Arthur M. Schlesinger Jr.
Richard M. Nixon Presidential Museum and Library, Yorba Linda, CA
      President's Office Files, White House Special Files: Staff Member and Office Files:
        John D. Ehrlichman, Alphabetical Subject Files, 1963–73
Southern Historical Collection, University of North Carolina, Chapel Hill, NC
    Papers of Jonathan Worth Daniels
Metropolitan Nashville and Davidson County Archives, Nashville, TN
    Papers of Richard H. Fulton
Albert Gore Research Center, Middle Tennessee State University, Murfreesboro, TN
    Papers of Buford Ellington
    Albert Gore House Papers
    Albert Gore Senate Papers
    Letters to the Vice President, Al Gore Jr.
    Albert Gore FBI File secured under the Freedom of Information Act, 37110 and
      161-12855
    Frank Ahlgren FBI File secured under the Freedom of Information Act, 94-47701
Julian P. Kanter Political Commercial Archive, University of Oklahoma, Norman, OK
    Adverts from Tennessee 1970 Senatorial Election
Carl Albert Congressional Research and Studies Center, University of Oklahoma,
  Norman, OK
    Papers of Robert Kerr
    Papers of A. S. "Mike" Monroney
    Periodic Log Maintained during the Discussions concerning the Passage of the
      Civil Rights Act of 1964 by Stephen Horn
Rare Books and Special Collections, Princeton University Library, Princeton, NJ
    Papers of David E. Lilienthal
    Papers of George McGovern
    Papers of Adlai Stevenson
Franklin D. Roosevelt Presidential Library, Hyde Park, NY
    Papers of John M. Carmody
    Papers of Democratic National Committee
    Papers of Harry Hopkins
    Papers of Gardner Jackson
    Papers of Isador Lubin
    Franklin D. Roosevelt, Presidential Papers—Vertical File
    Papers of Henry A. Wallace
Tennessee State Library and Archives, Nashville, TN
    Papers of Governor Prentice Cooper
    Papers of Thomas Jefferson Murray
    Papers of J. Percy Priest
Modern Political Archives, Howard H. Baker Center for Public Policy, University of
  Tennessee, Knoxville, TN

Papers of William Emerson Brock III, John Jennings, Estes Kefauver, Frank W
Wilson
Harry S. Truman Presidential Library, Independence, MS
President's Person File. Post-Presidential Papers, 1953–72
Special Collections, Alexander Heard Library, Vanderbilt University, Nashville, TN
Southern Politics Collection, Papers of Alexander Heard. Papers of James G.
Stahlman
Library of Congress, Washington, DC
Papers of the National Association for the Advancement of Colored People (microfilm
Part 26: Selected Branch Files, 1940–1955. Series A: The South, University Publications
of America)
State Historical Society of Wisconsin, Madison, WI
Papers of William Proxmire. Records of the Americans for Democratic Action,
1932–1999
American Heritage Center, University of Wyoming, Laramie, WY
Papers of Gale McGee

ORAL HISTORY
Interviews with the author
Lamar Alexander, 22 July 2015
Howard Baker, Jr., 7 April 2008
George Barrett, 10 January 2006
John Bragg, 12 July 2002
William E. Brock, 5 December 2006
David Broder, 20 April 2006
Dale Bumpers, 5 December 2005
Hodding Carter III, 21 September 2016
Hudley Crockett, July 2004, November 2006
John Culver, 8 December 2003
Winfield Dunn, 8 April 2008
Larry Daughtrey, 31 March 2004
John Egerton, 10 April 2008
Dante Fascell, 27 February 1997
Norman Ferris, 15 April 2006
Jerry Futrell, 10 January 2006
Albert Gore, Sr., 1 December 1990
Al Gore, Jr., 9 April 2005 and 19 March 2007
David Halberstam, 10 December 2006
Frank Hunger, 20 April 2007
Edward Kennedy, 10 December 2003
Harry McPherson, 17 September 2007
Gilbert Merritt, 24 February 2003
Roy Neel, 11 April 2008
Don Oberdorfer, 17 September 2007
Gordon Petty, 24 April 2004

Jack Robinson Sr., 26 January 2003, 4 December 2007
James Sasser, 10 December 2003
Mary Sasser, 2 September 2016
Karenna Gore Schiff, 11 December 2006
John Seigenthaler, 27 February 2003
Dalena Wright, 29 April 2015
Jim Wright, 18 November 1996
Jimmy Carter Presidential Library, Atlanta, GA
Gil Kujovich, Exit Interview Series, 1980
Lyndon B. Johnson Presidential Library, Austin, TX
Buford Ellington, 2 October 1970
Adrian Fisher, 31 October 1968
Bryce Harlow, 28 February 1979
George Reedy, 17 August 1983
Harry McPherson, 5 December,1968, 16 January, 24 March, 9 April 1969,
November 20, 1985, 7 February, and 13 May, 1986
William S. White, 5 March 1969, 21 July 1978
John F. Kennedy Presidential Library, Columbia Point, Boston, MA
JOHN F. KENNEDY ORAL HISTORY
Charles Bartlett, 6 January, 20 February 1965
Abram Cheyes interview with Eugene Gordon, 18 May 1964
Adrian S. Fisher, interview by Frank Sieverts, May 13, 1964
Albert Gore interview with Seth Tillman, 13 and 21 August 1964
Barbara Ward Jackson interview with Walt and Elizabeth Rostow, 28 June 1964
John Seigenthaler interview with William A. Geoghegan, 22 July 1964, interviews
with Ronald J. Grele, 21, 22, 23 February 1966
ROBERT F. KENNEDY ORAL HISTORY
John Seigenthaler, June 5, 1970, 1 July 1970
Memphis/Shelby County Public Library and Information Center, Memphis, TN
Gordon Browning: An Oral Memoir by Joseph H. Riggs, 1965 Memphis Public
Library, copy in Columbia Oral History Collection, Columbia University
University of Memphis Library, Memphis, TN
Frank Ahlgren interview with Charles W. Crawford, 31 March, 8 April, 13 May
1969, University of Memphis
Dan Kuykendall interview with Charles W. Crawford, 17 May 1976
Middle Tennessee Oral History Collection, Albert Gore Research Center, Murfreesboro, TN
Ivy Agee interview with Betty Rowland, 27 January 2003
Mary Elizabeth Arnold Basso and Dorothy Arnold Morris interview with
Michael S. Martin, 30 June 2003
Rollie Holden interview with Regina Forsythe, 29 August 1995, QMS 078
Larry Richards interview with Betty Rowland, 14 January 2003, MT 2000-154
Lucy Strickland interview with Kris McCusker, 2 May 2005, MT256
Richard Nixon Presidential Library and Museum, Yorba Linda, CA
Lamar Alexander, interviewed by Timothy Naftali, 27 June 2007
Senate Historical Office, Washington, DC
Francis R. Valeo, Secretary of the Senate, 1966–1977

Dennis Brezina, Staff, Science Policy Research Division, Legislative Reference
Service Staff, Senate Subcommittee on Government Research; Legislative
Assistant to Senator Gaylord Nelson
Carl M. Marcy, Chief of Staff, Foreign Relations Committee, 1955–1973
Southern Oral History Collection, University of North Carolina, Chapel Hill, NC
Albert Gore interview with Dewey Grantham and James Gardner, 13 March, 24
October 1976
Albert Gore, William E. Brock, William C. Carter and William L. Carter,
interviews with Jack Bass in Jack Bass and Walter De Vries Southern Politics
interviews, 1974
Harry S. Truman Presidential Library, Independence, MO
Lewis T. Barringer interview, with J. R. Fuchs, 15 April 1969
Leon Keyserling interview with Jerry Hess, 2, 10, 17 May 1971
Wesley McCune interview with Neil M. Johnson, 15, 16 September 1988
J. Leonard Reinsch interview with J. R. Fuchs, 13, 14 March 1967
Walter Trohan interview with Jerry N. Hess, 7 October 1970
Library of Congress, Washington DC
INTERVIEWS WITH FORMER MEMBERS OF CONGRESS
William E. Brock, 1979, and Wilbur Mills, 1979
Women in Politics Oral History Project, Bancroft Library, University of California,
Berkeley Regional Oral History Office, Berkeley, CA
Clara Shirpser, "One Woman's Role in Democratic Party Politics: National,
California, and Local, 1950–1973," interview with Malca Chall (University of
California: Berkeley, 1975)

PRINTED PRIMNARY SOURCES
Robert L. Branyan and Lawrence H. Larsen eds., *The Eisenhower Administration*
1953–1961: A Documentary History, vol. 1. (Greenwood: Wesport, CT, 1977)
Foreign Relations of the United States, 1958–1960. Volume I, Vietnam.
Foreign Relations of the United States, 1961–1963. Volume IV, Vietnam, August–
December 1963.
Foreign Relations of the United States, 1961–1963. Volume XX, Congo Crisis.
Foreign Relations of the United States, 1963. Volume XXI, Africa.
Foreign Relations of the United States, 1961–1963. Volume VII, Arms Control and
Disarmament.
Foreign Relations of the United States, 1964–1968. Volume IV, Vietnam, 1966–72.
Foreign Relations of the United States, 1964–1968. Volume V, Vietnam, 1967.
Louis Galambos and Daun Van Ee, eds., *The Papers of Dwight David Eisenhower:*
The Presidency: The Middle Way vol. 16 (Johns Hopkins University Press:
Baltimore, 1996).
Kent B. Germany and Robert David Johnson, *The Presidential Recordings of*
Lyndon B. Johnson, vols. 1–3, *The Kennedy Assassination and the Transfer of*
Power (Norton: New York, 2005).
Kent B. Germany and Robert David Johnson, *The Presidential Recordings of*
Lyndon B. Johnson, vols. 4–6, *Toward the Great Society* (Norton: New York,
2007).

Government Printing Office, "1956 General Election Campaign. Report of the Subcommittee on Rules and Administration submitted to the Committee on Rules and Administration." (Washington DC, 1956).

Walter Johnson, ed., *The Papers of Adlai Stevenson*, vol. 6, *Toward a New America* (Little, Brown: Boston, 1976).

Timothy Naftali and Philip Zelikow, *The Presidential Recordings of John F. Kennedy: The Great Crises*, vol. 2, September–October 21, 1962 (Norton: New York, 2001).

Donald A. Ritchie ed., *Minutes of the Senate Democratic Conference: Fifty-Eighth Congress through Eighty-Eighth Congress, 1903–1964* (U.S. Government Printing Office: Washington, DC, 1998).

MEMOIRS

Roger M. Anders, ed., *Forging the Atomic Shield: Excerpts from the Office Diary of Gordon E. Dean* (University of North Carolina Press: Chapel Hill, 1987).

Clinton P. Anderson (with Milton Viorst), *Outsider in the Senate: Senator Clinton Anderson's Memoirs* (World: New York, 1970).

Chester Bowles, *Promises to Keep: My Years in Public Life, 1941–1969* (Harper and Row: New York, 1971).

Carl Curtis, *Forty Years Against the Tide: Congress and the Welfare State* (Regnery: Washington DC, 1986).

Cartha DeLoach, *Hoover's FBI: The Inside Story by Hoover's Trusted Lieutenant* (Regnery: Washington, DC, 1997).

Larry Devlin, *Chief of Station, Congo: Fighting the Cold War in a Hot Zone* (Public Affairs: New York, 2007).

Paul H. Douglas, *In the Fullness of Time: The Memoirs of Paul H. Douglas* (Harcourt Brace Jovanovich: New York, 1973).

Winfield C. Dunn, *From a Standing Start: My Tennessee Political Odyssey* (Magellan Press: Brentwood, TN, 2007).

Dwight David Eisenhower, *At Ease: Stories I Tell My Friends* (Robert Hale: London, 1968).

Robert H. Ferrell, ed., *The Diary of James C. Hagerty: Eisenhower in Mid-Course 1954–1955* (Indiana University Press: Bloomington, 1983).

John Kenneth Galbraith, *Name-Dropping: From FDR On* (Aurum: London, 1999).

———, *A Life in Our Times: Memoirs* (Ballantine Books: New York, 1982).

Raymond L. Garthoff, *A Journey through the Cold War: A Memoir of Containment and Co-existence* (Brookings: Washington, DC, 2001).

Albert Gore, Sr., *Let the Glory Out: My South and Its Politics* (Viking: New York, 1972).

———, *The Eye of the Storm: A People's Politics for the Seventies* (Herder and Herder: New York, 1970).

Katharine Graham, *Personal History* (Knopf: New York, 1997).

Walter Mondale, with David Hage, *The Last Good Fight: A Life in Liberal Politics* (Scribner: New York, 2010).

Robert D. Novak, *The Prince of Darkness: 50 Years Reporting in Washington* (Crown Forum: New York, 2007).

Chalmers Roberts, *First Rough Draft: A Journalist's Journal of Our Time* (Praeger: New York, 1973).

Arthur Schlesinger, Jr., *Journals: 1952–2000* (Atlantic Books: London, 2007).

John G. Tower, *Consequences: A Personal and Political Memoir* (Little, Brown: Boston, 1991).

NEWSPAPERS AND PERIODICALS

Carthage Courier
Chattanooga Free-Press
Chattanooga News
Congressional Record
Knoxville News-Sentinel
Memphis Commercial Appeal
Memphis Press-Scimitar
Nashville Banner
New York Times
Raleigh News and Observer
Tennessean
Time
Vanderbilt Hustler
Wall Street Journal
Washington Post

NOTES

INTRODUCTION

1   Ted Kennedy interview with author, 10 December 2003. Gordon Petty interview with author, 24 April 2004.

2   The ads can be found in the Julian P. Kanter Political Commercial Archive, Carl Albert Center, University of Oklahoma, Norman.

3   Albert Gore to Frank Wilson, 8 February 1951, Albert Gore House Papers, Albert Gore Research Center, Middle Tennessee State University, Murfreesboro, TN. Albert Gore Sr., *Let the Glory Out: My South and Its Politics* (Viking: New York, 1972), 211–14. Al Gore interview with the author, 9 April 2005.

4   V. O. Key, *Southern Politics in State and Nation* (Knopf: New York, 1949), 670.

5   J. Douglas Smith has recently shown how the malapportionment, especially of state legislatures, served conservative interests across the nation. He documents how metropolitan leaders in Tennessee came together to challenge the bloated rural dominance of the state legislature in the case *Baker v. Carr* (Joe Carr, the Tennessee secretary of state). *On Democracy's Doorstep: The Inside Story of How the Supreme Court Brought "One Person, One Vote" to the United States* (Hill and Wang: New York, 2014), 5, 52–93.

6   Anthony J. Badger, "Whatever Happened to Roosevelt's New Generation of Southerners?" in Robert A. Garson and Stuart Kidd, eds., *The Roosevelt Years: New Essays on the United States, 1933–1945* (Edinburgh University Press, 1999), 122–38.

7   Anthony J. Badger, "Fatalism, Not Gradualism: Race and the Crisis of Southern Liberalism, 1945–1965," in B. Ward and T. Badger, eds., *The Making of Martin Luther King and the Civil Rights Movement* (Macmillan: London, 1996), 67–96. Anthony J. Badger, "'Closet Moderates': Why White Liberals Failed, 1940–1970," in Ted Ownby, ed., *The Role of Ideas in the Civil Rights South* (University Press of Mississippi: Jackson, 2002), 83–112.

8   David Halberstam, "The Air-Conditioned Crusade against Albert Gore," *The Reporter*, September 1958, 24–26.

9   For V. O. Key Jr., "In its grand outlines, the politics of the South revolves around the position of the Negro." Key, *Southern Politics*, 5. Dan T. Carter, "More than Race: Conservatism in the White South since V. O. Key Jr.," and Byron Shafer and Richard Johnston, "Partisan Change in the Post-Key South," in Angie Maxwell and Todd G. Shields, eds., *Unlocking V. O. Key Jr: Southern Politics in the Twenty-first Century* (Fayetteville: University of Arkansas Press, 2011), 129–84. Dan T. Carter, *From George Wallace to Newt Gingrich: Race*

in the Conservative Counterrevolution, 1963–1994 (Baton Rouge: Louisiana State University Press, 1999). Byron Shafer and Richard Johnston, *The End of Southern Exceptionalism: Class, Race, and Partisan Change in the Postwar South* (Harvard University Press: Cambridge, 2006), 2. Matthew D. Lassiter, *The Silent Majority: Politics in the Sunbelt South* (Princeton University Press: Princeton, NJ, 2006), 1–19. Glenn Feldman, ed., *Painting Dixie Red: When, Where, Why and How the South Became Republican* (University of Florida Press: Gainesville, 2011), 79–197.

10   Scholars argued that V. O. Key ignored religion; see Charles Reagan Wilson, "The Morality-Driven South: Populists, Prohibitionists and V. O. Key's *Southern Politics*," in Maxwell, *Unlocking V. O. Key Jr.*, 2–22. Also Carter, "More than Race," Shafer, "Partisan Change," and Wayne Parent, "Evaluating V. O. Key Jr. and Advancing Our Understanding of Southern Politics," in Maxwell, *Unlocking V. O. Key Jr.* Daniel K. Williams, "Voting for God and the GOP: The Role of Evangelical Religion in the Emergence of the Republican South," and Frederick V. Slocum, "With God on Our Side: Moral and Religious Issues, Southern Culture, and Republican Realignment in the South," in Feldman, ed., *Painting Dixie Red*, 21–37, 55–76.

11   Dale Bumpers interview with the author, 5 December 2005. John C. Culver interview with the author, 8 December 2003. Ira Shapiro, *The Last Great Senate: Courage and Statesmanship in Times of Crisis* (Public Affairs: New York, 2012). Michael Foley, *The New Senate: Liberal Influence in a Conservative Institution, 1959–1972* (Yale University Press: New Haven, CT, 1980).

12   John Norris, *Mary McGrory: The First Queen of Journalism* (Penguin: New York, 2010). William S. White, "The 'Club' That Is the U.S. Senate," *New York Times Magazine*, 7 November 1954, pp. 9, 30, 32–34. William S. White, *Citadel: The Story of the U.S. Senate* (Harper & Brothers: New York, 1956). William S. White, *The Making of a Journalist* (University Press of Kentucky: Lexington, 1986), 165. Lewis Gould, *The Most Exclusive Club: A History of the Modern United States Senate* (Basic Books: New York, 2005), 195–232.

13   William S. White Oral History Interview 3, July 21, 1978, by Michael L. Gillette, LBJ Library, 25–26. White, *The Making of a Journalist*, 167. Russell Baker, "Gore Also Runs—but for V.P.," *New York Times Magazine*, 10 April 1960.

14   Coates Redmon, *Come As You Are: The Peace Corps Story* (Harcourt Brace: New York, 1986), 147. Francis R. Valeo, Secretary of the Senate, 1966–1977, Oral History Interviews, Senate Historical Office, Washington, DC, 121–22. An anonymous source, when Gore was being vetted for a place on the Intelligence Oversight committee in 1977, spoke in a similar vein to Valeo's. The lone dissenter among the 58 people the FBI interviewed conceded Gore was a man of good intentions who no doubt meant well, but he "never sees any gray area—everything must be black and white." Gore "will stick with his decision even if wrong in a dogmatic manner" and "will jump at a decision and stick with it dogmatically." FBI File N 94-37110 and 161-12855, secured under the Freedom of Information Act by Rep. Bart Gordon, Albert Gore Research Center.

15   Political scientist Donald R. Matthews studied senators from 1947 to 1958 and largely confirmed White's picture of an "inner club" and of Senate "types." He concluded that conformity was the key to an individual senator's effectiveness. Donald R. Matthews, *U.S. Senators and Their World* (University of North Carolina Press: Chapel Hill, 1960), 115.

16   Anthony J. Badger, "Lyndon Johnson and Albert Gore: Southern New Dealers and

the Modern South," *The Historian* (Winter 2005), 9–15. Anthony J. Badger, "Lyndon Johnson and Albert Gore: Southern New Dealers and the Modern South," in Mark Newman and Suzanne Jones, eds., *Poverty and Progress in the South* (VU University Press: Amsterdam, 2007), 99–118.

17   Anthony J. Badger, "Southern New Dealers Confront the World: Lyndon Johnson and Albert Gore," in *New Deal/New South: The Anthony J. Badger Reader* (University of Arkansas Press: Fayetteville, 2007). Joseph A. Fry, *The American South and the Vietnam War: Belligerence, Protest, and Agony in Dixie* (University Press of Kentucky: Lexington, 2015).

18   *Economist*, 18 April 2015.

19   Tony Badger, "The New Deal Without FDR: What Biographies of Roosevelt Cannot Tell Us," in T. C. W. Blanning and David Cannadine, eds., *History and Biography: Essays in Honour of Derek Beales* (Cambridge University Press: Cambridge, 1996), 243–65.

CHAPTER 1

1   Lyndon Johnson (born Stonewall, Texas, 1908), Clinton Anderson (Centerville, South Dakota, 1895), Estes Kefauver (Madisonville, Tennessee, 1903), William Fulbright (Sumner, Missouri, 1905), Mike Mansfield (New York City, 1903, but grew up in Great Falls, Montana), John Stennis (Kemper County, Mississippi, 1901), Mike Monroney (Oklahoma City, 1902, when Oklahoma was still a territory), Hubert Humphrey (Wallace, South Dakota, 1911), and Richard Nixon (Yorba Linda, California, 1913). Donald Matthews, *U.S. Senators and Their World* (University of North Carolina Press: Chapel Hill, 1960), 12, noted how many members of the 1947–57 Senate grew up in rural and small towns in the age of national expansion. A large number of the Southern senators were lawyers.

2   Albert Gore, Sr., interview with Dewey W. Grantham and James B. Gardner, 13 March, 24 October1976, Interview A-0321, Southern Oral History Program Collection (#4007), University of North Carolina, Chapel Hill, NC (hereafter cited as Gore A-321 interview). Jeanette Keith, *Country People in the New South: Tennessee's Upper Cumberland* (University of North Carolina Press: Chapel Hill, 1995), 15–18. Lu Ann Jones, *Mama Learned Us to Work: Farm Women in the New South* (University of North Carolina Press: Chapel Hill, 2002), 1–7, 49–79. Melissa Walker, *All We Knew Was to Farm: Rural Women in the Upcountry South, 1919–41* (Johns Hopkins University Press: Baltimore, 2000), 69–141.

3   Gore A-321 interview.

4   Keith, *Country People in the New South*, 125–42. Ivy Agee interview with Betty Rowland, MT155, Gore Research Center.

5   Gore A-321 interview; Albert Gore Sr. interview with the author, 1 December 1990; Keith, *Country People in the New South*, 46–57; Karenna Gore Schiff interview with the author, 8 December 2006; Al Gore Jr. interview with the author, 19 March 2007.

6   Gore A-321 interview. Keith, *Country People in the New South*, 173; Elmore Messer Matthews, *Neighbor and Kin: Life in a Tennessee Ridge Community* (Vanderbilt University Press: Nashville, 1966), 74–78.

7   Gore A-321 interview; Lisa Pruitt, Nancy Morgan, and Holly Barnett, *Middle Tennessee State University* (Charleston, SC: Arcadia Publishing, 2001) 7–8, 39–65; Homer Pittard, *The First Fifty Years: Middle Tennessee State College, 1911–1961* (Murfreesboro, TN: MTSC, 1961), 93–139.

8   Robert Caro, *The Years of Lyndon Johnson: The Path to Power* (Knopf: New York,

1982), 141–65, 174–201. Gore A-321-1 interview; Albert Gore, *The Eye of the Storm: A People's Politics for the Seventies* (Herder and Herder: New York, 1970), 194–98.

9   Gore transcript held at Albert Gore Research Center, Middle Tennessee State University, Murfreesboro, TN. Louise Conditt to Albert Gore, 8 September 1951, Gore House Papers, Albert Gore Research Center. Rollie Holden interview with Regina Forsythe, 29 August 1995, QMS 078, Albert Gore Research Center.

10   Holden interview with Forsythe, 1995. Bob Abernathy to Albert Gore, 8 March 1952, Gore House Papers, and Gene Sloan to Albert Gore, 20 November 1969, Gore Senate Papers, Albert Gore Research Center.

11   Gore A-321 interview; Jerry Futrell interview with the author, 10 January 2006. Albert Gore Sr., *Let the Glory Out: My South and Its Politics* (Viking: New York, 1973), 39–40, 43. Gore, *The Eye of the Storm*, 194–98. Carroll Van West, *Tennessee's New Deal Landscape: A Guidebook* (University of Tennessee Press: Knoxville, 2001), 183.

12   John Dean Minton, *The New Deal in Tennessee, 1932–1938* (Garland: New York, 1979), 1–25.

13   Gore A-321 interview.

14   Interviews with Brainard Cheney and H. B. McGinniss, Southern Politics Collection, Alexander Heard Papers, Special Collections, Vanderbilt University.

15   Interview with Clint Beasley, Southern Politics Collection, Alexander Heard Papers. Keith, *Country People in the New South*, 64.

16   Mary S. Hoffschewelle, *Rebuilding the Southern Rural Community: Reformers, Schools, and Homes in Tennessee, 1900–1930* (University of Tennessee Press: Knoxville, 1998) 7, 34–60. *Carthage Courier*, 17 December 1998.

17   Remarks as Prepared for Delivery by Vice President Al Gore, Union University Luncheon Honoring Pauline LaFon, Monday, April 10, 2000. Billy Stair, *McWherter: The Life and Career of Ned McWherter* (Billy Stair, TN 2011), 5.

18   Gore A-321 interview. Al Gore Jr., "Words of Celebration and Thanks for the Life of Pauline LaFon Gore," 18 December 2004. Bill Turque, *Inventing Al Gore* (Houghton Mifflin: New York, 2000), 7–9; Pamela Hess, "The Perils of Pauline Gore," *George*, October 1998.

19   Gore A-321 interview.

20   For Martha Ragland, see Carole Bucy, "The Evolution of a Political Feminist," in Beverly Bond and Sarah Wilkerson Freeman, *Tennessee Women: Their Lives and Times*, vol. 1 (University of Georgia Press: Athens, 2009). Al Gore, Jr., "Words of Celebration"; Al Gore, Jr. interview with the author, 10 April 2005; John Seigenthaler interview with the author, 27 February 2003; John Bragg interview with the author, 12 July 2002. Remarks as Prepared for Delivery by Vice President Al Gore, April 10, 2000. "Democratic Convention: The Women Who Made Al Gore," *Time*, August 21, 2000. Turque, *Inventing Al Gore*, 24. Gail Sheehy, "The Son Also Rises," *Vanity Fair*, March 1988. David Maraniss and Ellen Nakashima, *The Prince of Tennessee* (Simon and Schuster: New York, 2000), 33. Bob Zelnick, *Gore: A Political Life* (Regnery: Washington, DC, 1999), 20. Hodding Carter III interview with the author, 22 September 2016.

21   The Murray boys who ran Madison County were the brothers Tom and Dave Murray. Tom was district attorney for the Twelfth Judicial District, based in Jackson, before going to Washington to work for the Post Office Department in 1933. He served in Congress from 1943 to 1966. His brother served as district attorney in Jackson for the reorganized

Twenty-sixth District for forty-one years. The Murrays were linked to the Crump machine but had their own power base. They were conservative and segregationist. LaFon, as district attorney and then circuit judge, was, like them, part of the legal establishment in Jackson. For the Murrays' involvement in the local White Citizens' Council in the 1950s, see http://orig.jacksonsun.com/civilrights/sec2_citizencouncil.shtml. accessed 4 April 2018. (In 2000, as part of a campaign against Al Gore, AIM and WorldNetDaily, right-wing Internet sources, made implausible allegations about drug running, bribery, and criminal coverups involving the then 82-year-old Whit LaFon: http://www.aim.org/aim-report/aim-report-al-gores-embarrassing-uncle/ accessed 4 April 2018.)

22   V. O. Key, *Southern Politics in State and Nation* (Knopf: New York, 1949), 75–81.

23   William D. Miller, "The Progressive Movement in Memphis," *Tennessee Historical Quarterly* 15, no. 1 (March 1956). William D. Miller, *Memphis During the Progressive Era: 1900–1917* (Brown University Press: Providence, RI, 1957). William D. Miller, *Mr. Crump of Memphis* (Greenwood: Westport, CT, 1981). G. Wayne Dowdy, *Mayor Crump Don't Like It: Machine Politics in Memphis* (University Press of Mississippi: Jackson, 2006), 3–54. Owen P. White, "Sinners in Dixie," *Collier's*, 26 January 1935. James Street, "Mista Crump Keeps Rolling Along," *Collier's*, 9 April 1938. Jonathan Daniels, "He Suits Memphis," *Saturday Evening Post*, 10 June 1939.

24   Dowdy, *Mayor Crump*, 6, 12–14, 19–20, 38–40, 49–50, 61–62, 88–89, 102.

25   Key, *Southern Politics*, 58–69. Roger Biles, *Memphis in the Great Depression* (Knox-ville: University of Tennessee Press, 1986), 96–107. Interview with Joe Hatcher, Southern Politics Collection. Dowdy, *Mayor Crump*, 109.

26   Key, *Southern Politics*, 61.

27   Ibid., 78.

28   Robert Dean Pope, "Senatorial Baron: The Long Political Career of Kenneth C. McKellar," Ph.D. diss., Yale University, 1975. Lyle W. Dorsett, *Franklin D. Roosevelt and the City Bosses* (Kennikat: Port Washington, NY, 1977), 35–48.

29   William R. Majors, *The End of Arcadia: Gordon Browning and Tennessee Politics* (Memphis State University Press: Memphis, 1982), 11–42. "Gordon Browning: An Oral Memoir by Joseph H. Riggs," Memphis Public Library, copy in Columbia Oral History Collection, Columbia University, New York.

30   Gore A-321 interview; Majors, *End of Arcadia*, 61–62.

31   Key, *Southern Politics*, 62.

32   Ibid., 62–63. Majors, *End of Arcadia*, 68–80. Gore A-321 interview. "City and County Crowd," *Time*, 17 August 1936.

33   Gore A321 interview. Key, *Southern Politics*, 62.

34   His wife, Pauline, recalled that she learned about Gore's decision to run when she went to his office and found him more excited than she had ever seen him. "'Pauline,' he burst out, 'You'll have to wean the baby and get ready to help me in my campaign.'" Sidney Shalett, "He Licked the Old Man of the Senate," *Saturday Evening Post*, 11 October 1952.

35   George F. Milton Jr., "The South Do Move," *Yale Review* 29 (September 1939): 138–52.

36   Fred Colvin, "Rogers Clark Caldwell," *Tennessee Encyclopedia of History and Culture.* http://tennesseeencyclopedia.net/entries/rogers-clark-caldwell/ accessed 5 April 2018.

37   Carroll Van West, *Tennessee's New Deal Landscape: A Guidebook* (University of Tennessee Press: Knoxville, 2001), 1–25.

38   Minton, *The New Deal in Tennessee, 1932–38* (Garland: New York, 1979), 157–59, 176–77, 191–93, 200, 212, 244.

39   Federal Writers' Project, *Tennessee; A Guide to the State* (Viking Press: New York, 1939), 96. Van West, *Tennessee's New Deal Landscape*, 96–98.

40   Van West, *Tennessee's New Deal Landscape*, 70–71, 116–18, 121–23, 183–85, 217–18, 228.

41   Gore A-321 interview.

42   Gore A-321 interview. Majors, *End of Arcadia*, 96.

43   Gore A-321 interview. Gore, *Let the Glory Out*, 58–59. Remarks as Prepared for Delivery by Vice President Al Gore, April 10, 2000. Ivy Agee interview, MT 155, Gore Research Center. Mary Elizabeth Arnold Basso and Dorothy Arnold Morris interview with Michael S. Martin, 30 June 2003, Gore Research Center.

44   Larry Richards interview, MT 2000-154, Gore Research Center. *Carthage Courier*, 16 June, 14, 21, 28 July 1938.

45   Gore A-321 interview. *Carthage Courier*, 5 May 1938.

46   *Carthage Courier* 5, 12 May 1938. Newspaper press release, 6 May 1939, Gore House Papers. Majors, *End of Arcadia*, 31.

47   Harry McPherson interview with the author, 17 September 2007.

48   *Carthage Courier,* 4 August 1938.

49   *Carthage Courier*, 11 August 1938. John Bragg interview with the author, 12 July 2002.

50   Albert Gore, Sr. interview with the author, 1 December 1990.

CHAPTER 2

1   Anthony J. Badger, "Whatever Happened to Roosevelt's New Generation of Southerners?" in Robert A. Garson and Stuart Kidd, eds., *The Roosevelt Years: New Perspectives on the United States, 1933–1945* (Edinburgh University Press: Edinburgh, 1999), 122–38.

2   Gore interview A321. Wilbur Mills interview with Charles Morrisey, 1979, Former Members of Congress Oral History Project, Library of Congress.

3   Gore interview A321.

4   The classic analysis of this bipartisan conservative coalition remains James T. Patterson, *Congressional Conservatism and the New Deal: The Growth of the Conservative Coalition in Congress, 1933–1939* (University of Kentucky Press: Lexington, 1967). For superb overviews of Congress during the New Deal and the war, see Patrick Maney, "The Forgotten New Deal Congress," and Alonzo L. Hamby, "World War II: Conservatism and Constituency Politics," in Julian E. Zelizer, ed., *The American Congress: The Building of Democracy* (Houghton Mifflin: Boston, 2004), 446–92.

5   *Tennessean*, 4 August 1939. *New York Times*, 4, 8 August 1939. Gore, *Let the Glory Out, Let the Glory Out: My South and Its Politics* (Viking: New York, 1972) 60–61. Carl Curtis, *Forty Years against the Tide: Congress and the Welfare State* (Regnery: New York, 1986), 115–16. "Blood on the Saddle," *Time*, 14 August 1939. As a result of his opposition to the housing bill, Gore in December 1939 was invited to speak to the New York State League of Savings and Loan Associations in New York City. The audience appreciated Gore's attacks

on federal housing programs and the United States Housing Authority for their excessive spending. The organization then unanimously approved a resolution opposing any expansion of federal housing projects. *New York Times*, 15 December 1939. Gore's hostility to the USHA did not diminish. In February 1941 he denounced USHA's spending requests, which included provisions for public relations and tenant education. "When we need billions and billions of dollars for national defense, we shouldn't waste money on such tommy-rot." WSM Transcript, 2 February 1941, Gore House Papers.

6   *Washington Post*, 4 August 1939. Jack Robinson interview with the author, 2003. Albert Gore to Bernard Baruch, 9 March 1953, Gore House Papers. Richard Lowitt's "The Enigma of Mike Monroney," *Chronicles of Oklahoma*, 91 (Spring 2013), 4–39, helps explain Gore's close affinity with Monroney. Lowitt describes Monroney as a self-consciously "level-headed moderate" with an independent streak who, with the exception of Vietnam, shared most of Gore's policy stances.

7   *Tennessean*, 6 July 1939, 5 January 1940. *Congressional Record*, 3, 4, 17 April 1939. Alfred O. Hero, *The Southerner and World Affairs* (Louisiana State University Press: Baton Rouge, 1965), 59–68.

8   Gore newsletter, June 1939, Gore House Papers.

9   Lynne Olson, *Those Angry Days: Roosevelt, Lindbergh, and America's Fight over World War II, 1939–1941* (Random House: New York, 2013).

10   Ibid. Joseph A. Fry, *Dixie Looks Abroad: The South and U.S. Foreign Relations, 1789–1973* (Louisiana State University Press: Baton Rouge, 2002), 188–203. Hero, *The Southerner and World Affairs*, 3–7, 73–75.

11   *Tennessean*, 1, 2 November 1939. Fry, *Dixie Looks Abroad*, 201–7.

12   *Tennessean*, 5 January 17, 19 July 1940. Hero, *The Southerner and World Affairs*, 5. Most Southern congressmen, like Gore, did not face any Republican opposition in the general election. They could support destroyers for bases and conscription in August and September 1940 with greater equanimity than could congressmen from other parts of the country who were in the midst of election battles.

13   Fry, *Dixie Looks Abroad*, 204. WSM Transcripts, 16 February, 11 May, 29 June 1941. Radio broadcast for Paul Kilday, 17 October 1941, Gore House Papers. *Tennessean*, 1, 3, 5, 8 June 1943. Hero, *The Southerner and World Affairs*, 91, 96. Susan Dunn, *1940: FDR, Willkie, Lindbergh, Hitler: The Election Amid the Storm* (Yale University Press: New Haven, CT, 2013), 281.What British observer Isaiah Berlin said of Wirt Courtney could have been said of Gore: "typical of the southern Democratic vote of complete support for the Administration's foreign policies." Thomas E. Hache, "American Profiles on Capitol Hill: A Confidential Study for the British Foreign Office in 1943," *Wisconsin Magazine of History*, 57, no. 2 (Winter 1973), 151.

14   *Time*, "The Great Debate," 12 July 1943; *Tennessean*, 4 July 1943. "Thoughts on Winning the Peace," "How Can We Win the Peace This Time?" Gore House Papers. Barbara Stuhler, *The Men of Minnesota and American Foreign Policy* (Minnesota Historical Society: St. Paul, 1973), 134. Fry, *Dixie Looks Abroad*, 220. Hero, *The Southerner and World Affairs*, 6.

15   *Tennessean*, 2, 3 May 1940. Gore, *Let the Glory Out*, 61. Gore interview A321.

16   Gore interview A-321. *Tennessean*, 22 September 1940.

17   *Tennessean*, 19 January 1943. Gore interview A321.

18   Gore interview A-321.

19   *Tennessean*, 1 October 1941. *Time*, "Brookings' Advice," 6 October 1941, "Doctor's Dilemma," 24 November 1941, "Price Mouse," 8 December 1941. WSM Transcript, "Inflation and Price Control," 26 September 1941; National Farm and Home Hour transcript, 11 October 1941.

20   Jordan A. Schwarz, *The Speculator: Bernard M. Baruch in Washington, 1917–1965* (University of North Carolina Press: Chapel Hill, 1981), 380–81. Nancy Beck Young, *Why We Fight: Congress and the Politics of World War II* (University of Kansas Press: Lawrence, KS, 2013), 62–64. *Congressional Record*, 77th Congress, 1st session 9247.

21   Schwarz, *The Speculator*, 532. Bernard Baruch to Albert Gore, 24 January 1945, 7 October 1952; Lyndon B. Johnson to Stuart Symington, 3 March 1953 (copy), Gore Senate Papers.

22   Richard Parker, *John Kenneth Galbraith: His Life, His Politics, His Economics* (Farrar, Straus and Giroux: New York, 2005), 139–52. Young, *Why We Fight*, 69. Congressional Record, 77th Congress, 1st session 9247. Albert Gore to Dale Chapman, 8 July 1959, Tight Money, 1959 File, Gore Senate Papers. Transcript, NBC radio, 28 May 1943, Gore House Papers.

23   Young, *Why We Fight*, 54–61, 93–99. Transcript, NBC radio, 28 May 1943, Gore House Papers.

24   "Gordon Browning: An Oral Memoir by Joseph H. Riggs," Memphis Public Library, held at Columbia Oral History Collection 77.

25   *The Journals of David E. Lilienthal*, vol. 2, *The Atomic Energy Years* (Harper and Row: New York, 1964), 396. In 1952, when Gore defeated McKellar, Lilienthal remembered it almost identically: "I recall taking Gore some years ago to look at construction on Douglas Dam, which set off the big row between McKellar and TVA—more particularly with me. As he looked out over the 'organized chaos' of the thing that so many bloody words had been spilled over, he said: 'This may be more than a dam; this may be the end of a political dynasty.'" David Lilienthal, *The Journal of David Lilienthal*, vol. 3: *The Venturesome Years, 1950–55* (Harper and Row: New York, 1964), 333. "Gordon Browning: An Oral Memoir."

26   Russell B. Olwell, *At Work in Atomic City: A Labor and Social History of Oak Ridge, Tennessee* (University of Tennessee Press: Knoxville, 2004), 9–25. Charles W. Johnson and Charles O. Jackson, *City Behind a Fence: Oak Ridge, Tennessee, 1942–1946* (University of Tennessee Press: Knoxville, 1981), xvii–xx. "Gordon Browning: An Oral Memoir." Robert Dean Pope, 'Senatorial Baron: The Long Political Career of Kenneth D. McKellar' (Ph.D. diss., Yale University, 1976).

27   Pope, "Senatorial Baron."

28   *Tennessean*, 8 January, 7 February 1943; 2, 7, 27 May and 2, 11 June 1944.

29   *Tennessean*, 2 June 1944. Erwin C. Hargrove, *Prisoners of Myth: The Leadership of the Tennessee Valley Authority, 1933–1990* (Princeton University Press: Princeton, NJ, 1994), 58. For the distinction between patronage-oriented and issue-oriented politicians, see James L. Sundquist, *Dynamics of the Party System: Alignment and Realignment of Political Parties in the United States* (Brookings Institution: Washington, DC, 1973), 183–217.

30   Ira Katznelson, Kim Geiger, and Daniel Kryder, "Limiting Liberalism: The Southern Vote in Congress," *Political Science Quarterly* 108 (1993), 283–306.

31   WSM Transcripts, 2 February, 11, 24 May 1941, Gore House Papers. *Tennessean*, 4

June 1944, 2 July 1944. Ira Katznelson, *Fear Itself: The New Deal and the Origins of Our Time* (W. W. Norton: New York, 2013), 16, 361.

32   Young, *Why We Fight*, 204–8.

33   Ibid., 208–9.

34   Ibid., 209–12. Clinton B. Anderson (with Milton Viorst), *Outside in the Senate: Senator Clinton Anderson's Memoirs* (World Publishing: New York, 1970). *Tennessean*, 14 February 1943.

35   Laura Kalman, *Abe Fortas: A Biography* (Yale University Press: New Haven, CT, 1990), 98. Young, *Why We Fight,* 213.

36   Young, *Why We Fight*, 217. For Estes Kefauver's lonely stand against anti-communist hysteria, see Joseph Bruce Gorman, *Kefauver: A Political Biography* (Oxford University Press: New York, 1972), 32–33, 49–51, 69–71, 170–72. Charles Fontenay, *Estes Kefauver: A Biography* (University of Tennessee Press: Knoxville, 1980), 240–47. For the doubts of Mike Mansfield and his staff about the Kerr Committee's definition of subversive activity, "so broad in scope and so lacking in specification of subversive acts as to jeopardize the fundamental rights of government employees as citizens of the United States, and to that extent imperiling the privileges of all citizens to enjoy their rights to free speech, free press and free assembly," see Memorandum Series 2, Box 2, Folder 9, Papers of Mike Mansfield, University of Montana, Missoula, Montana.

37   *Tennessean*, 18 June 1944. Randall B. Woods, *LBJ: Architect of American Ambition* (Free Press: New York, 2006), 162–69.

38   *Tennessean*, 4, 5, 7, 8, 29 November 1943; 11, 12, 14, 16 January; 4, 5 December 1944. *Time*, "Easing Up," 24 January 1944. Sidney Shalett, "He Licked the Old Man of the Senate," *Saturday Evening Post*, 11 October 1952.

39   *Tennessean*, 28 May, 26 June, 9 July, 4 August 1944. Bryce Harlow interview with Michael Gillette, 28 February 1979, Oral Histories, Lyndon B. Johnson Library, 2.

40   *Congressional Record*, vol. 91, 79th Congress, 1st Session, 19 March 1945, 2451–46.

41   Albert Gore to Jack Woodall, 18 March, 25 April 1950; 25, 31 January, 16 March 1951, Gore House Papers. Michael O'Brien, *Philip Hart: The Conscience of the Senate* (Michigan State University Press: East Lansing, 1995), 27–53.

42   *New York Times*, 20 July, 3 September 1944.

43   Gore, *Let the Glory Out*, 63.

CHAPTER 3

1   Gore interview A321.

2   John Egerton, *Speak Now Against the Day: The Generation Before the Civil Rights Movement in the South* (Knopf: New York, 1995), 10–11.

3   Robert G. Spinney, *World War II and Nashville: Transformation of the Homefront* (University of Tennessee Press: Knoxville, 1998). Robert G. Spinney, "Municipal Government in Nashville, Tennessee, 1938–1951: World War II and the Growth of the Public Sector," *Journal of Southern History* 61, no. 1 (February 1995) 81–83.

4   Notes of an interview with J. Percy Priest, 28 August 1947, Alexander Heard Papers. Clifford Davis to Thomas Jefferson Murray, 2 December 1948, Papers of Thomas Jefferson Murray, Tennessee State Library and Archives.

5   Thomas Jefferson Murray to Huffin Watters, 1946, Murray Papers.

6   WSM transcripts 15, 22 September 1946, 11 May 1947, CBS "In My Opinion," 14 March 1947, Gore House Papers. *Tennessean*, 13 March 1947.

7   WSM transcripts 14, 21 March 1948, 3 April 1949, Gore House Papers. Southern whites generally were more prepared to support the Truman Doctrine, the Marshall Plan, and the establishment of NATO than were people from other regions. But Southern representatives and senators were even more supportive than their constituents. Alfred O Hero Jr., *The Southerner and World Affairs* (Louisiana State University Press: Baton Rouge, 1965) 6, 197–202.

8   WSM transcripts 14, 21 March 1948, 3 April 1949, Gore House Papers.

9   Joseph A. Fry, *Dixie Looks Abroad: The South and U.S. Foreign Relations, 1789–1973* (Louisiana State University Press; Baton Rouge, 2002); Albert Gore to Harry S. Truman, 14 April 1951, Gore House Papers.

10   *Tennessean*, 15 June 1951.

11   *Tennessean*, 17 April 1951. Albert Gore telegram to Memphis Commercial Appeal, 31 October 1951, Gore House Papers.

12   These Southerners all figured in the list of young congressmen Gore recommended to Bernard Baruch. Albert Gore to Bernard Baruch, 1 November 1945, List of Members attending Baruch dinner, 25 October 1945; Albert Gore to Bernard Baruch, 2 June 1947, Gore House Papers.

13   *Tennessean*, 18, 19 February 1946.

14   *Tennessean*, 6 February, 13 March 1947.

15   *New York Times*, 5 March 1947.

16   Gore Newsletters, 1946–48, Gore House Papers.

17   *Tennessean*, 6, 18, 21, 22 January 1947; 7, 11 February 1947. Joseph P. Harris, *The Advice and Consent of the Senate: A Study of the Confirmation of Appointments by the United States Senate* (University of California Press: Berkeley, 1953), 155–77.

18   Allen J. Matusow, *Farm Policies and Politics in the Truman Years* (Harvard University Press: Cambridge, MA, 1967), 195–209.

19   Ibid., 209–10. Oral History Interview with Wesley McCune, 15 September 1988 and 16 September 1988, Harry S. Truman Library.

20   Matusow, *Farm Policies and Politics*, 216–19. Richard A. Baker, *Conservation Politics: The Senate Career of Clinton P. Anderson* (University of New Mexico Press: Albuquerque, 1985), 11–36, 282 n30. Anderson had intended to stay in Agriculture until the November 1948 elections, but Truman encouraged him to run for the New Mexico Senate seat when he appointed the incumbent, Carl Hatch, to the federal bench. Truman came to regard Anderson as someone who had quit when "the going got rough in 1948." By contrast he regarded Brannan as "the best one we've had since I've been in Washington." Address before the North Carolina Farm Bureau annual meeting, 14 February 1950, Gore House papers. Release, 7 June 1952, Speech on farm policy, 14 June 1952, Gore House Papers.

21   G. Wayne Dowdy, *Mayor Crump Don't Like It: Machine Politics in Memphis* (University Press of Mississippi: Jackson, 2006), 145–48. Michael K. Honey, *Southern Labor and Black Civil Rights: Organizing Memphis Workers* (University of Illinois Press: Urbana, 1993).

22   WSM Transcripts, 1 June 1946, 9 March 1947, 11 April 1948, Gore House Papers. George Barrett interview with the author, 10 January 2006.

23   Donald R. McCoy and Richard T. Ruetten, *Quest and Response: Minority Rights and the Truman Administration* (University Press of Kansas: Lawrence, 1973).

24   Spinney, *World War II and Nashville*, 52–72. Membership status of NAACP Tennessee branches as of 6 November 1947, Reel 19, Papers of the NAACP, Part 26: Selected Branch Files, 1940–1955, Series A: The South. "Address of Gloster B. Current, Director of Branches, November 16, 1947, for delivery at the Tennessee State Conference of Branches, Nashville, Tennessee" Reel 19, Papers of the NAACP, Part 26: Selected Branch Files, 1940–1955, Series A: The South. Notes on interview with Z. Alexander Looby, 21 August 1947, Heard Papers. Resolutions Adopted by the Sixth Annual Conference of Branches of the State of Tennessee, NAACP Reel 20, NAACP Papers. The Williams lynching that Looby was refer-ring to and the efforts of NAACP national officials to bring the perpetrators to justice are chronicled in Patricia Sullivan, *Lift Every Voice: The NAACP and the Civil Rights Movement* (New Press: New York, 2009), 237–42. Will Sarvis, "Leaders in the Court and Community: Z. Alexander Looby, Avon N. Williams, Jr., and the Legal Fight for Civil Rights in Tennessee, 1940–1970," *Journal of African American History* 88, no. 1 (Winter 2003), 47.

25   Notes on interview with Z. Alexander Looby, 27 August 1947, Notes on interview with Joe Hatcher, 29 August 1947, Southern Political Collection, Alexander Heard Papers, Special Collections, Vanderbilt University Library. Spinney, *World War II and Nashville*, 68.

26   David M. Tucker, *Memphis since Crump: Bossism, Blacks and Civic Reformers, 1948-1968* (University of Tennessee Press: Knoxville, 1980), 17–60.

27   Spinney, *World War II and Nashville*, 17–45. Don H. Doyle, *Nashville since the 1920s* (University of Tennessee Press: Knoxville, 1985), 167–68.

28   Gail O'Brien, *The Color of the Law: Race, Violence, and Justice in the Post-World War II South* (University of North Carolina Press: Chapel Hill, 1999), 89–108. Kenneth McKellar to E. H. Crump, 23 April 1946, Papers of Kenneth McKellar, Memphis Public Library. Bobby L. Lovett, *The Civil Rights Movement in Tennessee: A Narrative History* (University of Tennessee Press: Knoxville, 2005), 22.

29   Leroy Carter, assistant field secretary, to E. B. Cowan, 15 August 1947; E. B. Cowan to Gloster Current, 13 August 1947; Utilius R. Phillips, president, Tennessee State Conference, to Lucille Black, 24 May 1949; Black to officers and delegates, Tennessee State Conference, 24 August 1950; Phillips to Gloster Current, 25 October 1950; Ruby Hurley to Current, Phillips, and Black, 21 May 1951; Black to Hurley, 13 August 1951, reels 19 and 20, NAACP Papers, Part 26.

30   Lovett, *The Civil Rights Movement in Tennessee*.

31   Ibid.

32   Membership Status of NAACP Tennessee branches as of 6 November 1947. NAACP Memberships sent in 1 January to 17 August 1949, NAACP Papers. Pauline Gore interview with the author, 1 December 1990. Pamela Hess, "The Perils of Pauline Gore," *George* (October 1998), 98.

33   Jennings Perry, *Democracy Begins at Home: The Tennessee Fight on the Poll Tax* (J. B. Lippincott: Philadelphia, 1944).

34   *Tennessean*, 29 November, 31 December 1943; 14 January, 5 December 1944.

35   *Tennessean*, 4, 5, 9 March 1948.

36   WSM Transcripts, 26 February 1950, Gore House Papers.

37   Albert Gore to Bernard Baruch, 10 November 1952, Gore House Papers.

38   George Barrett interview with the author, 10 January 2006.

39   Jennifer L. Brooks, *Defining the Peace: Race, World War II Veterans, and the Remaking of Southern Political Tradition* (University of North Carolina Press: Chapel Hill, 2004). James B. Gardner, "Political Leadership in a Period of Transition: Frank G. Clement, Albert Gore and Estes Kefauver in Tennessee Politics, 1948–1956," PhD thesis, Vanderbilt University, 1978.

40   Albert Gore to Bernard Baruch, 14 January 1948, Gore House Papers.

41   Susan Graves, *Evins of Tennessee: Twenty-five Years in Congress* (New York: Popular Library, 1971), 44–47, 109–10, 114. John Bragg, interview with the author, August 2002. Joe Evins, *Understanding Congress* (Clarkson N. Potter, New York: 1963).

42   Albert Gore interview with Dewey Grantham and James B. Gardner, no. 2, A321-2, Southern Oral History Program.

43   E. H. Crump to K. D. McKellar, 5 August 1944; Evelyn Humphries to O. E. Godwin, 5 March 1948; E. H. Crump Collection, Memphis/Shelby Public Library and Information Center.

44   Will Gerber to Walter Winchell, 20 May 1947, E. H. Crump Collection; "Ring-Tailed Tooter," *Time*, 27 May 1946.

45   E. H. Crump to Edward J. Meeman, 22 May 1944, Crump Papers.

46   E. H. Crump to Silliman Evans, 22 May 1944, Crump Papers.

47   "Manipulation in Memphis," *Economist*, 21 August 1943; "Ring-Tailed Tooter."

48   "Ring-Tailed Tooter." Gordon Browning oral history interview, 1965, Columbia Oral History Collection. James B. Gardner, "Political Leadership in a Period of Transition: Frank G. Clement, Albert Gore and Estes Kefauver in Tennessee Politics, 1948–1956," PhD thesis, Vanderbilt University, 1978, 158–75, 239–76, 302–26. G. Wayne Dowdy, *Crusades for Freedom: Memphis and the Transformation of the American South* (University Press of Mississippi: Jackson, 2010), 10.

49   David M. Tucker, *Memphis Since Crump: Bossism, Blacks, and Civic Reformers, 1948–1968* (University of Tennessee Press: Knoxville, 1979), 40–60. George Barrett interview with the author, 10 January 2006. E. H. Crump to McKellar, 10 August 1948, Crump Papers. Dowdy, *Crusades for Freedom*, 15. Joseph B. Gorman, *Kefauver: A Political Biography* (Oxford University Press: New York, 1981), 35–63.

50   Gore interview A321.

51   Gore interview A321.

52   Crump wanted McKellar to announce to preempt possible opposition. He succeeded in deterring conservative Seventh District representative Pat Sutton and possibly Governor Browning, who decided to stay and fight for reelection as governor. Albert Gore to Frank Wilson, 19 June 1951, Papers of Frank Wilson, University of Tennessee Special Collections. Sutton would eventually run against Estes Kefauver for the Senate as a segregationist in 1954.

53   Gore interview A321. Bragg interview, *Washington Evening Star*, 18 February 1952.

54   Albert Gore to Bernard Baruch, 27 February 1951, Gore House Papers. Gore Interview A321-2. Albert Gore Sr., *Let the Glory Out: My South and Its Politics* (Viking: New York, 1972) 78. *Washington Evening Star*, 18 February 1952.

55   Gore Interview A321. John Jennings to Albert Gore, 23 January 1951, Papers of John Jennings, University of Tennessee Special Collections.

56   Gore Interview A321. Albert Gore to Frank Wilson, 8 February 1951, Albert Gore House Papers; Frank Wilson to Albert Gore, 21 February 1952, Papers of Frank Wilson, University of Tennessee Special Collections. Albert Gore to Mr. and Mrs. Marshall McNeil, 31 December 1951, Gore House Papers.

57   Gore Interview A321-2. Jack Robinson Sr., interview with the author, 23 January 2003. Gore raised hostile questions about the outsourcing of contract labor through the Arnold Research Organization at the Tullahoma base, which housed the Arnold Engineering Development Complex, one of the most advanced flight-testing and simulation facilities in the world.

58   Gordon Browning oral history interview, Columbia Oral History Collection.

59   *Memphis Commercial Appeal*, 3 February 1952. Gordon Browning oral history interview, Columbia Oral History Collection. Gore interview A321. William R. Majors, *The End of Arcadia: Gordon Browning and Tennessee Politics* (Memphis State University Press: Memphis, 1982)169–70, 191, 199. Gordon Browning to Lucius Burch, 10 February 1951, cited in Gardner, "Political Leadership," 163. Albert Gore to Bernard Baurch, 27 February 1951, Gore House Papers.

60   Gardner, "Political Leadership," 175–87. Dowdy, *Crusades for Freedom*, 25–26. *Tennessean*, 30 March 1952. John Seigenthaler interview with the author, 23 February 2003. Majors, *The End of Arcadia*, 207.

61   Albert Gore to E. H. Crump, Crump Papers. *Memphis Commercial Appeal*, 13 April 1952. Albert Gore to Avery Williams, 18 April 1952, Crump Papers. Gore attributed his success in attracting the support of Frank Ahlgren and the Commercial Appeal, in particular, to Bernard Baruch's influence with the Scripps Howard editorial conference; Albert Gore to Bernard Baruch, 21 April 1951, Gore House Papers. Gore's tactics of avoiding direct criticism of Crump meant that younger allies of Crump could associate with Gore. Congressman Cliff Davis told Frank Ahlgren, "Albert is able and is my friend. He always has something nice to say about me when he comes to Memphis. . . . There is no comparing Gore and Kefauver; Gore is so far out ahead that it is pitiful." Cliff Davis to Frank Ahlgren, 22 March 1952, copy in Gore House Papers.

62   Gore interview A321. Memo, 12 May 1952, Handwritten figures on Claridge Hotel notepaper, Crump Papers. Gore spent money very carefully. He was notoriously parsimonious in paying his staff and the expenses of campaign workers; Jack Robinson Sr., interview with the author, 2003.

63   Albert Gore to Frank W. Wilson, 29 August 1950; Wilson to Gore, 1 September 1950; Gore to Wilson, 9 March 1951, Wilson Papers. Albert Gore to Bernard Baruch, 16 March 1951, Gore House Papers.

64   Gore to Wilson, 22 April, 27 May 1951, Wilson Papers. "Tennessee Engagements 1951," in Box 25, Albert Gore to Bernard Baruch, 16 March 1951, Gore House Papers. Albert Gore to Charlie Gore, 6 October 1951, Gore House Papers. The Cumberland Feed Mill provided a modest but sustained income for Gore and his partner, Grady Nixon. In 1952–53 the mill yielded Gore a profit of $8,461.62 and his partner $4,228.40. A senator's annual salary at that time was $12,500.

65   Albert Gore to Bernard Baruch, 27 February 1952, Gore House Papers. *Tennessean*, 3 February 1952.

66   *Tennessean*, 21, 29, January, 3 February 1952. Oak Ridge residents after 1945 used

license plates that boasted that Oak Ridge was "The Atomic Capital of the World." Charles W. Johnson and Charles O. Jackson, *City Behind a Fence: Oak Ridge, Tennessee, 1942–1946* (University of Tennessee Press: Knoxville, 1981), 167–91.

67   Telecast, 30 June 1952, Gore House Papers. Lewis T. Barringer interview with J. R. Fuchs, 15 April 1969, Truman Presidential Library.

68   *Tennessean*, 13, 20 April 1952.

69   Dowdy, *Crusades for Freedom*, 26–28. K. D McKellar to E. H. Crump, 8 July 1946; Crump to McKellar, 6 June 1951; McKellar to Crump, 8, 15 January 1952; Crump to McKellar, 10 January 1952, McKellar Papers. E. H. Crump to Herbert S. Walters, 18 March 1952, McKellar Papers.

70   E. H. Crump to Frank Hobbs, 10 July 1946; Memo, 12 May 1952; Crump to Walters, 17 June 1952; Evelyn Humphries to K. D. McKellar, 28 July 1952, Crump Papers.

71   *Tennessean*, 6, 10, 16, 20 April 1952. K. D. McKellar to E. H. Crump, 15 May 1952, McKellar Papers. Dowdy, *Crusades for Freedom*, 27. McKellar's decision did not end the speculation.

72   *Tennessean*, 14, 16, 18, 19, 22, 23, 24, 25, 28, 29 July, 1 August 1952. John Bragg interview, with the author 2002.

73   *Tennessean*, 13, 15, 23, 25 July; 1, 3, 6 August 1952.

74   *Tennessea*n, 13, 15, 23, 25 July; 1, 3, 6 August 1952. Dowdy, *Crusades for Freedom*, 28.

75   *Tennessean*, 26 June, 13, 15, 26, 29 July 1952. "Paid advert Veterans Committee for McKellar," *Tennessee Legionnaire*, July 1952 (copy in Crump Papers). Browning interview.

76   *Tennessean*, 29 July, 30 July 1952. Gore, *Let the Glory Out*, 77–78. Washington Evening Star, 18 February 1952.

77   *Tennessean*, 13, 16, 19, 20, 22 July; 2, 3 August 1952.

78   *Memphis Commercial Appeal*, 3 February 1952. Gordon Browning oral history interview, Columbia Oral History Collection.

79   Labor Non-Partisan letter, 13 February 1952, Crump Papers; George Barrett interview with the author, 10 January 2006. Gardner, "Political Leadership," 269. David E. Lilienthal to Albert Gore, David E. Lilienthal Papers, Rare Books and Special Collections, Princeton University Library.

80   Mike Monroney to Albert Gore, 25 September 1952, 14 October 1952; "Mr. Gore's Engagements for 1952," Gore House Papers.

81   *Memphis Commercial-Appeal*, 30 November 1952. *New York Times*, 9 August 1952.

CHAPTER 4

1   Albert Gore to Lyndon B. Johnson, 9 January 1953, LBJ Congressional File, Box 44, Lyndon Johnson Papers, Lyndon B. Johnson Presidential Library, Austin, Texas.

2   Gore interview A321. Randall B. Woods, *LBJ: Architect of American Ambition* (Free Press: New York, 2006), 258–62. Robert Caro, *The Years of Lyndon Johnson: Master of the Senate*. (Knopf: New York, 2002). The Senate "class of 1952" has not been celebrated by historians in comparison with the classes of 1948 or 1958. But it was still a remarkable group. Elected to the Senate for the first time with Gore were John Kennedy, Mike Mansfield, Henry Jackson, Stuart Symington, and Price Daniel. Daniel would soon leave the Senate to return to Texas and serve as governor, but the others either ran for president or had long Senate careers in front of them.

3   Carl Albert Center, University of Oklahoma. Harry McPherson interview with the author, 17 September 2007. *Congressional Record*, 19 April 1967, 10164-5. George Smathers reported to LBJ in 1964 that Gore "finally got a big bull that he owns a third interest in. That's something that's worth $150,000. It's bred six calves and each one of them is sold for $6,000. Boy, he was just as proud of that as he can be." Kent B. Germany and Robert David Johnson, *The Presidential Recordings of Lyndon B. Johnson*, vol. 3, January 1964 (W. W. Norton: New York, 2011), 413.

4   83rd Congress, 2nd Session, *Congressional Record*, 100:2 (1 March 1954), 2824. R. C. Hendon to Clyde Tolson, 20 January 1947, FBI File N 94-37110 & 161-12855, secured under the Freedom of Information Act by Rep. Bart Gordon. Albert Gore Research Center.

5   Memo, L. B. Nichols to Clyde Tolson, n.d., FBI Files.

6   Director to SAC Memphis, 23 March 1954; M. A. Jones to L. B. Nichols, 30 March 1954, 19 June 1957; M. A. Jones to Wick, 2 March 1967, FBI Files.

7   L. B. Nichols to Clyde Tolson, 1 December 1954; M. A. Jones to L. B. Nichols, 30 March 1954, 19 June 1957; M. A. Jones to Wick, 2 March 1967, FBI Files. Cartha DeLoach, *Hoover's FBI: The Inside Story by Hoover's Trusted Lieutenant* (Regnery Publishing: Washington, DC, 1997), 351–70. The contrasting treatment of those favored by the FBI was summed up by what the FBI did for Frank Ahlgren, the editor of the *Memphis Commercial Appeal*, who with assistant editor Jack Carley had been contacts or sources for the FBI from at least 1944. The FBI valued him because he was a regent of the University of Tennessee, where several FBI suspects were enrolled. The FBI showed their appreciation for his cooperation, favorable press coverage, and friendship with Hoover by alerting local FBI agents whenever Ahlgren traveled. They extended to the editor and his party every courtesy, driving them to and from airports, for example, in San Francisco, Miami, and Honolulu, and sorting out hotel reservations. Carley ensured that there was a stream of personal notes of congratulation from Hoover whenever Ahlgren won an award. SAC Memphis to Director, 15 December 1954; L. B. Nichols to Clyde Tolson, 5 November 1956; SAC Memphis to Director, 5 July 1957; Director to SAC San Francisco, 8 July 1957, 94-47701.

8   Aaron Wildavsky provides an excellent account of the background to the controversy in *Dixon-Yates: A Study in Power Politics* (Yale University Press: New Haven, CT, 1962), 3–80. See also Wyatt Wells, "Public Power in the Eisenhower Administration," *Journal of Policy History*, 20, no. 2 (2008), 227–62.

9   Wildavsky, *Dixon-Yates*, 30–80; Wells, "Public Power," 223–34.

10   *Tennessean*, 22 April 1954.

11   Lewis L. Strauss, *Men and Decisions* (Macmillan: London, 1963), 296–312; 17 May 1955, Legislative Meeting Series, Eisenhower Papers. Wells, "Public Power," 232.

12   Robert Kerr to R. W. Roberson, 9 August 1955, Legislative Box 4, file 14, Kerr Papers.

13   Robert Kerr to Rev. William H. Travis, 15 June 1955, Legislative Box 4, file 14, Kerr Papers. 28 June 1955, Legislative Meetings Series, Eisenhower Papers. Wells "Public Power," agrees with Strauss that, since eventually Memphis built its own power plant that decision justified the position of the administration. "Public Power," 233.

14   Gore shared an appreciation of Gordon Dean with Harry Truman. Truman told Gore that Dean was a "wonderful man" when Gore was organizing pallbearers for Dean's funeral in 1958. He later agreed to serve as honorary chair of a memorial fund for Dean.

Harry Truman to Albert Gore, 21 August 1958, 11 June 1962, President's Personal File, Truman Papers, Harry S. Truman Presidential Library.

15   Clinton P. Anderson (with Milton Viorst), *Outsider in the Senate: Senator Clinton Anderson's Memoirs* (World: New York, 1970) 156. Roger M. Anders, ed., *Forging the Atomic Shield: Excerpts from the Office Diary of Gordon E. Dean* (University of North Carolina Press: Chapel Hill, 1987), 273. *New York Times*, 24 May 1956. *Tennessean*, 1, 24 May 1958.

16   Lyndon B. Johnson to Albert Gore, 3 August 1956, U.S. Senate 1949–61, Master File Index, Box 70. Lyndon B. Johnson Papers, Lyndon B. Johnson Presidential Library, Austin Texas. Robert Kerr to Albert Gore, 25 May 1956, Kerr Papers.

17   Richard W. Dyke and Francis X. Gannon, *Chet Holifield: Master Legislator and Nuclear Statesman* (University Press of America: Lanham, MD, 1996), 211. Tom Pickett to Robert Kerr, 29 March 1956, Kerr Papers. *Tennessean*, 24 June, 1 July 1956.

18   Albert Gore to Clinton Anderson (copy to Lyndon Johnson), 1 January 1957, Lyndon Johnson Papers. Albert Gore to Robert Kerr, 1 January 1957, Campaign Box 9, File 8, Kerr Papers.

19   Dyke and Gannon, *Holifield*, 212. Strauss, *Men and Decisions*, 334. Harry S. Truman to Albert Gore, 13 March 1957, President's Personal File, Truman Papers.

20   Jason Nicholas Wingerd Krupar, "The Rise of Institutional Confusion: A History of the United States Atomic Energy Commission's Early leadership and Culture," PhD diss., Case Western Reserve, May 2000, expertly delineates the changes in the AEC's decision-making that Strauss brought about. Dwight D. Eisenhower to Albert Gore, 19 June 1959, Alphabetical File, Eisenhower Papers.

21   Tom Lewis, *Divided Highways: Building the Interstate Highways, Transforming American Life* (Viking Penguin: New York, 1997), 47–92; Phil Patton, *The Open Road: A Celebration of the American Highway* (Simon & Schuster: New York, 1986), 79–91. Al Gore, interview with the author, 9 April 2005.

22   Mark H. Rose, *Interstate: Express Highway Politics, 1941–1956* (Lawrence: University Press of Kansas, 1979), 1–13.

23   Ibid., 15–28.

24   Ibid., 5, 11, 19.

25   Jason Scott Smith, *Building New Deal Liberalism: The Political Economy of Public Works, 1933–1956* (Cambridge University Press: Cambridge, 2006), 1–20, 258–66.

26   Patton, *Open Road*, 74. Smith, *Building New Deal Liberalism*, 251–52.

27   Patton, *Open Road*, 81. Lewis, *Divided Highways*, 89–90. Robert Weingroff, "Creating the Interstate System," Public Roads-On-Line (Summer 1956), 4–5. Dwight David Eisenhower, *At Ease: Stories I Tell My Friends* (Robert Hale: London, 1968), 155–60.

28   *New York Times*, 22 February 1955. *Tennessean*, 22 December 1992; Weingroff, "Creating the Interstate," 5. Lewis, *Divided Highways*, 24, 92. Eisenhower, *At Ease*, 166–67.

29   Robert L. Branyan and Lawrence H. Larsen, eds, *The Eisenhower Administration, 1953–1961: A Documentary History*, vol. 1 (Random House: New York, 1971), 537–39.

30   Robert H. Ferrell, ed., *The Diary of James C. Hagerty: Eisenhower in Mid-Course, 1954–1955* (Indiana University Press: Bloomington, 1983), 195. Branyan and Larsen, *The Eisenhower Administration*, 545. Legislative Meeting Series, 26 July 1955, Eisenhower Papers.

31   Lewis, *Divided Highways*, 107–13. Lucius Clay to Dwight D. Eisenhower, 11 January 1955, Official File Box 730, Eisenhower Papers.

32 Ferrell, *The Diary of James C. Hagerty*, 194.

33 *New York Times*, 19 March, 26 May, 28 July 1955.

34 Caro, *Master of the Senate*, 557–614.

35 Ibid., 678.

36 *New York Times*, 28 July 1955.

37 Dwight D. Eisenhower to Paul Roy Helms, 30 April 1955, in Louis Galambos and Daun Van Ee, eds., *The Papers of Dwight David Eisenhower: The Presidency: The Middle Way*, vol. 16 (Johns Hopkins University Press: Baltimore, 1996), 1691. The administration was much happier with the bills considered in the House. Legislative Meeting Series, 24 May 1955, Eisenhower Papers.

38 George Humphrey to Sherman Adams, 16 August 1955, Official File Box 730, Eisenhower Papers; Cabinet meeting, 28 October 1956, Ann Whitman File, Eisenhower Papers. *Tennessean*, 2 June 1956.

39 Lewis, *Divided Highways*, 20. Caro, *Master of the Senate*, 678. *Washington Post*, 6 July 1956.

40 Iwan Morgan, *Eisenhower versus "The Spenders": The Eisenhower Administration, the Democrats and the Budget, 1953–60* (Pinter Publishers: London, 1990), 109–10; Albert Gore to Dwight D. Eisenhower, 16 September 1959; Eisenhower to Gore, 9 October 1959, Alphabetical File, Eisenhower Papers.

41 Bartley, *The New South*, 403, 438.

42 *Tennessean*, 26 December 1992; Al Gore interview, 2005.

43 Wilma Dykeman, "Too Much Talent in Tennessee?" *Harper's* (March 1955), 48–53. Gorman, *Kefauver*, 224–48.

44 Dykeman, "Too Much Talent," 49. *Tennessean*, 11, 17 August 1956.

45 Gore, *Let the Glory Out*, 92. Adlai Stevenson to Abraham Ribicoff, 16 July 1956, in Walter Johnson ed., *The Papers of Adlai Stevenson*, vol. 6, *Toward a New America* (Little, Brown: Boston, 1976), 169. Gore interview A321.

46 Lee Greene, *Lead Me On: Frank Goad Clement and Tennessee Politics* (University of Tennessee Press: Knoxville, 1982), 221–46.

47 *Tennessean*, 17 August 1956.

48 Gore, *Let the Glory Out*, 93–94. David Broder, interview with the author, 3 April 2006.

49 Transcript, George Reedy Oral History Interview IX, 8/17/83, by Michael L. Gillette, LBJ Library, IX 6.

50 Reedy Interview IX 8. *Tennessean*, 17 August 1956. Clara Shirpser, "One Woman's Role in Democratic Party Politics: National, California, and Local, 1950–1973," interview with Malca Chall, Women in Politics Oral History Project, Bancroft Library, University of California, Berkeley Regional Oral History Office.

51 *Tennessean*, 18 August 1956.

52 Shirpser interview. *Tennessean*, 18 August 1956. It is the version John Seigenthaler also believed. Seigenthaler interview with the author, 2003. Martha Ragland believed that she had been instrumental in persuading Gore to release his delegates. Carol Bucy, "Martha Ragland: The Evolution of a Political Feminist," in Sarah Wilkerson Freeman and Beverly Bond, eds., *Tennessee Women: Their Lives and Times* (University of Georgia Press: Athens, 2009), vol. 1, 285. *Newsweek*, 27 August 1956.

53   Gore, *Let the Glory Out*, 95–96.

54   Ibid. Shirpser interview. *Tennessean,* 19 August 1956. The Stevenson Papers, Subseries 4B: 1956 Presidential Campaign, 1955–1957, Vice-Presidential Candidate Box 267, folders 4–6, contain the deluge of telegrams Stevenson received about the vice-presidential nomination. These were overwhelmingly in favor of Kefauver and Clement. Only two telegrams endorsed Gore. Rare Books and Special Collections, Princeton University Library.

55   Reedy interview. Woods, *LBJ*, 307–10.

56   Daniel Scroop, "A Faded Passion? Estes Kefauver and the Senate Subcommittee on Antitrust and Monopoly," *Business and Economic History*, 5 (2007), 1–17.

57   Larry Tye, *Robert Kennedy, The Making of a Liberal Icon* (Random House: New York, 2016). David Halberstam, *The Unfinished Odyssey of Robert Kennedy* (Random House: New York, 1968). Donald R. Matthews, *U.S. Senators and Their World* (University of North Carolina Press: Chapel Hill, 1960), 220.

58   Harry McPherson oral history interviews, Johnson Library. Keith M. Finley, *Delaying the Dream: Southern Senators and the Fight Against Civil Rights, 1938–1965* (Louisiana State University Press: Baton Rouge, 2008), 288.

59   Caro, *Master of the Senate*, 660–68. Randall B. Woods, *Fulbright: A Biography* (Cambridge University Press: Cambridge, 1996), 202–4.

60   Caro, *Master of the Senate*, 668–72. *Tennessean,* 12 February 1956.

61   *Tennessean,* 21, 24, 26 February, 1, 2, 4, 10, 11, 15, 18 March 1958. Caro, *Master of the Senate*, 673–75.

62   "1956 General Election Campaign. Report of the Subcommittee on Rules and Administration submitted to the Committee on Rules and Administration," 1–2. Statement of Alexander Heard, 8 October 1956, Boxes 52, 54, Gore Senate Papers. Heard later wrote *The Costs of Democracy* (University of North Carolina Press: Chapel Hill, 1960).

63   "1956 General Election Campaigns," 3, 9, 24. Albert Gore to ——, 31 January 1957, Box 52, 54, Gore Senate Papers.

64   Gore interview, 1990. Julian E. Zelizer, *On Capitol Hill: The Struggle to Reform Congress and Its Consequences, 1948–2000* (Cambridge University Press: Cambridge, 2006), 51–52. Julian E. Zelizer, "Seeds of Cynicism: The Struggle over Campaign Finance, 1956–1974," *Journal of Policy History*, 14, no. 1 (2002), 73–111.

65   Virginia Van der Veer Hamilton, *Lister Hill: Statesman from the South* (University of North Carolina Press: Chapel Hill, 1987), 230.

66   Ibid., 224–31.

67   Ibid., 212–23.

CHAPTER 5

1   John Kyle Day, *The Southern Manifesto and the Fight to Preserve Segregation* (University of Mississippi Press: Jackson, 2014), has provided a thoughtful and comprehensive account of the drafting of the manifesto and its regional and national implications. See also Anthony J. Badger, "The South Confronts the Supreme Court," *Journal of Policy History*, 20, no. 1 (January 2008), 126–42. The motivations of the nonsigners in the House and the Senate are discussed in Anthony J. Badger, "Southerners Who Did Not Sign the Southern Manifesto," *Historical Journal*, 42, no. 2 (1999), 517–34.

2   Badger, "Southerners Who Did Not Sign the Southern Manifesto," 512–22.

3   *New York Times*, 12 March, 3 April 1956. Speech draft, 1956, Estes Kefauver to P. L. Prattis, 19 May 1956; Kefauver to B. L. Fonville, 10 May 1956, Estes Kefauver Papers, University of Tennessee, Knoxville.

4   Albert Gore to Mrs. Talley, 12 October 1954, Gore Senate Papers; James B. Gardner, "Political Leadership in a Period of Transition: Frank G. Clement, Albert Gore, Estes Kefauver and Tennessee Politics, 1948–1956," PhD diss., Vanderbilt University, 1978, 500–670. Albert Gore interview with the author 1 December 1990.

5   Albert Gore, interview A 321.

6   Donald Davidson to Albert Gore, 12 March 1956; Fred Childress to Gore, 12 March 1956; Sims Crownover to Gore, 19 April 1956, Gore Senate Papers. David Halberstam, "The Air-Conditioned Crusade against Albert Gore," *Reporter* (September, 1958), 24–26.

7   Albert Gore interview with the author 1 December 1990.

8   Hugh Davis Graham, *Crisis in Print: Desegregation and the Press in Tennessee* (Vanderbilt University Press: Nashville, 1967), 29–90. Gore interview with the author 1 December 1990. Albert Gore to Pat Hughes, 12 April 1956, Gore Papers. *Nashville Tennessean*, 13 March, 18 March 1956. Ironically, Priest was challenged by young Richard Fulton, the future congressman and mayor of Nashville who, unlike Gore, would vote for the 1964 Civil Rights Act, as did Ross Bass.

9   Gore oral history A 321. Carl Elliott Sr. and Michael D'Orso, *The Cost of Courage: The Journey of an American Congressman* (Doubleday: New York, 1992), 178–82.

10   Miss Jean Scraggs to Albert Gore, 28 January 1956, Gore Senate Papers. Day, *The Southern Manifesto*, 114.

11   Michael Klarman, "Why Massive Resistance?" and Tony Badger, "Brown and Backlash," in Clive Webb ed., *Massive Resistance: Southern Opposition to the Second Reconstruction* (Oxford University Press: New York, 2005), 21–55. Bobby L. Lovett, *The Civil Rights Movement in Tennessee: A Narrative History* (University of Tennessee Press: Knoxville, 2005), 11–13, 24–25, 31–35. Benjamin Houston, *The Nashville Way: Racial Etiquette and the Struggle for Social Justice in a Southern City* (University of Georgia Press: Athens, 2012), 1–81.

12   J. W Anderson, *Eisenhower, Brownell, and the Congress: The Tangled Origins of the Civil Rights Bill of 1956–1957* (Inter-university Case Program series, University of Alabama Press: Tuscaloosa AL, 1964). David A. Nichols, A *Matter of Justice: Eisenhower and the Beginning of the Civil Rights Revolution* (Simon & Schuster: New York, 2007).

13   Robert Caro, *The Years of Lyndon Johnson*, vol. 3, *Master of the Senate* (Knopf: New York, 2003), 779–83, 788–800. Randall B. Woods, *LBJ: Architect of American Ambition* (Free Press: New York, 2006), 304–5. Hugh Davis Graham, *Crisis in Print: Desegregation and the Press in Tennessee* (Vanderbilt University Press: Nashville, 1967), 123–28. For an extensive discussion of the Powell amendment, see Day, *The Southern Manifesto*, 41–43.

14   Caro, *Master of the Senate*, 830–94. Woods, *LBJ*, 325–28. Robert Mann, *When Freedom Would Triumph: The Civil Rights Struggle in Congress, 1954–1968* (Louisiana State University Press: Baton Rouge, 2007), 22–48.

15   Graham, *Crisis in Print*. David Halberstam recalled that Frank Clement privately mused to reporters he trusted that the *Brown* decision was right and long overdue. "I'm not going to say that publicly, of course. All I am going to say is that we are going to obey the law in this state. And that's enough." David Halberstam, *The Children* (Random House: New York, 1998), 20–21.

16   In 1966 Rowland Evans and Robert Novak mapped out LBJ's strategy in their *Lyndon B. Johnson: The Exercise of Power—A Political Biography* (New American Library: New York, 1966). The subsequent accounts by Caro and Mann provide color and detail but no fresh analysis.

17   Caro, *Master of the Senate*, 895–1012. Woods, *LBJ*, 328–31. LeRoy Ashby and Rod Gramer, *Fighting the Odds: The Life of Senator Frank Church* (Washington State University Press: Pullman, 1994), 74–97. Mann, *When Freedom Would Triumph*, 49–60.

18   Graham, *Crisis in Print*, 130. Halberstam, "The Air-Conditioned Crusade against Albert Gore," 24–26. Draft jury trial speech, 1957, Gore Senate Papers. With some justification, Keith Finley argues that, for his constituents, Gore distorted and exaggerated his role in securing the amendments that watered down the bill. Keith M. Finley, *Delaying the Dream: Southern Senators and the Fight Against Civil Rights, 1938–1965* (Louisiana State University Press: Baton Rouge, 2008), 195–96.

19   Graham, *Crisis in Print*, 137, 140–69.

20   Ibid., 275.

21   Ibid., 276–27. Orgill told a constituent in 1956 that he did not believe in integration of the schools. But he thought "if Negroes were treated fairly, it would avoid trouble and discord and put off the day when they will try to force the issue of integration of the schools and parks in the courts." Edmund Orgill to Gordon Hollingsworth, 15 March 1956, Edmund Orgill Papers, University of Memphis Special Collections.

22   Anne-Leslie Owens, "William Prentice Cooper Jr.," *Tennessee Encyclopedia of History and Culture.* James H. S. Cooper, "Boss Crump and Governor Prentice Cooper: A Study of a Relationship, 1938–1944," History Honors Thesis, University of Chapel Hill, 1975, copy in Governor Prentice Cooper Papers, Tennessee State Library and Archives. Nikki Miller, "Roy Acuff, Born on This Day in Country Music History," www.citypages.com/.../roy-acuff-born-on-this-day-in-country-music-history-662486 accessed 12 April 2018. *Washington Post*, 24 December 1982.

23   Mrs. Julian Parks to Prentice Cooper, 24 April 1958; G. Patton to Prentice Cooper, 7 May, 22 April 1958, Prentice Cooper Papers. *Memphis Press-Scimitar*, 15, 17 May 1958.

24   Graham, *Crisis in Print*, 279–80. Halberstam, "The Air-Conditioned Crusade against Albert Gore." *Nashville Banner*, 27, 29, 31 May 1958. *Memphis Press-Scimitar*, 7 June 1958.

25   *Nashville Banner*, 25 July, 4 August 1958. *Memphis Press-Scimitar*, 22, 25 July 1958. *Memphis Commercial Appeal*, 17, 29, 30 July, 8 August 1958.

26   *Memphis Commercial Appeal*, 3 July 1958. *Nashville Banner*, 3, 26 July, 19 June, 2 July 1958.

27   Joseph A. Fry, *Dixie Looks Abroad: The South and U.S. Foreign Relations, 1789–1973* (Louisiana State University Press: Baton Rouge, 2002), 220–30, 251–54. *Nashville Banner*, 4, 16, 17 July 1958.

28   *Memphis Press-Scimitar*, 31 May, 28 June 1958. *Memphis Commercial Appeal*, 6 June, 6 July 1958.

29   *Memphis Commercial Appeal*, 20, 28 July 1958. *Memphis Press-Scimitar*, 16, 19, 23 July 1958. *Nashville Banner*, 31 July 1958. The only stop where he did not wave or mention the manifesto was in Blount County, an old unionist county right at the eastern border of the state, where Cooper was told it would not arouse any interest. Milton Britten, the *Press-Scimitar* Washington correspondent, took some mischievous pleasure in trying to track down the

"official" copy of the manifesto, which Cooper might actually sign. There was no copy in the Library of Congress. The papers of former senator Walter George, who introduced the manifesto, had been burned. Strom Thurmond's staff denied any knowledge of its whereabouts. (In fact Thurmond did gather up the various drafts of the manifesto, and they are currently in his papers at Clemson University.) *Memphis Commercial Appeal*, 5 August 1958 *Memphis Press-Scimitar*, 5 August 1958.

30   *Memphis Press-Scimitar*, 19 June 1958. *Nashville Banner*, 28 July, 4 August 1958.

31   *Memphis Press-Scimitar*, 10 July 1958. Don Oberdorfer interview with the author, 17 September 2007. Halberstam, "The Air-Conditioned Crusade against Albert Gore," 24–26.

32   *Memphis Commercial Appeal*, 15 June, 31 July, 7 August 1958. *Nashville Banner*, 1, 4 August 1958. Julius Edelstein to Herbert Lehman, 18 July 1958, Folder 512, Lehman Special Correspondence Files, Herbert H. Lehman Collection, Rare Book and Manuscript Library, Butler Library, Columbia University.

33   *Memphis Press-Scimitar*, 15 May 1958. *Nashville Banner*, 31 July 1958.

34   *Memphis Press-Scimitar*, 15 May, 14 July 1958; *New York Times*, 3, 8 August 1958. *Washington Post*, 9 August 1958. *Memphis Commercial Appeal*, 15 June 1958.

35   *Memphis Commercial Appeal*, 15 June 1958. *Washington Post*, 9 August 1958.

36   *New York Times*, 3 August 1958. *Memphis Commercial Appeal*, 27 July 1958. *Nashville Banner*, 4 June 1958. *Washington Post*, 9 August 1958.

37   *Memphis Commercial Appeal*, 1 July 1958.

38   Graham, *Crisis in Print*, 281. *Memphis Press-Scimitar*, 21 July 1958.

39   *Memphis Commercial Appeal*, 17, 19, 20 July 1958. *Memphis Press-Scimitar*, 14 June, 8, 26 July 1958.

40   *Memphis Commercial Appeal*, 5 July, 1 August 1958. *Nashville Banner*, 17 July 1958

41   *Memphis Press-Scimitar*, 13 June 1958.

42   *Memphis Press-Scimitar*, 5, 7, 30 June; 4, 5 July 1958. *Nashville Banner*, 15, 25 31 July 1958.

43   Bill Allen to Albert Gore, n.d., Gore Senate Papers.

44   *New York Times*, 3 August 1958. *Memphis Press-Scimitar*, 21, 23 June, 10 July, 19 July 1958. *Nashville Banner*, 6 July 1958.

45   *Washington Post*, 24 December 1982. In Keith Finley's fine study of Southern senators, he argues that the result was narrower than Gore expected over a "candidate who began the campaign with little name recognition." The closeness of the result made Gore more cautious on civil rights in the future. As a three-time elected governor, Cooper was scarcely a political unknown. His campaign was well financed. The scale of Gore's victory, his increase in the popular vote despite the racial issue, seem to me more compelling than the "narrowness" of the victory, Finley, *Delaying the Dream*, 196.

46   *Memphis Press-Scimitar*, 8 August 1958. *Memphis Commercial Appeal*, 15 July 1958, 12 August 1958.

CHAPTER 6

1   Robert D. Novak, *The Prince of Darkness: 50 Years Reporting in Washington* (Crown Forum: New York, 2007) 70.

2   Albert Gore, *Let the Glory Out: My South and Its Politics* (Viking: New York, 1972), 130.

3   Gore, *Let the Glory Out*, 133–63. Albert Gore oral history interview with Seth Tillman 13, 21 August 1965, John F. Kennedy Oral History Collection (JFKOH), John F. Kennedy Presidential Library, 9. Hereafter cited as Gore interview JFKOH.

4   Albert Gore to Lyndon Johnson, 9 November 1958, Box 369, Congressional File G, Papers of the Democratic Leader, Lyndon B. Johnson Library. Lyndon B. Johnson to Albert Gore, 15 November 1958, Box 44, LBJ Congressional File, Lyndon B. Johnson Library.

5   Gore, *Let the Glory Out*, 124. Gore Interview A-321. Randall B. Woods, *Fulbright: A Biography* (Cambridge University Press: Cambridge, 1995), 245–48. Paul Douglas, *In the Fullness of Time: The Memoirs of Paul H. Douglas* (Harcourt Brace Jovanovich: New York, 1973), 428.

6   Dominic Sandbrook, *Eugene McCarthy: The Rise and Fall of Postwar American Liberalism* (Knopf: New York, 2004), 94–95.

7   Toshihiro Higuchi, "Radioactive Fallout, the Politics of Risk, and the Making of a Global Environmental Crisis, 1954–1963," PhD diss., Georgetown University, 2011, 30–199. H. W. Brands, "The Age of Vulnerability: Eisenhower and the National Insecurity State," *American Historical Review*, 94, no. 4 (October 1989), 963–89.

8   Robert A. Divine, *Blowing in the Wind: The Nuclear Test Ban Treaty Debate, 1954–1960* (Oxford University Press: New York, 1978), 11, 33–35. Lewis L. Strauss, *Men and Decisions* (Macmillan: London, 1963), 336.

9   Divine, *Blowing in the Wind*, 143–52.

10   Ibid., 213–40.

11   Gore, *Let the Glory Out*, 123. Divine, *Blowing in the Wind*, 70.

12   Albert Gore to Lyndon Johnson, 9 November 1958, Papers of the Democratic Leader, Box 369, File G, Lyndon Johnson Library. *New York Times*, 14 November 1958.

13   Memo of Eisenhower-Gore conversation by Bryce Harlow, 17 November 1958; memo by Gore, 19 November 1958; Harlow to Gore, 15 January 1959, Dwight D. Eisenhower Papers OF 108-A, Dwight D. Eisenhower Library. Divine, *Blowing in the Wind*, 248, 257, 280, 301–14. *New York Times*, 12 January, 29 December 1959, 6 March 1960. *Tennessean*, 28, 29 March 1960.

14   Albert Gore to Robert Kerr, 15 April, 20 May 1959, Kerr Papers. Jack Robinson Sr. interview with the author 2003. Raymond L. Garthoff, *A Journey through the Cold War: A Memoir of Containment and Coexistence* (Brookings: Washington, DC, 2001), 64. *Tennessean*, 11 September 1959. Albert Gore to Robert L. Dew, May 29, 1958, Legislative Series File, "Finance-Excise Tax," 1958, Gore Senate Papers. *Tennessean*, 11 September 1959, 16, 17 February 1960. Albert Gore to Lyndon Johnson, 13 October 1959; Eliot Janeway to Albert Gore, blind copy to Walter Jenkins, 2 April 1959, Papers of the Democratic Leader, Box 369, Congressional File G, Lyndon Johnson Library. For Leon Keyserling's consistent advocacy for government seeding, see Leon Keyserling interview with Jerry Hess, 2, 10, 17 May 1971, Harry S. Truman Library. Don Paarlberg to William Strand, RNC Director of Public Relations, 27 March 1959, Eisenhower Alphabetical File, Eisenhower Papers. Harry Truman to Albert Gore, 10 September 1959; Gore to Truman, 19 September 1959, Personal File, Truman Papers.

15   Meg Jacobs, *Pocketbook Politics: Economic Citizenship in Twentieth-Century America* (Princeton University Press, Princeton, NJ, 2007), 221–61. Jonathan Bell, *California Crucible: The Forging of Modern American Liberalism* (University of Pennsylvania Press:

Philadelphia, 2012), 3–4, 55–155. Curtis, *Forty Years Against the Tide: Congress & the Welfare State* (Regnery: Washington, DC, 1986).167. Gore, *Let the Glory Out*, 127–28. *Tennessean*, 22, 28 June 1960. Albert Gore to Carl Jones, 30 June 1960, Finance Depletion Allowance, Gore Senate Papers.

16 *Tennessean*, 5 February 1960. Gore's Americans for Democratic Action score, an index of liberalism on roll-call votes, was always greater than 65 percent in the late 1950s. Indeed, he scored 93 percent in 1956 and 75 percent in 1960. Americans for Democratic Action records, 1932–1999, State Historical Society of Wisconsin.

17 The class of 1958 is the heart of Michael Foley's *The New Senate: Liberal Influence on a Conservative Institution, 1959–72* (Yale University Press: New Haven, CT, 1980). Donald A. Ritchie, ed., *Minutes of the Senate Democratic Conference: Fifty-Eighth Congress through Eighty-Eighth Congress, 1903–1964* (U.S. Government Printing Office: Washington, DC, 1998), 515–23.

18 Albert Gore to Lyndon Johnson, 12 January 1960, Box 44, LBJ Congressional File, Johnson Library; Ritchie, *Minutes*, 524–43; *Tennessean*, 12, 13 January 1960.

19 *Tennessean*, 13, 15, 18 January 1960. Transcript, *Face the Nation*, 17 January 1960, Gore Senate Papers.

20 *Tennessean*, 28 March 1960. Ben Houston, *The Nashville Way: Racial Etiquette and the Struggle for Social Justice in a Southern City* (University of Georgia Press: Athens, 2012), 82–122.

21 *Tennessean*, 7 March, 12 April 1960.

22 Gore, *Let the Glory Out*, 133. *Tennessean*, 21 June 1960.

23 Gore, *Let the Glory Out*, 133. Gore Interview A321. Gore interview JFKOH. Charles Bartlett interview JFKOH. CNN, *Larry King Live*, transcript 23 September 2003.

24 Gore, *Let the Glory Out*, 139. Gore interview JFKOH. John Seigenthaler Oral History interview, Robert F. Kennedy Oral History no. 2, 1 July 1970, John F. Kennedy Library.

25 Gore interview JFKOH. Seigenthaler, who was working for Bobby Kennedy, JFK's brother and campaign manager, recalled that he met with Gore periodically, but he "didn't think anything worthwhile ever came from that group that was effective. I wouldn't say nothing, but as I said, very little ever got into the dialogue of the campaign." Seigenthaler interview, 2 JFKOH.

26 Ken O'Donnell to Robert Kennedy, 26 October 1960, Box 1066, Campaign File, Folder 1, Pre-presidential Papers, John F. Kennedy Library. Gore's rhetoric was strikingly reminiscent of the rhetorical devices Nixon used when criticizing the Truman administration for being soft on communism. Alan D. Harper, *The Politics of Loyalty: The White House and the Communist Issue 1946–1952* (Greenwood: Westport, CT, 1970), 121.

27 Kent Syler, "JFK Asked Gore to Head Secret Debate Strategy Group," *Daily News Journal*, 26 September 2016.

28 Al Gore interview with the author, 19 March 2007. *Tennessean*, 9 November 1960. At the Al Smith Foundation Dinner in 2000, Al Gore recalled his father telling him about ministers in Tennessee preaching against Smith solely because of his religion. Louis Harris, 20 September 1960, Box 45, Robert F. Kennedy Pre-Administration Papers, Kennedy Library. There was speculation that Governor Ellington might be made secretary of agriculture. *Tennessean*, 13, 17, 18 November 1960. He made a trip to Texas when LBJ entertained Kennedy. Seigenthaler remembers it as more likely that Ellington was considered for post-

master general. But Kennedy knew that Ellington was in LBJ's pocket. Ellington had boasted that he could deliver Tennessee in the election and had failed. Seigenthaler told Kennedy's team that Ellington was popular with Southern governors but that he was an old-fashioned segregationist. Seigenthaler interview 4, JFKOH.

29   For Kennedy's use of Gore as a one-on-one sounding board, see Timothy Naftali and Philip Zelikow, eds., *The Presidential Recordings: John F. Kennedy—The Great Crises*, vol. 2, *September–October 21, 1962* (Norton: New York, 2001) 80, 365–68.

30   Richard Parker, *John Kenneth Galbraith: His Life, His Politics, His Economics* (Farrar, Straus, Giroux: New York, 2005), 348. Katharine Graham, *Personal History* (Knopf: New York, 1997). Gore, *Let the Glory Out*, 143.

31   Albert Gore to John F. Kennedy, 22 November 1960, John F. Kennedy Library. Gore, *Let the Glory Out*, 144–47. Gore Interview JFKOH.

32   Gore, *Let the Glory Out*, 146–47. Gore interview JFKOH. John Seigenthaler interviews 5 June, 1 July 1970, Robert F. Kennedy Oral History (RFKOH).

33   Albert Gore to T. I. McRee, February 15, 1960, Special Files, File "Tight Money and Inflation," 1960. Gore Senate Papers. *Wall Street Journal*, 26 April 1961; *New York Times*, 15, 26, 29 April, 18 September 1961. Albert Gore to Lucius E. Burch Jr., 22 September 1961, Legislative Series, File "Finance-Disposed Stock," 1961, Gore Senate Papers.

34   *Barron's National Business and Financial Weekly*, 28 August 1961.

35   Gore, *Let the Glory Out*, 152–54. *Washington Post*, 17 April 1962.

36   Robert David Johnson, "Congress," in Marc J. Selverstone, *A Companion to John F. Kennedy* (Wiley Blackwell: Chichester, 2014), 52–171. David J. Whalen, *The Rise and Fall of COMSAT: Technology, Business, and Government in Satellite Communications* (Macmillan: London, 2014), chap. 1. Joseph Bruce Gorman, *Kefauver* (Oxford University Press, New York, 1971), 360–62. The successful cloture vote was the first since 1927 and only the fifth in the history of the Senate. Apart from Russell Long the senators who joined Gore and Kefauver in opposition to the COMSAT bill were the "usual suspects" of outsider liberals—Ralph Yarborough from Texas, Maurine Neuberger and Wayne Morse from Oregon, Joseph Clark from Pennsylvania, Gruening's fellow Alaska senator, Bob Bartlett, and Quentin Burdick from North Dakota. Abram Cheyes, Harvard lawyer, early Kennedy backer and Legal Adviser to the State Department, reported that the administration thought some amendments might break Gore away from the others. But Gore was committed to Kefauver, and Robert Kerr was determined to crush the opposition. Cheyes noted that Kerr "loved to exercise power, and he loved to exercise it often in a brutal way." Abram Cheyes interview with Eugene Gordon, 18 May 1964, JFKOH.

37   Paul Douglas, *In the Fullness of Time: The Memoirs of Paul H. Douglas* (Harcourt Brace Jovanovich: New York, 1973), 428. Albert Gore to N. Campbell Craig, 12 May 1961, Legislative Series, File "Finance-Dividend Tax Credit 1961"; Gore to W. G. Polk, 25 May 1962; Gore to Walter S. Nunnelly, 13 July 1962, Legislative Series, File "Tax Dividend Tax Credit 1962," Gore Senate Papers.

38   Gore Interview, JFKOH. *New York Times*, 24, 29 August, 6 September 1962. *Washington Post*, 30, 31 August 1962. Roger Biles, *Crusading Liberal: Paul H. Douglas of Illinois* (Northern Illinois University Press: De Kalb, 2002), 159–60. Albert Gore to Fred Maggart, 10 January 1961, Legislative Series, File Finance–General, 1961. Gore to William E. Brock, 11 June 1962, Legislative Series, File Finance–General, 1962. Gore to W. R. Moyers Jr., 14 August, 1963,

Legislation Series, File "Finance–General," 1963; Gore to Mrs. A. M. Gregory, 8 September 1962, Legislative Series, File "Finance–General," 1962, Gore Senate Papers.

39   Gore, *Let the Glory Out*, 54–55. Gore Interview, JFKOH.

40   Gore, *Let the Glory Out*, 156–58. Gore Interview, JFKOH.

41   Robert Dallek, *An Unfinished Life: John F. Kennedy, 1917–1963* (Little, Brown: Boston, 2003), 585.

42   Albert Gore to Howard Hale, 12 January 1963, Gore to Marvin L. Ratner, January 26, 1963, Legislation Series, File Finance–Income Tax, 1963, Gore Senate Papers. 10 February 1963, 3 November 1963, Folder 13, Arthur Schlesinger Jr. Papers, New York Public Library.

43   Biles, *Crusading Liberal*, 161.

44   Albert Gore to Leon H. Keyserling, 15 August 1963; Gore to James Stahlman, 7 October 1963; Gore to Joe L. Evins, 23 October 1963, Legislation Series, File Finance–Income Tax, 1963, Gore Senate Papers. *Nashville Banner*, 29 October 1963.

45   *New York Times*, 27 September; 3, 12, 18, 31 October 1963. John F. Kennedy–Douglas Dillon, Henry Fowler, 30 September 1963, Audiotape 113.5, John F. Kennedy Library. *Nashville Banner*, 14, 15, 16 October 1963. Mike Manatos, Memo to Lawrence O'Brien, 4 November 1963, White House Staff Files, Lawrence O'Brien, Presidential Papers, Kennedy Papers.

46   For the best accounts of Kennedy's civil rights policies, see Carl Brauer, *John F. Kennedy and the Second Reconstruction* (Columbia University Press: New York, 1977); Mark Stern, *Calculating Visions: Kennedy, Johnson, and Civil Rights* (Rutgers University Press: New Brunswick, NJ, 1992); and Nick Bryant, *The Bystander: John F. Kennedy and the Struggle for Black Equality* (Basic Books: New York, 2006).

47   Draft statement, Albert Gore to Stephen K. Clark, 22 June 1963; Gore to Robert W. Hatcher, 1 August 1963, Gore Senate Papers.

48   May S. Newberry to Albert Gore, 13 June 1963; Grooms Herron to Gore, 15 June 1963; Mrs. Kenneth Garner to Gore, 15 June 1963; George Hutchinson to Gore, 22 June 1963; L. E. Wittenberg to Gore, 23 August 1963, Issue Mail Civil Rights 1963, Gore Senate Papers.

49   James Sasser, interview with the author, 10 December 2003. John Seigenthaler interview, 2003. John Seigenthaler interview RFKOH. Theodore Brown Jr. and Robert B. Allen, "Remembering Estes Kefauver," *The Progressive Populist* (1996). Joseph Bruce Gorman, *Kefauver* (Oxford University Press: New York, 1971), 368–69. Herbert Walters was an influential east Tennessee Democrat from Morristown. A former state highway commissioner, banker, and contractor, he was the point man in Republican east Tennessee for the Crump machine, Senator McKellar, and Buford Ellington. In return for delivering eastern votes, he was able to secure road and water development and natural gas that convinced firms like ENKA, the rayon manufacturers, to relocate to East Tennessee. A perennial figure on the state Democratic executive committee and often the Democratic national committeeman, he had been bitterly critical of Truman's civil rights' proposals. Howard L. Hill, *The Herbert Walters Story* (Kingsport Press: Kingsport, TN, 1963), 52–55, 57–60, 64–70, 83, 98.

50   Gore, *Let the Glory Out*, 148–50. Albert Gore Oral History, JFKOH. Alan Brinkley, *John F. Kennedy* (Times Books: New York, 2012), 71.

51   Adlai Stevenson, who played a memorable role on the Security Council during the missile crisis, told Fulbright that Gore had been "an enormous and invaluable help." J. William Fulbright to Albert Gore, 11 January 1963, Series 87, Box 46, folder 11, Papers of J. William Fulbright, Special Collections, University of Arkansas. For Stevenson's efforts to

get Gore to serve on the delegation, see Stevenson to Albert Gore, 17 June 1962; Gore to Stevenson, 24 July 1962; Gore to Stevenson, 9 May 1963, Stevenson Papers. It took Kennedy himself to persuade Gore to serve.

52   Philip E. Muehlenbeck, *Betting on the Africans: John F. Kennedy's Courting of African Nationalist Leaders* (Oxford University Press, New York, 2014), 34–57. Thomas J. Noer, *Soapy: A Biography of G. Mennen Williams* (University of Michigan Press: Ann Arbor, 2005), chap. 6; Robert B. Rakove, *Kennedy, Johnson and the Nonaligned World* (Cambridge University Press: New York, 2014), 27–93.

53   *New York Times*, 2 October, 1961. Telegram from the embassy in the Congo to the Department of State, Léopoldville, 13 October 1961, 5 PM. From Gullion, *Foreign Relations of the United States, 1961–1963. Volume XX, Congo Crisis.* Gore and his colleagues made a better impression in Leopoldville than Dodd, who followed Gore to the Congolese capital. According to CIA station chief Larry Devlin, Dodd was "a good example of some members of Congress who, when they travel overseas, feel they have to exercise their egos and browbeat embassy officials." Larry Devlin, *Chief of Station, Congo: Fighting the Cold War in a Hot Zone* (Public Affairs: New York, 2007). Dodd's account of one incident during his trip is in *Life*, 15 December 1961.

54   *New York Times*, 25, 27 October 1961, 14 January 1962. Gore's daughter, Nancy, was working for the Peace Corps in Washington.

55   *New York Times*, 17 December 1961, 14, 17 January 1962. Muehlenbeck, *Betting on the Africans*, 82–86, 239. Memorandum from the President's Special Assistant for National Security Affairs (Bundy) to President Kennedy, Washington, December 1, 1961. *Foreign Relations of the United States, 1961–1963, Volume XXI, Africa.* British leaders believed that the American refusal to fund the Aswan Dam in 1956 had driven Egyptian President Nasser to nationalize the Suez Canal. British development economist Barbara Ward believed that Nkrumah was more complex than Gore and Neuberger thought. She feared that turning Nkrumah down would push him to the Eastern Bloc. Barbara Ward Jackson interview, 28 June 1964, JFKOH.

56   *Tennessean*, 21 December 1960.

57   Ritchie, *Minutes*, 577–83. *New York Times*, 6 January 1961. Robert A. Caro, *Master of the Senate: The Years of Lyndon Johnson*, vol. 3 (Vintage: New York, 2002), 1034–40; *The Passage of Power: The Years of Lyndon Johnson* vol. 4 (Vintage: New York, 2012), 164–69.

58   Glenn T. Seaborg, *Kennedy, Khrushchev, and the Test Ban* (University of California Press: Berkeley, 1981), 45–48, 83. *New York Times*, 6 April, 5 May 1961. Adrian Fisher oral history interview with Paige Mulhollan, 31 October 1968, Lyndon B. Johnson Library. Gore, *Let the Glory Out*, 161. Gore did make a speech, drafted at the State Department, on nuclear testing, at the UN General Assembly on 3 December 1962, Extract from Glenn Seaborg, Journal, document 61 *Foreign Relations of the United States, 1961–1963, Volume VII: Arms Control and Disarmament.* Garthoff, *A Journey through the Cold War*, 160. Adrian Fisher describes the whole story of the test-ban negotiations under the Kennedy administration in Adrian Fisher oral history interview with by Frank Sieverts, 13 May 1964, JFKOH.

59   Background material on Indochina for possible use in speech by Senator Gore, Research-Foreign Policy-Indochina, 1954; Howard. L. Parsons to Albert Gore, 12 April 12 1954; C. C. Smith to Gore, 3 May 1954; Gore to R. G. Morrow, 3 May 1954; Indo-China, Policy, 1954, Gore Senate Papers. William Conrad Gibbons, *The U.S. Government and the Vietnam*

War: Executive and Legislative Roles and Relationships (Princeton University Press: Princeton, NJ, 1986), 191. The meeting actually took place at the State Department, and Eisenhower did not attend. The decision not to rescue the French was confirmed by the congressional leaders' reluctance to support intervention, but it owed as much to the failure to secure allied support and to the opposition of Army Chief of Staff Matthew Ridgeway, backed by the president. Journalist Chalmers Roberts reconstructed the meeting in "The Day We Didn't Go to War," *First Rough Draft: A Journalist's Journal of Our Time* (Praeger: New York, 1973), 133–22.

60 Albert Gore to William Fulbright, 16 September 1959, Papers of J. William Fulbright, Special Collections, University of Arkansas.

61 Donald A. Ritchie, "Advice and Dissent: Mike Mansfield and the Vietnam War," in Randall B. Woods, ed., *Vietnam and the American Political Tradition: The Politics of Dissent* (Cambridge University Press: New York, 2003), 177–80. John Ernst, *Forging a Fateful Alliance: Michigan State University and the Vietnam War* (Michigan State University Press: East Lansing, 1998), 1–20.

62 Mike Mansfield to William Fulbright, 12 September 1959; Fulbright to Albert Gore, 17 September 1959, Box 140, Folder 52, Fulbright Papers.

63 Ronald Bruce Frankum, Jr., *Vietnam's Year of the Rat: Eldridge Durbrow, Ngo Dinh Diem and the Turn in U S Relations, 1959–1961* (McFarland: Jefferson, NC, 2014). Fredrik Logevall, *Embers of War: The Fall of Empire and the Making of America's Vietnam* (Random House: New York, 2012), 674–701.

64 Albert Gore to Gale McGee, 10 December 1959, enclosing letter from Roy Essoyan of Associated Press, 10 December 1959, and his teletype, Associated Press World Service, 9 December 1959 Release. Papers of Gale McGee, American Heritage Center, University of Wyoming, Laramie.

65 Elbridge Dubrow to Gale McGee, 21 December 1959; Wesley R. Fishel to McGee, 28 December 1959. "Vietnam: A Living Example for Implementing the American Spirit," speech, speech by McGee, 9 February 1960. Senate Summary, February 1960. John W. O'Daniel to McGee, 10 May 1960. Later that year McGee received a copy of a letter from an American businessman in Saigon who talked about the way that the Vietcong controlled the roads out of Vietnam. Two hundred incidents in the previous month had left as many as sixty people killed. It was a "hopeless situation in its present set-up." The only solution was to get "a stronger military power than the Vietnam Army. . . behind the wheel." M. and R. to Ray and family, 18 September 1960, passed on by Raphael Kaufman, Papers of Gale McGee, American Heritage Center, University of Wyoming. Gore interview A321. James M. Carter, *Inventing Vietnam: The United States and State Building, 1954–68* (Cambridge University Press: Cambridge, 2008), 102–12, 99. Memorandum of a Conversation between Senator Mike Mansfield and the Under Secretary of State (Dillon), Department of State, Washington, 18 December 1959. *Foreign Relations of the United States, 1958–1960. Volume I: Vietnam.* Whatever Gore's skepticism about the Military Assistance Advisory Group and the military and economic assistance program, the champion of Diem, Samuel Williams, claimed he had been praised to the skies by Gore, who stated, "If the Pres should nominate you for a 4th Star I'd be the first to stand up in the Senate and say give it to him." Document 155 Letter from the Chief of the Military Assistance Advisory Group in Vietnam (Williams) to the Secretary of Defense's Deputy Assistant for Special Operations (Lansdale), Saigon, 9 May 1960, *Foreign*

Relations of the United States, 1958–1960 Volume I, Vietnam. Francis R. Valeo, Secretary of the Senate, 1966–1977, Oral History Interviews, Senate Historical Office, Washington, DC.

66   Albert Gore, letter to the editor, 10 January 1960; Pauline Gore to David Halberstam, 22 November 1963; Albert Gore to Halberstam, 6 May 1964, Gore Senate Papers.

67   Gore, *Let the Glory Out*, 161–62. Appointment Index–Albert Gore off record, 1 August 1963, Kennedy Library. Donald A. Ritchie, "Advice and Dissent: Mike Mansfield and the Vietnam War," and Thomas J. Knock, "'Come Home America': The Story of George McGovern," in Randall B. Woods, ed., *Vietnam and the American Political Tradition: The Politics of Dissent* (Cambridge University Press; New York, 2003), 83–84, 184–85. Thomas J. Knock, *The Rise of a Prairie Statesman: The Life and Times of George McGovern* (Princeton University Press: Princeton, NJ, 2016), 209–305.

68   Document 190 Memorandum from the Assistant Secretary of State for Congressional Relations (Dutton) to the Secretary of State, Washington, 8 October 1963, *Foreign Relations of the United States, 1961–1963 Volume IV, Vietnam, August–December 1963.*

69   William Conrad Gibbons, *The U.S. Government and the Vietnam War: Executive and Legislative Roles and Relationships, Part II* (Princeton University Press: Princeton, NJ, 1986), 242. Gore did not receive a lot of constituency correspondence on Vietnam at this stage, but a University of Tennessee professor summed up Gore's position well. L. D. Amick argued that "we are making a mockery of our nation's heritage and ideology in the name of 'fighting communism.'. . . spending vast sums in this foreign country to oppose religious freedom, to oppose the will of the majority, to support government oppression by brute force, to support nepotism in government." L. D. Amick, associate professor of medicine, University of Tennessee, to Albert Gore, 14 September 1963, Legislation, Foreign Relations, General, 1963, Gore Senate Papers.

70   Gore scored an astonishing 88 percent in 1962. Records of the Americans for Democratic Action, Wisconsin. David Maraniss and Ellen Nakashima, *The Prince of Tennessee* (Simon and Schuster: New York, 2000), 48, 53, 137. Mary Sasser interview with the author, 2 September 2016. Louise Gore became a force in Maryland GOP politics. In 1963 the Jockey Club was described in *Holiday* magazine as Washington's first elegant restaurant. The Gores moved to an apartment in the Methodist Building on Maryland Avenue in 1962.

71   Marannis and Nakashima, *The Prince of Tennessee*, 197. Mary Sasser interview, 2016.

72   Marannis and Nakashima, *The Prince of Tennessee*, 196–98. Mary Sasser interview 2016. Seigenthaler interview, 2003. Otis Graham to Tony Badger, 6 September 2016, email in the author's possession. Hodding Carter III interview with the author, 21 September 2016.

73   It was no coincidence that the executive order establishing the Peace Corps was modeled on Roosevelt's executive order establishing the Civilian Conservation Corps. Scott Stossel, *Sarge: The Life and Times of Sargent Shriver* (Other Press: New York, 2011), 207, 211, 246. Maraniss and Nakashima, *The Prince of Tennessee*, 198–204. William F. Haddad had come to the Kennedy entourage after working for Estes Kefauver. Coates Redmon, *Come As You Are: The Peace Corps Story* (Harcourt Brace: New York, 1986), 36–67, 77, 216. Gerard T. Rice, *The Bold Experiment: JFK's Peace Corps* (University of Notre Dame Press: Notre Dame, IN, 1985), 48, 91. David Halberstam, "Recruits Flocking to Join Corps," *New York Times*, 2 March 1961. Kevin Sack, "The 2000 Campaign: The Gore Family; Gore's Brother-in-Law Plays Crucial Role in the Campaign," *New York Times*, 14 October 2000.

74   Mary Sasser interview with the author, 2016. Hodding Carter III interview with the author, 2016. FBI File N 94-37110 and 161-12855, secured under the Freedom of Information Act by Rep. Bart Gordon. Albert Gore Research Center. Sack, "The 2000 Campaign." *Washington Post*, 31 July 2000.

CHAPTER 7

1   Jack Robinson, Sr. interview with the author, 26 January 2003.

2   *Nashville Banner*, 19 December 1963. *New York Times*, 9 January 1964. Albert Gore to Walter Lippmann, 4 January 1964. Gore sent a copy of the Lippmann letter to John Kenneth Galbraith and asked if he was free to give him a little aid on the tax bill; Gore to John Kenneth Galbraith, 4 January 1964, Legislative Files, File Finance-Tax Bill 1964, Gore Senate Papers.

3   Albert Gore to Robert E. Zang, 3 January 1964, Legislative Files, File Finance-Tax Bill, 1964, Gore Senate Papers.

4   Kent B. Germany and Robert David Johnson, *The Presidential Recordings of Lyndon B. Johnson*, vol. 3, *January 1964* (Norton: New York, 2011), 634–36.

5   Ibid., 199, 301, 305, 344, 411–12, 419–20, 737–39, 774. *New York Times*, 4 February 1964. On the Baker investigation Gore indicated that, he "did not want to stand before my country as one of 99 senators who didn't want to be investigated" *Nashville Banner*, 4 February 1964. The Baker case was also one that exercised John Williams. Johnson was furious with Gore: "What's this damn fool Gore want to investigate everybody for?" Kent B. Germany and Robert David Johnson, *The Presidential Recordings of Lyndon B. Johnson*, vol. 4, *February 1, 1964–March 8, 1964* (Norton: New York, 2011), 121, 178.

6   *Nashville Banner*, 23 August 1966. Albert Gore to Louis Chambers, 7 November 1967, Legislative Series, File Finance-Income Tax, 1967; Gore to Mary Lee Bowen, 8 February 1967, Legislative Series, File Finance-General, 1967, Gore Senate Papers.

7   Randall B. Woods, *LBJ: Architect of American Ambition* (Free Press: New York, 2006), 467–80. Robert Caro, *The Years of Lyndon Johnson*, vol. 4, *The Passage of Power* (Knopf: New York, 2012) 452–65, 484–99, 558–70.

8   Periodic Log Maintained during the Discussions Concerning the Passage of the Civil Rights Act of 1964 by Stephen Horn, Carl Albert Congressional Research and Studies Center, Congressional Archives, University of Oklahoma.

9   *Nashville Banner*, 24 March, 29 April, 11 May 1964.

10   Periodic Log Maintained during the Discussions Concerning the Passage of the Civil Rights Act of 1964, 143. Todd S. Purdom, *An Idea Whose Time Has Come: Two Presidents, Two Parties and the Battle for the Civil Rights Act of 1964* (Henry Holt: New York, 2014), 305, 309. John G. Stewart, "Thoughts on the Civil Rights Bill" and "Independence and Control," in Robert D. Loevy, *The Civil Rights Act of 1964: The Passage of the Law That Ended Racial Segregation* (State University Press of New York: Albany, NY 2011), 146, 311–12.

11   John Seigenthaler interview with the author, 2003. James Sasser interview with the author, 10 December 2003.

12   Purdom, *An Idea Whose Time Has Come*, 309. Jack Robinson, Sr. interview with the author 2003. Jim Wright interview with the author, 18 November 1996. Dante Fascell interview with the author, 27 February 1997. Tony Badger, "Southerners Who Refused to Sign the Southern Manifesto," in *New Deal/New South: An Anthony J. Badger Reader* (Fayette-

ville: University of Arkansas Press, 2007), 87. Gore did not have anybody on his staff who provided the sort of rationale for support of civil rights that, for example, Jake Yingling provided for William Fulbright—advice that Fulbright, as it happened, ignored. Randall B. Woods, *Fulbright: A Political Biography* (Cambridge University Press: New York, 1995), 300, 303, 328–332, 480.

13   Michael Foley, *The New Senate: Liberal Influence on a Conservative Institution, 1959–1972* (Yale University Press: New Haven, CT, 1980), 274–76.

14   Albert Gore to Dennis N. Duggins, 20 August 1960, Legislative Series, File Finance-Social Security, 1960, Gore Senate Papers.

15   Clinton P. Anderson (with Milton Viorst), *Outsider in the Senate: Senator Clinton Anderson's Memoirs* (World Publishing: New York, 1970), 265, 281–82. Sean J. Savage, *JFK, LBJ, and the Democratic Party* (State University of New York Press: Albany, 2004), 128–29. *Memphis Press-Scimitar*, 21 August, 16 September 1964. *Memphis Commercial-Appeal*, 5 August, 1, 16 September 1964. Albert Gore to Leonard P. Gonce, 21 September 1964, Legislative Files, File Finance-Medical Care for the Aged, 1964, Gore Senate Papers. Francis Valeo, *Mike Mansfield: Majority Leader; A Different Kind of Senate, 1961–76* (M. E. Sharpe: Armonk, NY 1999), 248–49. Albert Gore, *Eye of the Storm* (Herder and Herder: New York, 1970), 137–39. Albert Gore, *Let the Glory Out: My South and Its Politics* (Viking: New York, 1972), 177–86.

16   Frederik Logevall, *Choosing War: The Last Chance for Peace and the Escalation of the War in Vietnam* (University of California Press,: Berkeley, 1999), 144–48.

17   Edwin Moise, *Tonkin Gulf and the Escalation of the Vietnam War* (University of North Carolina Press: Chapel Hill, NC, 2004), for a full analysis of what we now know and do not know about the Tonkin Gulf incident.

18   Albert Gore interview, 1990. Randall B. Woods, *Fulbright: A Biography* (Cambridge University Press: New York, 1995), 348–56. William C. Berman, *William Fulbright and the Vietnam War: The Dissent of a Political Realist* (Kent State University Press, 1988), 19–29. Tony Badger, *Race and War: Lyndon Johnson and William Fulbright* (University of Reading: Reading, UK, 2000), 24–25. *Nashville Banner*, 4 August 1964. After the 1967 Foreign Relations Committee hearings on the Tonkin Gulf incident, Gore believed that the administration had "acted precipitately, inadvisably, unwisely" and "out of proportion" to the supposed "provocation." Joseph A. Fry, *The American South and the Vietnam War: Belligerence, Protest, and Agony in Dixie* (University Press of Kentucky: Lexington, 2015).

19   *Memphis Press-Scimitar*, 1 August 1964.

20   Interview with Hon. Dan Kuykendall, by Dr. Charles W. Crawford, 17 May 1976, University of Memphis Special Collections.

21   Ibid. For Goldwater, see Elizabeth Tandy Shermer, *Sunbelt Capitalism: Phoenix and the Transformation of American Politics* (University of Pennsylvania Press: Philadelphia, 2013); Elizabeth Tandy Shermer, ed., *Barry Goldwater and the Remaking of the American Political Landscape* (University of Arizona Press: Tucson, 2013); and Rick Perlstein, *Before the Storm: Barry Goldwater and the Unmaking of the American Consensus* (Hill and Wang: New York, 2001).

22   Seigenthaler interview 1970 RFKOH. *Memphis Press-Scimitar*, 8 August 1964. Robert David Johnson, *All the Way with LBJ: The 1964 Presidential Election* (Cambridge University Press: Cambridge, 2009), 226.

23   Jack Robinson to Tony Badger, 16 February 2009. Jack Robinson interview with the author, 4 December 2007. *Memphis Commercial Appeal*, 1, 8 August 1964. *Memphis Press-Scimitar* 8, 16 August 1964. Jim Sasser interview, 2007. David Halberstam, "The End of a Populist" *Harper's*, vol. 1 (January 1971), 37.

24   Kuykendall interview 1976. *Memphis Commercial Appeal*, 1 November 1964. *Memphis Press-Scimitar*, 8 August 1964. *Nashville Banner*, 14 September 1964.

25   *Memphis Commercial Appeal*, 28, 30 October 1964.

26   *Memphis Commercial Appeal*, 20 October 1964. *Tennessean*, 2, 21 October 1964. *Memphis Press-Scimitar*, 1, 28 September 1964.

27   *Memphis Press-Scimitar*, 10 September, 25 October 1964. *Memphis Commercial Appeal*, 22 October 1964.

28   *Memphis Press-Scimitar*, 1 September 1964; *Nashville Banner*, 24 October 1964.

29   *Memphis Press-Scimitar*, 25 October 1964.

30   *Memphis Press-Scimitar*, 1 August, 4 October 1964. *Memphis Commercial Appeal*, 16 October 1964. Howard H. Baker Jr. interview with the author, 7 April 2008.

31   *Memphis Commercial Appeal*, 6 September 1964.

32   Johnson, *All the Way with LBJ*, 1. *Memphis Press-Scimitar*, 8 August, 20, 26 October 1964. *Memphis Commercial Appeal*, 8 November 1964. *Nashville Banner*, 20 October 1964.

33   *Knoxville News-Sentinel*, 1 November 1964. *Nashville Banner*, 15 October 1964.

34   *Tennessean*, 12 September, 8 October 1964. *Memphis Commercial Appeal*, 10, 26 October 1964.

35   *Memphis Press-Scimitar*, 18 September, 13 October 1964. *Memphis Commercial Appeal*, 16, 17, 18 October 1964. *Nashville Banner*, 16 October 1964. For a vivid account of the Democratic television attack ads about the nuclear issue in 1964, see David Mark, *Going Dirty: The Art of Negative Campaigning* (Rowman and Littlefield: Lanham, MD, 2009), 39–53.

36   *Memphis Commercial Appeal*, 5 November 1964.

37   Foley, *The New Senate*, 274–78. The ADA scores reinforce Foley's calculations.

38   Gareth Davies, *See Government Grow: Education Politics from Johnson to Reagan* (University Press of Kansas, Lawrence, 2012).

39   William A. Pearman and Philip Starr, *Medicare: A Handbook on the History and Issues of Health Care Services for the Elderly* (Garland: New York, 1988). Robert M. Ball, "Reflections on How Medicare Came About," in Robert D. Reischauer et al., eds., *Medicare: Preparing for the Challenges of the 21st Century* (National Academy of Social Insurance: Washington, DC, 1998), 27–37.

40   *Memphis Press-Scimitar*, 30 September 1964.

41   M. W. Allen to Albert Gore, 10 March 1965; Albert Gore to —— (form letter), 25 March 1965, Gore Senate Papers. Ted Kennedy interview with the author, 2003. Bruce L. Clayton to Albert Gore, 15 March 1965, Gore Senate Papers.

42   James J. Justice to Albert Gore, 15 March 1965, Gore Senate Papers.

43   Walter Mondale, with David Hage, *The Last Good Fight: A Life in Liberal Politics* (Scribner: New York, 2010), 66.

44   Nelson Fuson to Albert Gore, 5 April 1968, J. L. Seay to Gore, 8 April 1968; T. L. Herbert IV to Gore, 10 April 1968; R. L. Pettigrew to Gore 10 April 1968; Mrs. Carney B. Nicks to Gore, 26 April 1968, Gore Senate Papers.

45 Julian Zelizer, "Seeds of Cynicism: The Struggle over Campaign Finance, 1956–1974," in *Governing America: The Revival of Political History* (Princeton University Press: Princeton, NJ, 2012). *Nashville Banner*, 25 March, 3 April 1964, 21, 22 October 1966.

46 Michael Manatos to Albert Gore, 17 June 1966, Presidential OF, Johnson Papers.

47 Logevall, *Choosing War*, 212–413.

48 J. W. Fulbright to Albert Gore, 23 September 1942, BCN3 Folder 22; Gore to J. W. Fulbright, 19 April 1955, BCN Folder 28; Gore to Fulbright, 10 April 1959, BCN 116, Folder 23; Gore to Fulbright, 2 November 1955; Fulbright to Gore, 22 November 1955, BN46, Box 116, Folder 49; Fulbright to Gore, 13 January 1961, Series 87, Box 46, Folder 11, J. William Fulbright Papers, Special Collections, University of Arkansas Libraries, Fayetteville.

49 Woods, *Fulbright*, 348–56, 366, 375. William C. Berman, *William Fulbright and the Vietnam War* (Kent State University Press: Kent, OH, 1988), 19–29, 40–44.

50 William Conrad Gibbons, *The U.S. Government and the Vietnam War: Executive and Legislative Roles and Relationships, Part III* (Princeton University Press: Princeton, NJ, 1989), 39. Frank Church, George McGovern, Gaylord Nelson, and Claiborne Pell were the others in the group. Albert Gore to Robert Hailey, 9 March 1968, Vietnam, Gore Senate Papers.

51 *Nashville Banner*, 1 February 1965. Gordon Petty, interview with the author, 24 April 2004.

52 Fry, *The American South and the Vietnam War*. *Nashville Banner*, 28 June, 28 July 1965. Gibbons, *The U.S. Government and the Vietnam War, Part III*, 448–49.

53 Joseph A. Fry, *Debating Vietnam: Fulbright, Stennis, and Their Senate Hearings* (Rowan and Littlefield: Lanham, MD, 2006), 20, 27.

54 Fry, *Debating Vietnam*, 27–29.

55 Ibid., 19, 31. William Conrad Gibbons, *The U.S. Government and the Vietnam War, Part IV* (Princeton University Press: Princeton, NJ, 1989), 814.

56 Fry, *Debating Vietnam*, 37, 77. Fry, *The American South and Vietnam*. C. Vann Woodward, "The Chaotic Politics of the South," *New York Review of Books*, 19, no. 10, 14 December 1972. Telephone Conversation between President Johnson and the Deputy Under Secretary of State for Political Affairs, *Foreign Relations of the United States, 1964–1968*, vol. 4, *Vietnam, 1966*, 72.

57 Memorandum from the Counsel to the President (McPherson) to President Johnson, *Foreign Relations of the United States, 1964–1968*, vol. 5, *Vietnam, 1967*, 431. Gibbons, *The U.S. Government and the Vietnam War, Part IV*, 911–13.

58 Senate Remarks, 16 February 1966; Albert Gore to Jeffrey B. Hamilton, 8 November 1966; Hubert Humphrey to Gore, 16 November 1967; Gore to Humphrey (not sent); Gore to Humphrey, 1 December 1967, Gore Senate Papers. Edward Jay Epstein, *Dossier: The Secret History of Armand Hammer* (Carroll and Graf: New York, 1996), 166, 173, 189, 199, 202, 208, 211. *New York Times*, 20 November 1968.

59 *Congressional Record*, 90th Congress, 1st Sess., 24 October 1967, 29802. *New York Times*, 25 October 1967. Fry, *The American South and the Vietnam War*.

60 *Tennessean*, 1 April 1968.

61 Joe Dolan to Edward M. Kennedy, 14 March 1968; Harold Vanderbilt to Robert Kennedy, 21 March 1968; Notes of meetings at Hickory Hill, 19, 27 April 1968, Box 14,

Robert F. Kennedy 1968 Presidential Campaign Papers, Papers of Robert F. Kennedy, John F. Kennedy Presidential Library.

62   *Tennessean*, 29 August 1968.

63   David Maraniss and Ellen Nakashima, *The Prince of Tennessee* (Simon and Schuster: New York, 2000), 87.

64   Timothy N. Thurber, *The Politics of Equality: Hubert H. Humphrey and the African American Freedom Struggle* (Columbia University Press: New York, 1999), 216. *Banner*, 1 November 1968.

65   Joseph A. Fry, *Dixie Looks Abroad: The South and U.S. Foreign Relations, 1789—1973* (Louisiana State University Press; Baton Rouge, 2002), 269. Fry, *The American South and the Vietnam War*. From the border states, John Sherman Cooper opposed the war, as did Republican Thurston Morton later. From the former Confederate states, Ralph Yarborough publicly only opposed the war once Lyndon Johnson announced that he would not run again. Albert Gore interview with author, 1 December 1990. Robert D. Johnson, *Ernest Gruening and the American Dissenting Tradition* (Harvard University Press: Cambridge, MA, 1998), 273–77.

66   Senator Gore, 90th Congress, 2nd Session, *Congressional Record*, 114:14 (26 June 1968), 18790.

67   Robert C. Albright, "New Quiz of Fortas Is Asked," *Washington Post*, 10 September 1968, A1, A9. Fred P. Graham, "Fortas Debate Drones on Before Vote Set Today," *New York Times*, 1 October 1968, 23. Robert C. Albright, "Fortas Cloture Vote Awaited," *Washington Post*, 1 October 1968, A1, A8.

68   *Washington Post*, 19 September 1968.

69   Transmittal of Memorandum of conversation, Moscow Embassy, 21 November 1968, Johnson Library. *New York Times*, 20 November 1968. *Tennessean*, 20, 21 November 1968.

70   Epstein, *Dossier*, and Steve Weinberg, *Armand Hammer: The Untold Story* (Ebury Press: London, 1989), are substantial biographies of Hammer that portray Styles Bridges and Gore as protectors of Hammer's interests in Washington and as easing his way through government bureaucracy. They claim that Gore made a "substantial profit" from the cattle-raising business.

71   Albert Gore to Armand Hammer, 31 December 1957; Hammer to Gore, 8 January 1958, Personal, Gore Senate Papers.

CHAPTER 8

1   Wilbur Mills, interview with Charles T. Morrisey, 1979, Former Members of Congress Project, Library of Congress, Washington, DC.

2   Richard Scammon and Ben Wattenberg, *The Real Majority: An Extraordinary Examination of the American Electorate* (Coward-McCann: New York, 1971). Robert Mason, *Richard Nixon and the Quest for a New Majority* (University of North Carolina Press: Chapel Hill, 2004), 81–85. Thomas B. Edsall, *Building Red America: The New Conservative Coalition and the Drive for Permanent Power* (Basic Books: New York, 2006), 98. Robert Mason has provided an excellent overview of the realignment Nixon sought: "Political Realignment," in Melvin Small, ed., *A Companion to Richard Nixon* (Wiley-Blackwell: Oxford, 2011).

3   Dan T. Carter, *The Politics of Rage: George Wallace, the Origins of the New Conservatism, and the Transformation of American Politics* (Simon and Schuster: New York, 1995). Numan V. Bartley and Hugh D. Graham, *Southern Politics and the Second Reconstruction* (Johns Hopkins University Press: Baltimore, 1975).

4   Laura Kalman, *Abe Fortas: A Biography* (Yale University Press: New Haven, CT, 1990), 345–76.

5   Albert Gore to Nolan Van Powell, 8 May 1969, Legislative, 1969, Judiciary, Supreme Court; Gore to Tom G. Litz, 14 May 1969, Issue Mail, 1969; Gore to Hayes M. Beard, 21 May 1969, Mail, 1969; Gore to W. B. Loflin, Sr., 21 May 1969, Legislative, 1969, Judiciary, Supreme Court, Gore Senate Papers. *Time*, 23 May 1969.

6   Albert Gore to Dr. Ewing J. Threet, 29 May 1969, Legislative, 1969, Judiciary-Supreme Court Nomination, 2 of 2; Joe M. Paisley to Gore, 18 September 1969, Issue Mail, 1969, "Supreme Court," Gore Senate Papers. *Nashville Banner*, 6, 21 October 1969. *Tennessean*, 23 September, 21 October 1969. For the argument that the opposition to Haynsworth was primarily about the judge's ideology, not any wrongdoing, see John P. Frank, *Clement Haynsworth, the Senate, and the Supreme Court* (University of Virginia Press: Charlottesville, 1991) 2, who thought the arguments against Haynsworth were "makeweight." As a judge for a moot court at the University of Virginia Law School, Haynsworth had decided in favor of a young Ted Kennedy. Kennedy himself was later said to have had doubts about the anti-Haynsworth battle. Ted Kennedy interview with the author 2003. Adam Clymer, *Edward M. Kennedy: A Biography* (Harper Perennial: New York, 2009), 155–61. For the ham-fisted lobbying efforts of Nixon and his staff, see Dean J. Kotlowski, "Trial by Error: Nixon, the Senate, and the Haynsworth Nomination," *Presidential Studies Quarterly*, 26, no. 1 (Winter 1996), 71–91.

7   *Tennessean*, 23 September 1969.

8   State Representative Howard G. Swafford to Albert Gore, 20 October 1969, Issue Mail, 1969; W. A. Bradfield to Gore, 6 November 1969; Joe E. Kerr to Gore, 8 November 1969; John E. and Ruth M. Lothers to Gore, 9 November 1969; W. M. Woods to Albert Gore, 25 October 1969, Issue Mail, 1969, Supreme Court, Gore Senate Papers.

9   *Banner*, 25 November 1969.

10   Albert Gore to M. I. Hedrick, 5 December 1969, Legislative, 1969, Judiciary-Supreme Court Nomination; Mrs. Glenda G. Grigsby, Nashville, to Gore, n.d., Issue Mail, 1969, Supreme Court, Gore Senate Papers. Frank, *Clement Haynsworth*, 76, 80.

11   *Tennessean*, 20, 24 January, 16 February, 15 March 1970; Jerry Wurf, international president, American Federation of State, County, and Municipal Employees (AFL-CIO), to Albert Gore, 17 February 1970, Legislative, 1970, Judiciary-Supreme Court Nomination, Gore Senate Papers. Richard Harris, *Decision* (E. P. Dutton: New York, 1971), 186–88. Harris notes that lobbyists on both sides did not want to be too visible in Tennessee because of Gore's resistance to outside influence, but the strategy group put together by Birch Bayh did finally stimulate labor to write to the senator.

12   Albert Gore to B. B. Gullett, 9 April 1970; William G. Allen to Noel Riley, 18 April 1970; William G. Allen to Hugh T. Shelton, 5 May 1970, Legislative, 1970, Judiciary-Supreme Court Nomination, Gore Senate Papers. *Nashville Banner*, 6 April 1970; *Tennessean*, 7 April 1970. Bruce H. Kalk, "The Carswell Affair: The Politics of a Supreme Court Nomination in the Nixon Administration," *American Journal of Legal History*, 47, no. 3 (July 1998), 261–87, shows how contemptuous Nixon's congressional liaison staff were about Carswell's qualifica-

tions. David Ballantyne, *New Politics in the Old South: Ernest F. Hollings in the Civil Rights Era* (University of South Carolina Press: Columbia, 2016), 131.

13   Thomas F. Eagleton to Albert Gore, 9 April 1970; Birch Bayh to Gore, 10 April 1970, Legislative, 1970, Judiciary-Supreme Court Nomination. Ted Kennedy interview with the author, 2003.

14   Hazel M. Land, state field director, to Albert Gore, 14 April 1970; Whitney M. Young Jr., executive director, National Urban League, to Gore, 16 April 1970; Ralph David Abernathy to Gore, 16 April 1970; Mrs. Maxine A. Smith to Gore, 20 April 1970, Legislative, 1970, Judiciary-Supreme Court Nomination, Gore Senate Papers.

15   Albert Gore to Marvin A. Neskang, 28 May 1970; Wade Brown to Gore, 17 April 1970, Legislative, 1970, Judiciary-Supreme Court Nomination, Gore Senate Papers.

16   Robert Clyde Hodges, "Senator Albert Gore Sr. and the Vietnam War," master's thesis, University of Kentucky, 86–96, provides an excellent account of Gore's response to the Nixon administration. Joseph A. Fry, "Southerners and the Decisions to Withdraw from Vietnam, 1968–70," in *The American South and the Vietnam War: Belligerence, Protest, and Agony in Dixie* (University Press of Kentucky: Lexington, 2015), is outstanding on Gore. Albert Gore to David M. Eisenberg, 23 May 1969, Dept. State Vietnam, Capitol Commentary week of 23 March 1969, Gore to Mrs. W. C. Jordan, Dept. State, Vietnam 1969, Gore Senate Papers. *Congressional Record*, 91st Congress, 1st Sess., 8 May 1969, 11826–28; 20 May 1969, 130092–94; 17 June 1969, 11,827; 19 June 1969, 16576. For a recent overview of Nixon's Vietnam policy, see Jeffrey P. Kimball. "The Vietnam War," in Small ed., *A Companion to Richard Nixon.*

17   Joes S. Carners to Albert Gore, 13 May 1970, Albert Gore Senate Papers.

18   *Congressional Record*, 91st Congress, 1st session, 17, 19, 24 June, 31 July, 7 August 1969, 16127, 16576, 21540, 17010, 22901–2.

19   *Congressional Record*, 91st Congress, 1st session, 4 November 1969, 32790–95. Nashville *Banner*, 5 November 1969. *Tennessean*, 5 November 1969. Albert Gore to Edward G. Humphrey, 18 November 1969, Dept. State Vietnam, 1969, Gore Senate Papers.

20   LeRoy Ashby and Rod Gramer, *Fighting the Odds: The Life of Senator Frank Church* (Washington State University Press, Pullman, WA, 1994), 299–305. *Nashville Banner*, 10, 23 February 1970. *Tennessean*, 24 February 1970.

21   Ashby and Gramer, *Fighting the Odds*, 309. *New York Times*, 2, 6 May 1970. *Tennessean*, 12 May 1970. *Congressional Record*, 91st Congress, 2nd Sess., 1, 14, 21 May 1970, 13832–33, 215568, 16523–28.

22   Ashby and Gramer, *Fighting the Odds*, 308–30. Thomas Dine to Bill Allen, 3 July 1970, Albert Gore Senate Papers.

23   *Congressional Record*, 91st Congress, 2nd Sess., 25 August 1970, 29938. *New York Times*, 2 September 1970. Albert Gore to John W. Miller, 17 September 1970, Dept. State Vietnam, 1970, Gore Senate Papers. *Tennessean*, 13 February 1971.

24   Albert Gore to Dr. Curtis B. Clark, 5 April 1969; Gore to J. G. Wilson, 20 May 1969, Dept. State Vietnam, 1969; S. S. Mathews to Albert Gore, 11 May 1970, Gore Senate Papers. *Tennessean*, 12 May 1970. For student protest in Tennessee and the South, see Joseph A. Fry, "Southern College Students," in *The American South and the Vietnam War;* and Kate Jernigan Ballantyne, "Student Radicalism in Tennessee, 1954–1970," PhD diss., University of Cambridge, 2017, chap. 6: "'Four White Students Had to Die Before Other Whites Understood What Black People Had Known All of Their Lives': Tennessee Student Activists and the

Vietnam War." Nixon asked Alexander Heard, chancellor of Vanderbilt, who had worked for Gore on election costs in the 1950s, to be his special adviser on campus unrest. But Nixon and his staff dismissed Heard's report, which they thought excused student unrest.

25   Al Gore interview with the author 2005. Melinda Henneberger, "For Gore, Army Years Mixed Vietnam and Family Politics," *New York Times*, 11 July 2000, A1, A20–A21.

26   Bill Turque, *Inventing Al Gore: A Biography* (Houghton Mifflin: New York, 2000), 60–67, is a measured assessment of Al Gore's decision and his assignment to army journalism. Dale Van Atta, in his fine biography of Melvin Laird, *With Honor: Melvin Laird in War, Peace, and Politics* (University of Wisconsin Press: Madison, 2008), 307, notes that Laird recalled that he had responded to a request from Senator Gore about a posting in Vietnam for Al. Laird, unbeknown to Al, found him an assignment to a desk job at *Stars and Stripes*. The assertion is based on interviews with Laird staffers Robert Pursley, Rady Johnson, and Richard Borda. Henneberger, "For Gore, Army Years Mixed Vietnam and Family Politics."

27   Gore to Gene H. Sloan, 20 November 1969, Gore Senate Papers.

28   Robert G. Kaufman, *Henry Jackson: A Life in Politics* (University of Washington Press: Seattle, 2000), 209–13. Jonathan H. Cook, "Senator Henry H. Jackson and the Cold War, c. 1953–83," PhD diss., University of Cambridge, 2014.

29   Dennis W. Brezina, 34–35, Oral History Interviews, Senate Historical Office, Washington, DC. Randall B. Woods, *Fulbright: A Biography* (Cambridge University Press: Cambridge, 1995), 521. Van Atta, *With Honor*, 189–90.

30   Woods, *Fulbright*, 524. Kaufman, *Henry Jackson*, 211–13. Cook, "Senator Henry Jackson."

31   Ted Kennedy interview with the author, 2003.

32   Julian Zelizer, *Taxing America: Wilbur Mills, Congress, and the State, 1945-1975* (Cambridge University Press: New York, 1998) 283–89.

33   W. Elliot Brownlee, *Federal Taxation in America: A Short History* (Cambridge University Press: New York, 2004), 133.

34   Zelizer, *Taxing America*, 300–306.

35   Albert Gore to Charles Stanley, 8 August 1969; Gore to J. A. Hadley, 17 September 1969, Legislative Series, File "Finance-Taxes," 1969, Gore Senate Papers. *New York Times*, 6 September, 12, 14, 24, 28, 31 October 1969. Michael S. Martin, *Russell Long: A Life in Politics* (University Press of Mississippi: Jackson, 2014), 164–65.

36   *New York Times*, 9, 26, 27, 30 November, 2, 4 December 1969. Martin, *Russell Long*, 164–65.

37   Michael Foley, *The New Senate: Liberal Influence on a Conservative Institution, 1959-72* (Yale University Press: New Haven, CT, 1980), 52.

38   For Agnew, see Justin P. Coffey, "Nixon and Agnew," in Small, ed., *A Companion to Richard Nixon*.

39   Adam Clymer, *Edward M. Kennedy: A Biography* (Harper Perennial: New York, 2009) 128. Martin, *Russell Long*, 159–60. Kent Syler has provided an excellent, vivid sampling of the conservative views of Tennessee voters in their letters to Gore in the 1960s about law and order, civil rights protests, Medicare, immigration, the Poor People's Movement, and gun control: "A Mirror of Today's Political Fray in Letters from 50 Years Ago," *New York Times*, 29 October 2017.

CHAPTER 9

1   Albert Gore, Sr., *Let the Glory Out: My South and Its Politics* (Viking: New York, 1972). 214. Al Gore interview with the author, 9 April 2005.

2   Buford Ellington, oral history interview, 2 October 1970, Lyndon B. Johnson Library; John Seigenthaler interview with the author, 2003; George Barrett interview with the author, 2006.

3   Von Russell Creel and Bob Burke, *Mike Monroney, Oklahoma Liberal* (Oklahoma Heritage Association: Oklahoma City, 1997). Von Russell Creel, "Monroney, Almer Stillwell 'Mike' (1902–1980)," *Encyclopedia of Oklahoma History and Culture* (Oklahoma Historical Society, Oklahoma City). Harry McPherson noted that the changing nature of Oklahoma— as Tulsa oil became more important than impoverished farmers—left Monroney with a "tenuous hold on the electorate." Assiduous attention to constituent services and the needs of defense workers in the state could not save him in the end. Harry McPherson, *A Political Education: Washington Memoir* (University of Texas Press: Austin, 1995), 46–47.

4   Cambridge Opinion Studies, Papers of William Emerson Brock III, Modern Political Archives, Howard H. Baker Center for Public Policy, University of Tennessee, Knoxville

5   Gore, *Let the Glory Out*, 214. Al Gore interview with the author, 2005. Jim Sasser interview with the author, 10 December 2003.

6   Frank Hunger interview with the author, 2006.

7   Albert Gore to Howard Baker, 1951, Gore House Papers.

8   Howard Baker interview with the author, 7 April 2008.

9   Robert Mason, *Richard Nixon and the Quest for a New Majority* (University of North Carolina Press: Chapel Hill, 2004), 36–112; Kevin Phillips, *The Emerging Republican Majority* (Arlington House: New York 1969); Richard Scammon and Ben Wattenberg, *The Real Majority* (Coward-McCann: New York, 1970). Republican National Committee chairman Rogers C. B. Morton sent all his campaign managers in September 1970 Pat Buchanan's summary of Scammon and Wattenberg. Wattenberg was correct, he said: Swing voters were "thus conservative on the Social issue but progressive on domestic issues." Morton to Campaign Managers, 25 September 1970, White House File Series, 1968–1973, Papers of Harry S. Dent, Special Collections, Clemson University Library. Timothy Stanley, *The Crusader: The Life and Tumultuous Times of Pat Buchanan* (St. Martin's Press: New York, 2012), 46–59.

10   Mason, *Richard Nixon and the Quest for a New Majority*, 3, 77–112.

11   John Sears Memorandum for the President, 27 March, 1 April 1969, Box 3, Folder 88, Dent Papers. The fifty-seven-year-old Democrat Ed Jones, who won that election, was a one-time Tennessee commissioner of agriculture who had chaired the ASC state committee since 1961. He would retain his House seat until he retired in 1988.

12   Lamar Alexander to Harry S. Dent, 20 December 1969. Dent Memorandum for President, 3 December 1969, Dent Papers. Alexander added, in a handwritten note, that though Jarman might be a bad GOP choice for governor, he did head Genesco, "a *billion-dollar* corporation, all because of Maxey Jarman. Therefore we should treat him courteously for future RN benefits, Inc., campaign contributions."

13   Harry S. Dent, Memorandum for Pres., 7 August, 9 October, 3 December 1969, Dent Papers.

14   William E. Brock interview with the author, 5 December 2006. William E. Brock interview in Former Members of Congress Collection, 1979, Library of Congress. Interviews with William E. Brock, William C. Cater, and William L. Carter, with Jack Bass and William De Vries, 1974, Southern Oral History Project, Southern Historical Collection, Chapel Hill. Jack Bass and William DeVries, *The Transformation of Southern Politics: Social Change and Political Consequence Since 1945* (Basic Books: New York, 1976), 292–95. Press Releases and clippings, Box 12, Brock Papers.

15   Brock interview with the author 2006.

16   Ibid. Bass and DeVries, *The Transformation of Southern Politics*, 292–95. Press Releases and clippings, Box 12, Brock Papers.

17   Brock interview wth the author, 2006.

18   Ibid. Harry Dent to Dwight Chapin, 8 September 1969; Harry Dent to President, 9 October 1969, Dent papers. Lamar Alexander interview with the author, 22 July 2015. Quillen was elected to long-term GOP stalwart Carroll Reece's seat in 1962. He served eighteen terms in the House, the longest uninterrupted term of any Tennessee congressman. A former newspaper publisher, he was renowned for his ability to "shake down" the business community. He never chaired a House committee: As one of his colleagues noted, "Jimmy's one helluva nice guy, but let's face it. He couldn't organize a one-car funeral." *Kingsport Times-News,* 4 October 1992.

19   Poll and Strategy, Box 14, Brock Papers.

20   *Tennessean,* 12 April, 5 May, 28 June, 23 July 1970. Howard Baker interview with the author, 7 April 2008. Lamar Alexander interview with the author, 22 July 2015. Alexander wryly noted that he tested the water about running for statewide office himself in 1969. Six weeks of soundings in the state convinced him that he should not run.

21   *Tennessean,* 6 January, 26 February, 12 April, 3, 26 May, 30 June, 7, 9, 31 July, 1 August 1970.

22   *Tennessean,* 12 April, 2 June, 7 June, 26 July 1970. Brock interview, 2006.

23   Patrick Cox, *Ralph W. Yarborough, The People's Senator* (University of Texas Press: Austin, 2001) 260–63.

24   *Chattanooga Free-Press,* 11 January 1970. *Memphis Press-Scimitar,* 26 February 1970. *Tennessean,* 7, 9, 16 May, 6 June, 9, 10 July 1970.

25   Hudley Crockett interviews with the author, July 2004, November 2006. Harry Dent thought Crockett had done Brock a favor by "putting the Gore record on the line." But both Brock and Dent recognized that Crockett was unlikely to defeat Gore because of the limited amount of time and money that was available to him. Dent to H. R. Haldeman, 2 June 1969, Dent Papers.

26   *Chattanooga Free-Press,* 21 June 1970. *Tennessean,* 11 July 1970. *Nashville Banner,* 27 May, 11, 24 June 1970.

27   Crockett interview, 2004. *Tennessean,* 9 August 1970. *Memphis Commercial Appeal,* 12 July 1970; *Chattanooga News,* 9 August 1970. *New York Times,* 10 August 1970.

28   William E. Timmons to President, 8 August 1970, President's Office Files, Richard M. Nixon Presidential Library and Museum. Jim Allison to Harry Dent, 9 October 1969; John Stuckey to Bill Brock, n.d., Box 31, Brock Papers.

29   Polls and Strategy, Box 14, Brock Papers. Kenneth Rietz to staff, 24 November 1969, Box 31, Brock Papers. Richard Harris, "Annals of Politics: How the People Feel," *New Yorker,* 10 July 1971, 39. *Tennessean,* 5 April 1970.

30 A complete set of Brock TV commercials is held at the Julian P. Kanter Political Commercial Archive, University of Oklahoma. "Electronic Politics: The Image Game," *Time*, 21 September 1970. David Broder interview with the author, April 2006. Al Gore interview, 2005. David Halberstam maintained that "Believes was a code word for Nigger" ("The End of a Populist," *Harper's* [January 1971], 38.

31 *Nashville Banner*, 22 May 1970. *Tennessean*, 13 June, 27 September 1970.

32 James G. Stahlman to Harry Dent, 21 October 1970; Stahlman to Richard Nixon, 21 October 1970, Papers of James G. Stahlman, Special Collections, Vanderbilt University. Harry Dent to Dwight Chapin and Bob Haldeman, 6 October 1969, Dent Papers. Lamar Alexander interviewed by Timothy Naftali, 27 June 2007, Richard Nixon Presidential Library and Museum National Archives and Records Administration. Stephen B. Miller notes that the Knoxville Billy Graham rally was unusual in that Nixon not merely attended but directly addressed the huge crowd. Stephen P. Miller, *Billy Graham and the Rise of the Republican South* (University of Pennsylvania Press: Philadelphia, 2009), 142. The three hundred rather forlorn chanting antiwar protesters who attended the rally served as a very useful rhetorical foil for both Graham and Nixon.

33 *Washington Post*, 22 November 1970. *New York Times*, 2 October 2007.

34 David Mark, *Going Dirty: The Art of Negative Campaigning* (Rowman & Little-field: New York, 2006), 81. H. R. Haldeman to Harry Dent, 23 September 1970, Dent Papers. Haldeman also worried that Howard Baker and his supporters might not be cooperating as fully as they might in the Brock campaign. Dent reassured Haldeman that (a) Ken Rietz was working on the society pages; (b) the country-music stars were on board; and (c) the Baker team was cooperating, but the relationship had got off to a bumpy start. Nevertheless, Dent was going to make it clear to Baker's team that they were expected to deliver "the usual Republican majority from their area." Dent to Haldeman, 25 September 1970, Dent Papers. Barry Werth, *31 Days: Gerald Ford, the Nixon Pardon, and a Government in Crisis* (Anchor Books: New York, 2007), 115.

35 Brock interview, 2006. Buchanan recalled that Agnew flew into Tennessee determined to "peel the hide off" Gore. When Air Force 2 arrived at the gate, they looked down to the bottom of the ramp "and there, to our horror, stood the Silver Fox in the receiving line." The sight caused "discombobulation" on the plane. In the end they had to come out laughing. "It was," concluded Buchanan, "a memorable class act by your father" (Pat Buchanan to Al Gore, 7 December 1998, Letters to the Vice President, Albert Gore Research Center). Haldeman did not want the vice president to visit Tennessee; William Safire had warned about letting candidates like Gore glory in being on top of the purge list, giving him the chance to capitalize on local resentment against national visitors. H. R. Haldeman to Harry Dent, 23 September 1970; William Safire to Vice President, 18 August 1970, Dent Papers. But it was Safire who coined the phrase about Gore as regional chairman. (Buchanan claimed the credit as well.) Alexander interview, 2015. Harris, "How the People Feel," 41.

36 *Nashville Banner*, 22 May 1970. *Tennessean*, 13 June, 27 September 1970. H. R. Haldeman to Harry Dent, 23 September 1970, Dent Papers. Henry Loeb to William O'Hara, copy to Gore, 5 June 1970, B44, Gore Papers. *Tennessean*, 26 July 1970. *Nashville Banner*, 6, 10, 31 October 1970.

37 Gore, *Let the Glory Out*, 249. Crockett interview, 2004.

38 Norman Ferris interview with the author, April 2006.

39   Gore *Let the Glory Out*, 245–49. Gilbert Merritt interview with the author, 2003; Seigenthaler interview, 2003; Crockett interview, 2004. Halberstam, "The End of a Populist," 42–43. Harris, "How the People Feel," 33.

40   Keel Hunt, *Coup: The Day the Democrats Ousted Their Governor, Put Lamar Alexander in Office Early and Stopped a Pardon Scandal* (Vanderbilt University Press, Nashville, 2013), 13. Alexander interview, 2015.

41   Hunger interview with the author, 2006. Ferris interview with the author, 2006.

42   Gene Graham, "Gore's Lost Cause," *New South* (1971), 26–34. Jim Sasser interview with the author, 2003. Sasser and his team overcame the strong support that Davidson County had given Wallace in 1968. Harris, "How People Feel," 34. Gore himself was ambivalent about the student effort. *Chicago Tribune* journalist Walter Trohan recalled, "As Albert Gore said the other day, he's afraid that if he has some young college kids running around, he'd drive away more votes than they will ever gain. That's possible." Walter Trohan interview with Jerry Hess, 7 October 1970, Harry S Truman Library.

43   "Electronic Politics," *NewsHour with Jim Lehrer* transcript online, Charles Guggenheim, July 2000. Ted Kennedy interview with the author, 2003.

44   Gore campaign ads, Julian P. Kanter collection. "Electronic Politics." Seigenthaler interview with the author, 2003, Broder interview with the author, 2006. After the election Ken Rietz admired the Guggenheim ads, which were "arty, very well produced and probably should win an award," but he doubted they were effective. They were too geared to the elderly and, given the president's popularity, Gore should not have questioned the president's Supreme Court choices in the ads. Ken Rietz to Gordon Strachan, 24 November 1970, Dent Papers. David Halberstam, by contrast, thought the ads were excellent. "The End of a Populist," 36.

45   Harris, "How the People Feel," 37. Winfield Dunn, *From a Standing Start: My Tennessee Political Odyssey* (Magellan Press: Brentwood, TN, 2007), 172–73. Winfield Dunn interview with the author, 8 April 2008. *New York Times*, 1 November 1970. Not everyone shared this view of Gore's speaking ability. Lucy Strickland in Murfreesboro voted for Gore in 1970, though she did not tell her Republican husband. She admired Gore's track record on civil rights. But when he came to MTSU to deliver the commencement address, she recalled, "He was not a speaker and I don't think anybody ever said he was. But I was sort of humiliated that here is a product of this college and a Senator." Lucy Strickland interview with Kris McCusker, 2 May 2005, MT256, Middle Tennessee Oral History Collection, Albert Gore Research Center.

46   Ferris interview with the author, 2006. Broder interview with the author, 20 April 2006. Mark, *Going Dirty*, 86.

47   *New York Times*, 3 July 1970. Harris, "How the People Feel," 47. Gore, *Let the Glory Out*, 266. H. R. Haldeman to Harry Dent, 23 September 1970, Dent Papers.

48   J. Lee Annis Jr., *Howard Baker: Conciliator in an Age of Crisis* (Madison Books: New York, 1995), 55–56. *Nashville Banner*, 19, 22 October 1970 Harris, "How the People Feel," 47.

49   Al Gore interview with the author, 2005; Jim Sasser interview with the author, 2003. Gore Final TV broadcast, Julian P. Kanter Political Commercial Archive, University of Oklahoma. Harris, "How the People Feel." Daniel K. Williams, "Voting for God and the GOP: The Role of Evangelical Religion in the Emergence of the Republican South," in Glenn Feldman ed., *Painting Dixie Red: When, Where, Why, And How The South Became Republican* (University of Florida Press; Gainesville, 2011).

50   Harris, "How the People Feel." Gene Graham, "Gore's Lost Cause," *New South* (1971), 26–34. Al Gore interview, 2005. *New York Times*, 1 November 1970.

51   Numan V. Bartley and Hugh D. Graham, *Southern Politics and the Second reconstruction* (Johns Hopkins University Press: Baltimore, 1975) 150.

52   James G. Stahlman telegram to Richard Nixon, 3 November 1970; Stahlman to Lyndon B. Johnson, 4 November 1970, Stahlman Papers.

53   Thad Stem Jr. to Jonathan Daniels, 27 October 1970; Daniels to Stem, 11 November 1970, Papers of Jonathan Worth Daniels, Southern Historical Collection, Chapel Hill, NC. George McGovern to Albert Gore, 4 November 1970, Papers of George McGovern, Rare and Special Books Collection, Princeton University Library.

54   Matthew D. Lassiter, *The Silent Majority: Suburban Politics in the Sunbelt South* (Princeton University Press, 2006) 271.

55   Nadine Cahodas, *Strom Thurmond and the Politics of Southern Change* (Simon and Schuster: New York, 1993), 411–12. Joseph Crespino, *Strom Thurmond's America* (Hill and Wang: New York, 2012), 245–46. Randy Sanders, *Mighty Peculiar Elections: The New South Gubernatorial Campaigns of 1970 and the Changing Politics of Race* (University of Florida Press: Gainesville, 2002), 1–10. White House Special Files: Staff Member and Office Files: John D. Ehrlichman, Alphabetical Subject Files, 1963–73, Box 23, 1970, Post-election analysis, Nixon Presidential Materials Project.

56   Seigenthaler interview with the author, 2003; Sasser interview with the author, 2003; Merritt interview with the author, 2003.

57   Annis, *Howard Baker* 56.

58   Sasser interview, 2003.

59   *Raleigh News and Observer*, 8 November 2014. In 1970 George Wallace ran his last explicitly racist and successful campaign against his former lieutenant governor, Albert Brewer, but as governor he made a clear attempt to woo the new African American voters with symbolic gestures on race and through populist economic policies.

60   David Broder interview with the author, 2006. Halberstam, "The End of a Populist," 39. Harris, "The Way People Feel," 49.

EPILOGUE

1   *Tennessean*, 5 February 1971.

2   *Tennessean*, 6, 13 February 1971.

3   *Tennessean*, 20 February 1971.

4   C. Vann Woodward, "The Chaotic Politics of the South," *New York Times Book Review*, 19, no. 10 (14 December 1972).

5   Godfrey Hodgson, "Recollections of a Political Man," *Washington Post Book World*, 8 October 1972), 3, 10.

6   J. William Fulbright to Albert Gore, 24 June 1971, 20 November 1972, 13 June 1974, Series 87, Box 46, Folder 11, Fulbright Papers.

7   Albert Gore interview with Jack Bass, 17 August 1974, Southern Oral History Prgoram. Albert Gore interview with the author, 1 December 1990. Bob Zelnick, *Gore: A Political Life* (Regnery: Washington, DC, 1999), 93.

8   FBI File N 94-37110 and 161-12855, secured under the Freedom of Information Act by Rep. Bart Gordon, Albert Gore Research Center.

9   Albert Gore interview with the author, 1 December 1990. Kyle Longley, *Senator Albert Gore Sr: Tennessee Maverick* (Louisiana State University Press: Baton Rouge, 2004) 253. *New York Times*, 3 July 1975; 31 May, 14 June 1977; 18 December, 1979; 29 March 1980; 23 March 1982. *Wall Street Journal*, 31 May 1977; 22 May 1979; 24 April 1980; 23, 26 March; 17 December 1982; 9 March, 20 July 1983.

10   Michael F. Melosi, "Environmental Policy." in Mitchell B. Lerner ed., *A Companion to Lyndon B. Johnson* (Wiley-Blackwell: New York, 2012), 189.

11   Ibid., 188. Otis Graham email to the author, 6 September 2016. Albert Gore, *Eye of the Storm: A People's Politics for the 1970s* (Herder and Herder, 1970) 88.

12   Gore, *Eye of the Storm*, 98, 103, 105

13   Dennis J. Mitchell, *Mississippi Liberal: A Biography of Frank E. Smith* (University Press of Mississippi: Jackson, 2001), 217. Gore, *Eye of the Storm*, 88, 94. As Otis Graham has noted, scholars were slow to pick up on the environmental dangers posed to the South as the fastest-growing region in the country. Southern historians who were Gore's contemporaries shared his views on the primacy of economic growth and the role of economic interests, rather than a belief in the environment as the determinant of the region's past—and future. Environmental history in the United States at that time, and for some time to come, had been largely written by Westerners about the West. Otis L. Graham, "Again the Backward Region? Environmental History in and of the American South," *Southern Cultures*, 6, no. 2 (2000), 50–72; Christopher Morris, "A More Southern Environmental History," *Journal of Southern History*, 75, no. 3 (August 2009), 581–98. Melosi, "Environmental Policy," 187. Bill Christofferson, *The Man from Clear Lake: Earth Day Founder Senator Gaylord Nelson* (University of Wisconsin Press: Madison, 2004), 334.

14   Harry McPherson interview with the author, 17 September 2007. William Fulbright to Albert Gore, 30 March 1973, Series 87, Box 46, Folder 11, Fulbright Papers.

15   Zelnick, *Gore: A Political Life*, 94.

16   David Maraniss and Ellen Nakashima, *The Prince of Tennessee* (Simon and Schuster: New York, 2000), 272.

17   John G. Tower, *Consequences: A Personal and Political Memoir* (Little, Brown: Boston, 1991), 68. Jerry Futrell interview with the author, 10 January 2006.

18   Albert Gore interview, 1990. Jerry Futrell interview with the author, 10 January 2006.

19   Carl M. Marcy, Chief of Staff, Foreign Relations Committee, 1955–1973, Oral History Interviews, Senate Historical Office, Washington, DC. *Tennessean*, 5 September 2012.

20   Gil Kujovich, exit interview, Intelligence Oversight Board, 22 February 1980, Jimmy Carter Presidential Library, Atlanta, GA.

21   Albert Gore interview with the author, 1 Decembe,1990. "Albert Gore Sr.: Young Al kept me out of his first campaign" audio interview with E. Thomas Wood uploaded on YouTube on 8 February 2008 .https://www.youtube.com/watch?v=RtEC6olA2DY accessed 19 March 2017. Maraniss and Nakashima, *The Prince of Tennessee*, 164–74.

22   Roy Neel interview with the author, 11 April 2008.

23   Dalena Wright interview with the author, 29 April 2015.

24   Dale Bumpers interview with the author, 5 December 2005.

25   Maraniss and Nakashima, *The Prince of Tennessee*, 207–31. Arthur Schlesinger Jr., *Journals: 1952–2000* (Atlantic Books: London, 2007), 21 April 1988, 651. Arlie Schardt Inter-

view, "The Choice 2000," *Frontline*, PBS https://www.pbs.org/wgbh/pages/frontline/shows/choice2000/gore/schardt.html accessed 29 March 2017. Lloyd N. Cutler to Al Gore, n.d., Letters to the Vice-President, Albert Gore Papers.

26   Maraniss and Nakashima, *The Prince of Tennessee*, 207–31. Zelnick, *Gore: A Political Life*, 154, 167, 169. Bill Turque, *Inventing Al Gore: A Political Biography* (Houghton Mifflin: New York, 2000), 203, 208. Roy Neel interview with the author, 11 April 2008.

27   Lamar Alexander interview with the author, 22 July 2015. Schlesinger, *Journals*, 21 April 1988, 651.

28   Schlesinger, *Journals*, 21 July 1992, 726. Maraniss and Nakashima, *The Prince of Tennessee*, 274. Turque, *Inventing Gore*, 20–21, 249–50, 260.

29   Karenna Gore Schiff interview with the author, 11 December 2006.

30   Maraniss and Nakashima, *The Prince of Tennessee*, 199.

31   Al Gore interview with the author, 2005.

32   Jerry Futrell interview with the author, 10 January 2006.

33   Roy Neel interview with the author, 11 April 2008. Carthage *Courier*, 10, 17 December 1998. Maraniss and Nakashima, *The Prince of Tennessee*, 19–42. Turque, *Inventing Al Gore*, 352–54.

34   Vice President Al Gore, remarks at Service of Celebration and Thanksgiving for the Life of Senator Albert Gore Sr., Nashville, December 9, 1998. Howard J. Baker Jr. to Al Gore, 18 December 1998, Letters to the Vice-President, Albert Gore Papers. Roy Neel, interview with the author, 11 April 2008.

35   *Carthage Courier*, 10, 17 December 1998. Maraniss and Nakashima, *The Prince of Tennessee*, 19–42. Turque, *Inventing Al Gore*, 352–54.

36   J. K. Galbraith to Al Gore, 9 December 1998; Charles D. Gersten to Gore, 7 December 1998; Frances A. Zwenig to Gore, 7 December 1998; Sheldon S. Cohen to Gore, 7 December 1998; Mortimer Caplin to Gore, 8 December 1998; Pierre Salinger to Gore, 6 December 1998; Edward M. Kennedy to Pauline Gore, 8 December 1998, Letters to the Vice-President, Albert Gore Research Center.

37   Al Gore Comments, April 2005, copy in the author's possession.

38   Numan V. Bartley, *The Rise of Massive Resistance: Race and Politics in the South During the 1950s* (Louisiana State University Press: Baton Rouge, 1969), 25.

39   Carole Bucy, "Martha Ragland: The Evolution of a Political Feminist," in Beverly Greene Bond and Sarah Wilkerson-Freeman, eds., *Tennessee Women: The Lives and Times*, vol. 1 (University of Georgia Press: Athens, 2015), File 125, Scrap/Fragment in Martha Ragland's hand, Martha Ragland Papers, Schlesinger Library, Harvard University.

INDEX

ACKNOWLEDGMENTS

AS ONE OF the three Southern senators who refused to sign the Southern Manifesto, Albert Gore, Sr. interested me as an example of how Southern New Dealers confronted the race issue after World War II when, unlike in the 1930s, they could not avoid the question. In December 1990 I made a first visit to Murfreesboro to visit the Albert Gore Research Center at Middle Tennessee State University (MTSU), which held the senator's papers that had been shipped to MTSU from Washington, DC, after his defeat in 1970. Jim Neal, the director of the center, not only provided me with expert guidance through the collections but also rang the Gore home in Carthage to see if I could visit. Pauline Gore responded firmly to my diffident inquiry that the senator, who was out on the farm, would want to see me. I drove to Carthage to the striking modern house on the bluffs overlooking the town and was rewarded by gracious hospitality and a leisurely interview with both Gores about the manifesto, Vietnam, the senator's post-1970 business career, and their pride in their son's performance in the Senate—as well as their fondness for David Halberstam, whose latest book lay on the coffee table.

In 1997 Jim, who had welcomed me so warmly in 1990, invited me to talk on Gore and civil rights at a symposium at the Albert Gore Research Center to mark the senator's ninetieth birthday. I was a small part of a remarkable program, attended by the senator and Mrs. Gore, that included many leading figures from the world of Tennessee politics, such as former governor Ned McWherter, and renowned journalists like John Seigenthaler and David Halberstam.

At this stage I had no intention of writing a biography of Albert Gore, but in 2001 I was invited by Jim's successor as director of the Gore Center, Lisa Pruitt, to write a biography. The Samuel Fleming Foundation had provided a challenge grant to MTSU to fund a biography of the senator. That grant was matched by donations from Albert Gore's friends and admirers. Both the center and I wish to acknowledge the generosity of the Samuel Fleming Foundation, the principal donor to the Gore Biography Fund, and particularly Fleming Wilt. This generosity was matched by other generous donors: James L. Bass, BellSouth Telecommunications, Cecil Dewey Branstetter Jr. and Charlotte C. Branstetter, Theodore Brown Jr., Martha Craig Daughtrey, Walter T. Durham, Jane G. Eskind, Dr. Norman B. Ferris, Dr. Henry W. Foster Jr., the Freedom Forum's First Amendment Center (Washington, DC), Friends of Ned McWherter, Dr. Jerry H. Futrell, the Gannett Foundation, Sandra T. Higgins, Rollie M. Holden Sr. and Katherine B. Holden, Eugene L. Joyce and Vivian N. Joyce, Richard LaRoche Jr. and Gloria LaRoche, the Occidental Petroleum Foundation, Frank Sutherland and Natilee M. Duning, John Tanner, Susan Turner Taylor and Royce Taylor, and Byron R. Trauger.

The heart of this biography lies in the political papers of Senator Gore at the Gore Center. The center could not be a more congenial place to work. Lisa Pruitt and her successors as director—Jim Williams, Mary Hoffschwelle, and Louis M. Kyriakoudes—have been constant supporters of this project and very patient when its completion was delayed by my new administrative responsibilities in Cambridge and too-frequent surgery. The staff made the center an unrivaled research resource. Under Lisa Pruitt's direction, Betty Rowland not only made it a very welcoming place but also conducted superb oral-history interviews in Murfreesboro and took on the painstaking task of transcribing all the interviews for the project.

Jack Robinson Sr., whose family members were close Carthage friends of Gore, worked for eight years in Gore's Senate office before the senator encouraged him to go to law school. No one is more knowledgeable about the senator, and no one could have been a more helpful and staunch supporter of this project. From the start I have been considerably in his debt.

The grant from the MTSU Foundation made it possible to hire a research assistant, Michael S. Martin. Michael's work on the Gore papers has been indispensable: It is the foundation of this biography. Michael displayed all the research skills, determination, and intellectual curiosity that would be shown in his own excellent biography of Russell Long. Sean Smith followed with a prodigious capacity for meticulous mining of the newspapers and the Congressional Record. Michael Fletcher was later very helpful in tracking down references and rogue documents.

The Paul Mellon Fund attached to my Cambridge chair paid for my transatlantic travel and research costs outside Tennessee and provided funds for two research assistants in Cambridge. The work of my former PhD students

Catherine Maddison and Adam Gilbert was invaluable. Cambridge American history graduate students, as they fanned out to archives all over the United States, helped me gather material in collections from Texas to Montana. I am extremely grateful to Tom Tunstall Allcock, James Blackstone, Jonathan Cook, Robert Freedman, Hannah Higgin, Katherine Ballantyne Jernigan, Katy Reeves, Olivia Sohns, and Tim Stanley for their detective work. Good friends David Chappell, Steve Gillon, Liz Lundeen, Jeff Norrell, and Jason Scott Smith followed up sources for me in Norman, Knoxville, Albuquerque, and Chapel Hill. Emily Charnock very generously shared material with me from the Americans for Democratic Action files.

It also helped me greatly that two of my former PhD students, Dominic Sandbrook and David Ballantyne, wrote excellent senatorial biographies of Eugene McCarthy and Fritz Hollings, respectively.

There are many oral-history interviews that concern the senator at MTSU, the presidential libraries, the Southern Historical Collection, the Senate Historical Office, and the Library of Congress. It is testimony to Albert Gore's influence that so many friends, family, and opponents of the senator were prepared to grant me interviews. I am also grateful to Donald Ritchie for guiding me through the Senate oral histories and, especially, to John Culver, who facilitated interviews with Gore's Senate colleagues and with David Broder. Al Gore was particularly generous in the time he gave me to talk about his father and to point me in crucial new directions.

My debt to the scholarship of others will be obvious in the pages that follow. Kyle Longley's biography is a starting point for all work on Albert Gore. I have learned much from Kyle. He is more of a foreign policy specialist; I am more of a Southern historian: I hope our work is complementary. There is a rich seam of modern Tennessee historiography: James B. Gardner's outstanding and sadly unpublished PhD on the state's postwar progressive politics in the state; Bobby Lovett and Ben Houston's work on civil rights; Wayne Dowdy's unequaled knowledge of Memphis and Boss Crump; Don Doyle on Nashville; Hugh Davis Graham's landmark study of the press and desegregation in Tennessee; and Carole Bucy's pioneering work on Martha Ragland. No one knows more about Southerners and foreign policy than Joseph A. Fry. Like other historians of the modern South, I have been much influenced by Bruce Schulman, Dan Carter, and the late Numan V. Bartley.

It has been my good fortune to be invited to talk about Gore at the universities of Boston, Columbia, East Anglia, Middle Tennessee, Oxford, South Carolina, Texas A&M, and Vanderbilt, and at Vassar College. For the invitations, generous hospitality, and helpful criticism, I am grateful to Robert K. Brigham, Alan Brinkley, Dan Carter, Richard Carwardine, Gareth Davies, Don H. Doyle, George C. Edwards, Adam Fairclough, Godfrey Hodgson, Ira Katznelson, Bruce Schulman, Marjorie Spruill, Stephen Tuck, and Julian Zelizer.

Opportunities to try out my ideas about Albert Gore came at conferences of the Tennessee Conference of Historians (2002, 2003), the Organization of American Historians (2003), the British Association of American Studies (2004), the European Southern Studies Forum (2005), the Princeton-Cambridge-Boston University American Political History Institute (2007, 2009), Historians of the Twentieth Century United States (2008), and the Biennial American History Symposium at Queen Mary University, London (2015), as well as at conferences on the Kennedy presidency (2013), the Johnson presidency (2014), and Selma (2015) at the Eccles Centre of the British Library, Cambridge University, and Northumbria University, respectively. For the invitations and the incisive comments, my thanks to Janet Beer, Jonathan Bell, David Blight, Joanna Cohen, Philip Davies, Kari Frederickson, Godfrey Hodgson, the late Walter Jackson, Henry Knight Lozano, Robert Mason, Iwan Morgan, Mark Newman, James T. Patterson, Bruce Schulman, Tim Stanley, Joe Street, and Julian Zelizer.

In Cambridge, Suzanne Donovan, Ann Holton, and Sophie King provided essential administrative and research support. My Americanist colleagues over the years—Joel Isaac, the late Mark Kaplanoff, Sarah Pearsall, Andrew Preston, Mike Sewell, Elizabeth Tandy Shermer, Colin Shindler, Betty Wood, and Joshua Zeitz—were a constant source of friendship and encouragement. John Thompson has offered wise counsel for more than forty years. The late Michael O'Brien and I were very different sorts of Southern historians, but he was a true friend. His return to Cambridge in the 1990s was a source of great personal satisfaction to me, and of great intellectual value to the wider community of British scholars of America. His untimely death came when he had exciting writing projects ahead and the eager anticipation of time to fulfill them.

Northumbria University has provided a welcoming academic base from which to complete this project. Brian Ward heads a team of outstanding and congenial Americanists: Patrick Andelic, David Gleeson, Henry Knight Lozano, Randall Stephens, and Joe Street. Sylvia Ellis and Michael Cullinane could not have made me more welcome before they left for Roehampton.

Ruth Badger has been a constant source of encouragement and support, as well as making a large contribution to the research in Tennessee, Hyde Park, New York, and Cambridge. She has always asked the best questions—that is, the awkward ones. I hope she knows what her love means to me. I am acutely aware of the sacrifices Ruth has had to make over the years. This book is inadequate recompense for those sacrifices, but like my other works, it could not have been completed without her.

It could also not have been completed without the enthusiasm and help of the wonderful people at the University of Pennsylvania Press. Tom Sugrue and Bob Lockhart were great cheerleaders, and Bob could not have been a more supportive and sympathetic editor. Mindy Brown copy-edited the text of a British author with wise and meticulous patience. Angela Hall produced the index with great skill and efficiency. Managing editor Noreen O'Connor-Abel has seen through the final stages of production with great good cheer.

Finally, the book is dedicated to the memory of the late Hugh Davis Graham. Hugh was a pioneer historian of racial crises in Tennessee in the 1950s and the racial and class electoral dynamics of postwar Southern politics. Subsequently he was a leader in the emerging field of policy history, a field he helped define. But he was a particularly generous supporter and mentor of younger British historians of the United States. Like others, I was the beneficiary of that open-hearted encouragement. More specifically his endorsement led to the invitation to write this book. The prospectus he promised I would deliver was a daunting one: I would, he asserted, use the biography of Gore to illuminate the transformation of Tennessee and the modern South, and the evolution of national policy in postwar America. I hope that, in however small a measure, this book lives up to his expectations.